THE PANAMA GUIDE

A CRUISING GUIDE TO THE ISTHMUS OF PANAMA

SECOND EDITION

by
Nancy Schwalbe Zydler
and
Tom Zydler

SEAWORTHY PUBLICATIONS, INC.
PORT WASHINGTON, WISCONSIN

Copyright ©1996, 2001 by Nancy Schwalbe Zydler and Tom Zydler

Published in the USA by: Seaworthy Publications, Inc. 215 S. Park St., Suite #1 Port Washington, WI 53074
Phone (262) 268-9250   Fax (262) 268 9208   www.seaworthy.com

All rights reserved. No part of this book may be reproduced, stored in a retrieval system, or transmitted in any form, or by any means, electronic, mechanical, photocopying, recording, or by any storage and retrieval system, without permission in writing from the Publisher.

CAUTION: Sketch charts are not to scale and are not to be used for navigational purposes. They are intended as supplements for NOAA, DMA, or British Admiralty charts and no warranties are either expressed or implied as to the usability of the information contained herein. The Author and Publisher take no responsibility for their misuse.

All photos, including the cover photos, whether or not a credit appears, were taken by Tom Zydler, except photo on page 31 of yachts transiting the Panama Canal courtesy of Phil Wade, a friend of the author.

Also by Nancy Schwalbe Zydler and Tom Zydler:
The Georgia Coast, Waterways and Islands

Library of Congress Cataloging-in-Publication Data

Zydler, Nancy Schwalbe, 1951-
    The Panama guide : a cruising guide to the Isthmus of Panama / by Nancy Schwalbe Zydler and Tom Zydler.
        p.   cm.
    Originally published: 1996.
    Includes bibliographical references.
    ISBN 1-892399-09-1 (alk. Paper)
    1. Pilot guides--Panama. 2. Yachting—Panama. I. Zylder, Tom, 1940-   II. Title.

VK970. P2 Z93 2001
623 . 89' 297287—dc21   2001031381

Dedication:

To Mieczyslaw Zydler, my father: I waited too long to admit you were always right.

To the memory of my father, Herman Louis Schwalbe whose every and many adventure stories were always accompanied by a twinkle in his eye.

PREFACE

It took four voyages to the waters of the Panamanian Isthmus to gather data for this cruising guide. During the last 2½ year long trip, which served to complete the surveys, the Panamanian people turned our work into an enjoyable adventure. They gave generously out of their store of local information, they taught us to cook the right way and they sincerely cared about our welfare. They made us feel safe and welcome.

Captain Cristóbal of the good ship Don Jaime III gave us the initial encouragement to take our 38 foot yawl up the Tuira to Yaviza. He divulged peculiarities of the other rivers in the area, "Just steer punta a punta," he said. Exactly the words we needed to send us on our merry ignorant way.

When on our travels on the lands of Darién we plopped right out of the blue dugout into the middle of Union de Chocó village, Tilila Valdespino, the first female chief in remembered Emberá history, gave up her bed and mosquito net to make us comfortable. In Cauchero, Laguna de Chiriquí, Lucrecia Chocón shared her family's food so, God forbid, we would not miss some special treat.

In Mulatupu, Sasardi, San Blas, Florentino Urrutia and his family explained Kuna history and tribal knowledge. Florentino made sure we learned about the forest and still made it in one piece over the hills of the Serrania del Darién to Rio Morti.

We encountered many good people in Panama and hope you will, too. Spanish is easy to learn and a visitor with a rudimentary knowledge of the language will find an audience who brushes aside mistakes but comprehends the gist.

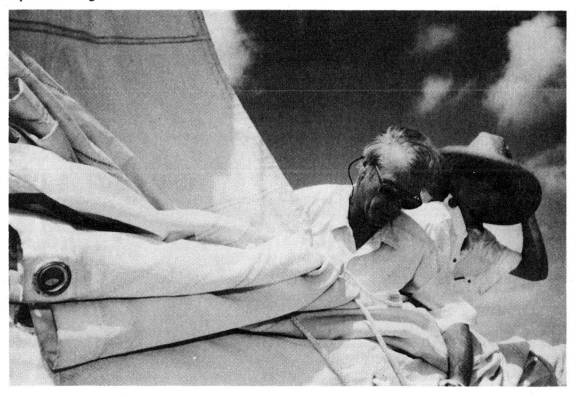

Tom Zydler and Nancy Schwalbe Zydler

TABLE OF CONTENTS

PREFACE v
TABLE OF CONTENTS vi

INTRODUCTION
PROVINCES OF PANAMA 2
WHY CRUISE PANAMA? 3
A SHORT HISTORY OF PANAMA 4
CLEARING IN AND OUT OF PANAMA 5
COMMUNICATIONS 6
HAM RADIO 6
POSTAL SERVICES 6
COURIERS 7
TRAVELING IN PANAMA 7
BUSINESS HOURS 8
HOLIDAYS 8
HEALTH MATTERS 9
NATIONAL PARKS 9
MUSEUMS 10
BOATYARD SERVICES 10
   THE ATLANTIC COAST 10
   IN THE PANAMA CANAL 10
   THE PACIFIC COAST 10
   DRYING OUT 11
AIDS TO NAVIGATION 11
   US DMA CHARTS TO PANAMA 11
   BRITISH ADMIRALTY CHARTS 12
   TOPOGRAPHICAL MAPS 12
   LIST OF LIGHTS 12
WEATHER FORECASTS 19
USING THIS GUIDE 21
SPECIAL SERVICES 21

CHAPTER I ~ PANAMA CANAL
PORT OF CRISTOBAL 23
   DIESEL, GASOLINE AND PROPANE 24
   MEDICAL HELP 24
   SAIL REPAIR 24
   SHIP BATTERIES 24
   MECHANICAL AND ELECTRICAL REPAIRS 24
   HARDWARE SUPPLIES 24
   FREE ZONE 24
   FOOD SHOPPING 24
   CHARTS 24
   INTERNATIONAL COURIERS 25
   CONNECTIONS WITH PANAMA CITY 25
THE PANAMA CANAL SYSTEM 27
   PANAMA CANAL TRANSIT 27
   PREPARING A YACHT FOR TRANSIT 27
THREE METHODS OF TRANSITING 28

CENTER OF THE LOCK 28
ALONGSIDE ANOTHER VESSEL 28
ALONGSIDE LOCK WALLS 28
IN THE PANAMA CANAL 28
RADIO COMMUNICATIONS FROM THE CANAL 28
THE TRANSIT 31
ALTERNATE ANCHORAGES IN BALBOA 37
BALBOA YACHT CLUB 37
CLEARING INTO PANAMA IN BALBOA 38
THE TOWN OF BALBOA 38
TRANSPORTATION FROM BALBOA TO PANAMA CITY 38
SHOPPING AND SERVICES IN PANAMA CITY 38
PLAYA KOBBE ANCHORAGE 40
VACAMONTE HARBOR 41
THROUGH THE PANAMA CANAL FROM THE PACIFIC 41

CHAPTER II ~ BAHÍA LAS MINAS TO PUERTO OBALDIA, INCLUDING THE SAN BLAS ISLANDS

WEATHER AND WINDS 43
CURRENTS AND TIDES 43
NAVIGATING WITH GPS 43
ANCHORAGES BETWEEN CRISTOBAL AND PUNTA SAN BLAS 45
BAHÍA LAS MINAS 45
ISLAS NARANJO 45
BUENAVENTURA 45
PORTOBELO 45
PLAYA BLANCA 47
JOSÉ POBRE 47
ISLA LINTON (ALSO JUAN JOAQUIN) 49
ISLA GRANDE 49
ENSENADA INDIO 51
NOMBRE DE DIOS 51
PUNTA MACOLLA 52
PLAYA CHIQUITA (details on DMA chart 26065) 52
ENSENADA BARRO (details on DMA chart 26065) 55
BAHÍA DE ESCRIBANOS 55
THE INNER ROUTE BETWEEN NOMBRE DE DIOS AND PUNTA SAN BLAS ...55
ROUTES INTO THE SAN BLAS ISLANDS 57
SAFE PASSES INTO THE SAN BLAS ISLANDS 57
CANAL DE SAN BLAS 57
HOLANDES CHANNEL 57
CAOBOS CHANNEL 57
IMPORTANT CAUTION FOR WATERS EAST OF LA COQUERA POINT LONGITUDE 58
ISLA PINOS CHANNEL 58
ESCOSÉS CHANNEL 58
PILOTING BY EYE 58
THE PEOPLE OF SAN BLAS 58
SHOPS AND SUPPLIES 61
CLEARING IN AND OUT OF SAN BLAS 61
PORVENIR AND THE NEIGHBORING ISLANDS 64
CHICHIME CAYS - UCHUTUPU PIPPI AND UCHUTUPU DUMAT 64
WESTERN LEMON CAYS 67
EDEN CHANNEL 67

EASTERN LEMON CAYS	67
YANSALADUP	67
NUINUDUP	67
HOLANDES CAYS, KAIMOU	70
WESTERN HOLANDES CAYS	70
EASTERN HOLANDES CAYS	70
THE GULF OF SAN BLAS	71
ANCHORAGES ON THE NORTH SHORE OF THE GULF OF SAN BLAS	71
NALIA (BAHÍA DE TIBURON)	71
NELOGUICHI	71
URUSUKUN	71
TADARGUANET - ISLAS ROBESON	71
TUPSUIT ISLANDS - ISLAS GERTIE AND ELSIE	75
TUWALA - ISLA GEORGE	75
UBICANTUPU - ISLA NELLIE	75
NUPNUTUPU	75
ARITUPU - ISLA LENA	75
RIO NICUESA - CHART 26065	75
ISLAS AMMEN - NARBAGANDUP DUMAT AND PIPI	79
ACUADUP	79
NONOMULU	79
CARTÍ ISLANDS	79
UARSADUP	80
NURDUPU	80
SOLEDAD MIRIA	80
MORMAKE TUPU - MAQUINA	80
RIO SIDRA	86
NUSATUPU	86
ARIDUP	86
GUNBOAT ISLAND - NUBASITUPU	87
TUBASANIKET	87
MORON ISLAND - NARASKANDUP	87
LOS GRULLOS - KUANIDUP	88
NAGUARGANDUP CAYS	88
THE WESTERN NAGUARGANDUP CAYS	88
EASTERN NAGUARGANDUP CAYS	88
TUBORGANA	93
ORTUPU	93
MADUNUNUDUP AND BANERDUP	93
LIGHTHOUSE ISLAND - SIMONDUP	93
GREEN ISLAND - KANILDUP AND SURROUNDING CAYS	93
COCO BANDERO CAYS	95
ORDUPTARBOAT	95
EAST END OF COCO BANDERO CAYS	95
RIO AZUCAR - UARGANDUP	95
RIO DIABLO (NARGANA) AND CORAZON DE JESUS	99
IGUANA ISLAND	99
PUYADAS - PUGADUP	99
FAREWELL ISLANDS PASSAGE	99
TIGRE - MAMARTUPU	99
NIADUP	104
PLAYON GRANDE CHANNEL	104
RATONES CAYS - ARIDUP	104
SNUG HARBOR	104

ISKARTUPU	108
PLAYON CHICO - UKUPSENI	108
PLAYON CHICO TO SAN IGNACIO DE TUPILE	108
SAN IGNACIO DE TUPILE (MONO VILLAGE ON CHART NO. 26042)	108
ISLA MONO	113
PUNTA BRAVA CHANNEL	113
PUNTA BRAVA TO MAMITUPU	113
AILIGANDI	113
ISLANDIA	113
ACHUTUPU	113
MAMITUPU	114
ACHUTUPU TO USTUPU	114
USTUPU	119
BAHÍA DE MASARGANDI	119
USTUPU TO ISLA PINOS	119
ISLA PINOS - TUPBAK	123
ISLA PINOS TO CALEDONIA	123
MULATUPU	123
TUBUALA AND NUBADUP	127
CALEDONIA - KANIRDUP	127
PUERTO ESCOSÉS - SUKUNYA	127
CARRETO	130
ANACHUCUNA AND PUERTO PERME	130
PUERTO OBALDIA	131
LA MIEL	132
SAPZURRO - COLOMBIA	132

CHAPTER III ~ RIO CHAGRES TO BOCA DEL DRAGO

WINDS, CURRENTS and TIDES	135
RIO CHAGRES	135
RIO CHAGRES TO TOBOBE CREEK, GOLFO DE LOS MOSQUITOS	137
AGUACATE	138
LIMÓN	138
RIO EUÉRO	138
BELÉN	138
BEJUCO	140
ESTERO SALADO	140
CALOVÉBORA	140
ESCUDO DE VERAGUAS	140
TOBOBE CREEK	141
LAGUNA DE CHIRIQUÍ	141
ENTRANCE INTO LAGUNA DE CHIRIQUÍ	143
LAGUNA DE BLUEFIELD	143
PUNTA ALLEGRE	143
PUNTA AVISPA	143
BAHÍA AZUL	143
PLAYA RAYA	148
EASTERN AND SOUTHERN ISLA POPA AND CAYO DE AGUA	148
ISLA TIGRE	148
PUNTA LAUREL BAY	148
CAYO PATTERSON	148
IRISH BAY AND RIO CRICAMOLA	151
CHIRIQUÍ GRANDE	151

- ENSENADA DELISCANOS 151
- ENSENADA TAPAO AND ITS ANCHORAGES 155
- CAUCHERO 155
- THE PASSAGES FROM LAGUNA DE CHIRIQUÍ INTO BAHÍA ALMIRANTE 155
  - SPLIT HILL CHANNEL - LOMA PARTIDA 155
  - SPLIT HILL - LOMA PARTIDA 155
  - SUMWOOD CHANNEL 155
- BAHÍA ALMIRANTE 159
- ANCHORAGES NORTH OF SPLIT HILL 159
  - ISLETS SOUTHEAST OF THEMUNG POINT 159
  - FINCA CORDOBA 159
  - ISLA POPA NUMERO UNO 159
  - ENSENADA POPA 159
  - ISLA POPA NUMERO DOS 159
  - VISCAINO CAYS 160
  - SHARK HOLE 172
- THE ROUTE TO BOCAS DEL TORO 172
- BOCAS DEL TORO 172
  - CARENERO - CAREENING ISLAND 174
- OCEAN ENTRANCES TO BAHÍA ALMIRANTE 174
  - BOCA DEL TORO 174
  - BOCA DEL DRAGO 174
- ISLA COLÓN ANCHORAGES 182
  - SAIGON 182
  - BIG BIGHT 182
  - CONCH POINT 182
  - GROUND CREEK 182
- ISLA BASTIMENTOS 182
  - BASTIMENTOS VILLAGE 182
  - HOSPITAL BIGHT 183
  - SHORT CUT 183
  - BAHÍA HONDA 183
- THE GAP 183
- NANCY CAY - SOLARTE 183
  - NORTHEAST OF BUTTONWOOD CAY 183
  - NORTH OF BUTTONWOOD CAY 183
- CRAWL CAY CHANNEL 184
- SALT CREEK 183
- CAYOS ZAPATILLA 188
- WESTERN PORTION OF BAHÍA ALMIRANTE 190
- ALMIRANTE 190
- AMBROSIO BIGHT ANCHORAGES 190
  - QUARY'S POINT 190
- ENSENADA SHEPHERD - PUNTA DE GALLINAZO 190
  - ISLA SHEPHERD 190
- ISLA CRISTOBAL 193
  - PIGEON CREEK 193
  - BAMBOO BIGHT 193
  - BAHÍA GRANDE 193
  - BERMUDEZ POINT CHANNEL 193
- PALOS LAGOON - DARK LAND 193
  - LAGUNA PALOS CUT 193
- BOCA TORRITOS 194
- CANAL BOCA TORRITO 194

SHARK HOLE LAGOON 194

CHAPTER IV ~ BALBOA TO PUNTA BURICA

- WINDS 203
- CURRENTS 203
- TIDES 203
- AIDS TO NAVIGATION 207
- ANCHORAGES AND HARBORS IN THE GULF OF PANAMA 207
  - TABOGA 207
  - ISLA OTOQUE 208
  - ISLA BONA 208
  - BAHÍA CHAMÉ, ISLA ENSENADA AND ISLA TABOR 208
  - AGUADULCE 212
- AZUERO PENINSULA 214
  - BAHÍA PARITA TO PUNTA MALA 214
  - ENSENADA BENAO 214
  - PUNTA GUANICO 214
  - PUNTA GUANICO TO PUNTA MARIATO 214
  - ENSENADA NARANJO 214
  - BAHÍA ARENAS 215
- CÉBACO 218
  - SOUTH COAST OF CÉBACO 218
  - NORTH COAST OF CÉBACO 218
- ISLA GOBERNADORA 223
- BAHÍA MONTIJO 223
  - PUERTO MUTIS 223
  - RIO DE JESUS 223
  - RIO PONUGA 225
  - ISLA VERDE 225
  - BOCA DE LA TRINIDAD 225
  - RIO SAN PABLO 225
  - ISLA LEONES 225
  - HICACO 225
  - RIO CATÉ 226
- SANTA CATALINA TO BAHÍA HONDA 230
  - ISLA SANTA CATALINA 230
  - FROM SANTA CATALINA TO PUNTA CATIVO 230
  - ISLAS CIMARRONES 230
  - ENSENADA DE CATIVON 230
  - PUERTO ESCONDIDO 230
  - HACHA 230
- BAHÍA HONDA 231
- CAUTIONARY NOTE 231
- ISLA MEDIDOR (on some charts, Isla Canal de Tierra) 231
- ISLA CANAL DE AFUERA 231
- COIBA 236
  - PUNTA MACHETE 236
  - RANCHERIA - COIBITA 236
  - GRANITO DE ORO 236
  - PLAYA ROSARIO and ENSENADA SANTA CRUZ 236
  - JICARON 236
- ISLAS DE CONTRERAS 239
- MAINLAND BAYS BETWEEN PUNTA ROBLE AND ENSENADA MUERTO 239

PUNTA ROBLE and ISLA MONA 239
   ENSENADA DE PIXVAE 239
   ENSENADA DE ROSARIO 239
   ENSENADA DE MUERTO 239
   ENSENADA DE PLAYA BRAVA 239
RIO SANTA LUCIA and SURROUNDINGS 239
   RIO SANTIAGO 245
   ISLA SILVA DE TIERRA 245
ISLAS SECAS 245
   ISLA CAVADA 245
   SOUTHERN ISLAS SECAS 245
ISLA VENADO TO PEDREGAL 248
   ISLA VENADO 248
   ENSENADA DE BEJUCO 248
   BOCA CHICA 248
PEDREGAL AND THE CHANNELS TO THAT PORT, INCLUDING PUERTO CABRITO 252
   BOCA BRAVA 253
   PUNTA CHALAPA 253
OFFSHORE ISLANDS SOUTH OF ISLA BOCA BRAVA (or south of BOCA CHICA) 253
   ISLAS SAN JOSE 254
   ISLA BOLAÑOS 254
   ISLA PARIDA - PUNTA JUREL 254
   PLAYA DEL SOCORRO 256
   ISLA GAMEZ 256
   NORTHWEST OF MOGOTE DE SEPULCRO 256
   ENSENADA DEL VAREDERO 256
   ENSENADA SANTA CRUZ 256
   ENSENADA LOS NEGROS 256
PUERTO ARMUELLES 256

CHAPTER V ~ LAS PERLAS AND EAST COAST OF THE GULF OF PANAMA

NAVIGATIONAL LIGHTS 262
SOUNDINGS 263
TIDES 263
LAS PERLAS 263
   CONTADORA, PACHECA, SABOGA 266
   ISLA CHAPERA AND MOGO MOGO 266
   BAJO BOYARENA 268
   CANAL GIBRALEON 268
   ISLA CASAYA 270
   ISLA BAYONETA 270
   ISLA MINA 270
   ISLA VIVEROS 270
ISLA DEL REY 270
   SAN MIGUEL 279
   ISLA ESPIRITU SANTO 279
   ISLA DE CAÑA 279
   PUNTA GORDA 279
   PLAYA DE SAN JUAN 280
   SANTELMITO CHANNEL 280
   BAHÍA SAN TELMO 280
   MORRO DE CACIQUE 280
   RIO CACIQUE 280

- ESMERALDA ... 280
- PUNTA DE COCOS ... 281
- THE WEST SHORE OF ISLA DEL REY ... 281
- ISLA DE SAN JOSE ... 283
  - ENSENADA PLAYA GRANDE ... 283
  - NORTH OF PUNTA TIMON ... 283
  - ENSENADA BODEGA ... 283
  - SOUTH TIP OF SAN JOSE ... 283
- ISLA PEDRO GONZALES ... 285
  - PEDRO GONZALES ... 285
  - ISLA SEÑORA ... 285
  - DON BERNARDO ... 285
- EAST COAST OF THE GULF OF PANAMA ... 288
  - ISLA CHEPILLO ... 288
  - RIO CHEPO ... 288
  - PUNTA BRUJAS ... 288
- GULF OF SAN MIGUEL ... 289
  - ISLA IGUANA ... 293
  - RIO CONGO ... 293
  - RIO SUCIO ... 295
  - RIO CUCUNATÍ ... 295
  - ISLA IGUANA TO BOCA GRANDE ... 298
  - ISLA CEDRO ... 298
  - PUNTA PLAYA GRANDE ... 298
  - BOCA GRANDE ... 299
  - ISLA BOCA GRANDE ... 299
  - LA PALMA ... 301
- RIO SABANA ... 302
  - ESTERO ÑOPO ... 306
  - ESTERO GREGORIO DIAZ ... 306
  - RIO IGLESIAS ... 306
- RIO TUIRA AND RIO BALSAS ... 306
  - CHEPIGANA ... 306
  - RIO TUIRA ... 306
  - RIO BALSAS ... 307
  - ISLA MANGLE ... 307
- ANCHORAGES ON SOUTHERN SHORES OF THE GULF OF SAN MIGUEL ... 309
  - PUNTA ALLEGRE ... 309
  - PUNTA PATIÑO ... 309
  - PUNTA GARACHINÉ ... 309
- THE PACIFIC COAST TO THE BORDER WITH COLOMBIA ... 311
  - BAHÍA PIÑAS ... 311
  - JAQUÉ ... 311
  - FONDEADERO GRANDE ... 311
  - GUAYABO ... 311
  - A WORD OF CAUTION ... 312
- APPENDIX ... 315
- FOOD! ... 315
  - Pifa, Pijiba, Pejibaye, Piba, Pixbae ... 315
  - Boiled Pifas ... 315
  - Pifa and Okra ... 315
  - Pifa Dasheen Soup ... 316
  - Roots ... 316
  - Corn ... 317

Irene Castrellón's Tortillas and Bollos	317
Kuna Cakes	317
Coconut Bread	317
Lucrecia Chocón's Coconut Bread	317
A Few Fruits	318
Bibliography	319
Index	320

The mountains of the continental divide loom high over Laguna de Chiriquí as The Zydler's engineless yawl, Mollymawk, glides silently by.

THE PANAMA GUIDE

A CRUISING GUIDE TO THE ISTHMUS OF PANAMA

SECOND EDITION

INTRODUCTION

WHY CRUISE PANAMA?

While the Panama Canal stands out as a wonder of technology and for many people is worth a visit for its own sake, the Republic of Panama has a lot more to offer to a cruising sailor. The Atlantic coast measuring 350 nautical miles as a grackle flies between the borders with Costa Rica in the west and Colombia to the east is twice that length if one goes into bays and around islands of which there are over 360 just in the San Blas area. Similarly, the straight line length of 510 nautical miles on the Pacific coast grew to over a 1,000 miles after surveyors included all the coastal indentations and islands. These numbers reveal a wealth of anchorages that provide months of exploring, and the coasts remain very uncrowded. Almost half of the 2.4 million citizens of this country, about twice the size of Netherlands and slightly smaller than Lake Superior, dwell in Panama City, Colón and David. However, meeting Panamanians adds a fascinating aspect to cruising. While exploring Panama's waters a yachtsman will interact with Latinos, Orientals, Afro-Antilleans as well as three thriving indigenous groups. The majority of Kunas live on offshore islands in the San Blas area of the Caribbean coast. Guaymi, (a generic term which refers mostly to Ngöbe people) populate many hamlets on the shores of Bahía Almirante and Chiriquí Grande, two large bays in the Caribbean west of the Panama Canal. Finally, the Chocó (another generic term which embraces the Emberá and Wounaan linguistic groups) live along the banks of the navigable Rio Tuira and its navigable tributaries far inside the Darién province in Pacific Panama. And remember that irrespective of their ethnic backgrounds Panamanians treat visitors warmly. Regrettably, and similarly to other large urban centers, one has to avoid parts of Panama City and Colón because of recurring street robberies.

Climate-wise living is easy in Panamanian waters. Located on the isthmus between 7°N and 10°N, Panama lies south of hurricane paths. With an average annual temperature of 80°F (26° Centigrade) you will find the country a lot cooler than the east coast of the USA during summer months. Wet and dry seasons approximate the division into winter and summer in high latitudes. With the exception of Darién, the Pacific coast receives relatively little rain even during the wet months between May and December. On the other hand it can rain like the devil on the Caribbean side during November and December as well as July and August.

Handling the yacht's business in Panama, which uses the US dollar as currency and calls it a Balboa, is easier than in other Central American countries. Since Panama is the commercial center of Central and South America, companies in Panama City stock most U.S. industrial products and obtaining spare parts presents little difficulty. What is not immediately available can be shipped either by fast couriers, air freight or ship freight and released to customers with relatively little customs hassles and charges.

Few people realize that Panama has set aside more land as National Parks and protected forests than Costa Rica, so famous a destination for thousands of ecotourists. In Panama a yachtsman who leaves the boat for some land exploration will not have to pay excessive park fees or jostle on trails with others. In fact, park rangers welcome visitors and exhibit genuine pleasure when showing off their treasures. Several travel agencies organize nature tours, but Eco Tours in Panama City certainly has the widest itinerary and experienced guides. They will take you trekking across the mountains of the isthmus from Atlantic to Pacific or provide a lunch and a boat to visit Barro Colorado, a condensed package of tropical nature under the Smithsonian Institute's care. Or, if you do not mind traveling by bus with the country people you can have an equally rewarding experience all by yourself. Even without leaving the boat you can get close to tropical nature here. In several deep rivers in Darién and Rio Chagres on the Atlantic a yacht may anchor in the middle of forests and be surrounded by several species of birds from ibis and parrots to fork tailed kites and toucans. In Panama one can slip out of a bustling urban center and two hours later be swimming in a secluded anchorage.

Sport fishermen will find a convenient base in Taboga or Las Perlas to fish the Gulf of Panama in water filled with large game fish like Blue and Black Marlin, Yellow Fin Tuna and others. A sport fishing resort in Bahía Piña on the Darién coast not only offers eight of their own boats for charter but will supply guides to visiting yachts. Tropic Star Lodge clients have broken more I.G.F.A. records there than anywhere else in the world. The author Zane Grey was the first "gringo" to stumble on these rich fishing waters and somehow the Lodge has managed to attract only the real devotees of deep sea fishing.

The Pacific waters near Isla Coiba also have had very little fishing pressure and the hot spot over Hannibal Bank attracts only an occasional sport fishing yacht in search of hard fighting Tiger Sharks. The Caribbean off Panama has tarpon and snook (locally called robalo) as the best known quarries. Rio Chagres draws many fishermen casting for large tarpon while Bocas del Toro is a good destination for snook, tarpon and large snappers.

A SHORT HISTORY OF PANAMA

Scientists estimate that the land bridging the Americas on the isthmus of Panama emerged about three million years ago. From excavations anthropologists surmise that humans, probably the descendants of the first migrants from Asia who entered North America across Bering strait, lived here eleven thousand years ago. Later, several nations who cultivated corn and beans left distinct traces of their sophisticated cultures, first on the southern side of the Cordillera Central and later on the northern and eastern slopes.

At the time of the Spanish arrival the indigenous people of various linguistic groups numbered between 500,000 and 900,000, estimates vary. Columbus himself started cruising Panamanian waters in October, 1502 by entering a large bay now called, after his own title, Bahía Almirante. Vasco Nuñez de Balboa, commemorated on Panamanian coins, acquired fame through his 1513 crossing of the Isthmus from the Atlantic coast near Punta Escosés to a bay on the shores of the Pacific which he named Golfo de San Miguel. His fairly good relations with the natives ended with the arrival of the royal appointee Pedrarias Dávila who pillaged and murdered, eventually succeeding even in beheading Balboa himself. Finally Pedrarias moved his base to the Pacific coast to the village of Panama, whose name some say, meant plenty of fish and would be apt even today. After the Spanish shifted the focus of their attentions to southwestern Panama, the area of the original Spanish entry, Comarca de San Blas, parts of Darién and eastern Panama, reverted to wilderness. European diseases and warfare had reduced the population and dense forests returned even to the central planes, near today's Chepo and Bayano where Balboa once saw thousands of people and cultivated fields.

Meanwhile, Panama had become an important transhipment point for the gold and silver from Peru. This thriving commerce attracted privateers. Some of them made fortunes and acquired fame like Francis Drake, who in 1570 raided Nombre de Dios, and Henry Morgan who in 1668 made successful forays on the new transhipment port of Portobelo. Even Panama City on the Pacific side was not safe from buccaneers and Henry Morgan looted the town in 1671. When the trading laws imposed by the Spanish Crown were relaxed and the riches of Peru were depleted, Panama lost its important role and in 1751 became a part of Nueva Granada, a vast Spanish viceroyalty which also included Colombia, Ecuador and Venezuela.

A wave of revolutionary movements among South American colonies to separate from Spain eventually led to Panama becoming part of Gran Colombia in 1821. Three attempts by Panamanian politicians to secede from Colombia failed and Panama stagnated. Then came the gold rush of the 1840's in California which brought the American financed Panama Railroad across the isthmus. Within ten years the prosperity of Panama greatly improved as 375,000 people crossed to the Pacific side and 225,000 came back, all contributing to the flow of money. This activity renewed the idea of constructing a canal between the oceans. In 1879, a French company headed by Ferdinand de Lesseps obtained a concession from Colombia. Through faulty planning and mismanagement the project went bankrupt nine years later. Meanwhile, political turmoil in Colombia lead to the resumption of Panamanian attempts to gain independence. Americans, now committed to building a canal in Panama, were watching very closely. Faced with strong opposition in Colombia to an American owned canal, the United States government ordered its naval forces to support the Panamanian independence efforts. After some skirmishes between Panamanian junta rebels and Colombian troops in November 1903, President Theodore Roosevelt recognized the junta leaders as the government of an independent Republic of Panama. A year later the United States had ratified a treaty which gave them control over a large strip of land across the isthmus in perpetuity, a cause for serious conflict in the years to come.

Soon after its commencement the management of the canal project was transferred to the US Army Corps of Engineers and Colonel William Gorgas took charge of sanitation. By successfully removing the breeding opportunities for mosquitoes, which transmitted malaria and yellow fever to humans often killing thousands, he probably contributed more than anyone else to the successful construction of the canal just by keeping the workers alive. Realizing the difficulties of building a sea level canal as the French planned, the American engineers decided to utilize the Chagres river by damming it and creating an artificial lake. The lake provided the water for operating a system of locks and also served as a ready made waterway. It took ten years and about 75,000 people to slice through mountains, blast through rocks, build the largest locks in the world and complete the canal, which opened in August 1914.

The original treaty, however, haunted the relationship between the two countries. The Canal Zone, owned by the US, created a country within a country. Canal Zone employees lived in a system of privileges open only to American citizens. The resentment resulting from glaring inequalities of life styles and US military interventions in the political life of the republic gradually led to clashes between Panamanian protesters and the National Guard of the Republic. In 1964 a violent three day battle broke out over the displaying of the Panamanian flag in the Zone and led to the killing of over twenty students. It became obvious that all the minor adjustments to the original treaty were inadequate. The new negotiations which started in 1969 and promised the transfer of the Canal to Panama in 1999 eased the tensions. Finally, in 1977 during President Carter's administration a new treaty was signed with General Omar Torrijos, the left leaning populist head of the National Guard and de facto ruler of Panama. The new treaty expired on December 31, 1999 when Panama took over the ownership and administration of the canal.

The new treaty did not stop US involvement in Panamanian politics. In 1981 General Torrijos died in an airplane crash and another prolonged period of political instability followed. Eventually the unsavory General Manuel Noriega with shady connections to the CIA, Cuba and Colombian drug cartels took over complete control of the country which slipped into political anarchy. After the U.S. imposed economic sanctions in order to force Noriega out, he declared himself Head of Government and announced a state of war with the United States. American armed forces moved in and Noriega escaped to the residence of the papal representation in Panama City but finally gave himself up. He was later tried and convicted in Miami where he is now serving his sentence. For the first time in many decades Panama is a real democracy with clean elections and a rapidly growing economy which is based on trade and services to South American countries.

CLEARING IN AND OUT OF PANAMA

In order to enter the Republic of Panama all visitors must have a valid passport. The citizens of the U.S.A, Canada, UK, Switzerland, Spain, and Germany do not have to obtain a visa beforehand. Australians and New Zealanders must get visas from Panamanian consulates before they enter Panama. However, even if you do not need a visa but plan to enter the Republic's territory in a place other than Porvenir (San Blas), Colón or Balboa try to get a visa beforehand. In places like Armuelles they will send arrivals without visas to a fairly distant border immigration post even when their nationality entitles them to enter without visas. This may happen also in Bocas del Toro and Chiriquí Grande if they run out of the forms to fill. UK citizens can get a 90 day permit but U.S. citizens receive 30 day tourist visas on entering. This permit can be extended to a total of 90 days in the "migration" offices in Panama City, Diablo Heights, Colón, Changuinola, David, Santiago and Chitre. In Panama City the main immigration offices are on Avenida Cuba and Calle 29. The extension means you will be fingerprinted and photographed in order to issue a "cedula", a plasticized ID card which costs $11.00. Usually these offices use their own camera to take mug shots. If their equipment does not work you will be asked to bring two passport size photos. Once you have received the extension you will not be allowed to leave the country without first getting a Paz y Salvo form (.25) from the Ministerio de Hacienda y Tesoro. With this form you go to the "migration" office and they will stamp a "permiso de salida" in your passport. Remember this procedure before flying out as no persuasion will work on the immigration officer at the airport who cannot issue a "permiso de salida". If you sail to Costa Rica without the "salida" stamp from Panama a strict immigration officer there may send you back. Yachtsmen whose 90 days terms are expiring usually leave their boats in one of the clubs and depart from the Republic of Panama for 72 hours, the minimum time out of the country before one can start the new cycle over.

To clear the boat in you will have to go to the Direccion Consular y de Naves office where they want to see the clearance from the previous port and the vessel's document. These offices in the main harbors issue a Permiso de Navegacion which costs according to the size of the boat. Yachts up to 6 meters or 20 feet pay a total of 30 dollars. Yachts between 6 and 10 meters or between 20 feet 11 inches and 33 feet pay 45 dollars and vessels over 10 meters or 33 feet long have to cough up 75 dollars. These charges are now actually lower than the rates enforced in 1995.

This navigation permit allows a yacht to cruise and to enter Panamanian ports for three months without any further paperwork. However, port captains in some remote places insist on issuing a clearance between harbors called a "zarpe" which usually costs $8.40. The cruising permit system started relatively recently and since all Panamanian vessels must use the "zarpe" system these port captains just follow the good old practices. A clearance out of the country, also called a "zarpe", costs $ 25.00.

The Department of Agriculture in Armuelles charges a $10.00 inspection fee, even though they do not inspect anything. Occasionally an officer from the customs office (Aduana) tries to extract money from a yacht, but such charges are totally illegitimate so refuse to pay. You should complain about such demands to the Port Captain or the Direccion Consular y de Naves office.

When a yacht arrives from foreign ports in Balboa Yacht Club or at the Panama Canal Yacht Club in Cristobal, the skipper has to clear initially with the immigration officer who has an office in each club. He will fill some forms and then send the skipper to the main offices to complete the clearing procedures. If you carry arms aboard write down their serial numbers for the Direccion Consular y de Naves office. They will put them on your cruising permit. If possible bring proof of purchase for the weapons, some offices may ask to see them.

COMMUNICATIONS

The offices of the Panamanian telecommunications company, INTEL, handle international phone calls and operate fax machines between 7:30 AM and 10:00 PM. Their services are reasonably priced and the offices are air-conditioned. One can also make international phone calls from pay phones located around the country and maintained by INTEL. To reach the AT&T operator in the U.S. dial 109, MCI dial 108 or dial 106 to reach the INTEL operator for overseas calls.

The INTEL office in Cristobal is accustomed to receiving faxes for yachtsmen and if the fax includes the name of your boat they will notify the Panama Canal Yacht Club of its arrival. Their fax number is 507-441-4649, and the phone number is 507-445-0131. P.C.Y.C. sends and receives faxes at 507(country code) 441-7752, their phone number is 441-5882. The Balboa Yacht Club sends and receives faxes at 507-228-5440, their phone number is 228-5794. Pedro Miguel Boat Club also has a fax machine with number 507-252-8105, their phone number is 232-4509.

To call the police dial 104. Firemen receive emergency calls at 103. In a medical emergency call 225-1536 (Hospital Santo Tomas) or 229-2001 (Hospital San Fernando).

HAM RADIO

Amateur radio operators licensed in their countries of origin and visiting the Republic of Panama on yachts may use their call signs for 30 days by adding HP2 if they are located on the Atlantic coast and HP1 on the Pacific side. It appears that getting a Panamanian amateur radio license would involve several months worth of paperwork.

POSTAL SERVICES

The postal services in Panama are reliable and reasonably priced. Remember to add POR AVION on outgoing mail otherwise it will travel by surface mail.

Post offices here do not deliver mail and citizens and businesses use post office boxes - Apartados - and pick up the mail personally. So do the yacht clubs, perhaps only every other day or even less frequently. The fastest possible way to get mail is to have letters addressed to your name, Entrega General, name of the post office closest to you, Republic of Panama. (Use Balboa-Ancon when in Balboa and Cristobal when in Colón.) Post offices hold such letters for about a month.

You can receive mail from the U.S. by U.S. Express Mail Service. You will find its office next door to the post office in the bottom of the El Dorado shopping mall in Panama City. A customs officer stays on duty there to clear packages through. Cristobal Post Office also has this service and its own customs officer on the premises.

To receive mail at the Panama Canal Yacht Club use the following address: name, yacht name, c/o Panama Canal Yacht Club, Apartado 5041, Cristobal, Republic of Panama. In Balboa use: c/o of Balboa Yacht Club, Apartado 552, Balboa Ancon, Republic of Panama. Or: c/o Pedro Miguel Boat Club, Apartado 2613, Balboa Ancon, Republic of Panama.

COURIERS

UPS has offices in the Free Zone, Colón, phone 445-2778, 441-2283. The phone number in Panama City for UPS is 269-9222, in Colón 445-2778.

DHL has an office in Colón, Free Zone, phone 441-6639, 441-6766, an office in Panama City, phone 236-0111, and an office in David, phone 775-7664.

Federal Express has a branch office in Colón, Free Zone, phone 430-8495 or 430-8496. The number for the FedEx center in Panama City is 507-800-1122, you may also reach them at 271-3838 or 775-7664. They have recently opened a Jetex office in David.

Shipments from the continental U.S. take about four days to reach you in Panama and all these companies deliver to the P.C.Y.C. in Cristobal directly to yachts at the docks. They will leave a note in the club office for yachts at the anchorage. Balboa Yacht Club refuses to keep the packages in the office. Apparently a yacht occasionally claims a package that belongs to another. The couriers leave notices in the club and you will have to phone them and arrange a contact or go to their offices. Or you can have the package sent by courier to your name for "customer pick up".

Small packages, which arrive by courier service usually, go through customs immediately without involving the recipient. Large shipments may entail a visit to customs.

There are several Panamanian courier companies, also reliable, and slightly less expensive although shipments to or from cities other than Miami and New York may take longer. These Panamanian companies often have offices in smaller towns, too.

Skynet Courier, phone 569-1145

Trans Express Worldwide, phone: 274-2233, fax: 274-2311

TRAVELING IN PANAMA

One can travel within the republic and reach remote places by boat, bus and airplane efficiently and at reasonable expense. Small freighters maintain commercial links between Muelle Fiscal in Panama City and the Darién oceanic coast and interior rivers as far as Yaviza. The ships are small, in poor shape and passengers sleep on deck using their own bedding. It takes two nights to reach Yaviza. The Kuna owned trading coasters, which sail between Coco Solo and San Blas Islands are in much better condition to respond to the more demanding weather conditions. Their passenger accommodations are crude but adequate for the trip, which takes just a few days. Their routes vary but one ship goes as far as Puerto Obaldia. Meals are included in the ticket price on all ships.

Some yachtsmen choose to anchor their boats in Taboga and then commute to the City on ferryboats which leave from Balboa harbor pier number 17. During the weekdays one ferry makes two trips a day, another only one. On weekends and holidays all ferries make three runs a day. A round trip cost $6 and should a ferry break down you can always find a boat to charter to take you back to Taboga.

If you have no fear of flying small airplanes, you can find in the Paitilla airport in downtown Panama City several companies flying to Contadora, San Miguel (Las Perlas), Chitre, David, Santiago, Changuinola, Colón, as well as Porvenir and several other villages in San Blas, and to La Palma, El Real, Garachiné, Sambú in Darién. To get a seat to the San Blas destinations on holidays buy a ticket in the Paitilla airport a day before your departure.

Bus transportation varies greatly. Expreso buses between major towns have air-conditioning and comfortable seats. Other than that you will travel in a converted American school bus or a Japanese made mini bus. All towns have well organized bus terminals which serve long distance and local lines. From Colón one can travel along the coast to the east called Costa Arriba as far as Cuango. You can also travel west on the coast, called Costa Abajo, as far Miguel de la Borda. Both routes may be closed at their limits during rainy season.

In Panama City there are several bus terminals, which serve as hubs to other parts of Panama. The terminals are often in streets that are downright dangerous for a "gringo" to enter. Always take a taxi and explain to the driver to where in Panama you will be traveling. The cab drivers know the terminals. The bus network to the western parts of Panama is very well developed. Eastward of Panama City this changes soon after Chepo on the Pan-American Highway. Buses can always travel as far as Canglon and will continue to Yaviza in dry weather but it takes only one serious rainstorm to stop the bus short of Yaviza and the Darién Gap. The Pan-American Highway stops in Yaviza.

BUSINESS HOURS

Government offices open at 8 AM and stay open until 3 or 4 PM without a lunch break Monday through Friday. Banks open at 9 AM and close at 1 PM Monday through Friday. Other businesses open at 8:00 AM and close for a break at noon until 1:30 PM when they open again until 4:30 or 5:00 PM. Almost all private enterprises stay open on Saturdays but often only until noon.

HOLIDAYS

January 1 New Year's Day

January 9 Martyr's Day to commemorate the students shot in 1964.

February 21 The anniversary of the Kuna revolution, celebrated in most villages, especially Tigre, Playon Chico, Ailigandi, and Ustupu, San Blas.

February/March For four days before Ash Wednesday and the beginning of Lent Panama City and other towns devotedly celebrate Carnaval. Ash Wednesday may occur between the second half of February and beginning of March in different years.

March 12 Patronales of San Francisco in Yaviza. (Patron saint's day.)

March (third week) Festival de Bunde y el Bullerengue in La Palma

March 20 Patronales of San Felipe in Portobelo. (Patron saint's day.)

March/April Good Friday through Easter Sunday - Semana Santa everything closes during this important holiday.

May 1 Labor Day

July 8 Anniversary of Inapakiña in Mulatupu

July 15 Fiesta in El Real

July 16 Patronales of Virgen de la Carmen in Taboga (an aquatic procession), also in Bocas del Toro, Isla Grande and Jaque (Darién). (Patron saint's day.)

August 15 Founding of Old Panama (Observed only in Panama City)

August 20 Anniversary of Charles Robinson, Nargana, San Blas

August 20 The annual festival of Congo dancing in communities along the coast east (Costa Arriba) and west (Costa Abajo) of Colón on the Caribbean.

August 30 Festival la Cuadrilla, Bocas del Toro, Isla Colón

September 3 Anniversary of Nele Kantule, Ustupu, San Blas

September 11 Anniversary of Yabilikiña, Tuwala, Sasardi, San Blas

September 15 Anniversary of Alcibiades Iglesias, Ailigandi, San Blas

September 15 to 17 depending on the year, Feria del Mar (boat races, too) in Bocas del Toro, Isla Colón.

September 24 Fiesta of the Virgin of the Mercedes, Garachiné, Darién

October 12 Hispanic Day-Dia de la Raza

October 21 Festival of Cristo Negro (Black Christ) in Portobelo.

November 3 Independence Day (Independence from Colombia)

November 4 Flag day (only government offices close)

November 10 National day in Los Santos - the first cry of Independence

November 28 Independence from Spain day

December 8 Mother's Day

December 25 Christmas Day

HEALTH MATTERS

Panamanian regulations do not require any vaccinations. For your own peace of mind you should have immunizations for yellow fever, tetanus and gamma globulin against hepatitis A. There may be a risk of dengue fever, hantavirus, malaria, yellow fever and rabies. The water in the urban communities in Panama is of excellent quality. If you have to use river water add water treatment tablets or small quantities of chlorine otherwise you will probably catch giardia parasites. Call the U.S. Embassy (227-1777) for the latest update on health hazards.

NATIONAL PARKS

14.5% of the land mass of Panama is under the protection of INRENARE (National Institute of Renewable Resources) aided by a strong non-governmental environmental organization, ANCON. Some of the National Parks, like Isla Bastimentos and Cayos Zapatillos in Bocas del Toro (Chapter III), can be visited on your boat. If you sail along the eastern Pacific coast down towards Colombia and stop in the Guayabo bays (Chapter V) you will find yourself in the National Park of Darién. Bahía Piña on the same coast is excluded from the park but adjacent to it. Coiba Island (Chapter IV) is a National Park in its own right. Enter Rio Chagres (Chapter III) and you will be in Parque Nacional Interoceanico de Las Americas. Even Portobelo, Isla Linton and Isla Grande (Chapter II) are within the borders of the Portobelo National Park.

The National Park, La Amistad, second largest in Panama, stretches into Costa Rica and requires a visit by land. You can get there by taking a bus from David to the town of Cerro Punta located high enough to get cool at night. From the town, which has both cheap "pensiones" and a nice hotel, it only takes a short cab ride to get to the rangers' station. You can camp in the park station by using an inflatable mattress or a hammock. Bring your food, which you can cook, on their stove. Several good trails meander through the forest at various altitudes and lesser trails go to indigenous hamlets far in. You would have to find a guide to go on these. You can hike or take a bus to Boquete, a well-known tourist destination with hotels, to visit the Volcan Barú National Park with the highest point in Panama at 3,475 meters (11,400 ft.).

The National Park of Darién includes large portions of the province and continues into Colombia. To visit the park you should get a permit at the INRENARE office in Panama City (232-4325 in Paraiso near Balboa), otherwise you will have to track down the INRENARE chief in El Real and get him to approve of your visit.

From El Real, a very pleasant town on Rio Tuira, reached by plane or hired cayuco from Yaviza, one can trek to the Rancho Frio park station. You can hire a man and a horse to carry your supply of food and camping equipment up hill.

Another park station in the Darién Park, Cruce de Mono, requires a boat trip up Rio Tuira to Boca de Cupe, where you can again hire a man with a horse to get your stuff up hill. On Rio Turia you will pass a few Embera villages and you can either camp or get accommodations in Union de Chocó. Both park ranger stations have bunk houses and cooking facilities for visitors but you must bring your own food. The water comes from forest streams. Personally, we consider our Darién visit as the highlight of our land trips, but bear in mind that one has to walk a lot there, often uphill. Best do it in dry season.

ANCON (264-8100, Panama City) maintains a station in Cana, the location of an old gold mine in Darién, and visitors can fly there on chartered planes arranged by travel agencies. A road from Cana descends to the Cruce de Mono station.

Several smaller national parks and protected forests lie near Panama City and with limited time a visit to Barro Colorado Island will give the visitor a very good idea of the natural wonders in Panama. Or visit Pemasky Nature Park in Kuna Yala and operated by the Kunas, call 282-3226 to speak to Guillermo Archibold.

MUSEUMS

Several museums in Panama City and other towns exhibit examples of many facets of colonial times in Panama. The anthropological museum Reina Torres de Arauz has a good selection of pre-Columbian indigenous art and should not be missed. It is located in Panama City on Pláza 5 de Mayo, open from 9:30 AM until 5:00 PM weekdays, 8:30 AM until 3:30 PM on Saturdays and is closed on holidays and Sundays. The museum does not have air-conditioning so start your tour early in the day when it is still cool.

BOATYARD SERVICES

THE ATLANTIC COAST

The Panama Canal Yacht Club has two haul out railways. The smaller one can handle boats under 35 ft. LOA and the larger has a 20-ton capacity with the draft limited to about 7 feet. It costs $75 to haul and launch. The club charges $1.50 per foot a day for each day on land. Boat owners are required to shore up their own vessels. You can do the work yourself or use the available help. Shelter Cover Marina located in the old Ft. Sherman will operate a 70-ton travel lift. The marina is scheduled to open October 2002. See page 25.

IN THE PANAMA CANAL

Pedro Miguel Boat Club located on Miraflores Lake to the side of Pedro Miguel Locks welcomes yachts whether they intend to do repairs or just stay in port. The Panama Canal Commission requires a statement from Pedro Miguel Boat Club that the yacht has a place in the facility. Only then will PCC allow a yacht to stop the transit at Pedro Miguel. The Club monitors VHF Ch. 72 during office hours Monday through Friday 1:00 PM-5:00 PM, Saturdays and Sundays 9:00 AM-3:00 PM. The phone numbers are 252-8654 or 232-4509, and the fax number 252-8105.

To haul boats out of the water the club uses a 15-ton crane. For many boats this entails unstepping the masts. The club charges $160 for the first hour of crane use and $80 for each additional hour. Jack stands to support a yacht on land cost $5 a month each. The responsibility for proper shoring rests with the boat owner. An additional fee is charged for the rental of the land space during the time on the hard.

The club allows do-it-yourself work and will recommend help if needed. A main bus route to Panama City and Colón passes near the club.

Occasionally tugboats bring a ship along the retaining wall before the lock and next to the marina. While the tugs push against the ship their props create turbulence that witnesses compare to rapids moving at 20 knots towards the moored boats. Bear that in mind when choosing dock lines and fenders for a stay there.

THE PACIFIC COAST

The Balboa Yacht Club operates two busy haul out railways. The smaller handles boats up to 15 tons and costs $50 per day. The larger one with a maximum capacity of 25 tons cost $75 a day. Do-it-yourself work is allowed and help is available, also. Good reports are coming from yachts using the yard located in Vacamonte. Contact Juan Rodriguez at Provada, S.A. Muelles de Atun. Telephone 507-251-0866, 251-0635, 251-1614, or 251-1236.

DRYING OUT

A few yachtsmen take advantage of the considerable Pacific tides to dry out when they need to work on the underwater parts of the hull. Only antifouling paint designed to be submerged soon after application will work in such a project. To dry out, yachts other than multihulls, will need a support to lean against and they usually use the wreck of a large ferrocement yacht in Taboga. It lies in the southern end of the harbor. Before taking your yacht there examine the place at low tide to see where some additional wreckage litters the bottom. Also, be sure to choose a period of calm weather as northerly and northeasterly winds raise a heavy chop off the town in Taboga.

AIDS TO NAVIGATION

Islamorada Int., S.A. 808 Balboa Rd., Balboa, stocks U.S. DMA and NOS charts and publications. They also stock British Admiralty publications and charts. Fax 228-1234, phone 228-4348, 228-6069, 228-4947.

US DMA CHARTS TO PANAMA	1:
21580 Cabo Matapalo to Morro de Puercos	Scale 300,000
21581 Plans within Bahía de Charco Azul	
A. Puerto Armuelles	Scale 25,000
B. Approaches to Pedregal	Scale 15,000
21582 Bahía Montijo	Scale 45,000
Continuation of Rio San Pedro	Scale 45,000
21583 Isla de Coiba	Scale 80,000
21584 Approaches to Puerto Armuelles and Pedregal	Scale 75,000
21601 Morro de Puercos to Panama	Scale 200,000
Plan: Aguadulce anchorage	Scale 50,000
21603 Approaches to Balboa	Scale 25,000
Plan: Balboa Harbor	Scale 10,000
21604 The Panama Canal	Scale 30,000
Plan: Gamboa	Scale 10,000
21605 Panama to Bahía Piña	Scale 25,000
22040 Bahía Piña to Boca Docampado	Scale 300,000
26042 Bahía Concepcion to Punta Brava	Scale 50,000
26060 Puerto Cristobal to Cabo Tiburon	Scale 300,000
26063 Punta San Blas to Bahía Concepcion	Scale 48,640

26065 Cayos Chichime to Punta Rincon and Approach	Scale 75,000
to Golfo de San Blas	Scale 35,000
26066 Approaches to Cristobal	Scale 75,000
Plans:	
A. Portobelo	Scale 25,000
B. Puerto de La Bahía de Las Minas	Scale 15,000
26068 Puerto Cristobal	Scale 15,000
26070 Rio Colorado to Cristobal	Scale 300,000
28041 Approaches to Bocas del Toro and Laguna Chiriquí	Scale 75,000
28042 Entrance to Laguna Chiriquí and Chiriquí Grande	Scale 35,000
Plan: Chiriquí Grande	Scale 15,000
28052 Canal de Bocas del Toro	Scale 20,000
28053 Boca del Drago-Northwestern Passage in Bahía Almirante	Scale 20,000
28054 Bahía Almirante (Southwestern Part)	Scale 20,000

BRITISH ADMIRALTY CHARTS

1278 Isla Fuerte to Punta de Mosquitos	Scale 200,000
Plan: Golfo del Darién	
1299 Panama Canal	Scale 50,000
Plan: Balboa Harbor	Scale 10,000
1300 Approaches to the Panama Canal at Cristobal	Scale 150,000
Plan: Bahía de Panama	Scale 150,000
Plan: Bahía Las Minas	Scale 50,000
1793 Bahía Almirante and Laguna de Chiriquí	Scale 103,000
1799 Anchorages on the north coast of Panama and Costa Rica	
Plan: Boca del Toro	Scale 22,800
Plan: Boca del Drago	Scale 18,200
Plan: Bahía Almirante	Scale 75,000
Plan: Bahía Moin and approaches	Scale 50,000
Plan: Puerto Limon	Scale 25,000
1929 Gulf of Panama	Scale 300,000

TOPOGRAPHICAL MAPS

Instituto Tommy Guardia in Panama City located on Tumba Muerto across from the Catholic University sells topographical maps with a scale of 1:50,000. Although not intended for navigational use we have referred to them occasionally for verifying land outlines. They do not supply coverage for several remote parts of the coast in eastern Panama. In the United States, topographical maps of Panama can be bought from **Map Link**, phone 805-965-4402, Monday through Saturday 10 AM to 6 PM, Pacific Time.

LIST OF LIGHTS

Key to abbreviations:

(T) = temporary

ec = eclipse

lt = light phase

L Fl = long flash

Oc = occulting - total duration of light is longer than total duration of darkness

Racon = Radar responder beacon

Fl = Flashing

Fl( )= Group Flashing

FFL = fixed + flashing

FFl( ) = fixed + group flashing

(vert) = vertical

Iso = isophase, equal periods of dark and light

Q = Quick repeating

IQ = Interrupted quick

F = fixed light

W = white   R = red

G = green   Y = yellow

Mo = Morse alphabet

ext = extinguished, rep ext = reported extinguished

The lights are described in the following manner: Name or number of the light, latitude and longitude, characteristics of the light (period and color), height, range, light description.

Caribbean Coast	
Puerto Obaldia	08°40.0'N, 077°25.0'W, L Fl W 10s, 39ft., 8M, White framework tower.
Isla Grande	09°38.3'N, 079°33.5'W, Fl 5s, 305ft., 24M.
Los Farallones	09°38.5'N, 079°38.2'W, Fl R 5s, 110ft., 10M.
Bahía Las Minas	Range front 09°23.9'N, 079°49.5'W, F G, Orange diamond daymark on beacon.
	Range rear, 80m 170° from front, F G, orange diamond daymark on beacon.
	Range front 09°23.4'N, 079°48.8'W, F G, Orange diamond daymark on beacon.

	Range rear, 160m 148°45' from front, F G, Orange diamond daymark on beacon.
	New pier - N end, 09°23.8'N, 079°49.1'W, F R.
Bahía Las Minas (cont'd)	Tanker jetty - N end, 09°23.6'N, 079°49.1'W, F R.
Colón - Cristobal	
Toro Point, W. side of entrance to Limón Bay	09°22.4'N, 079°57.1'W, L Fl W 30s, 108ft., 16M, White metal tower, stone base.
Cristobal Approach	Buoy A, 09°26.3'N, 079°55'W, Iso W 6s, Red and white stripes. Reported missing (1989).
W Breakwater head	09°23.4'N, 079°55.5'W, V Q (2) R 2s, 100ft., 16M, Red square on metal tower. Radar reflector.
E Breakwater head	09°23.3'N, 079°54.9'W, Mo (U) G 20s, 100ft., 16M, Green triangle on green metal tower.
Explosive Anchorage	09°22.4'N, 079°56.7'W, Fl Y 2s, 19ft., Special yellow near W limit Buoy E of Toro Point 09°22.3'N, 079°56.3'W, Fl Y 2s, Yellow light.
Panama Canal, Atlantic Entrance	Range front 09°17.7'N, 079°55.4'W, F G, Red lights shown on W side and Green lights shown on E side of dredged channel and in Limón Bay. The canal is marked by lights and leading lights mark the center of the channel.
Panama Canal, Entrance Range (middle)	1037 meters, 180°15' from front, F G, 98ft, 15M, Concrete conical tower, visible on range line only. Rear, 2278 meters, 180°15' from front, Oc G, 158ft., 15M, Concrete conical tower. Visible on range line only, F R lights shown on each of 2 radio towers 1.1 miles NE.
Northwest Coast of Panama	
Escudo de Veraguas	09°05.3'N, 081°32.2'W, Fl W 7s, 120ft., 6M, White square framework tower.
Chiriquí Range	Front, 08°56.5'N, 082°06.8'W, Q W, White cylindrical tower with black stripe. F R obstruction lights on tower 1.4M, W F Y on oil tanks 1.5 miles W, visible 202°-222° Rear, 60m, 212° from front, F W 4s, White cylindrical tower with black stripe visible 202°-222°.
Roca Tigre	09°13.0'N, 081°56.5'W, Fl W 5s, 50ft., Metal tower. Racon P.
Hospital Point	09°19.9'N, 082°13.2'W, Fl (2) W 10s, 36ft., 13M, Metal pedestal, F R lights on radio masts 1.2M, 1.9M and 2.2 WNW.
Buoy 8	09°20.4'N, 082°13.6'W, Q R, 15ft.

INTRODUCTION 15

Buoy 9	09°19.9'N, 082°13.5'W, Q G.
Beacon 11	09°18.0'N, 082°17.6'W, W.
Bocas del Toro	09°20.0'N, 082°14.4'W, Fl G, 27ft., White pedestal pier NE point.
Pier, SW corner	Fl R.
Juan Point	09°18.2'N, 082°17.8'W, Fl G 4s, 15ft., 5M, Green tower.
Pondsock Reef	09°17.3'N, 082°19.8'W, Fl W 6s, 15ft., 5M, Red pipe beacon.
Almirante, pier	09°17.3'N, 082°23.5'W, Fl R, Post Occasional.
Isla Pastores, NW end	09°14.7'N, 082°21.2'W, Fl W 10s, 60ft., 9M, Metal windmill tower.
Gulf of Panama	
Punta Piñas	07°33.5'N, 078°12.5'W, Fl W 5s, 222ft., 5M, White metal framework tower.
Punta Santa Barbara (Garachiné)	08°05.4'N, 078°24.7'W, Fl W 4s, 51ft., 5M, White metal framework tower.
Islote Patiñito, summit	08°15.5'N, 078°18.7'W, Fl (2) 15s, 165ft., 4M, White pyramidal concrete tower. Visible 338.6°-222.4° (248.8°).
Punta Bagochiquito, Boca Chica	08°24.9'N, 078°09.8'W, Fl W 5s, 7ft., 4M, White pyramidal concrete tower, Visible 047°-222° (175°).
Isla Batatilla	08°19.4'N, 078°22.8'W, Fl W 5s, 36ft., 5M, White metal framework tower.
Punta Brujas	08°34.0'N, 078°32.0'W, Fl W 4s, 141ft., 5M, White metal framework tower.
Archipelago de las Perlas	
Isla Galera	08°11.7'N, 078°46.6'W, Fl W 15s, 105ft., 12M, White metal framework tower on 4 legs.
Isla de San José near SW end	08°13.0'N, 079°17.8'W, L Fl W 6s, 216ft., 14M, White metal framework tower.
Isla del Rey, San Miguel	08°27.2'N, 078°56.2'W, Fl W 5s, 79ft., 5M, White metal framework tower.
Islote El Pelado	08°38.1'N, 078°42.4'W, Fl W 5s, 79ft., 5M, White metal framework tower.
Isla Pacheca	08°40'N, 079°03'W, Fl W 6s, 39.5ft., 7M, White metal framework tower.
Isla Chepillo	08°57'N, 079°08'W, Fl W 5s, 193ft., 5M, White metal framework tower.

Panama Canal	
Flamenco Island SW side	08°54.5'N, 079°31.4'W, Oc(2) W R 5s, 161ft., White square concrete pedestal. W 267°-003° (96°). R 003°-054° (51°), Storm signals Iso Y 2s + F R lights on radio tower 3.4M NNW. Racon.
Canal Entrance W side	Front 08°57.6'N, 079°34.8'W. F G 65ft., 14M, Concrete tower. Ldg Lts 322°. Visible on leading line only.
	Rear: 2.2M from front, Oc G 5s, 200ft., 20M, Concrete tower. Visible on leading line only.
Naos Island, Jetty	08°55.0'N, 079°32.3'W, 2 F Y (vert).
MI	08°55.0'N, 079°32.3'W, Fl Y 2s, Yellow beacon on pile fl 0.5. The canal is marked by lights and leading lights indicate center of the channel.
Tocumen	09°05'N, 079°23'W, Aero Al Fl W G 10s, 200ft., 9M Tower.
Cerro Cedro	08°59.8'N, 079°33.1'W, Aero Fl R 2s, 508ft.
Corozal	08°58.8'N, 079°34.1'W, Aero Al Fl W G 6.6s, 380ft., 17M, Metal tower.
Howard	08°54.9'N, 079°35.3'W, Aero Al Fl W G 5s, 298ft.
Isla Taboguilla, summit on E side	08°48.4'N, 079°30.7'W, L Fl W R 7s, 190ft., 14M, White metal framework tower.
N end	08°49.0'N, 079°30.8'W, L Fl W 20s, 59ft., 7M, White tower.
Terapa Island	08°46.1'N, 079°32.5'W, Fl W 5s, 46ft., 9M, White tower.
Perique Rock	08°44.7'N, 079°34.8'W, L Fl W 15s, 75ft., 9M, White tower.
Valladolid Rock	08°42.9'N, 079°36.2'W, Fl (2) W 30s, 75ft., 11M, White tower.
Vacamonte, Ldg Lts 321° approx.	Front 08°52.0'N, 079°40.2'W, F W, 18ft., 13M, White up triangle on tower.
	Rear 150m from front, F W, 72ft., 13M, White down triangle on tower.
Vacamonte, Breakwater head	08°51.7'N, 079°40.2'W, Fl (2) W 10s, 29.5ft., 7M, White tower.
Vacamonte, Lts in line	Front 08°52.0'N, 079°40.5'W, F G, 26.2ft., 9M, White up triangle on mast.
	Rear 70m from front, F G, 33ft., 9M, White down triangle on mast.

Isla Bona, Roca Bald	08°34.3'N, 079°35.5'W, L Fl W 13s, 165ft., 15M, White metal framework tower. Visible 211°-104.5° (253.5°) Rep. ext. 1985.
Aguadulce No 13	08°12.3'N, 080°28.2'W, Fl W, 3.25ft., 2M, Black beacon.
Aguadulce No 14	Fl R, 3.25ft., 2M, Red beacon.
Isla Villa	07°56.1'N, 080°18.1'W, 111ft., 8M, White framework tower.
Punta Mala	07°28.1'N, 080°00.0'W, L Fl W 10s, 145ft., 15M, Black metal framework tower.
Isla Iguana, SE end	07°37.6'N, 079°59.9'W, Fl W 14s, 75ft., 8M, White frame-work tower. Visible 184.8°-090° (265.2°) Reported at 18M.
Southwest Coast of Panama	
Frailes del Sur	07°20.3'N, 080°08.7'W, Fl R 4s, 65ft., 12M, White pyramidal concrete tower. Rep. ext. 1988.
Morro de Puercos	07°15'N, 080°26'W, Fl W 7.5s, 270ft., 19M, White metal framework tower. Visible 245°-072° (187°) Rep. ext. 1988.
Northwards	07°40'N, 080°26'W, Aero F R Obstruction, W R lights close by, Reported at 35 miles.
Punta Mariato	07°12.3'N, 080°53.2'W, L Fl W 25s, 170ft., 15M, White metal framework tower.
Isla de Cebaco, Pta. Zurrones	07°29.2'N, 081°15.3'W, Fl W 3s, 347ft., 5M, White square framework tower.
Isla Canal de Afuera	07°41.1'N, 081°37.7'W, L Fl W 2s, 85ft., 5M, White square framework tower.
Isla Jicarita, S end	07°12.7'N, 081°48.0'W, 2 Fl W 15s (vert), 347ft., 19M, White metal framework tower. Visible 270°-118° (208°) synchronized. Rep. reduced range 1985.
Isla Montuosa	07°28.0'N, 082°14.3'W, L Fl W 8s, 95ft., 11M, White metal framework tower. Rep. ext. 1988.
Islas Ladrones	07°51.9'N, 082°26.5'W, L Fl W 9s, 210ft., 12M, White metal framework tower.
Islas Secas	07°56.7'N, 082°00.5'W, L Fl W 9s, 167ft., 7M, White metal framework tower.
Islas Contreras, Isla Uva	07°47.9'N, 081°46.1'W, Fl W 12s, 285ft., 8M, White metal framework tower.
Isla Parida	08°06.0'N, 082°22.3'W, L Fl W 8s, 122ft., 7M, White metal framework tower.

Isla Monitas	08°09.1'N, 082°09.8'W, Fl W 5s, 162ft., 5M, White framework tower.
Puerto Armuelles Pier head	08°16.1'N, 082°51.5'W, Oc R 2s F R (vert), 70ft., 9M, Rep. ext. (1994).
	08°17.3'N, 082°52.2'W, Fl R, Red and white framework tower.
Petroterminal de Panama	08°12'N, 082°53'W, Q R.
Berth 2	Q R.
Berth 3	Q W.
Isla Burica	08°01.5'N, 082°52.5'W, Fl W 10s, 112ft., 12M, Post on white metal framework tower. Rep. ext. (1995).

These lights have been taken from the government list of lights but in the waters around the Isthmus light maintenance has lagged behind the light failure rate. Generally speaking, the lights close to the Panama Canal entrances work, but others get less reliable as a vessel increases the distance from the Canal. Some lights have been charted in wrong locations on the government charts and we have marked them on the sketch chart in the actual locations whenever we saw a discrepancy. As a rule, when making a landfall a navigator should not count on a lighthouse or a buoy to warn him of a hazard to navigation.

Balboa Harbor, Bridge of Americas.

WEATHER FORECASTS

Shipping weather forecasts are not available for the coastal waters of Panama. Yachts equipped with television sets and within range of the stations can get good analyses of the weather on TV.

The SSB (Upper side band) weather broadcasts from the U.S. Coast Guard Chesapeake station include the southwest Caribbean as far south as 10°N. These forecasts will have warnings about a cold front bringing strong northerlies to the Isthmus which happens from the end of December to April. The schedule follows:

UTC	1000	on channels	424, 601, 816
UTC	1130	on channels	601, 816, 1205
UTC	1600	on channels	601, 816, 1205
UTC	1730	on channels	816, 1205, 1625
UTC	2200	on channels	601, 816, 1205
UTC	2330	on channels	601, 816, 1205
UTC	0400	on channels	424, 601, 816
UTC	0530	on channels	424, 601, 816

The SSB channels translate to frequencies as follows:

Channel 403 = 4363.0 kHz

Channel 424 = 4426.0 kHz

Channel 601 = 6501.0 kHz

Channel 802 = 8722.0 kHz

Channel 816 = 8764.0 kHz

Channel 1205 = 13089.0 kHz

Channel 1206 = 13092.0 kHz

Channel 1601 = 17242.0 kHz

Channel 1625 = 17314.0 kHz

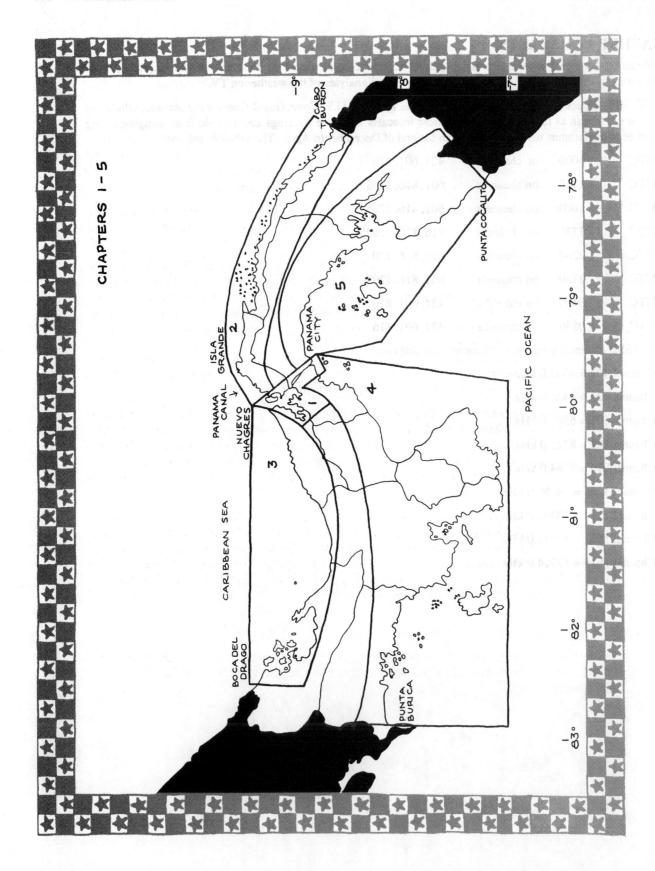

USING THIS GUIDE

Important note : The chartlets are drawn in the Mercator projection and all depths are in feet.

The authors assume that the user has mastered the principles of terrestrial navigation like converting True courses and bearings to Magnetic and Compass values, and back again, that is that the user is aware of magnetic errors like deviation and annually changing variation. These chartlets and the sailing directions are intended to serve an auxiliary function to the full size government marine charts. The guide chartlets illustrate the general trends of the depths and suggest the recommended routes but because of the inadequate scale cannot be used for plotting accurate fixes. Only the full size government charts are designed for this purpose.

We also assume that the user will use common sense and previous experience to decide when a recommended approach or an anchorage becomes dangerous because of weather factors like violent wave action or the lack of appropriate daylight.

The guide alone cannot serve as a tool to safe navigation and the user must refer to other aids like depth sounders, radar, compass bearings and most importantly eyesight. On the Caribbean side of the isthmus the prolific coral growth demands constant vigilance and ability to pilot by eye. Some of the passages described are simply too narrow and winding for the GPS to be a real service except to indicate the location of an anchorage or the initial approach point. The chartlets, which have all soundings in feet, have only one distance scale, latitudes marked on the meridians, where in this Mercator projection, 1 minute of latitude equals 1 nautical mile. We avoided placing an auxiliary distance scale at the bottom of the chartlets as it often leads to taking distance mistakenly from the scale of longitude. While at lower latitudes the difference between 1 minute of longitude and 1 minute of latitude is negligible it becomes considerable at higher latitudes.

We have placed as many soundings as possible on each sketch chart in order to illustrate the trends in depths. Although we suggest possible anchorages by GPS coordinates, bearings or graphic anchor symbols we feel that the wealth of soundings gives the navigator an opportunity to pick an alternate anchorage to better suit weather conditions at the time. Also, many locations have more than one possible anchorage and the navigator should decide where to drop the hook. We often describe the sea bottom characteristics in the sailing directions for each place.

We have visited, often several times, every location we describe in this guide and performed countless soundings and taken countless fixes to ensure accuracy. Still, considering our limited resources, all these chartlets indicate is that our vessel made a safe entry into the area and encountered certain depths. It is likely that without the back-up of aerial support and auxiliary vessels dragging wires at predetermined depths which government surveyors use and still miss things, we made mistakes, too. And so neither the publisher nor the authors can assume responsibility for errors in the sailing directions or the chartlets.

SPECIAL SERVICES

Panama Yacht Services offers an easy means of getting provisions, parts, mail and just about any other logistical support while in remote areas of Panama such as San Blas. Contact Julie Arias at 507-229-7110 or email at ariasjul@pananet.com.

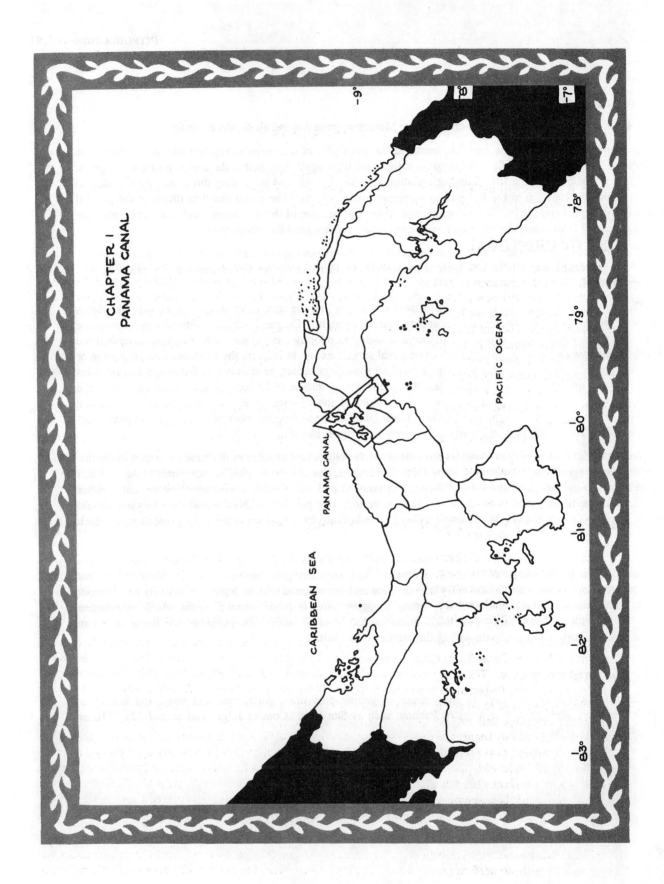

CHAPTER 1
PANAMA CANAL

CHAPTER I

PANAMA CANAL

Chapter I begins with the approaches to the Atlantic entrance to the Panama Canal at the port of Cristobal, continues with the canal itself until the Pacific canal entrance in Balboa. The chapter ends with Playa Kobbe anchorage and a small ship harbor in Vacamonte, west of Balboa.

PORT OF CRISTOBAL

Increased ship traffic and then several anchored ships announce that a yacht is coming near the port of Cristobal. The main entrance is marked by a 100 foot high tower with a 2 second red flashing light at the end of the west breakwater and with a 100 foot tower flashing green Morse letter U (dot dot dash) every 20 seconds on the east breakwater. Inside the harbor several pairs of red and green buoys assisted by a green range lead the way to the Gatun locks. The traffic through the 500 foot wide main entrance was relieved in 1995 by the opening of another narrower entrance in the east part of the breakwater. A white flashing buoy located 09°24.6'N and 079°53.8'W or 2 ½ miles from the breakwater opening marks the beginning of this new channel. The 45-foot deep channel has two sets of lit red and green buoys and a lit range of 180°T further assists the ships entering this way. The range has black crosses on white diamonds mounted low on the mainland. Its lights will easily disappear at night against the town lights. The east and west ends of this breakwater opening also have small green and red lights. This entrance serves vessels heading for Coco Solo ship basin and container ships, which dock at the new Manzanillo container terminal. Less ship traffic through here and also diminished surge reflected from the breakwater walls make this a recommended entrance for yachts during daylight. The three mile long and three mile wide area within the breakwater has ample space for several ships to anchor and still have room for others to sail by. Yachts must anchor on the F anchorage, the Flats, off the fueling wharf and close to the French Canal unless they choose to tie up at the Panama Canal Yacht Club located in the French Canal. The anchorage has depths between 36 and 41 feet with a mud bottom. Take care to dig and test the anchor as sometimes the garbage on the bottom fouls anchor flukes.

The P.C.Y.C. has several slips equipped with electricity and water at .45 a foot per day, $7.00 a foot per month. The Club does not take reservations and it is "first come first served" in this popular marina. Outer slips have ample depth, which diminishes rapidly towards the shore so watch the depth sounder. The club's fuel dock is at the end of the marina adjacent to a long wall where yachts moor stern to after dropping anchor out in about 30 feet of water. Two small striped-lit buoys mark a wreck. Do not drop your anchor between them!

The friendly P.C.Y.C. offers showers, laundry machines, a bar and a restaurant. The office holds mail addressed c/o Panama Canal Yacht Club, Apartado 5041, Cristobal, Republic of Panama. Use the yacht's name after the addressee name. Their fax number is 441-7752, country code 507, phone 441-5882. The phone at the bar is 441-5883. The Panamanian Immigration office on the premises of the Y.C. will check in arrivals and instruct them where to go to complete the formalities. Remember that once out of the gates you enter a real urban jungle where muggings and robbery occur. Behave accordingly by not wearing jewelry, not showing large amounts of money and by keeping an eye on shady characters following you. It is fairly safe to walk to the offices in the harbor complex, post office there and the INTEL, the telecommunications company open every day of the year, 7:30 AM till 10:00 PM. INTEL takes good care of the faxes for yachtsmen; have the boat's name included on faxes. To go anywhere else, you should use taxis until you get more familiar with the town. To get cash go to the Free Zone, which has, several banks equipped to give cash advances on various credit cards. Carry your passport in order to obtain a pass into the Free Zone grounds. El Rey supermarket in the Arco Iris area, a .20 bus ride, also has an ATM machine to get cash with credit cards.

P.C.Y.C. has two railway type haul-outs. The smaller can handle boats under 35 feet LOA and the larger has 20 ton capacity with the draft normally limited to about 7 feet. The tide range really determines the maximum draft for this railway. The railway master would like to see a drawing or at least a photograph of the keel configuration. The railway costs $75.00 in and out plus $1.50 per foot a day on the hard. Yacht owners are required to shore up their vessels.

DIESEL, GASOLINE AND PROPANE

The Club dispenses diesel fuel at its fuel dock but to get gasoline one must carry containers to a gas station in town - use a taxi. All propane bottles other than the Panamanian exchange bottles have to be filled in Panama City. Normally somebody does this service for yachtsmen at a reasonable charge - inquire in the club office for details.

MEDICAL HELP

Several clinics have physicians and dentists available all day but specialists often receive patients only on certain days. The standard of care and charges are lower than in Panama City. Definitely seek recommendations from long term liveaboards. The American Embassy in Panama City at 227-1777 has a list of English speaking doctors.

SAIL REPAIR

Manuel Pretelt has repaired countless sails and has done other canvas work for yachts earning much praise, he can be reached at 441- 2389.

SHIP BATTERIES

TASCO, a Panama City company builds heavy duty marine batteries. Call them at 228-0555 to find the right sizes and models to suit your needs as well as their current distributor in Colón.

MECHANICAL AND ELECTRICAL REPAIRS

Best inquire in the Club office for the latest recommendations and do not fail to talk to the long time dock residents in the marina.

HARDWARE SUPPLIES

Several stores specialize in general merchandise or focus on paints, high pressure equipment, wood products etc. Seek current information from long time residents of the marina.

FREE ZONE

The Free Zone, Zona Libre in Spanish, is a sprawling commercial center of businesses selling about everything from footwear and clothing to electronics. Some merchants sell only wholesale, others also retail at prices comparable to the ones outside the zone. Bring your passport to obtain a pass to enter.

FOOD SHOPPING

The closest to the Club and safest to go to is El Rey in Arco Iris. It carries a substantial inventory of Panamanian and imported products. What you cannot find there might be available in Super 99 downtown. Use a taxi to go there and back. A small fruit and vegetable market sits on the town side of the railway tracks at the northern perimeter of the Cristobal harbor area and is safe. Another, larger central market is in the middle of the town. A row of vegetable stalls lines Avenida Bolivar just north of the bus terminal and a good bakery, Peter Pan, occupies the corner across from the bus station.

CHARTS

Islamorada International in Balboa acts as agents for British Admiralty and U.S. Defense Mapping Agency and has a very complete inventory of charts for the whole world as well as Lists of Lights, Tide Tables, Pilots and Cruising Guides. Employees speak English. Phones 228-4348, 228-6069, 228-4947.

INTERNATIONAL COURIERS

Federal Express Company uses the Jetex company which has offices in the Free Zone, Colón, Panama City and the town of David. Both DHL and UPS have offices both in the Free Zone, Colón and in Panama City while DHL also has a branch in David. All companies deliver to Panama Canal Yacht Club. For details see page 7.

CONNECTIONS WITH PANAMA CITY

Inexpensive air-conditioned express buses leave for Panama City every half hour from the main bus station in Colón. The driver will drop you off in the City after you call loudly "Parada!" Pay on arrival at the destination. These buses leave Panama City from two terminals, on Avenida Central and on Avenida Peru and Calle 30. Of the two, the latter is safer and serves only the express buses. The bus ride takes about an hour and a half. If that is too slow you can take a commuter plane from Colón to Paitilla Airport in Panama City in the morning and return in the evening. Prices are very reasonable but one must add the taxi fare to the airport in Colón.

SHELTER COVE MARINA & LODGE

Shelter Cove Marina & Lodge located at the base of the west breakwater in the old Ft. Sherman is scheduled to be fully operational in October, 2002. The 120-slip facility with full dockside amenities will accommodate yachts up to 200 feet long and will include two restaurants and a small upscale hotel. A ship's chandlery is planned along with a boat yard.

26 THE PANAMA GUIDE

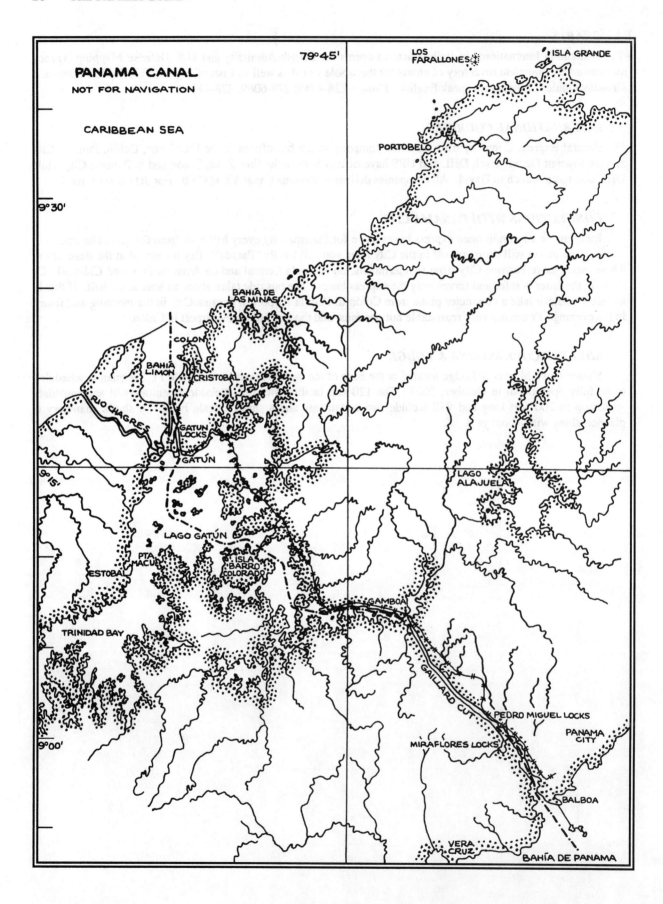

THE PANAMA CANAL SYSTEM

The Panama Canal transfers ships from one ocean to another through a system of locks. A vessel entering at the Atlantic side has to be lifted 85 feet in three steps to the level of Gatun Lake. After crossing 31 miles of the lake, the vessel drops 31 feet in one step at Pedro Miguel and enters Miraflores Lake. A mile further south the vessel enters double lockage at Miraflores and drops a further 54 feet to the level of the Pacific Ocean.

The 1000 foot long lock chambers limit the maximum ship length to 950 feet and the chamber width of 110 feet allows ships with beams of up to 106 feet. Maximum allowed ship draft is 39 feet 6 inches in freshwater.

Gatun Lake, created by damming River Chagres, holds the water necessary for the operation of the locks. Propelled by gravity the water reaches the locks via a system of main culverts located in the central and side walls and nearly as big as the tubes of the Penn Central Railroad crossing under the Hudson River. Next, the water enters several lateral culverts which run under the lock chamber. Each lateral culvert has 5 holes measuring 4½ feet in diameter. These culverts distribute the water through 100 holes in the chamber floor. The 52 million gallons of fresh water necessary to lock a ship from one ocean to another flows into the ocean after having done its work.

PANAMA CANAL TRANSIT

In order to organize a transit a skipper calls 443-2293 when the yacht lies in Cristobal or 272-4571 when in Balboa. An inspection by a Canal employee follows and validates a transit within 14 days after paying the transit fee. The fees are now $500 for yachts up to 50 feet LOA, $750 for yachts between 50 and 80 feet, $1,000 for craft between 80 and 100 feet and $1,500 for those over 100 feet LOA. These fees are, of course, subject to change. Yachtsmen should be aware that in addition refundable buffer fees will also be charged. These are deposits held against the possibility of pilot delays caused by the yacht and damage or uncollected wharfage a yacht might ensue. The refundable buffer fees are $800 for yachts up to 50 feet (fees are based on Canal stastics of incidents), $650 for vessels between 50 and 80 feet, $700 for boats between 80 and 100 feet and those over 100 feet deposit $900. These monies are paid directly to the bank.

PREPARING A YACHT FOR TRANSIT

Signing the indemnity form should alert all skippers to prepare their boats thoroughly against collisions with other vessels and lock walls. The regulations require four 125 foot long continuous locklines (no knotted pieces). Yachts up to 45 ft. LOA will find 3/4 inch nylon lines quite adequate, yachts up to 65 ft. LOA should upgrade to 7/8 inch diameter and vessels up to 120 ft. will do fine with 1 inch. The loops in the ends should be big enough to go over 18 inch bollard heads. Quite often the locklines will go almost vertically up from the boat. Make sure they do not jump out of chocks and catch under the bow and stern railings. Strong, through bolted closed chocks are ideal but few yachts have them. If necessary rig heavy blocks to lead the lines clear of all railings. Make sure all cleats are bolted through backplates.

The Canal requires one handler for each line and they should have the experience and strength to deal with sudden extreme loads. The water in the locks boils when gravity pushes it through a hundred holes in the lock floor in under 15 minutes. Fender the boat generously on both sides. You may collect a quantity of tires that other yachts have left in the P.C.Y.C. and the Balboa Y.C. Wrap the tires in heavy duty garbage bags to protect the topside paint.

Most of the smaller yachts transiting need to find additional crew. Fortunately, yachtsmen from other boats often want to experience their first canal passage on somebody else's yacht. They understand handling a small boat and the limitations of living in a confined space - important since a yacht transit usually takes two days and involves providing meals and bunks for extra crew. People from other yachts are also on hand to inform when your schedule changes unexpectedly. In the 24 hours before the transit one should keep in touch with the scheduling office by phone. Even then the Canal may delay your passage at the last minute without as much as saying sorry while a yacht which cancels a transit later than a day before faces a fine of $295.

Sometimes in the absence of fellow yachties one must seek others. Try some of the military personnel in the area - obtain phone numbers from the yacht clubs. Professional Panamanian linehandlers charge between $40 and

$50 a passage. Check their credentials with the yacht club managers. If you take Panamanians make sure that you can communicate with them enough to request moving fenders, adjusting lock lines and even adding a spring line when tying to a tug boat in a lock - one of the ways to transit.

THREE METHODS OF TRANSITING

CENTER OF THE LOCK

This entails placing a yacht in the center of the lock with bow lines and stern lines holding her in place. Providing the locklines are of adequate strength and free of knots and splices, the center lock transit is the safest. The only problem arises when several yachts lock at the same time and the lock controllers decide to raft three, sometimes four of the boats side by side. As a result the two outside boats hold the entire assembly. Failure of one of their lines or mishandling usually causes some of the hulls to crash into the walls. Be sure to use spring lines between boats in a raft and stagger masts so they cannot tangle when the boats roll.

ALONGSIDE ANOTHER VESSEL

Tying alongside a tugboat is least troublesome. The tugboat will already be attached to the wall and the yacht will tie up alongside with bow, stern and spring lines. Use a lot of fenders. The yacht will separate from the tugboat before proceeding to the next lock chamber and tie again there. Locking alongside a tugboat must be requested. Some yachtsmen avoid this method because tugs are often festooned with oily tires used as fenders.

ALONGSIDE LOCK WALLS

Transiting against a lock wall should only be done by very large yachts equipped with large fenders as the jagged hollows and rough surface of the concrete can damage the topsides. Also, a smaller yacht can roll in the turbulence far enough for the spreaders to hit the wall. Controlling the yacht can be difficult because the lines will lead straight up when the water level in the lock is very low.

IN THE PANAMA CANAL

RADIO COMMUNICATIONS FROM THE CANAL

VHF channel 12 is reserved for canal operations and pilot information. VHF channels 20, 63, 05 have a relay station which enables VHF transmissions from one end of the canal to reach vessels at the other end.

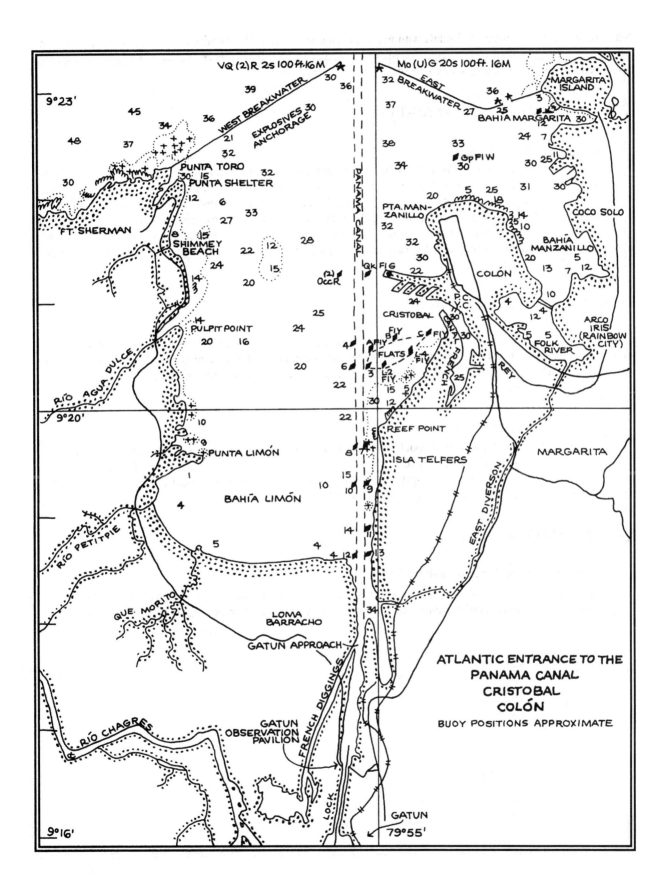

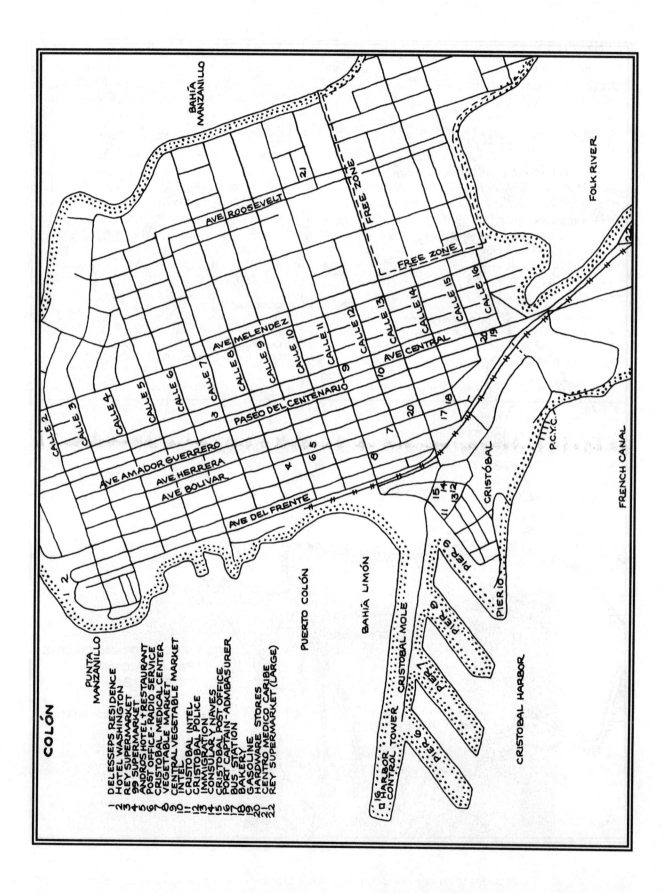

THE TRANSIT

In the port of Cristobal a pilot boards a yacht from a pilot boat at the anchorage. Boardings commonly happen in the early mornings so yachts moored at the P.C.Y.C. leave the dock early enough to move to the Flats to meet the pilot boat. The man who boards a yacht over 65 foot LOA will have a Panama Canal pilot license. Smaller vessels receive advisors. These advisors, usually young men in training to become pilots, have considerably less experience so yacht skippers should offer full information about any handling peculiarities or power limitations of their boats.

A south bound yacht will proceed from the anchorage to Gatun Locks where it will enter behind a larger vessel. As the yacht enters the locks the men on the walls above will throw heaving lines armed with monkey fists to the line handlers on deck. The line handlers should know how to tie the heaving line to their lock warps with a slip clove hitch then slack the line until it can be thrown over the bollards above. The crew on the yacht will then take up the slack as the water in the lock rises. When the gates ahead open and the warps are let go, the yacht handlers take them in until the eye of the line arrives. They should not untie the heaving line. The lock men will then walk with the single yacht or the raft of yachts to the next chamber with the heaving lines still attached to the warps. The three chambers of Gatun Locks raise the vessel 85 feet to the level of fresh water Lake Gatun. A southbound vessel will then motor 31 miles to Pedro Miguel lock. Some pilots and advisors take yachts through a narrow short cut called Banana Cut. It begins at buoys 5 and 7, runs close to beautiful lush islets and exits between buoys 35 and 37 off the north shore of Barro Colorado Island. The Smithsonian Tropical Research Institute maintains a research center there to study most of the isthmus animals and plant life in a low rain forest environment. This famous site is open to tourism.

Smaller yachts often have to anchor in Gamboa Reach to spend the night while vessels with licensed pilots as a rule continue to complete the transit in one day. At Gamboa a Pacific bound vessel enters Gaillard Cut - a nine mile long cut carved through rock and shale. The hardest excavation work during the canal construction had to cope with repeated landslides here. Eventually the worst spot, Contractor's Hill on the west bank of the canal, was sliced from 410 feet to 370 feet high to stabilize the earth, but landslides may still occur - the most recent was in 1987. The canal section north of the area was widened from 300 feet to the present day 500 feet to allow larger ships to pass each other. As the ships grow larger still the latest project aims at widening Gaillard Cut to 630 feet on the straight and to 730 feet at the curves.

Photo courtesy of Phil Wade

Three yachts transit Pedro Miguel Locks in the center of lock in front of a large ship.

32 THE PANAMA GUIDE

The Panama Canal

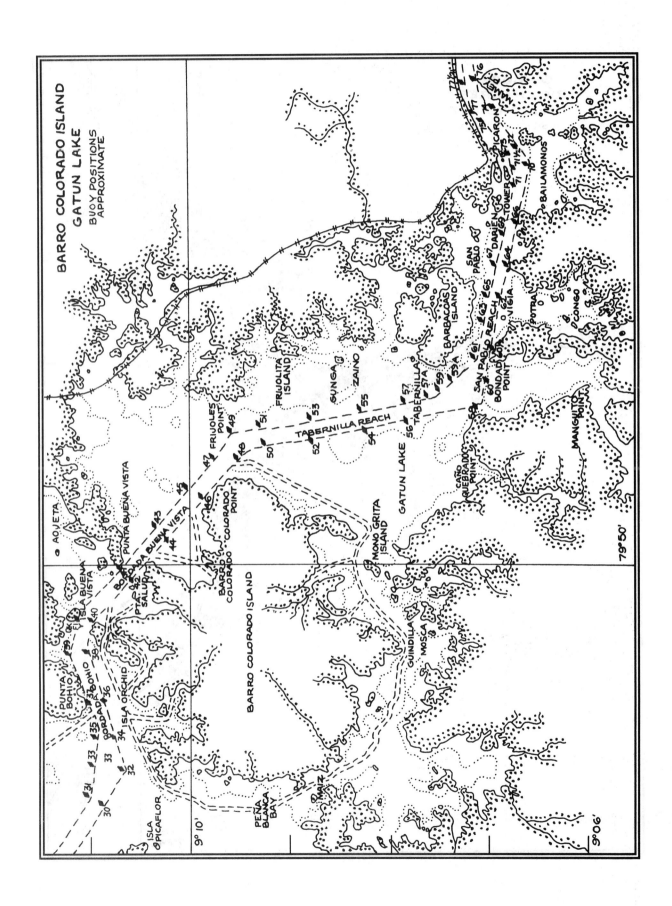

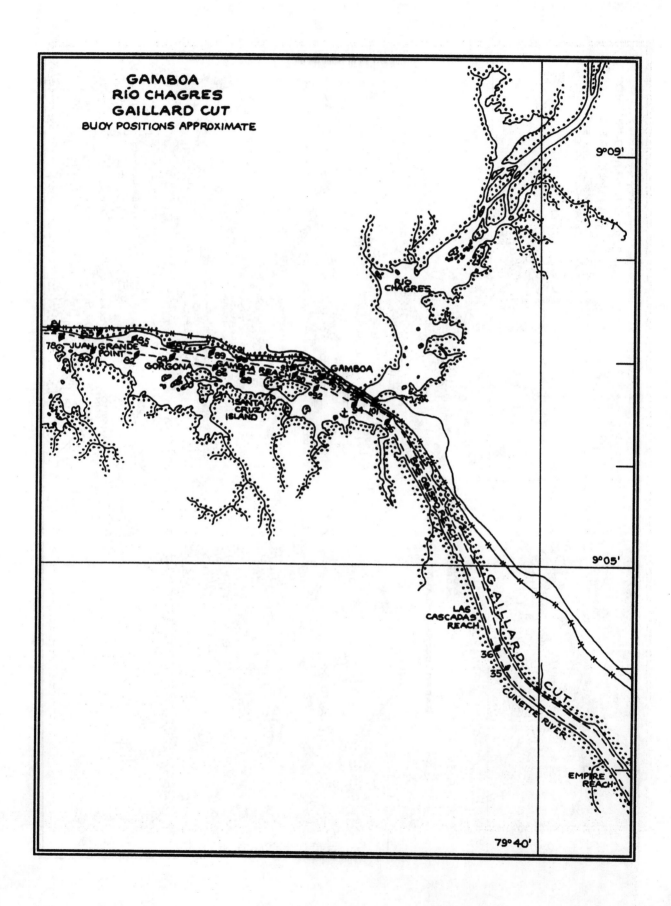

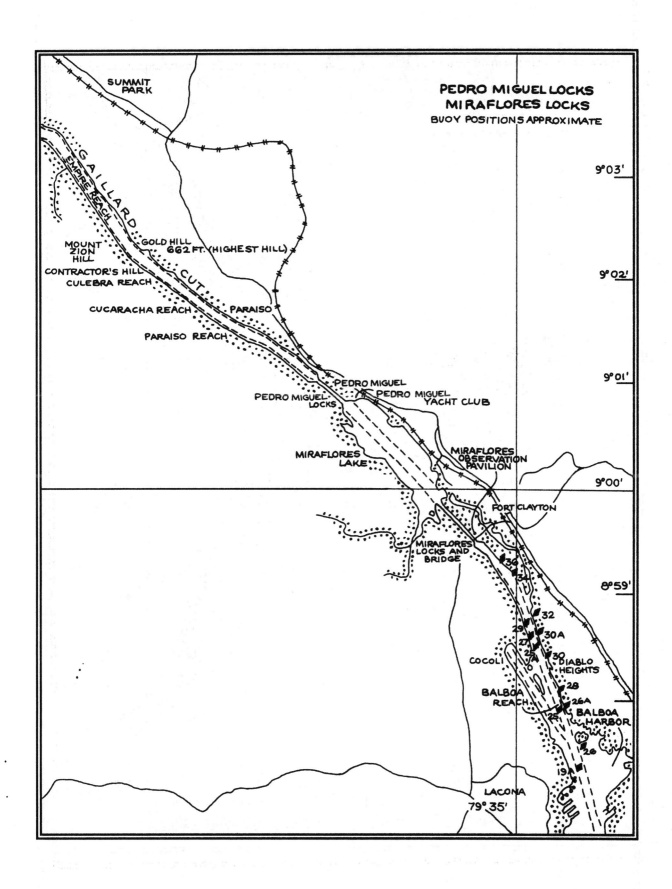

36 THE PANAMA GUIDE

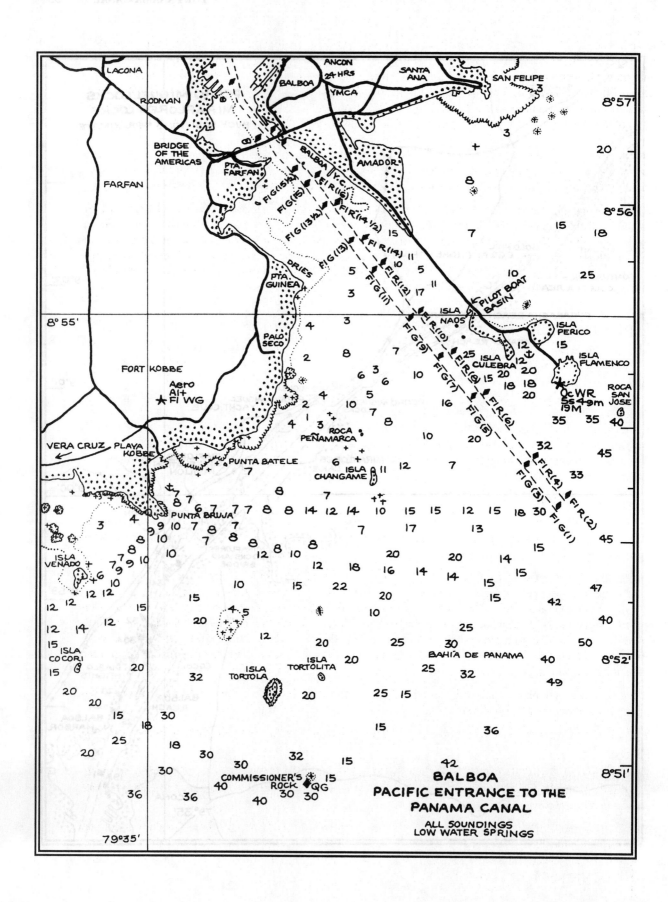

A Pacific bound yacht will enter the Pedro Miguel lock ahead of a ship and receive the heaving lines from the lock crew. After dropping 31 feet in the first chamber a vessel then passes the Pedro Miguel Yacht Club (see information in the section on boatyard services) and proceeds through the mile long Miraflores Lake to the two chambered Miraflores Lock, the last step before reaching the Pacific Ocean and the port of Balboa. Yachts enter here ahead of ships. When the lock doors open after the last chamber levels out do not let the advisor rush with letting go of the lock lines. A tricky current eddy often develops at the door edges and takes a few minutes to settle.

The pilot will leave the yacht on the canal boat off the Balboa Yacht Club. Most yachts then pick up a mooring at Balboa Y.C. The additional linehandlers who assisted in the transit can leave on the Balboa Y.C. launch. If the fuel dock is free a yacht may tie up to top up fuel and water tanks and let the extra crew go then.

When choosing a mooring remember a drying shoal which starts about 150 feet northeast of red buoy no.14½ and goes towards the club building. Some moorings close to it can only take 2 to 3 foot draft boats at low tide, so consult the tide tables. Yachts over 80 ft. LOA should pick only the outer mooring buoys and keep a person on watch in case a strong current combined with gusty wind causes the mooring to drag. Anchoring among moorings is forbidden. The moorings cost .50 ft/day plus a US$25 one time administrative fee. Long term users can obtain lower rates.

ALTERNATE ANCHORAGES IN BALBOA

Occasionally, when all the club moorings have been taken, new arrivals can anchor temporarily between the ship channel and the Fort Amador sea wall-causeway on the stretch of water from buoys #14 and #10. When sounding your way in remember to allow for the considerable tidal range on the Pacific shores. The low tide depths outside the channel vary from over 20 feet to as little as 6 feet. As the Balboa Y.C. does not allow leaving yacht tenders at their pier, going ashore from an anchored yacht will require a crew person to operate the dinghy. Another temporary anchorage used by yachts is in the cove between Perico Island and Isla Culebra where the bottom is mud. Again going to town requires a dinghy operator. Reaching the road on the causeway involves climbing over the sea wall rocks and then walking 2 nautical miles to the bus stop at the foot of the causeway.

BALBOA YACHT CLUB

Balboa Yacht Club maintains a 24 hours launch service and yachts are not permitted to leave their dinghies at the dock area. However, other crewmembers can drop somebody off on the dock and then return to the mother ship. To call the launch use a loud horn or call on VHF channels 06, 16 or 63.

The Club office receives and will send faxes for you. Fax no. 507-228-5446, phone no. 507-228-5794, and the email address is bycbma@sinfo.net. The office hours are 8AM to 5PM Monday through Friday, 8AM to noon on Saturday and closed on Sunday. The Club holds letters addressed to your name and the boat's name c/o Balboa Yacht Club, Apartado 552, Balboa, Republic of Panama. There is no mail delivery in Panama so a Club employee occasionally goes to the Balboa post office to collect the mail - about once a week. We found it more efficient to have letters addressed to your name, Entrega General, Balboa-Ancon, Republic of Panama. They keep the letters for about a month.

Overseas faxes and phone calls can be made and received in the air-conditioned INTEL (Panamanian telecommunications company) office in Balboa.

The club has showers at the swimming pool. A $10 per year membership fee is required to gain entry into the swimming pool area.

The smaller haulout railway in BYC costs $50 per day and can take boats up to 15 tons. The larger one costs $75 a day and can handle up to 25 tons. The railways are quite busy with the boats that belong to club members so make reservations well in advance.

The floating fuel dock at the end of the Club pier dispenses diesel and gasoline to visiting yachtsmen Mondays through Thursdays. One must pay in advance in the office and show the receipt to the dock pump operator. Water is available on the fuel dock. Four slips with floating docks can be rented on an hourly or daily basis when no club member yachts are using them.

To fill propane bottles hire a taxi for a round trip ($6) to the Tropigas filling station in the City. Taxis await customers at the club parking lot.

CLEARING INTO PANAMA IN BALBOA

At the top of the steps from the club pier you will find a small post with an immigration officer. He will do the initial entry formalities and instruct you on further proceedings and locations of the other offices. Taxi drivers at the club know their locations, also.

THE TOWN OF BALBOA

Balboa is safe to walk around and has restaurants, take-outs and small stores including a 24 Hours grocery near the YMCA building. Nearby you will also find two banks with ATM machines, a post office and Islamorada Chart Agents. Steven's Circle opposite the post office has a Panamanian crafts market with Kuna molas, Embera baskets and "jagua" carvings in ivory nuts, Guaymi dresses and much more. It takes about twenty minutes to walk there from BYC or you can take a bus which stops close to the yacht club in front of the golf club.

TRANSPORTATION FROM BALBOA TO PANAMA CITY

The yellow SACA bus which stops near the yacht club ends its run on Plaza 5 de Mayo in Panama City. So do the tiny beat-up buses which stop near the 24 Hours store in Balboa. From Plaza 5 de Mayo it is best to take a taxi to other destinations until you become more familiar with the city. Some yachtsmen with many errands to do hire a taxi on an hourly basis - usually US$8 an hour.

SHOPPING AND SERVICES IN PANAMA CITY

Panama City has several US style supermarkets: "Super 99", "El Rey", "Casa de la Carne" and "Gago". The El Dorado area on Tumba Muerto has a "Super 99" and an "El Rey", a large post office including the Express Mail branch for packages from the US and a customs desk right there to clear them through. Two copying enterprises, one inside El Dorado Mall and the other across the street, have machines large enough to copy charts. Inside El Dorado Mall you will find restaurants, shoe and clothing stores, a hardware store and the Gran Morrison department store with a good selection of English language books and magazines. At the back of El Dorado is a street with an oriental foods store and a vegetarian restaurant. Further down that way the "Do It Center", a large two floor store, sells tools, outboards and home improvement items. A couple of blocks away from El Dorado on Tumba Muerto, side by side, stand a huge branch of the Novey hardware store and Arrocha, a big drugstore.

To stock up on fresh vegetables and fruit for long passages go to Mercado Abasto, a sprawling farmer's market on the road from Balboa to the City. Inside you can hire a guy with a trolley cart. Ask him to get a wooden crate for .25 - .30 and then follow you and load the purchases. When finished get a small truck to drive all the stuff to the yacht club. The cart guys earn between $1 and $2 and a truck will cost between $4 and $6 depending on your bargaining skills.

In Panama City, the capital of the country which claims to be the commercial focus of Central and South America, one can obtain most industrial products made in the US. Finding them may take some time, though, as many businesses carry what seem to be unrelated items. Asking the local boatowners, boat captains or long term expats helps a lot. Here is a list of some important distributors.

Centro Marino on Avenida Nacional has a good supply of marine supplies, including Mariner outboards and has a busy outboard service and repair shop. Use a taxi in this bad area.

Abernathy on Transistmica has marine hardware, sport fishing and diving equipment as well as yachtie clothing. They repair fishing rods and reels.

Panama Outdoors on Avenida Justo Arosemena and Calle 30 sells marine supplies and Mercury outboards.

Pesqueros, S.A. on Avenida Balboa and Calle 27 sells workboat marine hardware from shackles to chain.

TASCO builds batteries including deep cycle marine batteries of good quality. Call 228-0555 for advice on models, sizes and distributors.

Motor Sport Panama, S.A. on Tumba Muerto sells Suzuki outboards.

Toyopan Tesa on Tumba Muerto and Centro Yamaha on Via Brasil both have an excellent stock of spare parts for Yamaha outboards, of which some are identical to Mariner motors, and also Yamaha generators and parts.

Novey Servi Center on Avenida Central sells Johnson outboards and parts and other marine hardware. Novey Servi Center is a chain of very large hardware stores all of which carry paints, tools and household items.

Central de Tuercas y Tornillos on Avenida Nacional has all kinds of fasteners in metric and standard sizes - use a taxi in that area.

Centro Industrial on Via Cincuentenario carries fasteners, tools, chain, O rings, pumps, hydraulic equipment, heavy marine hardware, electric motors.

Dimar, S.A. in Edificio La Balinera on Vista Hermosa sells bearings, seals and fan belts, as well as Jabsco pumps and Jabsco parts.

Electro Diesel on Via Fernandez de Cordoba sells hoses and Racor filters.

Rodelag on Transistmica sells power tools, gaskets, seals, bearings.

Protecsa deals in marine transmissions of all sizes.

Egeo stores in several locations sell fiberglass materials, resins and plumbing fittings.

Radicom Icom, S.A. on Tumba Muerto across from El Dorado Mall sells and services Icom radios.

Radio Shack on Tumba Muerto, a couple of doors from Radicom Icom has the usual Radio Shack inventory.

Several companies service marine electronics - definitely seek advice from yacht club residents as to the recommended outfit.

Liferaft service and certification is performed by Gamdare International on Avenida 28 North.

Centro Decorativo on 4 de Julio has a large inventory of fabrics including fabrics for marine use.

Siufer, S.A. on Tumba Muerto opposite Cerveceria Nacional does expert welding on stainless steel and aluminum. They also have a good stock of tube, pipe, sheet and plate of these metals. Call 236-1450 and ask for ingeniero Siu, the owner, who speaks English.

Max E. Jimenez on a side street of Tumba Muerto opposite of Cerveceria Nacional sells industrial chemicals among them silica gel (drying agent) crystals, additives for purifying water, etc.

Camera repair - go to Photo Zoom store on Via España close to Hotel Panama and across from Hotel Continental. They are dealers for major camera makers and take in repairs.

English language books are sold in all branches of Gran Morrison in Paitilla, Via España, and El Dorado. Argosy on Via Argentina close to Via España carries literary and art books in several languages. The Smithsonian Institute up hill from Plaza 5 de Mayo has a bookstore with several titles covering all aspects of tropical natural history as well as a rich library open to visitors.

Restaurants. Via Argentina hosts several restaurants from low priced to very sophisticated.

For any additional business or services information one should consult the yellow and blue pages of the phone directory.

Medical services. Panama City has several large hospitals and clinics with experienced physicians many of whom had training in the US and speak English. Still, it is highly advisable to inquire among the expats or the BYC office personnel for recommendations. Many drugs which in the US require a doctor's prescription can be bought directly from pharmacies. The American Embassy at 227-1777 keeps a list of the English speaking doctors. The ambulance numbers are 225-1436, 228-2786, 228-2787. The number for Hospital Santo Tomas is 225-1436. Dial 104 for police.

PLAYA KOBBE ANCHORAGE

For yachtsmen who have to spend time near Panama City but would like to avoid the polluted air and water off the Balboa Yacht Club, Playa Kobbe provides a convenient escape. The anchorage off the public beach has a safe dinghy landing right under the eyes of friendly 24 hour watchmen. The showers and bathrooms stay open all week while a restaurant opens during weekends and holidays. A short walk brings you to the main road to catch a bus to Panama City. Buses pass quite often on this route between the City and Vera Cruz.

Study the sketch chart of the Balboa entrance to the Panama Canal to get to this anchorage. From the green channel buoy no.1 or GPS Lat. 08°53.2'N and Long. 079°31.9'W steer 270°T for Punta Brujas and pass through GPS point 08°53.1'N and 079°32.9'W south of Isla Changame in a least depth of 10-11 feet. Carry on 270°T over 7-8 foot depths until close to Punta Brujas when you should turn to about 345°T and anchor in depths suitable to the draft of your yacht. The bottom is all mud. In depths of less then 6 feet the bottom has scattered rocks imbedded in sand. Bear in mind that the rocks south of Isla Changame disappear under a rising tide. Also the depths on the sketch chart (page 36) refer to the lowest spring tides and most of the time you will have deeper water.

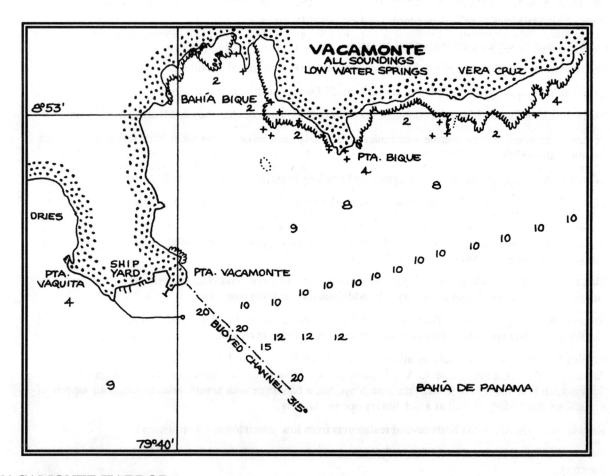

VACAMONTE HARBOR

This fishing vessel port has several sets of large docks and a large shipyard, Astillero Nacional, capable of hauling out boats from 40ft LOA to small freighters. The use of synchrolifts costs several hundred dollars and would probably be of interest only to large yachts. However, the labor rates are quite reasonable by US or European standards. The port and the yard welcome yachts but during fishing season are filled with hundreds of fishing boats through January till the middle of April. A 20 foot deep buoyed channel and a range of 315°T leads into the harbor. The treeless 80 foot high Isla Melones rises from the sea about 4½ miles offshore from Vacamonte and makes a good starting point to find the channel. The shipyard has a well supplied chandlery oriented towards the needs of working vessels. Scheduled buses connect Vacamonte with Panama City. Vicamonte has added facilities for yachts. At a duty free dock yachts can obtain water and fuel at duty free prices. Call 507-251-0866, 251-0635, 251-1614, or 251-1236. The manager is Juan Rodriguez.

THROUGH THE PANAMA CANAL FROM THE PACIFIC

Approaching Balboa from the south presents no problem. The thousand foot high Isla Taboga makes a good landmark even on hazy days. Next you will see Flamenco Island, 363 feet high and armed with a powerful lighthouse. When entering the buoyed channel into Balboa stay out of the way of commercial traffic and favor the northeastern side of the channel where the water is deep even outside the buoys. Plan to arrive off the Balboa Yacht Club moorings area during daylight and a launchman may come out to direct you to an available mooring open to visiting yachts. Generally, the moorings south of the pier are for visitors. Calling ahead on VHF 6, 16, or 63 may help if the launch operators are by the radio on the fuel dock - the launches have no radios. After picking up a mooring new arrivals should report to the immigration officer on the club premises only if they have not cleared into Panama previously.

To arrange a canal transit call 272-4571 to ask the Admeasurer's office to send a man to your boat. After that comes a visit to the Treasurer's office to pay for the transit in cash only, to receive the Ship Identification Number and only then schedule the transit. Mega yachts often hire shipping agents, such as Associated Steamship Agency which has handled yachts before, who will take care of all formalities including clearing into the country, flying out crew, shipping equipment, finding additional line handlers and even dealing with medical emergencies. Transcanal Yacht Services also helps dozens of yachts annually. A smaller agency and consequently less costly and more flexible, Transcanal will organize all aspects of a transit or will help with particular problems like locating line handlers or renting you their pre-made lock lines. Call Tina McBride at 228-8056, 637-2999 or email at tinamc@sinfo.net. All these agents operate on both sides of the canal.

The transit to the Atlantic is the reverse of the south bound passage. The advisor and pilots board yachts from the club launch at Balboa Yacht Club. Yachts enter the Miraflores and Pedro Miguel locks behind large vessels. Very often north bound yachts are left to anchor for a night off a small boat club on the east shore from the entrance to Gatun Locks. The anchorage is 50 to 60 feet deep and has a mud bottom. In the Gatun Locks yachts enter ahead of ships. When the last lock door opens onto the Caribbean ask your advisor to hold on to the lock warps until the turbulence ahead subsides. The pilots and advisors leave yachts on the Flats using a Canal pilot boat but you must take your extra line handlers ashore in a dinghy after anchoring on the Flats or after docking in the Panama Canal Yacht Club.

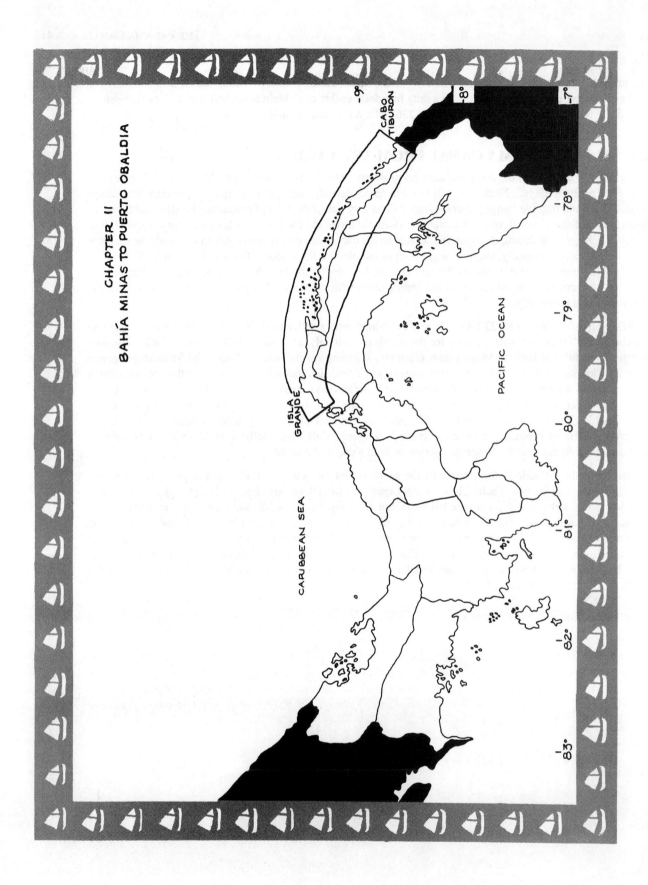

CHAPTER II

BAHÍA LAS MINAS TO PUERTO OBALDIA, INCLUDING THE SAN BLAS ISLANDS

This chapter describes the anchorages along the 60 miles of coast between Cristobal and Punta San Blas. It then continues with details of the San Blas Islands which are scattered along 120 miles of the mainland from Golfo de San Blas to Cape Tiburon on the border with Colombia. These coastal waters and the narrow belt of land up to the continental divide have been designated as the Comarca de San Blas in Spanish or Kuna Yala in the language of the indigenous Kuna people.

WEATHER AND WINDS

This part of the coastline lies outside the direct influence of the Caribbean Trade winds and only the constant swell from the northeast reminds one of the trades. The area lies blissfully south of the hurricane tracks, too. Winds from north to northeast blow between the end of December through April sometimes at 25 to 30 knots. An occasional cold front from north Central America brings even stronger northerly winds. All these onshore winds draw a curtain of haze reducing visibility down to 2 miles. The dry weather season usually begins in January and lasts through March although it may come as late as February and stay through April. At the height of the dry season the offshore islands receive no rain although showers still fall in the mountains.

It rains, at times very heavily, during all the other months of the year. Visibility, however, improves dramatically and the forested mountains of Cordillera de San Blas and Serrania del Darién stand dark and bold as a backdrop to the offshore islands.

During the rainy season winds become variable. On sunny days the onshore breeze starts around noon. The offshore cool mountain breeze may come in the early evening if it rains heavily in the mountains or late at night on drier days. The rainy months also have a lot of winds, at times quite fresh, from the west semicircle. This variable winds region reaches out over the offshore waters as far as about 10°30'N latitude sometimes even further. Powerful "chocosana" squalls with driving rain and blinding lightning occur occasionally and often travel pretty far offshore.

CURRENTS AND TIDES

The prevailing current offshore flows eastward paralleling the general curve of the coastline and westerly winds during the rainy season will reinforce it. A very strong easterly blow close to shore may temporarily stop this easterly flow or even reverse it. Strong trade winds far out in the Caribbean, on the other hand, may intensify this persistent countercurrent. Inside the San Blas Islands currents become variable and because of the presence of many rivers a heavy rainfall in the mountains will cause a general outflow of water towards the ocean. Maximum tide range does not exceed 1.3 ft.

NAVIGATING WITH GPS

The latitude and longitude grid on some governmental navigation charts for the area of this chapter have not been adjusted for GPS users. For example, while the 1984 issue of DMA 26065 has a correct grid, the 1982 DMA 20063 has not. Both charts are sold now. Hence, before plotting your own GPS fixes on older charts you should add about one tenth of a minute to all latitude readings and two tenths of a minute to all longitude readings. These corrections will relate your fixes more accurately to the charted features. However, the suggested corrections are approximate as some places are charted with different errors.

44 The Panama Guide

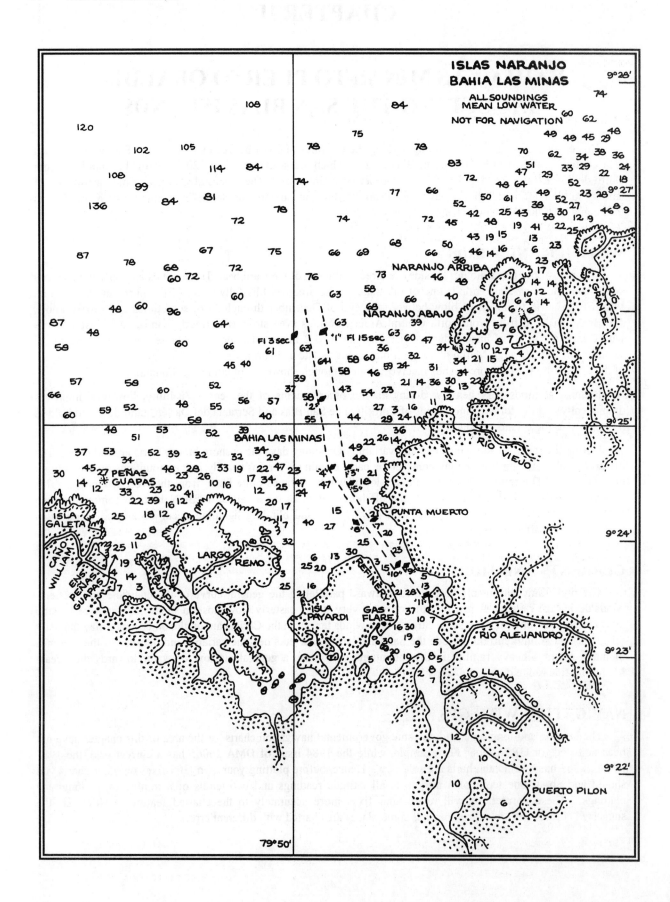

To double check your chart, plot a GPS fix after you have anchored and then confirm the position with compass bearings or transits of land features around you. All GPS positions in this text and the latitude/longitude grids on our chartlets are based on GPS readings we received in the area.

ANCHORAGES BETWEEN CRISTOBAL AND PUNTA SAN BLAS

BAHÍA LAS MINAS

Six nautical miles east-northeast from the main entrance to Cristobal breakwater one will find a red and white buoy (GPS 09°25.7'N, 079°50.0'W) marking the beginning of a buoyed channel to Bahía Las Minas tanker wharf. Two sets of ranges topped by red diamonds with a white stripe in the middle further indicate the deep approach. Yachts can sail into this mangrove lined bay and find several places to anchor. However, the binding stench from the refinery stacks fills the air all over the bay even during days with fresh northeasterly wind.

ISLAS NARANJO

These two lovely wooded cays lie only a mile further east from Las Minas entrance channel. A very good anchorage 10 feet deep and with a mud bottom exists under the south shore of Naranjo Abajo, GPS 09°25.58'N, 079°48.19'W. Approaching from the west pass close to the red/white sea buoy for Las Minas channel and then head for the south tip of the reef extending from the west shore of Naranjo Abajo. From the east one should parallel the fringing reefs extending seaward from the Naranjo Islands, continue southwest, then south and around the south tip of Naranjo Abajo. Do not enter between Naranjo Arriba and the mainland. Ocean swells roll into that area and the passage southward is blocked by several shoals hard to see in the murky water.

The proximity of the Naranjo Abajo anchorage to Cristobal makes it ideal as a stop to scrape the bottom growth acquired during a stay on the Flats or in the yacht club.

BUENAVENTURA

The two tall masts of an old coaster from Helsinki, which is slowly sinking into the mud in the south corner of the harbor, are the best landmark for Buenaventura Bay. One can drop anchor into good holding mud about 20 feet deep just south of a small point on the north shore and a quarter of a mile west from the bridge over a stream flowing out of the easternmost corner of the bay. A deeper anchorage with 30 foot depths lies further out and towards Isla Mogote. The bay stays smooth between January and April but the westerly winds of the rainy season will make it very uncomfortable. For shallow draft boats there is a totally protected 15 foot deep pool between Isla Mogote and Punta Escucha. A narrow channel 5 to 6 feet deep leads into it along the south side of Isla Mogote. A good high sun is essential to pilot a boat into there.

When going ashore one can safely leave the dinghy at the landing for the Cañones Restaurant. The bus to Colón stops on the main road by the entrance to this restaurant and you will find a pay phone there, too.

PORTOBELO

Columbus called this bay Puerto Bello when he stumbled in with his weary ships in November 1502. Portobelo, as it is now known, rose to importance in 1597 when the annual meeting of colonial merchants with the fleet from Spain was moved here from Nombre de Dios. Francis Drake used the port in 1570 as a base to rob Spanish merchantmen. He returned in the 1590s and promptly destroyed the beginnings of the Spanish fortifications. Drake died during the same voyage and was reputedly buried at sea near a little island recently named Isla Drake.

The riches plundered from the native nations of South America were sailed to the Pacific port of Panama and then conveyed by mule trains to the Atlantic side of the isthmus for the meeting with the "flota". According to Thomas Gage, an English born Jesuit, the warehouses of Portobelo would get so full of gold that silver ingots lay in the streets, unguarded. No wonder the place attracted constant raids by buccaneers, including Henry Morgan in 1668. British Admiral Vernon destroyed the Portobelo forts in 1739 and the great commercial fair never returned to the bay after the Spanish Crown finally allowed trading voyages around Cape Horn.

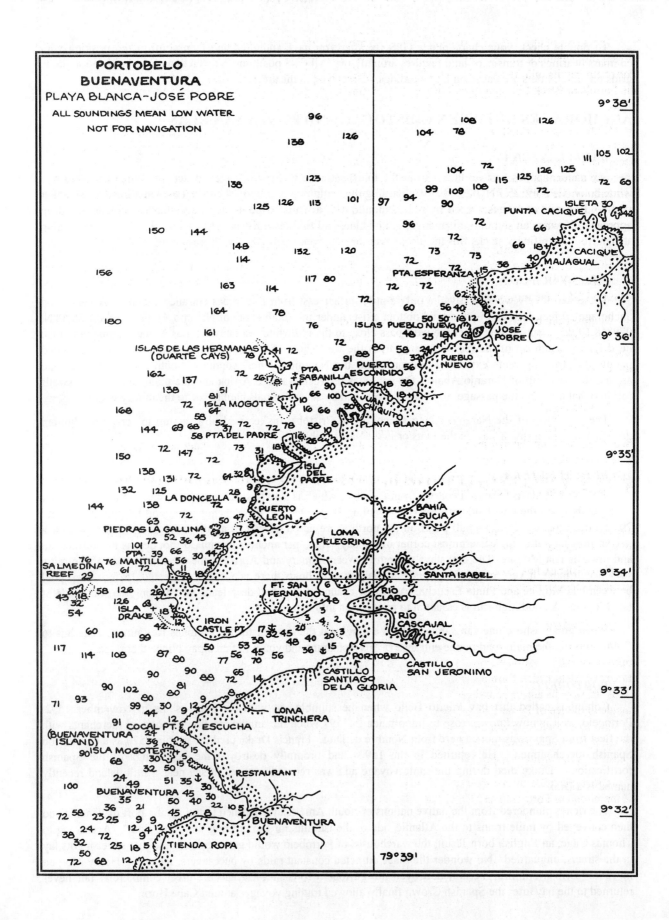

The ruins of the largest fort supplied rock material for the construction of the first Cristobal breakwater during the Panama Canal project from 1904 to 1914. However, enough of the four forts remains today to give Portobelo bay its unique character and to bring occasional buses of tourists. Once a year, in October, a fiesta for the Portobelo Black Christ, a patron of pickpockets among others, attracts crowds to the church originally built in 1776.

High hills to north and south surround the harbor while to the east several rivers drain into the bay through lowlands of marsh and pastureland. Protection is excellent during the dry season but rainy season brings occasional westerly winds and waves into the harbor. The deep water entry point of 09°33.4'N, 079°41.0'W opens up a clear approach from the sea. Yachts will find the smoothest anchorage under the remains of Fort San Fernando on the north shore where the depths vary from 6 feet near shore to 30 and 40 further out. You will find good holding mud and 31 feet at GPS 09°33.57'N and 079°39.98'W. The normally good anchorage off the town becomes rolly when on some days the swell from the ocean meets the river outflow.

Do not plan any painting here - Portobelo is one of the rainiest places on this coast. Ashore in town you will find basic groceries and fresh bread in the mornings. The Chinese grocery near the old church sells gasoline, too. Water is available from a spigot on the side of the police station. Since 1996 police come to the visiting yachts to collect a US$15 fee imposed by the town council.

Dinghies can be left at a little dock by a red and yellow painted house or on a beach landing further west by the houses under the Castillo de la Gloria. Regular buses make the one hour run to Colón. If you plan to go to Panama City leave the bus in Sabanitas on the main highway and catch an Express bus which stops on the other side of the road.

PLAYA BLANCA

2.5 miles northeast from Isla Drake one will find Playa Blanca, a small bay protected by Punta Sabanilla. Two white roofs on the southwest point of the bay make a good landmark. The inner cove has good holding in sand 10 to 8 feet deep and will easily accommodate two forty-foot boats. More yachts would have to run stern lines ashore in order to fit in. Protection is good except in strong northerlies and northwesterlies of any strength. Get out early when they occur.

Coming this way from Portobelo you will find smooth and deep water by going between Salmedina Reef (almost always breaking) and Isla Drake, then continuing along the coast and inside Isla Mogote. Enter the inner cove half way between the reefs growing from the points on both sides.

Playa Blanca has no road or any facilities except the hospitality of Mike Starbuck, an active ham radio operator who also monitors VHF 68.

JOSÉ POBRE

A Swiss sailor and a French cruising couple who have settled in the village of José Pobre invite other cruisers to visit. Many European yachts of very shallow draft do go there and get inside the string of reefy mangrove islets which form a natural and perfect breakwater. The entrance channel, good for about 3 feet draft, winds its way in among coral heads and the resident expats plan to blast a deeper entrance. The anchorage outside in the lee of Punta Esperanza is rolly. With our 5½ foot draft we anchored with two anchors seaward and the stern to a small mooring buoy in the mouth of the channel to the lagoon. The extremely shallow reefs which flank the channel were only 50 feet apart and it would have been very difficult to recover the anchors and leave in case of a bad onshore wind.

A road passable in dry season runs from José Pobre to the village of Cacique and then to a crossroads with the main road to Portobelo and Colón.

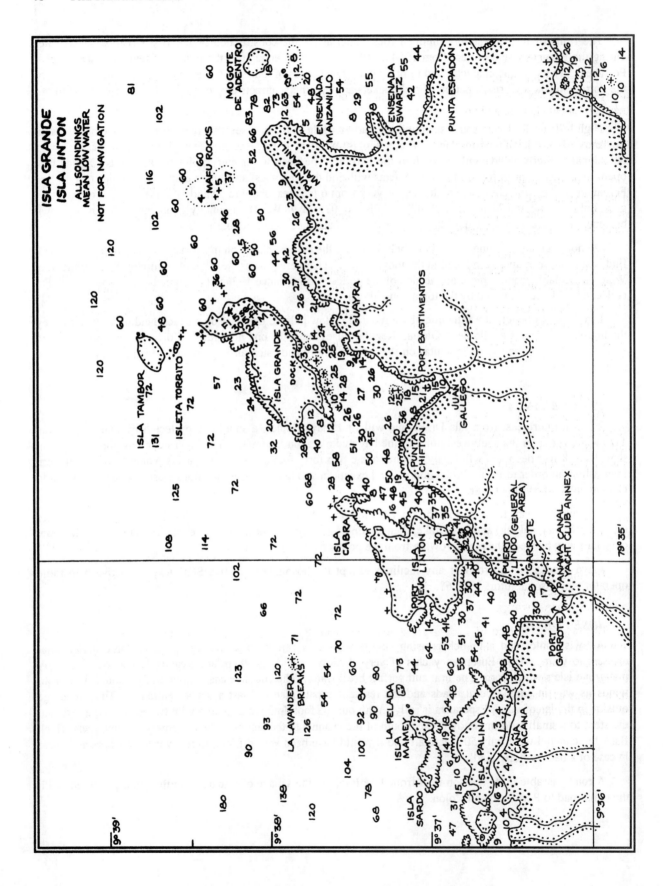

BAHÍA LAS MINAS TO PUERTO OBALDIA   49

ISLA LINTON (ALSO JUAN JOAQUIN)

The best harbor on this coast lies only 8 miles eastward from Portobelo. To enter the Isla Linton anchorage arrive at 09°37.5'N and 079°35.8'W keeping an eye out for La Lavandera shoal, then steer about south to pass between La Pelada rock and the northwest point of Isla Linton. Abeam of Isla Linton steer well clear of the reefs extending from Porto Viejo which is too reef bound and shallow to enter. Gradually swing eastward and anchor in depths between 28 and 44 feet with good holding in mud. You will find 43 feet at 09°36.8'N and 079°35.0'W and plenty of room to swing clear of any shoals.

The shallow reef which, bristling with several piles, sits smack in the middle of the inner passage eastward from the anchorage has deep water on both sides. The northern channel usually has plastic jugs marking the shallow edges. Get familiar with the channel in the dinghy before heading out that way. With high sun the deep water stands out clearly against the yellow shoals.

Mr. Allan Baitel, the owner of Isla Linton and the land opposite, very kindly allows visiting yachtsmen to leave their dinghies at his dock. Right outside the gate of his property runs the road connecting the coastal villages to the main road and eventually Colón via Portobelo. The bus ride to Colón takes about 2 hours.

The village of Garote in Puerto Lindo has a pay phone, a tiny grocery, an accessible water faucet and a beach to land the dinghy. In the very end of that bay the Panama Canal Yacht Club is expanding its facilities with a branch. The club's stone pier has about 7 feet at the seaward end and considerably less on its west side. Unfortunately, ocean swell enters this part of the bay.

ISLA GRANDE

The access to the south side of Isla Grande from the west is via a wide and deep channel free of dangers. Coming from the east a navigator should keep both eyes open for the breakers on Mafu Rocks and a smaller rock half a mile southwest from them. The safest course leads close to the north shores of two very conspicuous islands, Los Mogotes and Punta Manzanillo. All of them have deep water along their north sides.

The best anchorage in any weather lies close to the beach on the south side of the southwest point of the island. At 09°37.62'N and 079°34.0'W one will have 10 feet depth with excellent holding in sand. Another good anchorage is off the village dock which gets protection from reefs extending south from the shore. Trading vessels use this anchorage so space may be limited. Sometimes yachts anchor in the cove on the west side of Isla Grande - a good spot in settled dry season weather but dangerous during rainy season with its westerlies.

The inhabitants of the clean and prosperous Isla Grande village make their living from weekend visitors. Several small restaurants serve local seafood. The village pay phone will connect you to an ATT operator (109) in the U.S. when it works.

The mainland village of La Guayra across the channel from Isla Grande also has a pay phone with a connection to ATT. The Chinese store in the village sells groceries, refrigerated and frozen goods, vegetables as well as gasoline and some hardware items. They take foreign propane bottles for a refill and return them in three to four days. On Fridays at midday small trucks come to the village to sell fruit and some greens. One of the trucks stops off the gate to Allan Baitel's house if there are a few yachts in the anchorage there. Buses leave several times daily from La Guayra to make the run to Colón.

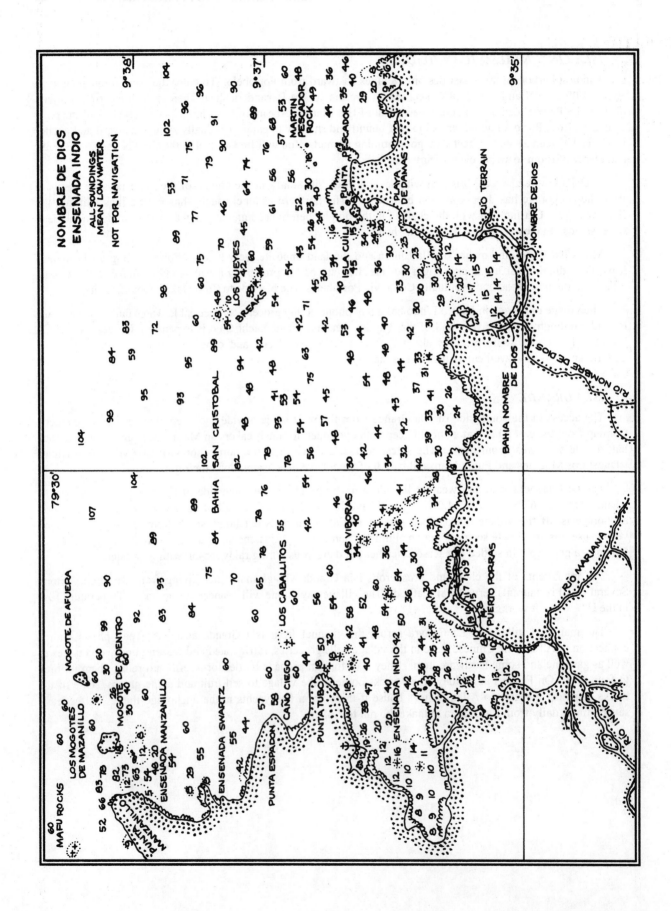

ENSENADA INDIO

This large bay around the corner and south from Isla Grande and Punta Manzanillo has a well protected and scenic cove on its north shore. The north shore is hilly with some pastureland but to the south one looks at distant densely forested mountains. To get there from Isla Grande head for Punta Manzanillo and then steer south in the deep water between Punta Manzanillo and Mogote de Adentro. Carry on to pass between Punta Tubo and a breaking shoal, Los Caballitos, then give a wide berth to the shoals south of Punta Tubo - swells break on them most of the time. Follow along the north shore and you will come to a cove bordered by a reef breaking the surface on the southwest side. Enter north of this reef and anchor in 12 feet shoaling to 8 feet, good holding in soft sand with some grass. Make sure your boat can swing clear of the coral patch further in the bay. GPS 09°36.1'N and 079°31.9'W is a good spot. Half a mile southwest you can anchor in another bay with 6 to 8 feet depths.

The large bay in the southern arm of Ensenada Indio receives too much swell for a long term anchorage. However, one can dinghy into the mouth of Rio Indio and Rio Mariana - two creeks full of fish. You might meet Mr. Molinar whose family has lived in the area for many years. He remembers the times when a freighter called Medio Million used to come to Puerto Porras to fill with half a million coconuts hence the name. Today only broken fragments remain of a 1913 dock at the mouth of a creek which ends at a shallow reef. Many species of land and water birds frequent this quiet backwater.

NOMBRE DE DIOS

Nombre de Dios served as the main shipping point of colonial products to Spain from 1520 until 1574 when it lost this distinction to Portobelo, a harbor better protected from weather and sea robbers. It recovered somewhat at the beginning of the 20th century. Cuili Cay acquired a pier for small freighters to load coconuts which came from the mainland by a narrow gauge train. At the same time a manganese ore loading pier was built at the other end of the bay and this operation still continues. Half of the present day Nombre de Dios village sits on a sandy spit created when Rio Terrain was dredged for sand necessary in the construction of the Panama Canal. Nombre de Dios today has a clinic with two resident doctors, good small grocery stores, schools, outboard and diesel mechanics, several bars and a pay phone.

Yachts approaching Nombre de Dios from the west should pass south of Los Bueyes, a large area of shoals. From the east a safe course leads close to the north side of Martin Pescador rocks and then well outside the reefs extending from Isla Cuili. The anchorage between Isla Cuili and Playa de Damas beach has good holding in sand but can get rolly and even untenable with strong north and northwesterly winds. The same applies to the second anchorage closer to the village and off the mouth of Rio Terrain. You will find 14 foot depths and a mud bottom with the mouth of Terrain bearing 120°T and the end of the reef to the north bearing 350°T. Both anchorages suffer the annoying presence of biting sandflies on some windless days. Perhaps that is why trading vessels anchor further south off the semicircular beach which is more exposed to swells.

Isla Cuili once had a pier on its south side for small freighters. The pier is gone but a 20 foot deep very narrow channel remains. It runs from the south towards Isla Cuili, passes west of a 5 foot high rock on the edge of coral shelf and continues eastward past the house with a dock on the mainland side. The depths there stay around 12 to 14 feet but then diminish to 6 and 5 feet east of small mangrove islets. Eventually the outer reef flats totally block the passage.

PUNTA MACOLLA

A bay with a lovely sandy beach lies on the southwest side of Punta Macolla, a prominent headland about one mile east southeast from Martin Pescador rocks. Protection is good unless north or northwest winds arrive. To enter this anchorage favor the west side of Punta Macolla while keeping a safe distance from the shallow reef extending from it. The GPS position in the anchorage of 09°36.0'N and 079°26.5'W has a sandy bottom and a depth of 18 feet.

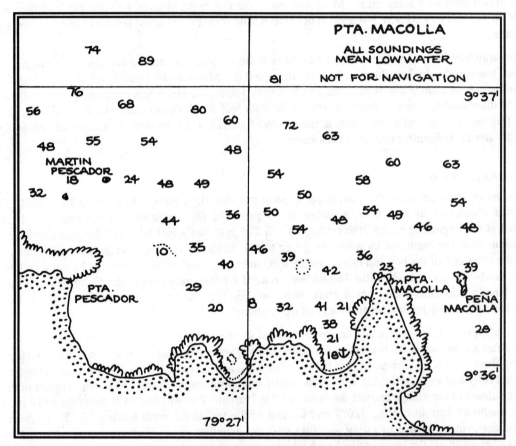

We found overlooking the crescent edge of the beach here several barringtonia trees whose seeds reputedly can be crushed into the water to stun fish. The heartshaped four edged fruit of this tree floats to disperse seeds. The shaving brush shaped flowers of barringtonias come into bloom in August and September.

PLAYA CHIQUITA (details on DMA chart 26065)

Eleven miles eastward from Nombre de Dios one can anchor comfortably in the lee of Punta Playa Chiquita. See the Isla Grande to Escribanos Shoals sketch chart. Protection is good unless it comes to blow from the north and northwest but then the place is easy to exit even at night. The approach from the west is free of dangers. When coming from the east give a wide berth to a shoal about 300 yards north of Punta Playa Chiquita and another close to the west side of the point. The anchorage at GPS 09°34.0'N and 079°17.66'W has good holding in sand at a 12 foot depth. Check that your anchor has dug in since there are a few patches of flat coral scattered in the sand. The depths vary between 14 and 10 feet close to the shore. However, do not come in too close as there is a shallow reef off the base of the headland and another in front of the village. You will find a smooth dinghy landing at the north end of the beach.

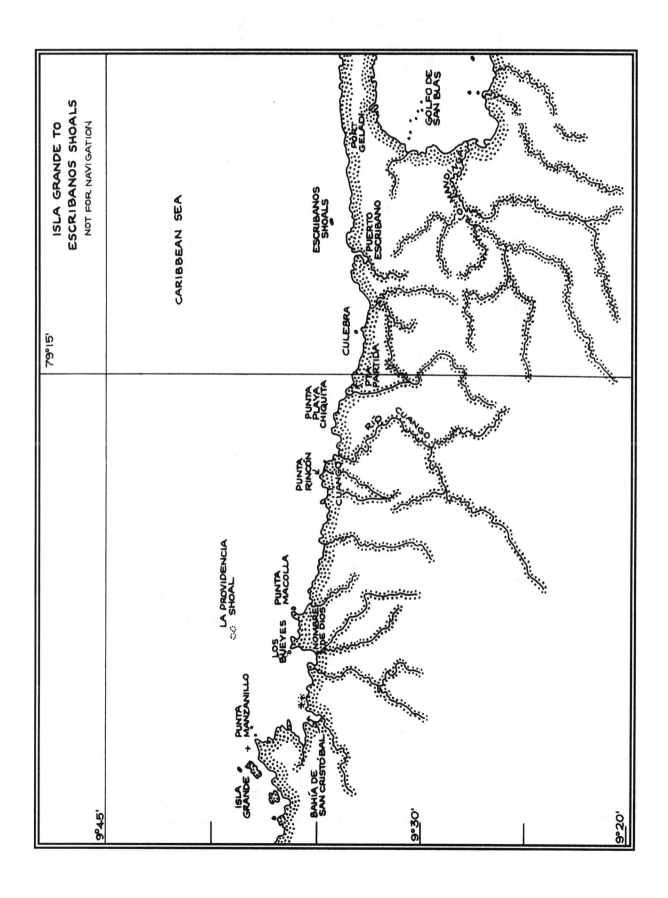

54 THE PANAMA GUIDE

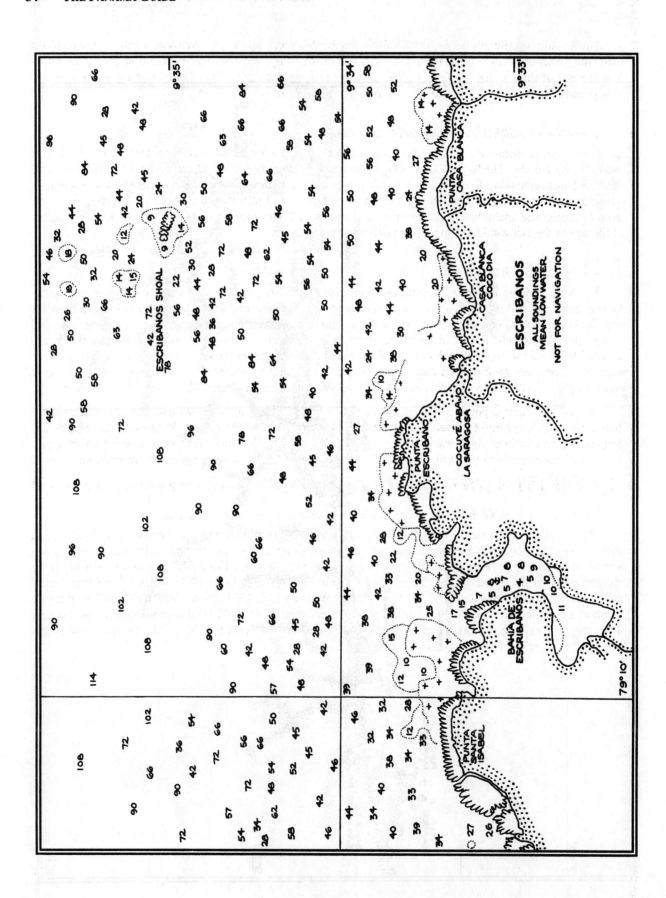

The friendly inhabitants of the village live off agriculture and fishing and welcome visitors. A rough dirt road with plenty of bird life starts behind the west end of the village and goes westward to Cuango village which is at the end of the bus service from Colón. Another path crosses Punta Playa Chiquita at the east end of the village and goes to a spectacular beach on the east side of the point.

ENSENADA BARRO (details on DMA chart 26065)

Two miles southeast from Playa Chiquita an indentation in the coastline makes an anchorage on the west side of Punta Partida. The bay has an inviting white beach but to enter one must have a high sun to see and avoid large reef areas extending from the east side of the bay into the middle of it. The best anchorage is the southeast corner away from the fringing reef along the west side of the bay. The reefs in the middle of the entrance are too deep to protect the anchorage in the event of a northerly or northwesterly winds and swells. Use it as a day anchorage as the exit would be too tricky in unfavorable conditions.

BAHÍA DE ESCRIBANOS

For boats drawing less than 7 feet this vast mangrove lined bay provides an extremely protected anchorage. Deeper boats can still use Escribanos if they anchor close to the entrance between the reefs extending from the low sandy points with coconut palms. The water is smooth even there and the bottom consists of soft sand and some grass. The depths further in the bay changed in the few years between our visits. In the past the deeper channel followed the west shore but in 1996 we found deeper water to the east. Several rivers flow into the lagoon and perhaps the increased outflow in that particularly wet season caused the change. Or it may have something to do with the construction of a dock on the inner west corner of the harbor.

The GPS anchorage position of 09°33.1'N and 079°09.29'W has a mud bottom with patches of grass and 8 foot depths. To enter into Escribanos arrive at 09°34.0'N and 079°09.3'W and then head south for the entrance keeping a good lookout for breaking edges of the outer reefs. The inner reefs may at some point appear continuous because of an overlapping effect. Adjust the course slightly to westward and the deep channel should soon open to view.

THE INNER ROUTE BETWEEN NOMBRE DE DIOS AND PUNTA SAN BLAS

Both westbound and eastbound yachts will find it advantageous to sail close to the coastline. When going east a yacht will encounter smoother water on this course at least until east of the Escribanos Shoals. Going westward on this route a yacht will avoid bucking a contrary current. Three GPS waypoints help avoid the dangers posed by the unmarked Escribanos Shoals. When eastbound steer from 09°35.0'N, 079°12.8'W (or half a mile north of Culebra island) to 09°34.5'N, 079°07.26'W and then to 09°34.57'N, 079°04.0'W (or 0.6 of a mile north of a conspicuous wreck at Port Geladi) and continue to 09°35.0'N, 079°00.0'W to maintain a safe distance from the reefs extending from the coast a couple of miles west of Punta San Blas. On the way west simply reverse the sequence of the waypoints.

56 THE PANAMA GUIDE

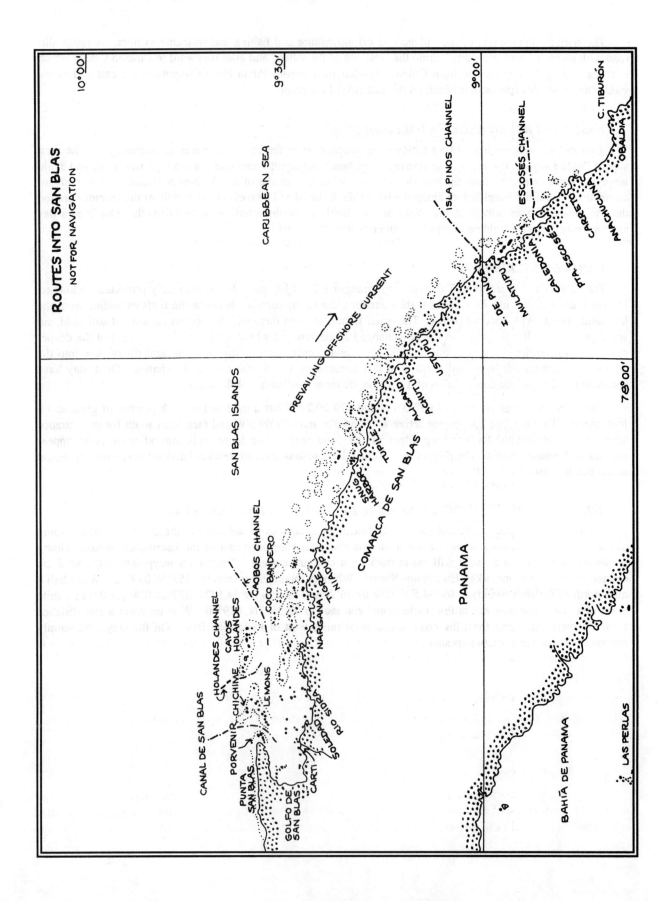

ROUTES INTO THE SAN BLAS ISLANDS

Yachts which come to San Blas typically follow one of three routes. The annual fleet of yachts heading for the Panama Canal from the West Indies, Venezuela and the ABC Islands will enter the San Blas area from far offshore. They sail during the months of strong northeasterlies when the eastgoing current is strong, visibility none too good and waves along the abruptly shoaling continental shelf quite intimidating. They should enter the San Blas area as suggested in Safe Passes into the San Blas Islands paragraph below.

Since Cartagena has become a popular destination many yachts sail from there to San Blas and the Panama Canal during the rainy season months between May and January. On occasion they may find the contrary current and the westerly winds frustrating as the chop from the west fights the swells from northeast. Entering the San Blas inshore route is the solution. See Safe Passes into the San Blas Islands section below.

A sizable group of yachts comes to Panama down the west coast of Central America. After transiting the Panama Canal they head east to the islands along the Caribbean coast of Panama. After a San Blas cruise some of them sail north into the Caribbean while others continue to Cartagena, Colombia. Going either way can be very rough between December and May. A northbound yacht can avoid the worst of the rough conditions outside by going eastward on the inshore San Blas route until, let us say, Isla Pinos. From there the sail to northern destinations like Providencia or the Bay Islands of Honduras will be a relatively comfortable reach instead of a teeth jarring beat from Colón or Isla Grande. A yacht trying to reach Cartagena at that time of the year can also benefit from going east on the inshore route as far as Puerto Escosés. See Safe Passes into the San Blas Islands section for information on entering or exiting the area.

SAFE PASSES INTO THE SAN BLAS ISLANDS

The continental shelf of the San Blas area reaches out into the Atlantic like a tray topped with gifts of countless beautiful islands. However, just before it drops off to 100 fathoms and more there is a step - a string of shallower outcrops, typically 20 to 30 feet deep with a few even shallower spots that remain uncharted. During the dry season the big swells driven by strong winds break on many of these banks. Most yachts at this time of the year arrive with following winds and waves which make it hard to distinguish the backs of shallow water breakers among wind driven white crests. At such time yachts should enter the continental shelf through the deep safe passes listed below.

CANAL DE SAN BLAS

This 3 mile wide pass has an extensive bank with the shallowest spot only 8 feet deep lying about 4 miles east-northeast from Punta San Blas. Cruise ships use the deep water entry to the west of the bank. The pass between the east edge of the bank and Chichime Cays is narrower but perfectly safe during daylight and reasonable weather conditions. Refer to US DMA 26063 or 26065.

HOLANDES CHANNEL

Cruise ships also use this over 2 mile wide, hazard free, pass between Icacos Island to the west and the westernmost island of the Holandes group. Refer to US DMA 26063 or 26065.

CAOBOS CHANNEL

The 2 mile wide deep water pass enters between the shoals (which break in boisterous conditions) lying south of the easternmost of Holandes Cays and the edge of the reef of the western Coco Bandero group. A yacht wreck on that reef testifies to the need of vigilance even in this wide pass. Refer to US DMA 26063 or 26065.

IMPORTANT CAUTION FOR WATERS EAST OF LA COQUERA POINT LONGITUDE

Between Spokeshave Reef with its center at 09°25'N and 078°21'W until the longitude of Isla Pinos at 077°45'W one encounters offshore banks with spots only 20 feet deep which should always be avoided. They are poorly charted or uncharted completely east of Punta Brava.

ISLA PINOS CHANNEL

From the offshore entry point of 09°03'N and 077°40'W steer southwest to a point at 08°59.2'N and 077°44.7'W off the east side of the very conspicuous Isla Pinos, or Tup Bak (whale) in the Kuna language. Refer to the Isla Pinos sketch chart for details.

ESCOSÉS CHANNEL

Make a landfall close to Punta Escosés at 08°51.4'N and 077°38.0'W and then refer to the Escosés sketch chart for charted hazards near shore. Be aware of Roca Escosés approximately one mile west of Punta Escosés.

PILOTING BY EYE

Among the hundreds of lovely coconut palm clad islands of the San Blas you will find even more islands under water and covered by coral. Some of them used to carry villages until the earthquake of 1882. Later, in 1887, the torrential rains of the great mother of all floods, Mu Dummat, washed away others. Sometimes in order to reach an interesting anchorage, village or a particularly good dive site yachts have to weave a course to find a way among these dangers to navigation. Deep water channels occasionally only a boat length wide defy the abilities of GPS and other electronic miracles so one must resort to using plain eyesight.

Piloting by eye, especially reinforced by a pair of polarized sunglasses, is easy for a navigator perched high and having high sunlight from behind shining on breeze ruffled waters. Many yachts already have mast steps installed, others lash ratlines of rope or wood to the shrouds to get their reef spotter well above water. In San Blas, due to the short distances between anchorages, one can always plan to move when the sun is high between 10 AM and 3PM. However, even the still high sun of the early afternoon will blind the reef spotter when it shines over the bow. Moving safely among reefs may call for a deviation from the most direct course in order to have the sun at a better angle.

One can best spot reefs and sand banks in clear water over a sandy bottom when colors give a good indication of the depth. Generally. the darker the blue the deeper the water. Unfortunately, in San Blas you will encounter such ideal conditions only in the outer islands. Closer to the mainland the water tends to become less translucent and the bottom darker on account of the mud deposited by the rivers. However, most of the channels tend to be very deep and the shoal tops very shallow. In these darker waters reefs appear to the observer as brownish or yellowish patches on the surface. Occasionally moving clouds cast shadows which look like shoals. Slow down to see whether the suspect spot is moving downwind or stays put and needs to be avoided.

On days with whitish overcast and on windless days when the sea surface looks like a mirror stay anchored or move with extreme caution. The lookout will not spot the reefs until the bow arrives over the shallow water.

THE PEOPLE OF SAN BLAS

The Comarca de San Blas or, Kuna Yala, appears little changed from the times before the Spanish Conquista, a result of the tenacity of the Kuna people. According to their oral tradition, the Kunas' forefathers lived in the Darién mountains. Anthropologists estimate they numbered between 500,000 and 750,000 at the time of the Spanish arrival. Linguistically they belong to the Chibcha family of languages once widespread in Central America and the northern parts of western South America. Under pressure from other tribes, or possibly the Spanish invaders, the majority of Kunas moved to the coast and later to the offshore islands. Some communities still survive in the forests of the Atlantic and Pacific slopes of the continental divide with a couple of villages over the border in Colombia. After suffering from violent inroads by outsiders the Kunas rebelled in 1925. In the process they killed many of the Panamanian policemen and children of mixed blood living in the islands. Only the intervention of the U.S. prevented a bloody retribution by the armed forces of Panama. Eventually in

1938 the government of Panama granted the Kuna leaders almost autonomous rule in the officially recognized Comarca de San Blas. The traditional hierarchy of tribal leaders on national and village levels has provided the cohesion that makes the 55,000 Kunas one of the strongest nations among indigenous Americans. Their law that the land belongs to all Kunas has prevented a division of the people into "haves" and "have nots" and helped them perceive themselves as the blessed co-owners of a wonderful country.

Through the turmoil of their history the Kunas developed a sociopolitical system equal to any of developed western countries. Carta Organica, their constitution, sets the governing principles for the three districts of the Comarca, each headed by an elected cacique, or high chief. The supreme cacique chairs the semi-annual General Congreso. A different village hosts each meeting and the villagers have to pull together to provide food for representatives of the remaining 48 communities.

The first sahila (chief, pronounced sila, like silo), the highest position on the village level, presides over a local daily congreso and has two or three deputy sahilas as well as one or more "arkar" or interpreters of the metaphorical pronouncements of the first sahila, a man versed in Kuna traditions. Then come the "sualipetmar" men, roughly equivalent to our police, who maintain order in the village and carry carved batons to advertise their position. Additionally each community has minor sahilas in charge of cemeteries, airstrips, hut building, communal agricultural projects, etc. Secretaries in congresos interpret for the first sahila from Spanish into Kuna. They also maintain records and write out countless permits. Every Kuna must pay for a permit to go to another village, a distant coconut grove or another town in Panama. A complex system of various penalties exists, from fines to expulsion or ostracism, for those who ignore permits or commit other infractions of scores of rules. Kunas who live and work in major towns outside the Comarca must report and pay dues to a chapter of their district or village. To take care of spiritual, mental or physical well being Kunas can turn to one of three specialized healers. Of these, one kind, "summaket" or chanters of sacred words, is further divided into twelve specialists focusing on various soul and body ailments. They may use "nuchus" (uchus in some islands), human figures carved from wood and believed to be alive, who help to seek the missing parts of a patient's soul. A "nele", or shaman, also uses "nuchus" to help find the causes of sickness. Since he can accuse another person in the community of harmful sorcery he holds a powerful position. Historically, the coconut trees have always been individually owned and the nuts have provided bartering power and later cash. Yankee schooners used to trade here and left linguistic traces in words such as "mani" for money, "watchee" for a time piece, and "merki" (from American) for a fair-haired foreigner. Today the talented Kuna women have another source of cash. They dress very colorfully and apart from golden rings in their noses, earrings, breast plates, intricate beadwork on their arms and legs (uini), some face painting and orange scarves, the most eye catching item is their blouse, "mola", with intricately designed and sewn panels on front and back. These reverse applique designs are quite famous and sell world wide turning the women into serious cash earners and reinforcing their already traditional central position in matrilineal Kuna society, where a new husband moves into his wife's family's compound. Often he brings only some clothes and a machete. As soon as he can afford to buy a mask and fins he will probably join other young men who dive for lobster and octopus and contribute to the inflow of dollars. However, the coconut trade is still of prime importance and picturesque Colombian schooners, most of them motorized nowadays, regularly trade in San Blas seeking this important commodity. Consequently, never help yourself to any coconuts, even on uninhabited islands.

Apart from the distant mountain villages, the majority of Kunas live on offshore islands and the coastal fringe. They use the mainland rivers to obtain water, hunt and grow basic crops. Their transportation is in dugout canoes, or "ulus", of advanced design which are in sight everywhere propelled by paddle and sail. The constant use of the canoe has produced a unison between the islanders and their boats - women, men and children are expert boat handlers and sailors. A Kuna paddling a canoe is the epitome of the boundless energy these people possess. Although very small in stature, they are perfectly proportioned and well muscled. The Kunas' indomitable spirit and stamina have maintained the continuity of their legendary reputation as fierce warriors. To this day squatters fear to intrude upon Kuna territory.

As a result, in a world of shrinking rain forests the Kuna Yala stands out as a notable exception. Kuna huts need no hardwood in their construction. Palm fronds make the thatch roofs and reeds or canes form the sides. A small number of large trees go down to make canoes but the hills remain densely wooded. Farming is on subsistence level and often only an experienced eye will spot a cultivated plot within the jungle greenery. Cattle breeding is alien to their culture so no vegetation disappears to open up fields for grazing. The thick forests resound with the screech of parrots and the blood curdling roar of howler monkeys while the rivers run clear and pure.

The Kuna's working day starts before dawn when fleets of canoes head for the mainland or for a day of fishing. By midday most of the men return for a rest. The later hours of the day are devoted to family life and to village matters which are always thrashed out in the large meeting hut, or congreso. This enviable and balanced scheme of life allots enough time for food gathering and still allows the Kunas to be good parents and citizens. Cruising yachtsmen wandering from island to island can immerse themselves in this ancient pattern of island life in an environment of rare beauty.

The interaction with the friendly and welcoming Kuna people is easy. They are as curious about the visiting yacht as the yachtsman is about them. English is spoken by someone in nearly every village but a little bit of Spanish helps tremendously. The schools that operate in all villages teach in Spanish so the younger generation speaks the language fluently. The notable exception are the adult women who have not gone to school. That will not stop them from trying to sell you their quota of molas, and being good family providers, they view each new arrival as a financial Godsend. Yachtsmen should realize that they can relieve heavy selling pressure through a joke or simply by saying "mola (or morr) bakke suli", phonetically, which means "we do not buy molas". Ask for plantains or fish or buy an inexpensive necklace to maintain good relations if you are not buying molas. One can barter for molas, too, especially with women's clothing, undergarments, sheets or towels.

Arrival in some villages may require a visit to a congreso, preferably in the afternoon as in the mornings even the chiefs have to provide food for their families and the congresos are empty. When you land in a village the people there will let you know whether a congreso visit is required. Inside the congreso hut the men in authority will swing in hammocks while the lesser beings share hard benches. Often a secretary will interpret for the sahila as a sign of respect for him. A visiting yachtsman will be charged a fee, usually five dollars. That grants the right to voice any grievances, like any cases of petty theft such as pieces of line missing from the deck. To keep relations smooth we prefer to lock everything and stow loose items in lockers.

While still in the congreso ask permission to visit the river and forest paths. The rivers vary greatly but are always fascinating be it for the tangle of vegetation, bird life or the scene of women scrubbing laundry and bathing. Some villages do not allow running motors past certain points since they use the river water for drinking, but when paddling silently you will see a lot more wild life in the trees. Kuna cemeteries are usually close to the rivers. Thatched roofs on poles shade deep clay graves accompanied by everyday utensils for cooking and traveling in the afterlife. The cemeteries are on choice sites with the best views of the islands and the rivers. Kunas are proud of them and visitors are free to roam around. The funerals are all day affairs when friends and relatives of the dead chant advice on how to deal with the perils of going through several layers of the underworld. Everyone can come to this haunting event although cameras are definitely out of place.

Photographing Kunas is a shaky business. The most picturesque subjects, the women, often cover their faces or even get angry. In some places they demand .50 as payment yet in other villages they welcome photographers. Of course you can photograph children to your heart's content and you will not lack willing subjects. Kids will keep you company wherever you go and as they are the pride and joy of every family nobody will discipline them. They will show you the way to the stores and smile a lot. Among them you will spot a few albinos, a result of intermarriage, a left-over from the times when traditional laws restricted movement between different villages. Albinos suffer from various infirmities even when young, especially of the eyes and skin. The old practice of eliminating albinos and other handicapped babies at birth has all but disappeared and in most places a few very white and badly sunburned villagers stand conspicuously above their brothers.

Every village sports two exceptionally large huts. One is a congreso and the other a chicha hut. The chicha of Kuna Yala is a mild alcoholic drink made from fermented sugar cane juice. Puberty rites for girls, anniversaries of the Kuna Independence Revolution or even Christian religious celebrations provide legitimate excuses for a little boozing. Collecting the cane, pressing the juice, and then several days of tasting the fermenting concoction terminates in two, sometimes three days of fiesta. The mild intoxication induced by chicha does not incite violence, just general relaxed stupefaction. People come for chicha from neighboring islands and you can join too, the only obligation being getting equally plastered. On the whole Kunas drink very rarely and only recently has beer appeared in stores on some islands.

SHOPS AND SUPPLIES

Stores in the islands sell cloth for blouses and wrap around skirts, scarves, beads, rice, sugar, salt, poor quality canned meats and fish, Coca Cola and other soft drinks as well as Kuna home baked bread - good stuff! The fancy ones may also sell spear gun rubber and screwdrivers. In other words, yachts cruising San Blas should carry all necessary supplies. One can always buy plantains and fish or lobster, while during the rainy season fruit like mangoes and avocados appear, too. All villages have a place that sells gasoline brought by the Colombian traders and generally of bad quality. Some places or traders may have diesel fuel for sale. You will have to strain a lot of water and dirt from it unless you order a full drum from a Kuna owned trading freighter it will come from Colón.

Unexpectedly, it is easy to obtain spare parts that are available in Panama City. What's more, you can have them in a couple of days. It all comes from the World War II era when the US Army built landing strips in San Blas. Later every village pulled together and built one for the small planes used by octopus and lobster buyers. Today these jungle pilots maintain regular traffic and for a charge, which you should discuss beforehand, they will track down the item you need and fly it to you in the islands. Most US manufactured equipment is available in Panama City but it helps to have the name and part number. Some pilots require a deposit. We even had our cooking gas bottles filled with butane and delivered by one of these planes. Allowing a week or so for a round trip, propane bottles may also be filled by Kuna freight boat captains.

You can fly to Panama City yourself or have friends flown in and out by one of the small passenger planes which make scheduled flights between the capital and San Blas.

CLEARING IN AND OUT OF SAN BLAS

Very conveniently there is Puerto Obaldia, a port of entry at the east end of the Comarca and Porvenir, also a port of entry, at the west. Both ports have immigration offices and port captains to admit vessels into Panamanian waters or to issue clearances for vessels bound to other countries. In Porvenir they do not issue cruising permits so yachts which sail to Colón after San Blas must obtain a cruising permit there. On the other hand, a yacht which only cruised San Blas without entering other Panamanian ports can return to Porvenir to obtain a clearance out.

San Blas islands.

62 THE PANAMA GUIDE

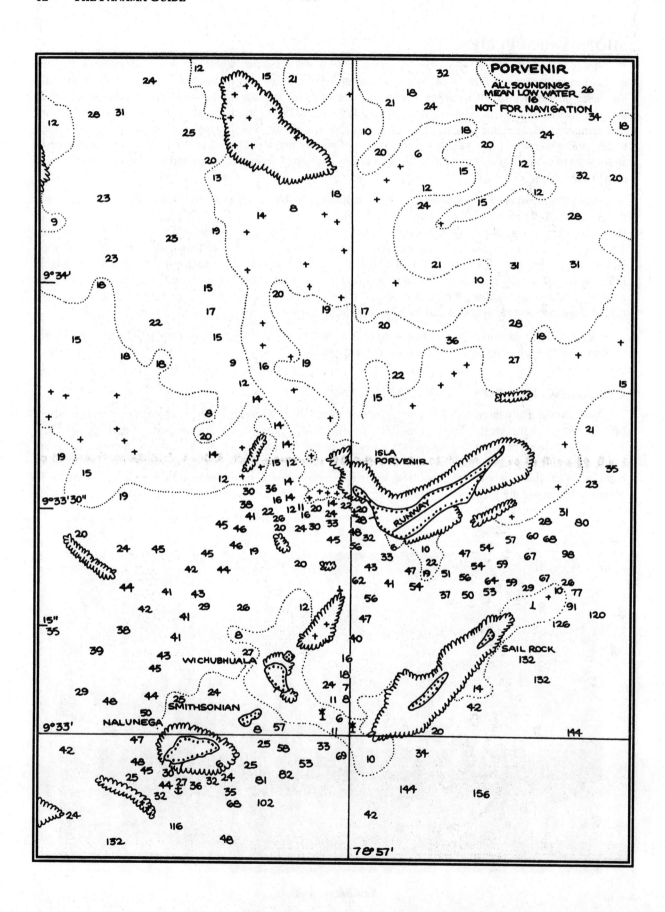

BAHÍA LAS MINAS TO PUERTO OBALDIA

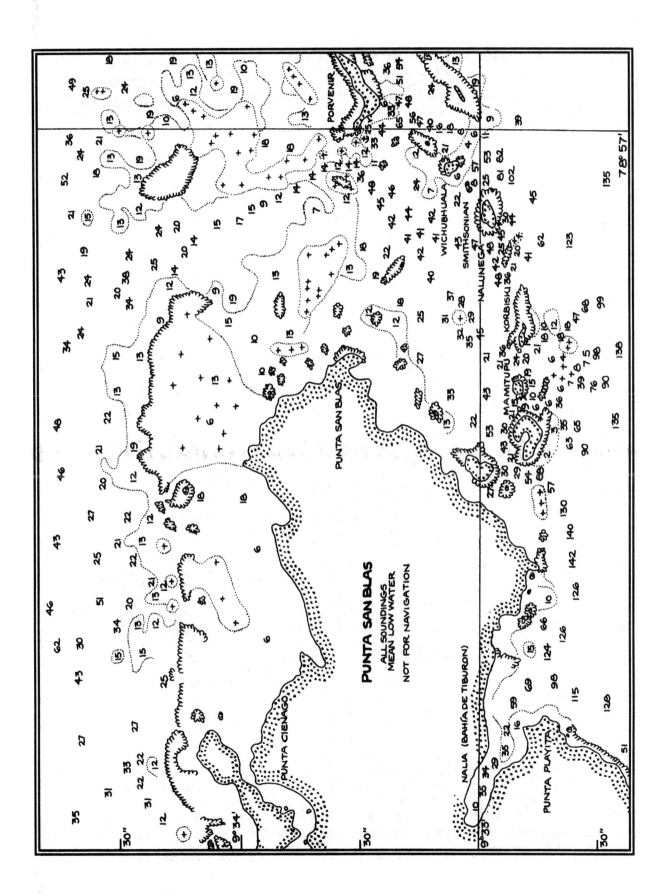

PORVENIR AND THE NEIGHBORING ISLANDS

The "Intendencia" in Porvenir is headed by a Kuna official and looks after the interests of both the Panamanian government and the Kuna Yala nation. The office takes care of immigration matters and controls the traffic of domestic and foreign vessels. Yachts which arrive here with a valid cruising permit do not have to check in but will be asked to pay US$10 as a fee for the Kuna Yala general purse.

Porvenir, which receives several flights from Panama City a day, is a good place to meet friends coming to join you for a cruise. Some cruisers come to use the pay phone which has a direct connection to an ATT (109) operator in the U.S., and at times works!

The safest way into the lee of Porvenir from the Caribbean is via Canal de San Blas (San Blas Channel) although local freighters use the reef passage northwest of Porvenir. This requires a high sun to see the way between the reefs extending from the westernmost point of Porvenir. Coming from San Blas Channel head for Porvenir when its southernmost point bears 270°T. The 21 foot deep anchorage spot at 09°33.5' N and 078°56.98'W, a short distance northwest from the pier, has very good holding in sand and the best overall protection. The depths in the area vary from 6 feet close to the beach to 33 feet further out. Leave good access to the pier which is used by small freighters almost every day. When anchoring south of the pier stay out of the line of the airstrip as the airplanes approach at very low altitudes.

While Porvenir has no village, immediately south you will see the islands of Wichubhuala and Nalunega with huts spilling over the edges. A low building between them houses a research station of the Smithsonian Institute. To get to these islands go along the south shore of Porvenir and north of Sail Rock before turning south and then west when clear of the reefs. Shallow draft yachts can take the inner passage west of Sail Rock and its reefs. Again good light is essential. The deepest spot on the bar has 6 feet and is marked on either side by wooden boards saying "Ocean Breezes". The most popular yacht anchorage lies south of the dock on Nalunega. Depths vary between 27 and 44 feet with the bottom consisting of sand with coral patches so take care to dig the anchor well.

Nalunega and Wichubhuala are both very tourist oriented with friendly people. Each village has hotels, small stores and lots of molas for sale.

One can get to the anchorage off Nalunega by going southwest from the Porvenir anchorage. However, the existence of several shoals in the way calls for skilled piloting by eye and strong high sun. West from Nalunega you will see more islands, two of them inhabited despite their negligible acreage. Korbiski has a protected anchorage close to the dock at 09°32.82'N and 078°57.89'W, see the Punta San Blas sketch chart. The depths are about 20 feet and the bottom firm sand with grass. When approaching from the south you will have to pass between two shoals of which the one to the west usually has a stick marker. Good sunshine helps see the limits of the reefs. Both Korbiski and the next island Mamitupu have only a few families crowding the edges while leaving room in the middle for basketball courts - a very popular sport in San Blas. Both islands have only thatched huts under tall coconut palms and breadfruit trees. Another protected anchorage is off the south side of Mamitupu. At 09°32.84'N and 078°58.04'W you will have 8 foot depths.

CHICHIME CAYS - UCHUTUPU PIPPI AND UCHUTUPU DUMAT

These two islands lying 4 miles northeast from Porvenir have become so popular with visiting yachts that Kunas sometimes call them Puerto Yate. The islands have no permanent village but just a few huts scattered in the thick groves of towering coconut palms. The pool of deep water between the islands receives additional protection from a shallow reef shelf reaching about half a mile out into the ocean. The safest approach to the only entrance is from southwest and the channel leads close to the west side of a small islet topped with a few palms about 300 yards west from Uchutupu Dumat. Inside you will find excellent holding in soft sand 34 feet deep at 09°35.2'N and 078°52.9'W. A pocket of 8 to 10 foot deep water tempts one to anchor close to the east side of Uchutupu Pippi. However, the coarse sand on the bottom there is so loose that any anchor will slip through it when the wind pipes up.

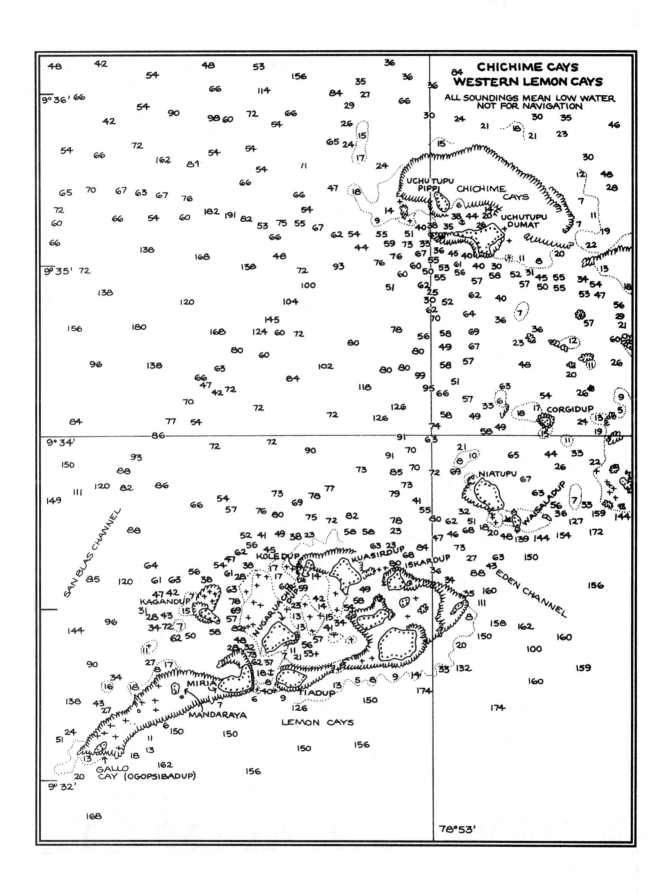

66 THE PANAMA GUIDE

WESTERN LEMON CAYS

This large group of extremely scenic islands has perfectly protected anchorages between the islets in its southern part. Three channels lead from the north inside the Lemon Cays. Of these the passage along the east side of Kagandup is the most straightforward. Since the north side of the whole group is exposed to ocean swells all the shoals break conspicuously except on very calm days. The only entrance from the sheltered south side has 8 feet on the bar and leads between Miria and Tiadup islands. Inside there is a 7 foot bar between the north side of Tiadup and Nugaruachirdup to the north. You can find a 30 foot deep anchorage in soft sand at 09°32.7'N and 078°54.0'W on the west side of that bar or 11 to 20 foot deep spot on the east side at 09°32.72'N and 078°53.93'W, also in soft sand.

EDEN CHANNEL

When approaching this deep hazard free channel from Chichime one may find this opening between islands difficult to distinguish from the others. You can start steering southeast from 09°33.8'N and 078°53.2W. See the Lemon Cays chartlets.

EASTERN LEMON CAYS

The vast area southeast of Chichime Cays not only has some beautiful coconut palm covered islets but also a maze of coral shoals and banks which stop yachts from exploring east of the Yansaladup - Nuinudup line. However, these two available anchorages make superb bases for some interesting dinghy adventures.

YANSALADUP

After leaving the Chichime entrance channel turn to steer about east southeast along the south shore of Uchutupu Dumat, then along the south edges of the northern outer reefs passing between a small sand bar to north and two large sandbars to south. Anchor either close to Yansaladup and its fringing reef in good holding sand at 09°34.53'N and 078°51.23'W or in a basin formed by shallow banks at 09°34.4'N and 078°51.34'W - a smooth place when the wind comes on strong from the west. Both anchorages have excellent holding in sand. Yanasaladup has only one hut that houses coconut caretakers.

NUINUDUP

Although Nuinudup lies less than a mile south of Yansaladup only very shallow draft boats with skilled eye pilots can attempt a direct crossing of the bank. The safest approach is from the south side of the eastern Lemon Cays. After identifying Nuinudup, which has a tiny satellite islet with four skinny tall palms off its eastern side, approach it from south steering 060°T on its north end. The depths at the entrance rise abruptly from 105 to 40 feet and then to 12 feet on the bar after which a deep water pool with deep coral heads lies close to the middle of the west shore of the island.

With GPS you can arrive at 09°33.62'N and 078°51.7'W (105 feet deep) and carry on to 09°33.69'N and 078°51.7'W with 15 feet. At this point steer 050°T on the north tip of Nuinudup and have a lookout on the bow. A high sun will help see the shallow bank growing towards the bar from the south end of Nuinudup and the coral shoals on the northwest side of the channel. There is a good anchorage in a pocket 29 to 32 feet deep northwest from the south end of Nuinudup. A shallower water anchorage with depths from 21 to 12 feet further in can be found west and northwest from the north end of Nuinudup. At 09°33.87'N and 078°51.5'W you will have 22 feet and a sand bottom.

No one lives on Nuinudup full time but a family from Banedup comes to get water from the well. Nuinudup trees are owned by families from Tupsuit in the Gulf of San Blas. On good weather days they sail here from Tupsuit to check on the coconuts and do some fishing.

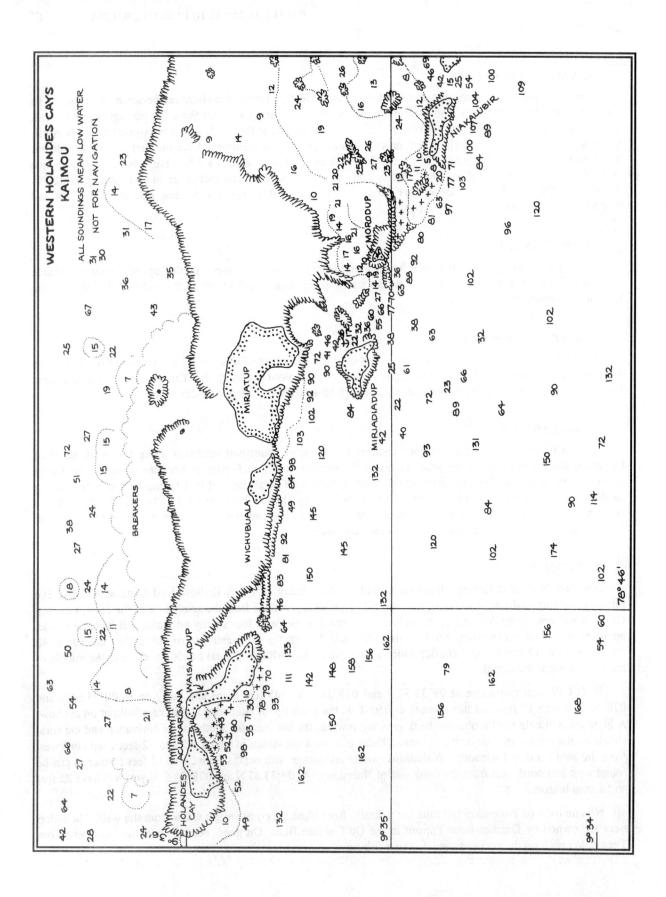

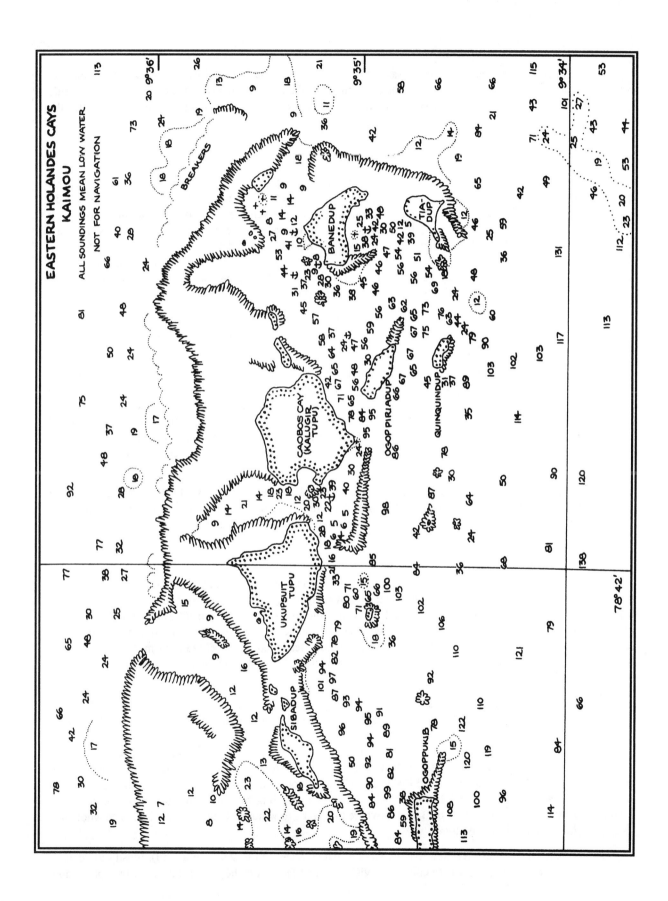

HOLANDES CAYS, KAIMOU

This outermost of all island groups in San Blas (Kaimou in Kuna but also called Mauki by Colombian traders) attracts a good number of yachts which come to enjoy the clear, protected waters within the seven mile long area of fringing reefs which shelter sixteen palm clad islands from the ocean action. Divers consider this the best of the San Blas.

WESTERN HOLANDES CAYS

The anchorage off the submerged coral shelf joining Acuakargana and Waisaladup has 30 to 50 feet depending how close you want to approach the coral edges. At 09°35.85'N and 078°46.56'W you will find 36 feet and good holding in sand. Outside the dry season months do not venture close to the coral unless you drop another anchor to the south. The wind between May and January often comes from the south semicircle. Snorkeling off the nearby reefs is very rewarding and Waisaladup has easy paths under the palms. They lead to a few huts at the east end which house coconut caretakers. Six villages claim the ownership of Kaimou coconut trees - Tigre, Nargana, Corazon de Jesus, Rio Azucar, Ticantiqui and Maiquipgandi. Kunas on coconut duty in Kaimou come to collect 5 dollars which allows a stay of three months. They issue proper receipts, too.

Going east from Waisaladup you can next anchor off the east side of Miriadiadup. At 09°35.17'N and 078°44.66'W you will have 30 foot depths and a sand bottom. During the dry months the breeze whistles through here but the water stays smooth.

Less than half a mile eastward from Miriadiadup one can enter the main bank through a channel on the west side of Morodup. You really need good sunlight to go through the bar and coral heaps on the bank. You can approach this channel from 09°35.05'N and 078°44.49'W which has 55 feet of depth and steer 045°T until you get to about 22 feet. From there you will cross a coral bar 9 to 10 feet deep after which the depths drop to around 20 feet. You can anchor in very good holding soft sand and grass when Morodup bears about south. GPS 09°35.12'N and 078°44.31'W has 18 feet. One can meander far onto the bank in depths around 20 feet by avoiding scattered shallow banks.

Further east one can pass between Niakalubir and Ogoppukib (meaning plenty of coconuts) islands to get closer to the lee of all the reefs and islands to the north, a useful dodge on the way to the east part of Kaimou. In particularly windy dry seasons ocean swells sweep into the south side of Holandes Cays.

EASTERN HOLANDES CAYS

Water too deep for an average cruising yacht to anchor comes right up the southern edge of the reef north of Ogoppukib. However, a little further east an all weather anchorage lies off the west side of Caobos Cay or Kalugirtupu. A good channel from the west leads alongside the south shore of Ukupsuit Tupu. For the first-time entry a good light is essential. From the anchorage indicated on the sketch chart one can move northward to get closer to the outer reef. Another, deeper but narrower channel, leads into this anchorage from the east along the south shore of Caobos Cay. A good light is also essential there. The anchorage bottom is mostly soft sand at a variety of depths.

Next east one finds the most popular yacht anchorages with easy entries, good protection and depths to suit even the mega yachts. The most foolproof approach is from due south of Quiquindup. Then pass close to the west of it and carry on 345°T to pass a short distance west of Ogoppiriadup. After rounding that island steer east-northeast and keep your eyes open for a large coral bank in the middle of the channel west of Banedup and later for a less distinct coral shoal much closer to Banedup. After that one can anchor in the desired depths in good holding sand. At 09°35.25'N and 078°40.59'W you will find smooth water 8 feet deep close enough to the beach on Banedup to land the dinghy and go for a stroll. When the whistling breezes of the dry season become too much one can move to the south side of Banedup where the palms to windward cut out the wind. The whole bay has good holding in a soft sand bottom.

The only Kunas in Eastern Kaimou live on Tiadup (which means an island with a well), mostly as coconut caretakers. Some of them may come to collect the visiting yacht fee unless they have run out of receipts. Show them your receipt from the other end of Kaimou if you already paid. One of the huts belongs to Sr. Robinson from Rio Sidra, a good friend to visiting yachtsmen for many years. In an advanced age now he only rarely visits Tiadup but some of his family are always there.

THE GULF OF SAN BLAS

The long arm of Punta San Blas wraps around the northern end of Comarca de San Blas in a protective embrace. The island communities in that extreme hook follow the traditional Kuna values more devotedly than in the other parts of San Blas, despite the intrusion of towering white giant modern cruise ships on their horizon. The cruise ships anchor either off the islands near Porvenir or near Cartí Islands described later in this chapter. Each year for the few months of northern winter "ulu" (dugout) fleets from far and near join in the selling fever of the outdoor markets in Porvenir, Nalunega and Cartí Sugdup. When northern climes warm up in the spring, cruise ships head for Alaska and things cool off in the Gulf of San Blas.

ANCHORAGES ON THE NORTH SHORE OF THE GULF OF SAN BLAS

NALIA (BAHÍA DE TIBURON)

Nalia bay lies 3 miles west from Nalunega and is shown on the Punta San Blas sketch chart. The deep water channel runs down the centerline until the last basin where it shoals rapidly. No one lives here permanently but sailing "ulus" come this way when Kuna men go to work their farm plots in the hills. One can walk on the trails as far as the other side of Punta San Blas.

NELOGUICHI

This mangrove lined inlet is named after a tree used as medicine by Kuna healers. All Kuna names here say interesting things about the places. The bay a mile to the east of Neloguichi and too shallow to enter bears the name of Parsamosukun - the place of the "parsamo" tree from which the first Kunas descended according to legend.

The Neloguichi entrance about 3 miles west from Nalia is best entered along the east shore. One can anchor before coming to a large reef 4 feet deep in the middle of the bay or continue along the east side. Avoid another reef complex in the middle of the last basin. A good entry point from 94 feet deep water lies at 09°32'N and 079°02.0'W.

URUSUKUN

Around the corner to the west one can anchor in a smaller inlet free of obvious reefs and lined by low mangroves with a few landings to paths on the mainland.

TADARGUANET - ISLAS ROBESON

The Kuna name for this vast archipelago means "where the sun sets", a more appropriate term than the name of George M. Robeson who was secretary of the US Navy in the 1870's.

The rains of the wet season send rivers of mud into this part of the Gulf making piloting by eye difficult. During the dry season the northern perimeter of the islands receives strong wave action which stirs up the mud and also reduces water clarity. When approaching the islands from the north in such conditions use Canal Porter (see Gulf of San Blas sketch chart), a 3 mile wide deep channel east of the group. Swing northwest into the lee of the islands after rounding Cayo Guardo which today is no more than a coral shoal. Local freighters use deep and narrow passes between the southeastern islands. A useable entry channel runs along the mainland to the north. Complex and numerous shoals present difficulty when passing through there and require favorable conditions for eye piloting even for very experienced reef spotters. Notice that the channel goes west of Tupsuit Dumat (Isla Gertie), see the Tadarguanet sketch chart, along the shores of the bay off the mouth of Rio Tortí, then south between the mainland and three clumps of mangroves on a large shoal.

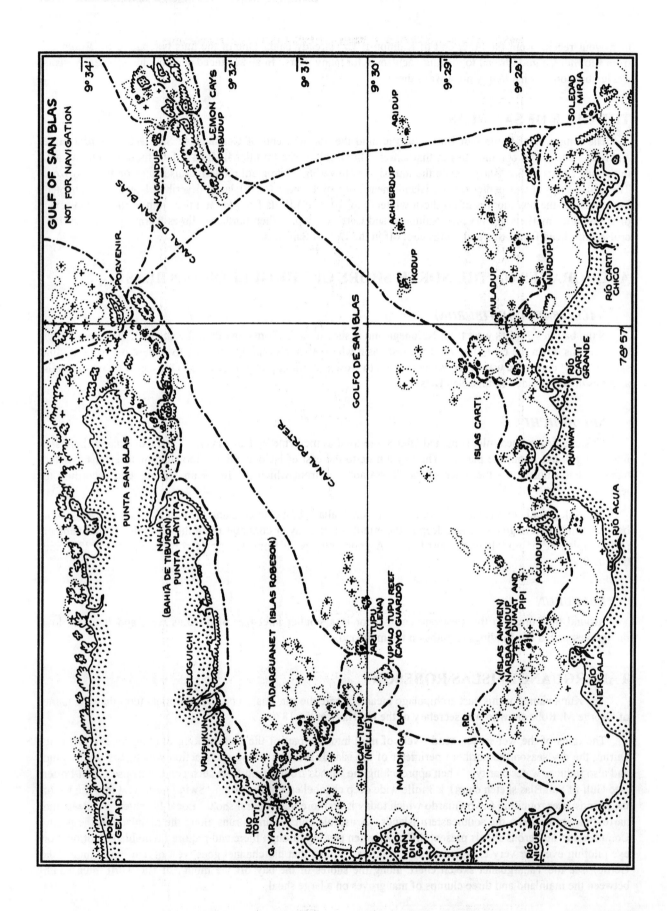

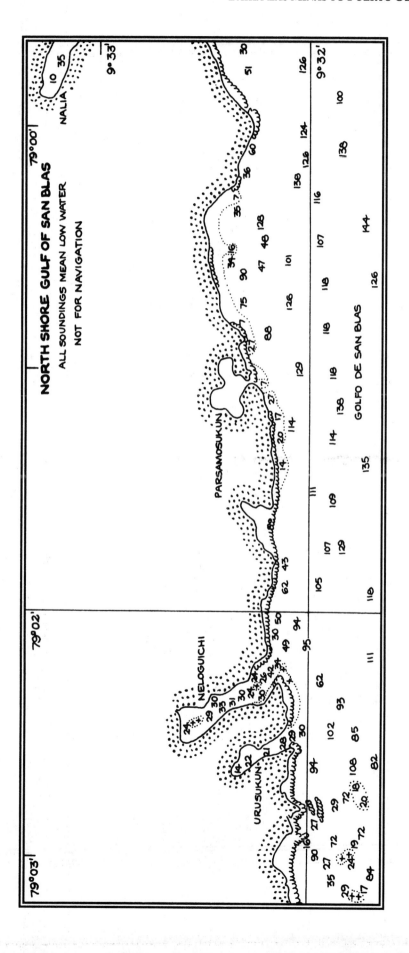

74 THE PANAMA GUIDE

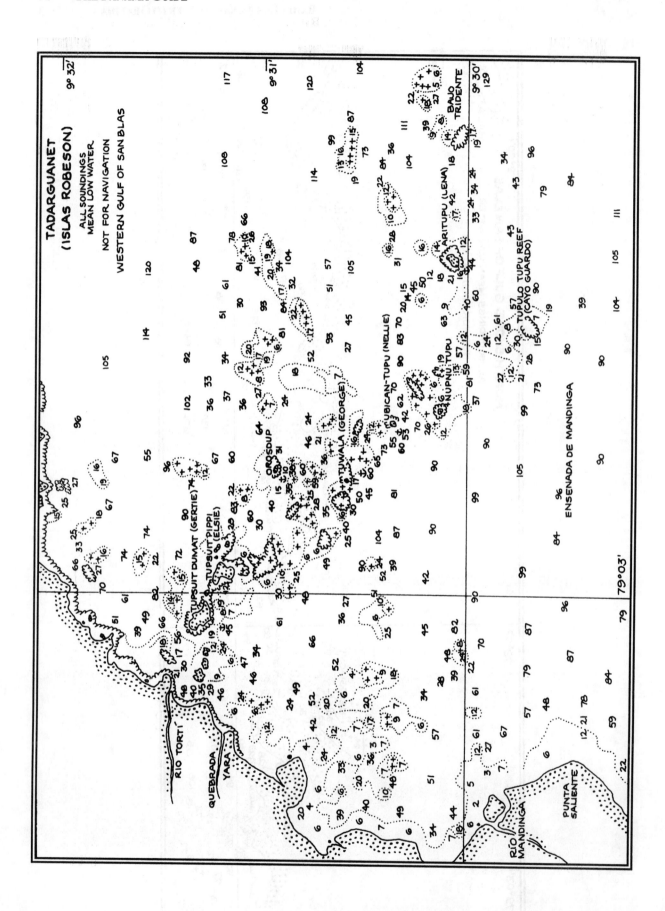

TUPSUIT ISLANDS - ISLAS GERTIE AND ELSIE

Tupsuit Dumat is also called Alitupu by Kunas. The anchorage off the village at 09°31.2'N and 079°03.4'W in 45 feet and good holding in mud gives a yacht access by dinghy to visit Tupsuit Pippi and Rio Tortí. Make a visit to the tiny stores to ask for Kuna bread, an excuse for a walk between the huts. People are very friendly and happy. You will find somebody speaking English among the older men or Spanish among the young ones. On the whole, few of the villagers here speak Spanish as they follow Kuna traditions to the point of not having a school, a clinic or a church in this part of the islands.

Rio Tortí near Tupsuit Dumat deserves a visit in a dinghy. Soon after entering you will pass a cemetery on the right. Further on the river narrows and winds between small clay banks overgrown by trees. Most of the villages of the Tadarguanet group use this small river as the main source of drinking water and the main access to their farm plots so "ulu" (dugouts) come and go all day.

From the Tupsuit anchorage one can also make a dinghy trip to Rio Mandinga, a long narrow river with plenty of birds in evidence as people rarely come here.

TUWALA - ISLA GEORGE

Only a couple of extended families live on this tiny islet shaded by tall coconut palms. They live very traditionally and make their own kitchen utensils like rice mortars, soup spoons, stirrers and plantain mashers. As in the other islands here their "ulus" exhibit first class workmanship. These people like to see visitors and show their molas and necklaces that they have for sale.

At 09°30.49'N and 079°02.65'W we had 55 feet, muddy bottom. Anchoring in shallower water puts the anchor in coral and will place the boat on the edge of the reef should the wind arrive from the mainland.

From Tuwala one can take a half a mile dinghy ride north to Orosdup (Rice Island), another tiny village under the palms.

UBICANTUPU - ISLA NELLIE

To avoid anchoring in coral one has to drop the hook deeper than 45 feet. We had 57 feet at 09°30.32'N and 079°02.49'W. The island is the most populated in the whole group with shoulder width lanes crisscrossing the island. It has a school, several stores and the water edge bristles with "ulus" hauled out onto wooden racks and ready to launch.

NUPNUTUPU

Another tiny cay which has a spot of 30 foot deep water at 09°30.11'N and 079°02.44'W.

ARITUPU - ISLA LENA

With 400 inhabitants Aritupu (Iguana Island) equals Ubicantupu in population density. The village has a school and stores. The best anchorage south of the dock has 39 feet at 09°30.0'N and 079°01.68'W. One can approach the anchorage from south or north along the west shore of the island. Good light is recommended as for all the other inter island shortcuts shown on the sketch chart of routes in the Gulf of San Blas.

RIO NICUESA - CHART 26065

The 1984 edition of this DMA chart correctly shows the route through the shoals to a bay receiving Rio Nicuesa. (See the Gulf of San Blas sketch chart.) Good light is essential to avoid the shallow banks surrounded by murky water. The anchorage off the remains of a dock once used by a banana company has complete solitude, perfect protection and excellent holding in mud. You will have 23 feet at 09°27.14'N and 079°03.80'W. You can make interesting dinghy trips to Rio Nicuesa and Rio Chiwadi.

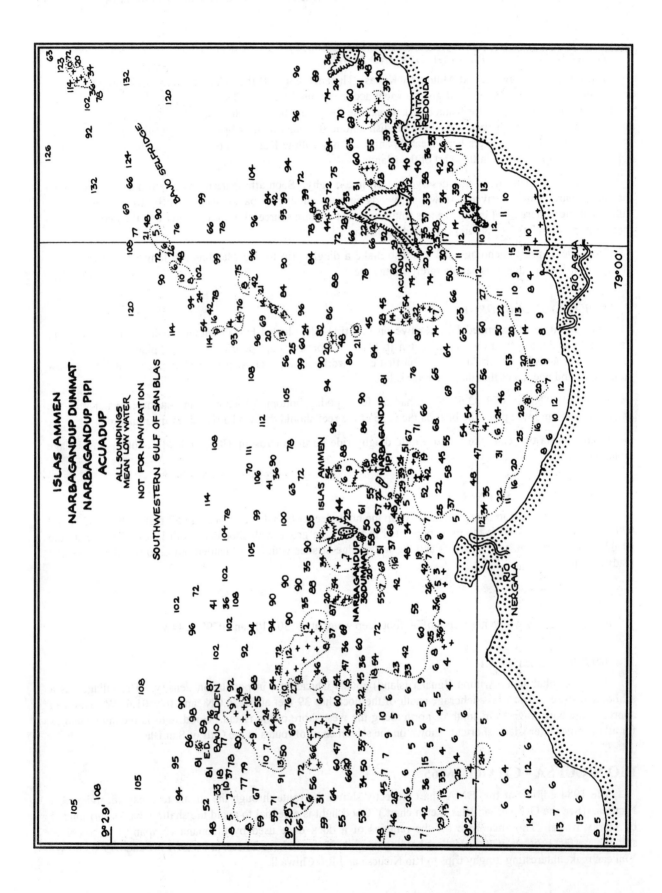

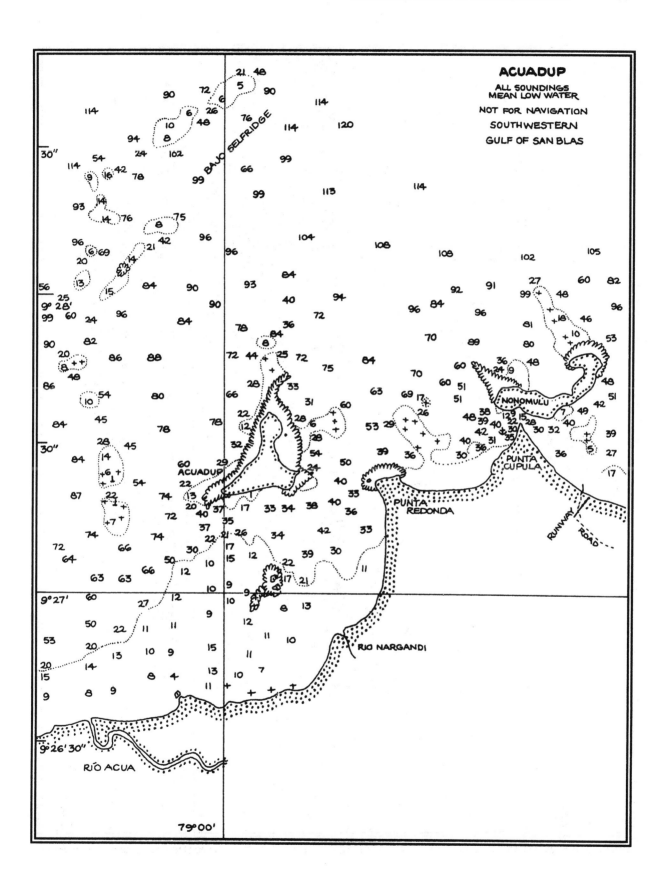

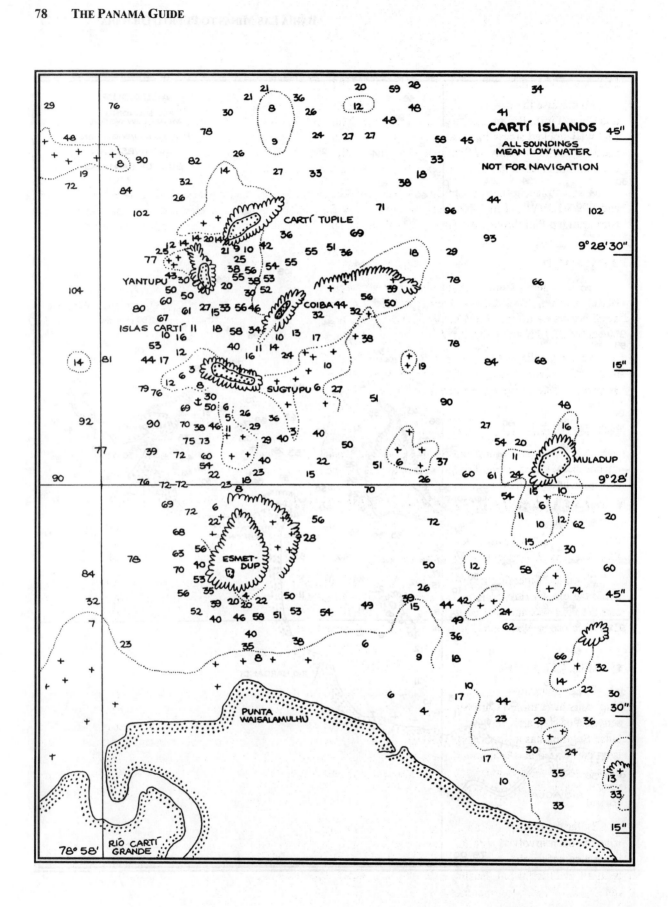

ISLAS AMMEN - NARBAGANDUP DUMAT AND PIPI

To confuse the nomenclature even more some Kunas and traders call these islands Naranjo Grande(Dumat) and Chico(Pipi). Both islands are packed tight with huts leaving only Kuna width alleys between them. You will find well stocked stores in both villages. Only Dumat has a school. Many of the welcoming inhabitants do not speak Spanish but kids will translate eagerly. Rio Nergala turns fresh soon after entering and the use of outboards is prohibited. The cemetery is more than a forty minute row up stream.

A smooth anchorage near an islet off Narbagandup Pipi has good holding in mud 50 feet deep at 09°27.45'N and 079°01.39'W. The recommended approach is from the north but if bound east you can leave south of Narbagandup Pipi through a good channel along the south edge of the bank which extends from the village.

ACUADUP

When coming from Narbagandup approach Acuadup steering northeast on the westernmost point of the island. Coming from the east one has to keep eyes opened for several shoals flanking the channel. Usually the swell breaks on them. Good holding sand makes anchoring easy along the south side of Acuadup. We had 17 feet at 09°27.18'N and 079°00.0'W.

Acuadup village has only a handful of huts nestling under towering palms leaving plenty of room for a basketball court and banana plots. You will not find a school in this traditional village. Stores have very basic inventory. One cannot use an outboard motor in their two rivers on the mainland.

NONOMULU

This mangrove island makes for a smooth inside passage by Punta Cupula and protects a couple of anchorages. When going through to the east follow the south edge of the channel and you should have 20 to 24 feet in this very narrow passage. A good anchorage lies off the southwestern tip of Nonomulu in 30 feet of water.

Southeast of Punta Cupula you will see on the mainland a conspicuous dock. It belongs to the busy airstrip which serves the Cartí Islands. The inland end of the landing strip continues as a very rough dirt road, the only one to the San Blas, which further on crosses a bridge over Rio Cartí Grande, widens, and goes on to join the Pan-American Highway to Panama City.

If you are expecting friends to fly in, Nonomulu anchorage would be an excellent place to wait for them and avoid the dinghy ride from the Cartí anchorages to the airport. In the windy season this mile and a half long trip can get very wet and one never knows which plane will bring your crew. One can even anchor east of Punta Cupula, close to Nonomulu, and have a clear view of the landing planes.

CARTÍ ISLANDS

The communities on these heavily populated islands must be the busiest in all of San Blas. Regular cruise ship visits have turned Cartí Sugtupu island into a Kuna handicrafts emporium. The post office here displays the schedule of ship arrivals. The money from the trade has added a number of ugly concrete houses rising over the huts. Sugtupu has a small Kuna museum, a library, several stores, restaurants, schools, hotel and a clinic. There is no pay phone as all communications go by way of a SSB radio in the post office. (Occasionally working pay phones are located in Porvenir, Rio Sidra, Nargana and Tigre.) No one tries hard to sell molas to a few stray yachtsmen as the village is geared towards hundreds of cruise ship passengers, which makes it relaxing to stroll around.

By far the prettiest of the Cartí group, Yantupu is a smaller and cleaner village with a good store. John Mann who has been involved with Kunas for decades starts the February sailing "ulu" races in Yantupu. Cartí Tupile has a nice cafe right on the dock and pleasant walkways shaded by breadfruit trees. Cartí Muladup definitely beats all records for hut density. Even the slim Kunas have to walk sideways in the alleyway maze between the cane walls of family compounds.

One can approach the Cartís from the northeast, pass between shoals extending from Cartí Tupile and Coiba and come out through the middle of the group south of Yantupu. Do not anchor between the islands. Most of the time swell reaches in there and boat and freighter traffic is heavy. One can anchor southwest of the old cement dock at Yantupu in about 50 feet which allows the boat to swing around clear of all obstacles. Another smooth anchorage is southwest of the west end of Sugtupu at 09°28.16'N and 078°57.81'W. There you drop anchor in 50 feet with good holding in a mixture of sand, shells and mud.

Visiting Rio Cartí Grande in your dinghy is practically impossible. The congreso regulations demand leaving the motor on the river bank at the entrance or you will be fined 10 dollars. As the current runs swiftly, rowing would not get you very far. However, a small river exits the mainland not far west from Cartí Grande. One can enter it along the shore from the west and south of a breaking bank which curves north and west from the east bank of the river. You may use the outboard to follow the meandering of this interesting stream until it joins Cartí Grande where you should turn back.

Water clarity around Cartí Islands depends on wind direction and rainfall but close to the mainland is always muddy. To go east from Cartí Islands one should head north into the deep water again before exploring the little cays east of Cartí Muladup.

UARSADUP

The Lopez family lives in the six huts on this tiny heap of sand topped by a few palms and papayas. The anchorage at 09°27.94'N and 078°56.40'W can get rolly on windy days.

NURDUPU

This one has all the aspects of a perfect little tropical island. Huts here have nice shady spots under breadfruit trees and coconut palms many of which have been pierced to take the levers of sugar cane presses to make juice for chicha. Perfectly shaped "ulus" (dugouts) line up on the miniature beach. The people welcome visitors. The isle houses the headquarters of the Jehovah witnesses with two resident missionaries. The anchorage off the south beach with the dock bearing about northeast lies at 09°27.53'N and 078°56.45'W.

SOLEDAD MIRIA

Young men from this village have the distinction of winning most of the sailing "ulu" races organized by John Mann every February in Cartí Yantupu. As shown on the sketch chart the safest approaches are either from northeast or from north along the west side of the village. Along the south side of the village the depths will jump from about 18 feet to 11 if one strays off the deep channel. All anchorages near the village have sand pockets intermixed with heavy coral unless one drops the anchor in 50 feet southwest of the village. At 09°26.72'N and 078°54.0'W you will have sand with some coral around 30 feet deep. A mile southwest from the village one can hide in the perfectly sheltered mangrove bordered bay on the south side of Punta Playa.

MORMAKE TUPU - MAQUINA

This small picturesque island whose name means in Kuna "shirt makers' island" has a very traditional community with congreso chiefs firmly in control. One can anchor off the south tip of the village in about 25 feet with a sand and coral bottom. However, the congreso encourages yachts to anchor in Gaigar, a totally protected place surrounded by mangrove isles about a mile south. In the past there were complaints from yachts about getting the topsides banged by curious kids in "ulus". From Gaigar one can easily make a dinghy trip to visit the pretty village to buy fresh bread or even some of their very good molas. In Gaigar at 09°26.20'N and 078°51.0'W you will have 46 feet and excellent holding in mud. The westernmost islet in Gaigar serves as a night roost for ibis, herons and pelicans. If you like snorkeling try the reefs west of Gaigar.

In the congreso you should ask for permission to visit Rio Esadi, the northernmost of the two streams in that bay. One can anchor a yacht there and at 09°25.48'N 078°51.33'W you will have 33 feet and mud bottom. Getting permission to go there will probably cost five dollars on top of the first five they charge you when you arrive. Enter the stream which discharges at the point on the west side of the bay and continue until you come to small reddish cliff on the left. Moor the dinghy there and climb the path. After about forty five minutes of easy hill walking the path goes down into a wetter area and the plants in that shady wet forest, which is often visited by howler monkeys, will give a good sample of a lowland rain forest environment.

Above: Nancy in Anachucuna village, San Blas Islands. Left: Village healer on Soledad Miria, San Blas. Below: Mamitupu, San Blas Islands.

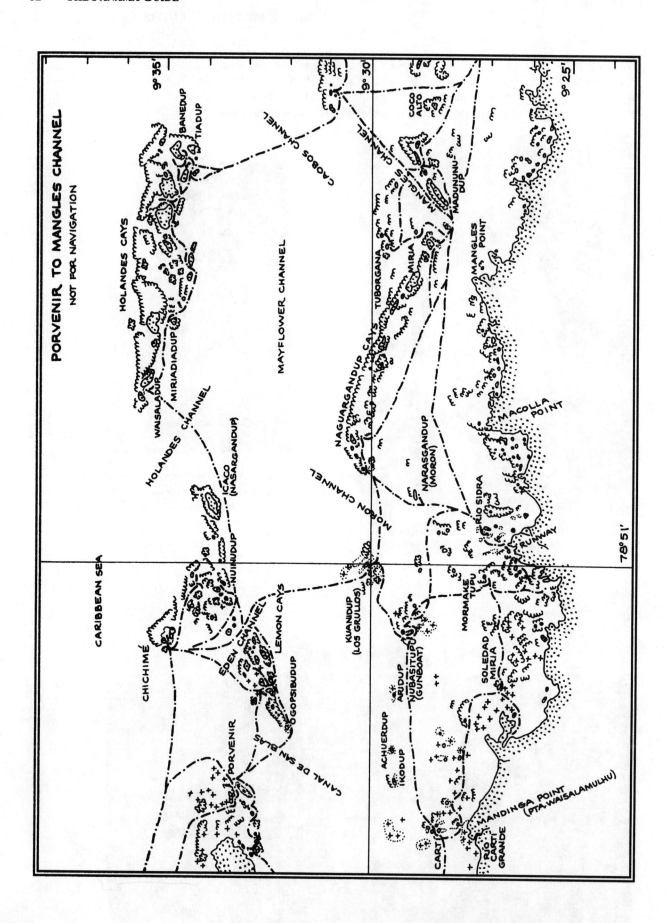

Bahía Las Minas to Puerto Obaldia

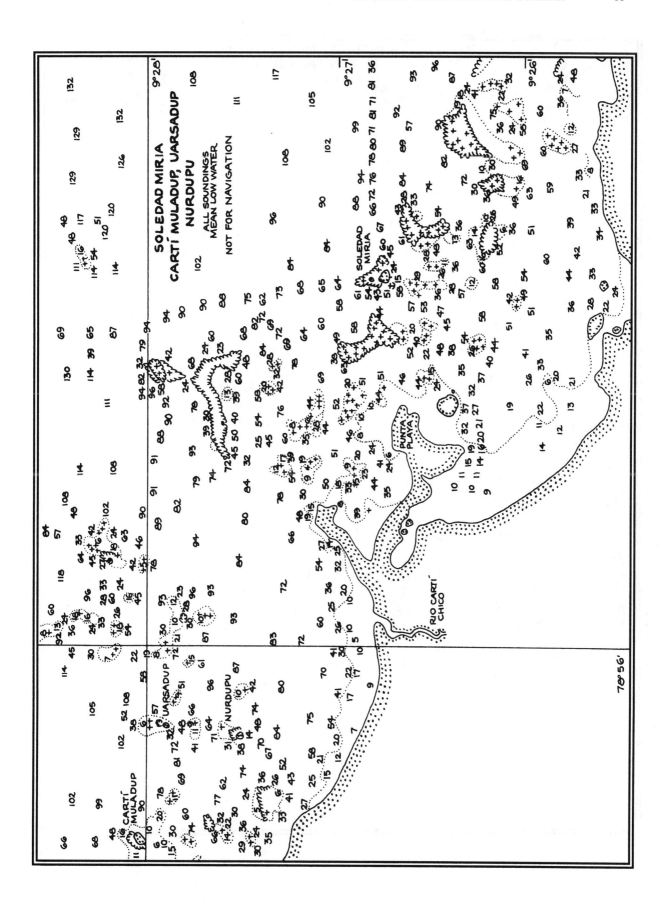

84 THE PANAMA GUIDE

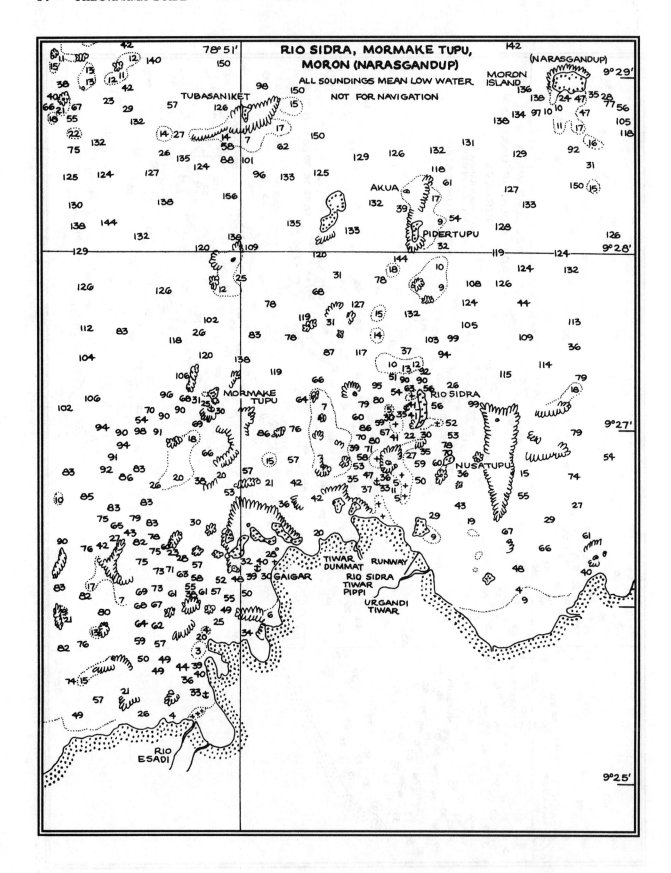

Bahía Las Minas to Puerto Obaldia

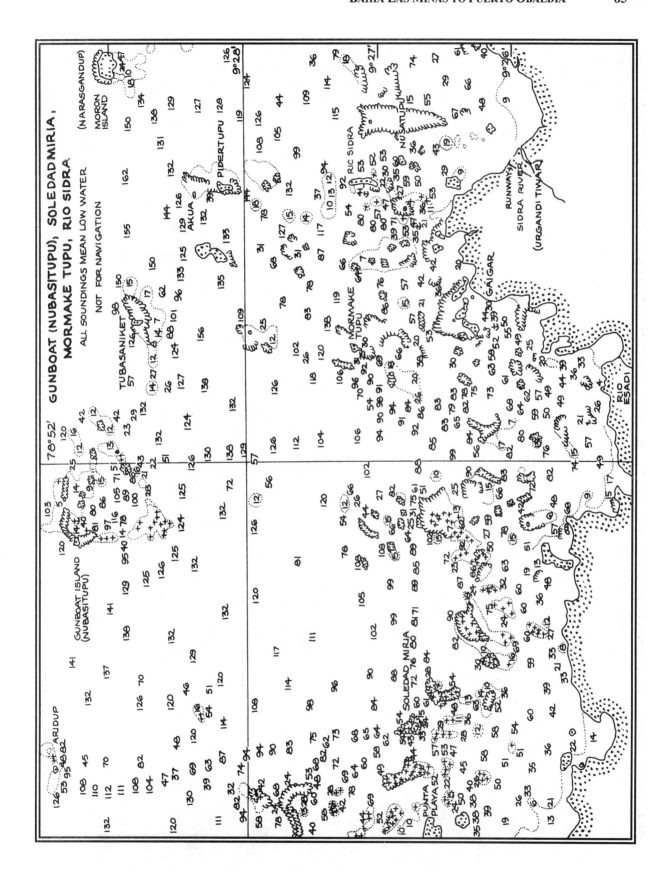

RIO SIDRA

Rio Sidra consists of two old villages, Mamartupu and Urgandi, now joined by a filled canal between the islands. However, two congresos are still in power and trading boats must change to the proper pier before doing business in either part of the village. Quite deservedly Rio Sidra has a reputation for high quality molas. Many stores with varying prices operate in the villages. A pay phone works occasionally but SSB radio is the real communications link for the Kunas. You can buy gasoline from a compound on a tiny islet off the south end of the island. Rio Sidra is so densely populated that its mainland airstrip receives several flights a day, sometimes even on Sundays, a rarity on the other airstrips. To photograph in the village or even the mainland landscape requires a special permit from the congreso. When a yacht arrives a congreso sends a dugout with some kids to collect the fee. They will give you a receipt for the five dollars. The anchorage off the two village piers gets quite a bit of swell and boat traffic goes right through it. Outhouses along the waterfront add to the attractions. Depths there vary between 41 and 46 feet. Make sure your anchor has dug in as much garbage litters the bottom. A lot better anchorage with overall protection is southwest of a small islet with a house on it. At 09°26.7'N and 078°50.17'W you will find depths around 30 feet and a sand bottom with some coral scattered around. Getting into that spot requires high sunlight. Yachts have also anchored in the channel close to the south side of the island and had good protection in fair holding in sand with clumps of coral.

NUSATUPU

The small community of Nusatupu, or Rat Island, has none of the self-confidence of Rio Sidrans. They are very traditional people whose women are also talented mola makers. You can tie your dinghy to the dock which belongs to the new hotel Arnulfo.

ARIDUP

This lovely uninhabited island 2½ miles north of Soledad Miria, see the Gunboat, Soledad Miria, Mormake Tupu, Rio Sidra chartlet, has deep water right up to the shore. The anchorage at 09°29.4'N and 078°54.4'W should be treated as day stop only. Ari, meaning iguana, is a popular island name.

Mollymawk at anchor off Nubasitupu (Gunboat Island), San Blas Islands.

GUNBOAT ISLAND - NUBASITUPU

This uninhabited densely palmed island, whose name means Dove Island, is fringed by reefs which give the anchorage off its east side a fair protection. One can enter the deep basin inside from the west by taking a channel with a 14 foot bar just south of a long reef running south from Nubasitupu. Go into this break when the sandbars at the far east bear 095°T - 100°T. Good light is necessary. Or one can enter from southeast through a channel passing close to the west side of the westernmost of the sandbars. You should have at least 16 feet there. Yet another pass with slightly more depth but harder to locate lies a little further west. High sunlight helps when negotiating any of these passes. The anchorage close to east side of Nubasitupu has between 18 and 30 feet with a sand and coral bottom. At 09°29.22'N and 078°52.54'W you will have 28 feet. Deeper water a little further east has better holding in sand. The snorkeling reefs lie nearby.

TUBASANIKET

Tubasaniket sits on a wide shallow coral shelf. Good only as a day stop because of almost constant swell.

MORON ISLAND - NARASKANDUP

Only occasionally coconut caretakers occupy the huts facing the beach. To reach the best anchorage (always slightly rolly) enter from the east via a deep water channel or from the west by rounding a shallow spit which extends southward from the southwestern shore of Naraskandup. The bar at the end of the spit has 10 feet of water. The anchorage off the sandspit and south of the huts has 24 feet at 09°28.8'N and 078°49.10'W and a sand bottom.

Kuna people sail their dugouts daily as we drive cars. The man pictured above is heading to a farming plot on Urgandi River.

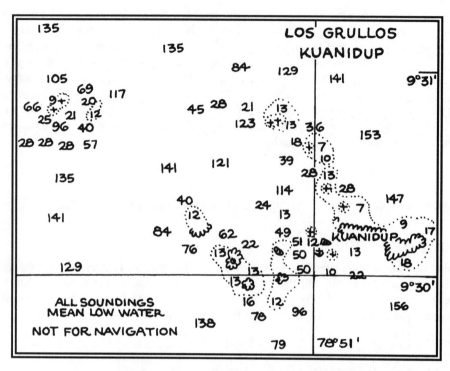

LOS GRULLOS - KUANIDUP

The safest entrance, from the south, leads on 005°T bearing on the dock. The best anchorage in sand is close and slightly southeast of the dock in 35 feet.

Otherwise you will have 55 feet with a sand bottom to the southwest of Kuanidup between the two islands or 14 to 18 feet with a sand bottom and coral to the west of the Kuanidup at 09°30.14'N and 078°51.03'W.

Kuanidup has a Kuna owned hotel which will take care of your garbage (they burn it) and serve meals (after a reasonable notice) and cold drinks.

NAGUARGANDUP CAYS

Two miles directly east from Los Grullos (Kuanidup) and one and a half miles northeast from Moron (Naraskandup) begins a six mile long group of reefs and islands called by the Kunas Naguargandup. It has picturesque islands to anchor off at its east and west ends. It also protects a long inshore ship channel from the usual northerly swell.

THE WESTERN NAGUARGANDUP CAYS

One can anchor off the southeast shore of Salar, the easternmost and the largest of the six cays at the west end of Naguargandup. Two entries lead into a very deep basin formed by these islands. From the west one can pass between Ukupsui to the north and a small cay to the south. The bar has 12 feet with a hard coral bottom and high sunlight is essential for the first time entry. Another wider pass leads into the area from the southeast. From the deep water in the channel south of the islands steer about 330°T on the gap between Salar and Achutupu islands. This bar has a least depth of 24 feet. Once inside, the problem is to find a shallow enough spot to anchor. Close to the south side of the east point of Salar there is a 12 foot deep bank with grass and sand. Further off one can drop anchor in sand pockets between coral outcroppings in depths between 30 - 45 feet at 09°30.41'N and 078°47.57'W. The reef to the east gives fair protection even in boisterous winds from the northeast but when the wind comes from southwest during the rainy months this basin gets uncomfortably choppy. Plenty of dinghy exploration and snorkeling will keep everyone entertained. A few coconut caretakers guard the palms on some of the islands.

EASTERN NAGUARGANDUP CAYS

The south side of Cangombia has the best protection in this area. One family stays permanently in the two huts you see ashore and they make long shopping sailing trips either to Nargana or Rio Sidra.

Cangombia has very good paths under the coconut trees and a front view of the towering hill on the mainland to the south.

One can pilot in from the southeast steering about 318°T on the opening in the islands west of Cangombia. The 9 foot deep coral bar lies between the tip of a shoal running south from the east end of Cangombia and a brown circle of coral 4-6 feet deep to west southwest. Good high sunlight really helps with eyeballing in this entrance. From the west one can steer for this anchorage along the northern edge of the offshore shoals as indicated in the sketch chart. Again the high sun will bring out the outlines of the shoals here. Yet another channel comes into this anchorage from the north along the west side of Cangombia. The depths in the anchorage vary from 57 feet in the middle to 20 feet near shore, all in good holding soft mud.

Nancy and a friend on Mulatupu, San Blas Islands.

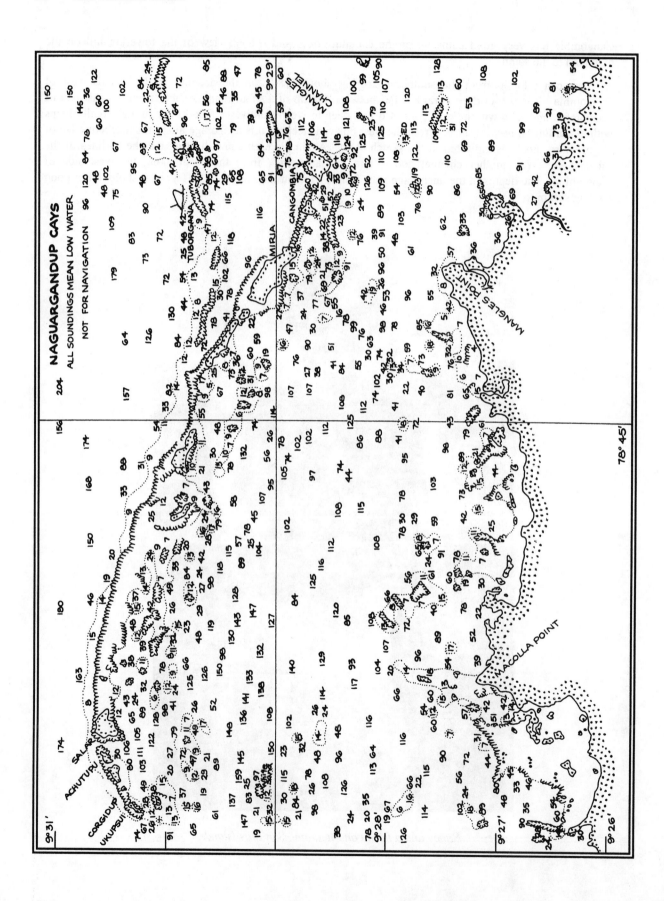

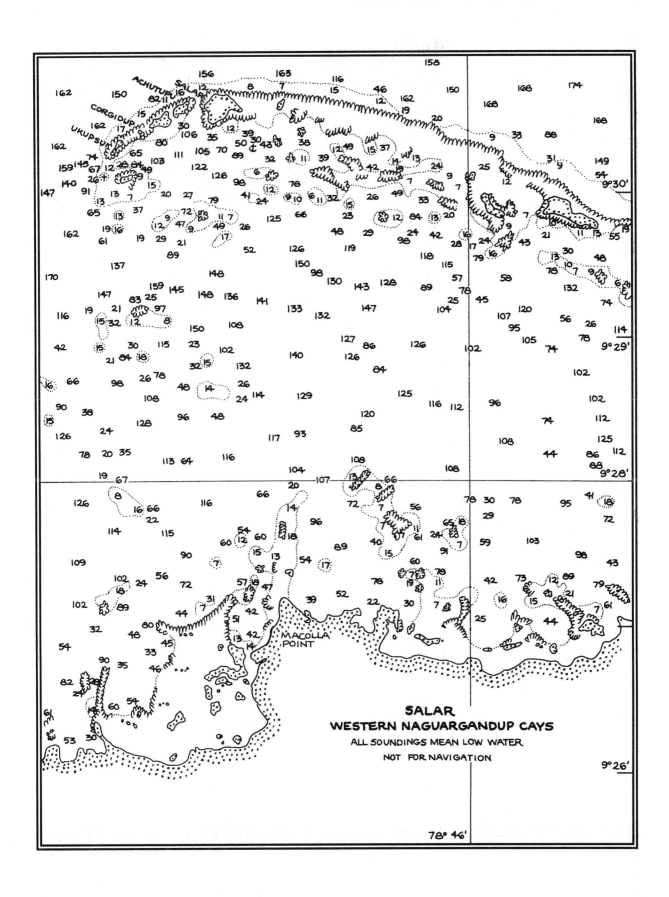

92 THE PANAMA GUIDE

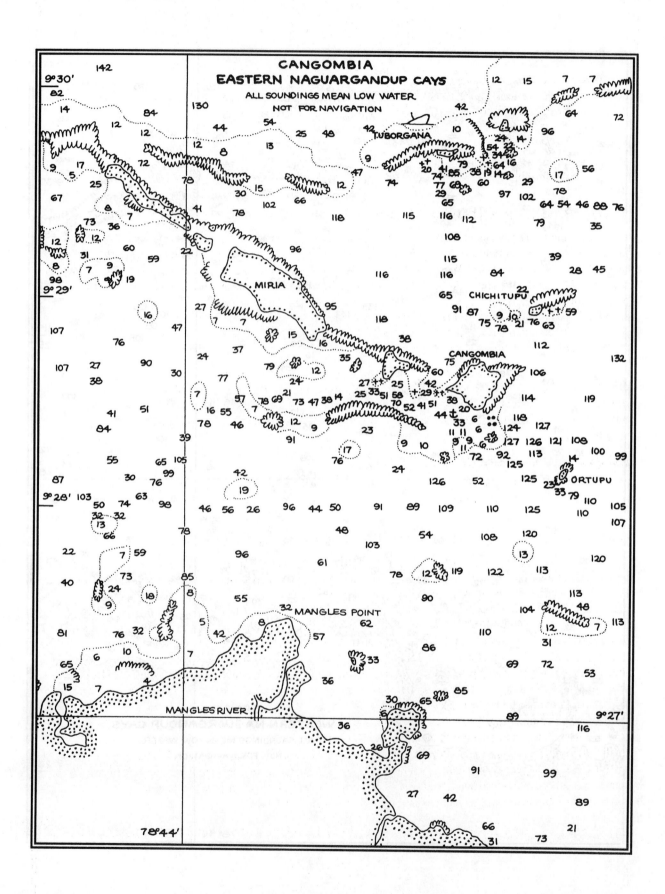

TUBORGANA

This spectacular uninhabited island about one mile north of Cangombia has great diving spots nearby, especially if you are looking for sharks. You will have to drop the hook in very deep water to avoid destroying the coral nearer the shore. Be prepared to move with any shift in the weather.

ORTUPU

The two huts under the towering palms are usually empty except during coconut harvests.

MADUNUNUDUP AND BANERDUP

An easy anchorage to enter from the main southern inshore channel lies off the east shore of the south end of the uninhabited Madununudup. Steer about 040°T on the northeast end of Madununudup. First you will pass over 19 to 30 foot deep spots. When they drop to 60 feet steer northeast and anchor when you reach 20ish foot depths in firm sand with grass. At 09°28.16'N and 078°41.56'W we had 49 feet and good holding soft sand. The narrow cut at the northeast tip of Madununudup has good looking reefs for snorkeling. The narrow beach surrounding Madununudup provides an interesting walk. The area between Madununudup and Banerdup is full of shallow banks often with less than 6 feet over them. Channels 40 - 60 feet deep snake between those shoals but one should only attempt these passages in the best high sunlight.

You will find the best anchorage with a sandy bottom at the Banerdup end of this group on the south side of the smaller island or even between the islands. Further west at 09°28.8'N and 078°40.73'W we had good protection but also plenty of coral outcroppings at 38 feet. Banerdup, Frigate Bird Island, supports a mixture of bush and palms, with very little beach exposed. The diving possibilities are the main attraction.

LIGHTHOUSE ISLAND - SIMONDUP

The usual inshore channel passage runs to the north of Lighthouse Island and the shoal to its west. Simondup, now reduced to a sandbar, once had a hut on it where Simon lived.

GREEN ISLAND - KANILDUP AND SURROUNDING CAYS

The well protected anchorage at the southeastern end of Kanildup has good holding in a sand bottom between 20 and 30 feet deep at 09°28.8'N and 078°38.1'W. Waisaladup, a small island loaded with coconut trees about half a mile south of Kanildup has an excellent anchorage off its south side. At 09°28.31'N and 078°38.15'W you will have 30 feet of depth and a sand bottom. The best approach to Waisaladup is from northwest on a bearing of 155°T on the islet. The bar has 14 feet, a sudden jump from 57 feet. After the bar the depth drops again to 50 feet until closer to Waisaladup. Skirt the shoal extending southwest from the islet keeping in 14 to 20 feet and anchor when the depth drops to about 30 feet. This anchorage stays empty when several other boats have anchored off Kanildup. The views from both anchorages will twang the artistic cords of your soul and the acres of coral banks will appeal to the snorkeler. Note that the islands to southeast of Waisaladup have other excellent anchorages. To reach them from Waisaladup you will have to go all the way to the deep water channel to the south of the group, by the way you arrived. Enter from the south by the west shore of Sugar Island, pass to the west of a small islet to its northwest and then swing westward to pass between another small islet leaving it to the south and a larger one to north. See the Rio Azucar, Green Island sketch chart. You will find there a protected area with at least two anchorages available. Ogopsibudup, another uninhabited island located east of Kanildup also has a temporary anchorage on its south side. A brilliant white beach runs along the north shore of Ogopsibudup, which means plenty of coconuts.

Above: Green Island (Kanildup), taken from Waisaladup, San Blas Islands. Below: Mollymawk at anchor off Ordupbanedup, East Coco Bandero Cays, San Blas Islands.

COCO BANDERO CAYS

This long offshore reef about 2 miles north of Green island has good anchorages off the islets at either end of the group. The snorkeling around numerous reefs there is superb.

ORDUPTARBOAT

A good anchorage at 09°31.15'N and 078°38.95'W has 42 feet depth and sandy bottom. A shallow reef and an island protects it from the west and southwest while a large island provides complete coverage from the north semicircle and a small islet on top of a reef covers it from the east. The entry channel leads from the south along the west edge of a bank running south from the islet with three palm trees. Be sure to avoid an extensive bank surrounding the sandbar to the west of the channel. Once inside one can also anchor close to the west side of the palm islet in depths between 20 and 14 feet with a sand and weeds bottom. A conspicuous wreck of a large ferrocement yacht lies on a reef north of the islet. When approaching this whole group of islands from the west give a wide berth to the shoals extending half a mile to the west from Orduptarboat.

EAST END OF COCO BANDERO CAYS

At the other end of the Coco Bandero group one can find superb protection between Tuala and Ordupbanedup at 09°30.61'N and 078°37.0'W in 28 feet of water with a sandy bottom. Note that deep water runs close to the west and south shore of Ordupbanedup. Yachts also anchor between Ordupbanedup and Esnatupile and between Tiadup and the north side of Ordupbanedup. These last anchorages become rolly in strong blows from the north semicircle. The tiny palm crowded cays and translucent water colors make this area one of the prettiest in the islands.

One can enter the anchorages from the east by a wide channel south of Tiadup (the most straightforward) or by another channel south of Ordupbanedup. The channel from the south leads east of the long reef running south from Esnatupile. Beware of the extensive shoals extending southwest from Tuala. This channel requires high sun to see the reefs as do the other channels from the east.

Nabsadup and Ordup, the two islands three quarters of a mile southeast from Tuala and conspicuous for their towering coconut trees do not have good places to anchor. Swell sweeps around them limiting the exploration of the area to dinghy trips.

RIO AZUCAR - UARGANDUP

The village seems in a transition away from the traditional Kuna lifestyle although during the 1925 Kuna revolution against Panamanian rule Azucar villagers took strong action against the pro-Christian Kuna faction. However, the congreso here is still in charge. You will see few women wearing mola blouses and many concrete houses crowd out the huts. Stores here have a reasonable supply of the basics and you can get fresh water from a faucet on the dock at a reasonable charge. The people are quite friendly. There is a rule against using outboard motors in Azucar River where you can do laundry. You will see the entrance flats to the river west of the village marked by scores of stranded trees. Enter along the mangroves on the east side then cut across between two shoals sprouting mangrove shoots and some stranded trees.

Two channels lead into the anchorage off the west side of the village. The access from northeast is easier and the channel passes close to the south edge of the village. The anchorage at 09°25.89'N and 078°37.69'W has 36 feet of depth over a mud bottom. One can leave through the channel going north between the village and the reefs to the west when the sun is high and all the numerous shoals stand out. This channel is a lot trickier to use when entering than leaving. When the sun is high and behind you can approach it by steering 185° - 190°T on the west side of the village and then start eyeballing your way in when close to the reefs.

96 THE PANAMA GUIDE

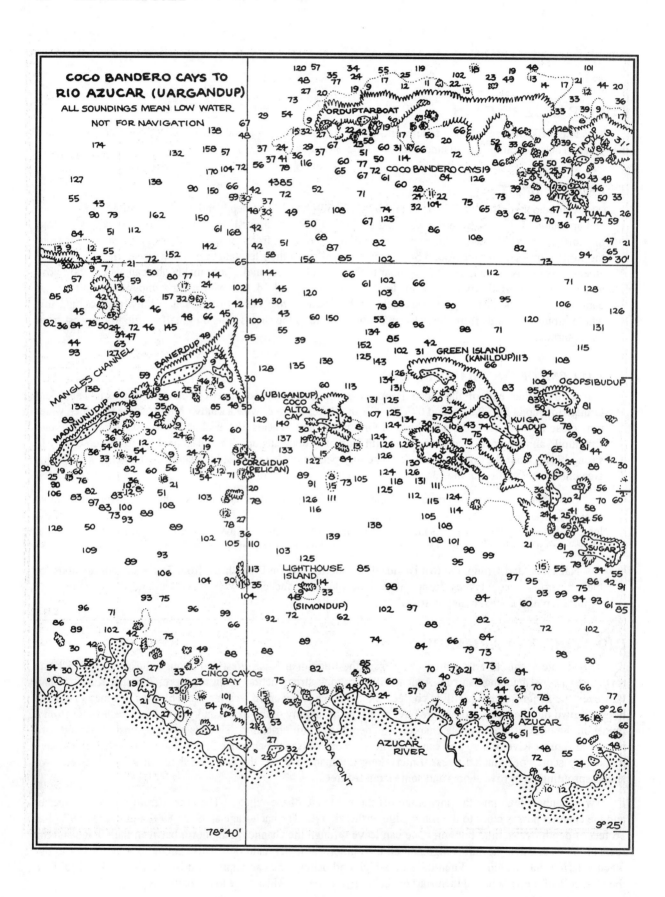

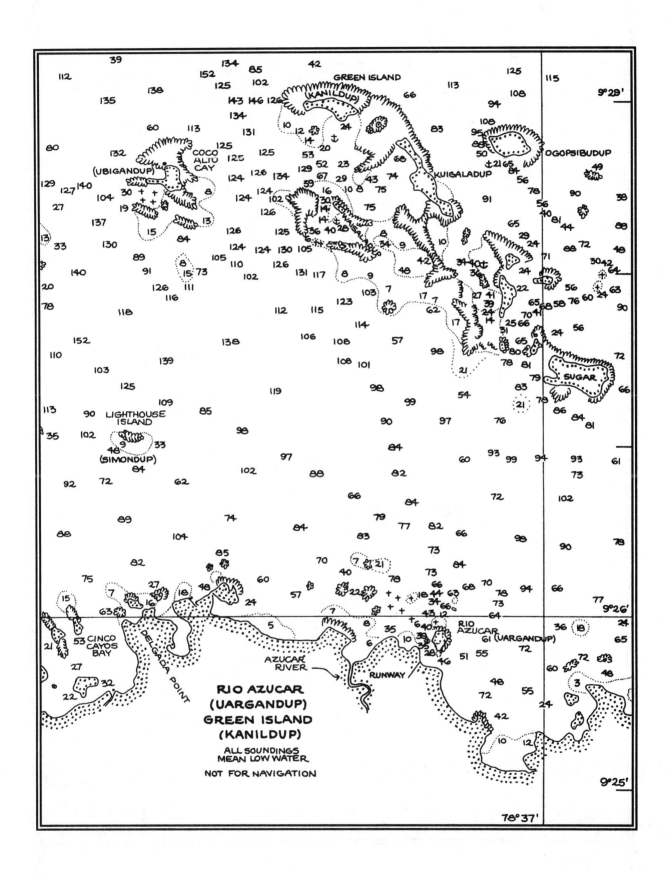

98 THE PANAMA GUIDE

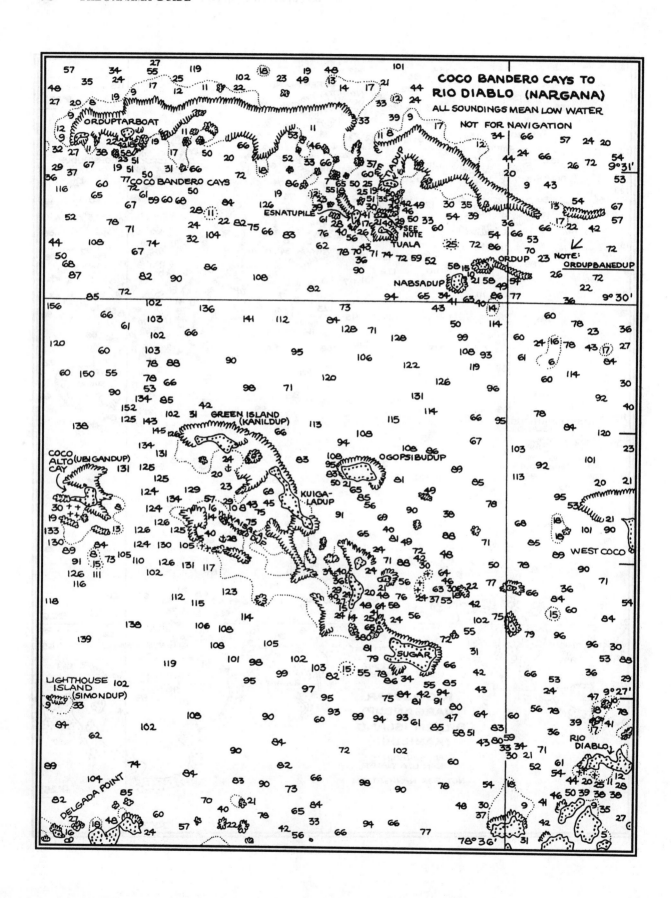

RIO DIABLO (NARGANA) AND CORAZON DE JESUS

Only the US DMA charts perpetuate Rio Diablo as the name for these two villages known in **Panama as** Nargana and Corazon de Jesus. In the Kuna language Corazon de Jesus bears the name of Akuanusatupu and Nargana - Yandup. A bridge connects the two communities of Kuna people who have decided to abandon their traditional beliefs and the colorful dressing ways of the women. You will find here hotels, restaurants, clinics, post office, churches, many stores (some with ice) and even a bank where you can change large dollar bills. No cash advances or check cashing here. Nargana is the main base of the defense force for the Comarca and has a jail. Sometimes police ask to see passports of the visiting yachtsmen but only to keep up their register of visitors. Yachts cannot make a formal entry here into the Republic of Panama. The pay phone which works only in the evenings when the generator starts (around 5 PM) does so much business that you must get a number from the kiosk next to the booth. Distribution of numbers begins at 4 PM, the generator is turned off at 10 PM. The phone is connected to an ATT operator by dialing 109, an international operator by dialing 106. It is not possible to call Europe from the San Blas. There is a busy airstrip on Nargana which makes it a convenient place to meet friends who arrive from Panama City. The longer airstrip of Corazon de Jesus is on a separate island to the east. Yachtsmen visiting ashore can safely leave dinghies at docks in either village at the foot of the bridge.

The anchorage off the south side of the villages has complete protection. At 09°26.47'N and 078°35.24'W you will have 28 feet of depth and a mud bottom. An easy channel from the northwest leads into the anchorage. When close to the west end of Nargana favor the south side of the channel to avoid a shallow bank and a reef off the southwest end of the island. Another entry channel from northeast passes close to the southeast shore of Corazon de Jesus and is easier to use for leaving than for entering unless the sun is high enough for eyeballing the few detached shoals and the edges of the banks growing out from the mainland.

You can make a dinghy trip with the outboard on up Rio Diablo where you will almost certainly see a troop of white faced monkeys. They might even watch you doing the laundry.

IGUANA ISLAND

The Iguana Island, located two miles northeast from Nargana, has a Kuna run hotel on the eastern island of the two, Kuadule. See the Puyadas Channel sketch chart. Ernest Diaz, the chef, invites yachts to anchor off the southwest tip of the island where you will find a 15 foot deep anchorage in a sandy bottom at 09°28.13'N and 078°34.02'W. You can have a drink or a meal (after reasonable notice) in their restaurant overlooking the sea and several islands to the north.

PUYADAS - PUGADUP

In mild weather conditions you can anchor about southwest from the two easternmost islets at 09°28.22'N and 078°30.74'W in 33 feet of water with a sand and grass bottom. South of this spot you will find deep coral outcroppings and closer to the shore you find a coral shelf running out from the island. A few coconut caretakers live in the huts on the north shore. Good paths go all over the island and snorkeling is very good in clear water.

FAREWELL ISLANDS PASSAGE

The deep channel used by local traders runs close to the south side of this island and continues southeastward passing between two reef banks over an 11 foot bar.

TIGRE - MAMARTUPU

The village does not look its best from the water due to many mildewing concrete houses along the waterfront but once you enter between the huts the island transforms itself into a little paradise. By order of the congreso people do not visit yachts. Ashore, apart from the usual stores you will find a Kuna handicraft store carrying molas, wood carvings and good models of their dugouts or "ulus" in their language. They also have rare items like traditional combs made from black palm. There is a pay phone with connections to ATT US operators by dialing

109, international operators by dialing 106, European calls are not possible. Conveniently, the runway is on the island. A faucet on the dock has fresh water and they charge .20 for five gallons (not always enforced).

The water comes from the mainland via a PVC pipe so do not anchor off the water tower. The smoothest anchorage is off the south side of the northwestern point near a concrete house with an outhouse. You will find 18 - 20 feet of water over sandy bottom at 09°25.95'N and 078°31.43'W. Several reef patches lie south of this position. Except during the strong winds of the dry season, the wind at night often comes from the mainland so you may want to put another anchor in that direction to prevent swinging onto the shoals near shore. The deep channel which runs along the south shore of the village allows a passage to the east.

Bahía Las Minas to Puerto Obaldia

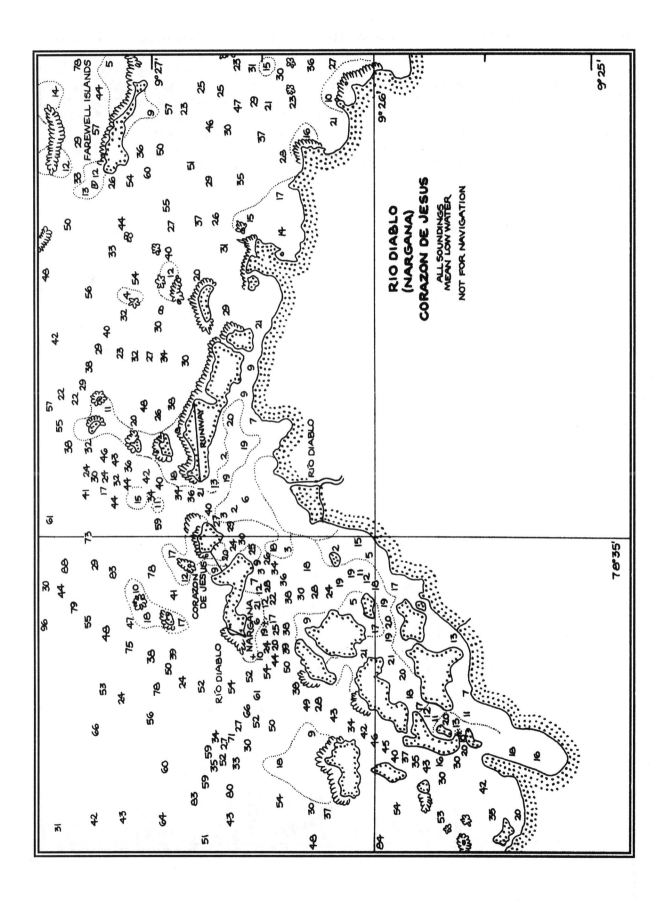

102 THE PANAMA GUIDE

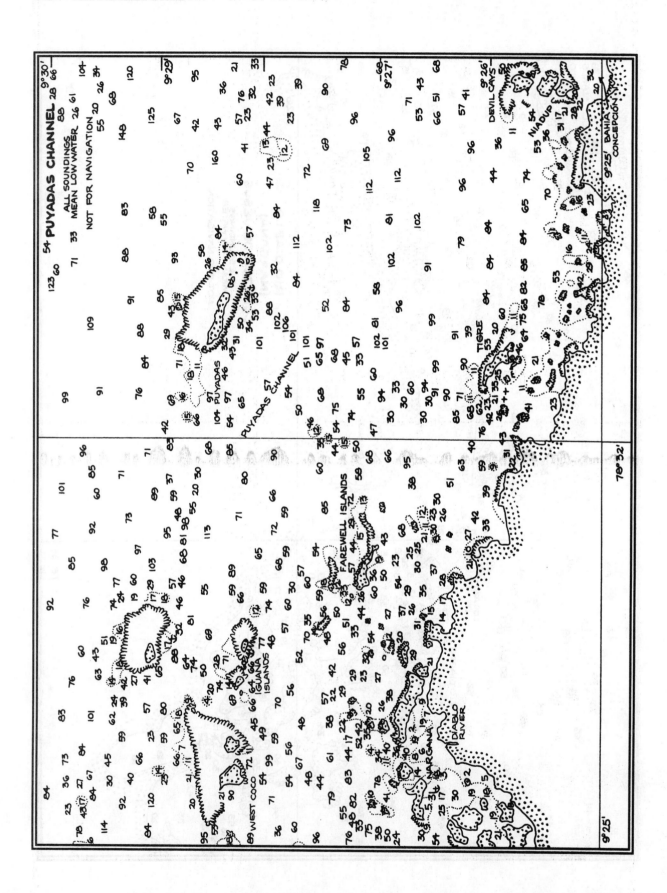

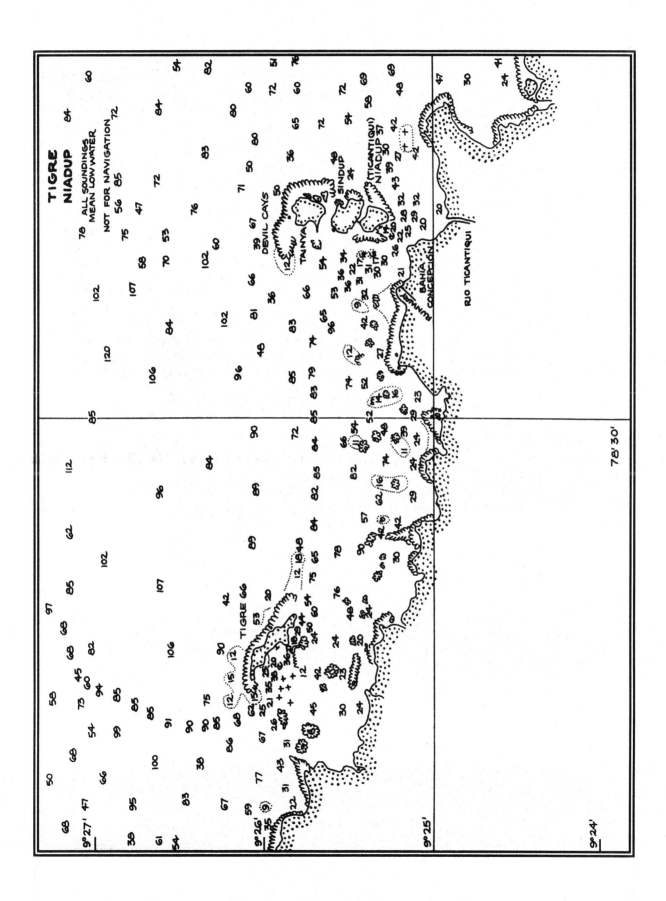

NIADUP

Nia means devil in Kuna and the villages prefer to call their main, southernmost, island Ticantiqui. Sindup, the next island to north has a clinic. Two stores sell wooden carvings and other artifacts along with basic supplies. Similarly to Tigre people here do not come to yachts to visit. On the other hand, visitors are requested to leave the island at 7 PM, a custom which persists in most of the small Kuna communities. The local congreso does not charge yachts any fees. Luis Ortiz, the first sahila, designs and sews molas.

Protection southwest of the dock is better than it appears from the chart. You should anchor in 20-22 feet and at 09°25.20'N and 078°28.90'W you will have good holding in sand mixed with mud. Check the anchor for there is a lot of debris on the bottom. Do not come closer to the dock as you will block the approach for the trading boats. Further out your boat will probably roll. The deep channel swings around the south tip of Ticantiqui from the northwest to the northeast as the sketch chart indicates.

PLAYON GRANDE CHANNEL

From Punta La Coquera to Culebra Rock the traders use the deep channel which is flanked by several reef patches on either side. They break in heavy swells and probably contain shallower spots than the officially charted 11 feet. With high sun these shallow places stand out clearly against the deeper water. Spokeshave Reef always breaks. The inshore channel after Culebra demands a lot of attention and a good high sun for eye piloting. In favorable conditions a yacht can go by this channel all the way to Snug Harbor. In overcast and calm weather one should head out further offshore to pass south and close to Ratones Cays (Aridup).

The chartlets do not cover the area which has a large breaking reef 1 mile northwest of Ratones Cays.

RATONES CAYS - ARIDUP

Approach the anchorage off the island from the south along the edge of the reef extending from the south tip of Aridup to two small islets further south. You can find depths between 23 and 30 feet, the bottom is flat coral with patches of sand, at 09°21.92'N and 078°15.47'W. Several families from Achutupu and Playon Chico keep watch over their coconuts. They maintain the island in perfect shape for strolling around. Prolific coral growth makes for exceptionally good snorkeling in clear waters.

SNUG HARBOR

Several islands give perfect protection to a deep basin off the mainland named Snug Harbor by the New England schoonermen who used to sail here to trade for coconuts. See the Playon Chico, Ukupseni sketch chart. Possibly the best anchorage for yachts lies close to the west side of Kaymatar. Approach from south between two large reef patches, one extending from Kaymatar, usually easily spotted. At 09°19.66'N and 078°15.08'W you will find 33 to 40 feet with good holding in mud. One can also pass through the narrow channel north of Kaymatar and anchor in a deep pool on the south side of Ogumnaga.

Men from Playon Chico sail by this anchorage to go fishing or working on the coconut trees covering islets nearby. Sometimes store owners from Playon Chico come to take orders for delivery. All the islands around invite trips ashore and in gentle weather one should not miss snorkeling on the outside reefs easily reached by dinghy.

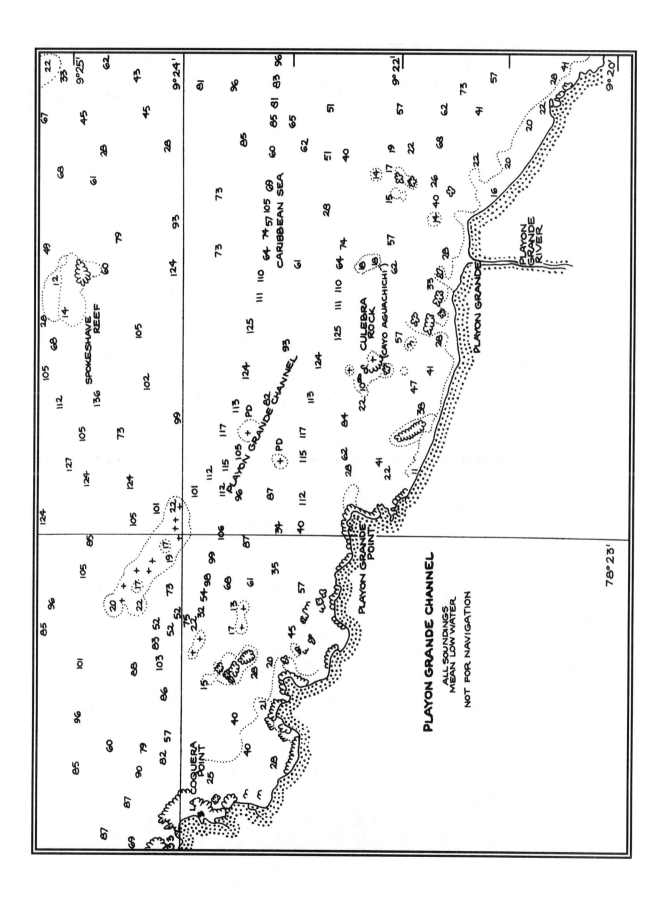

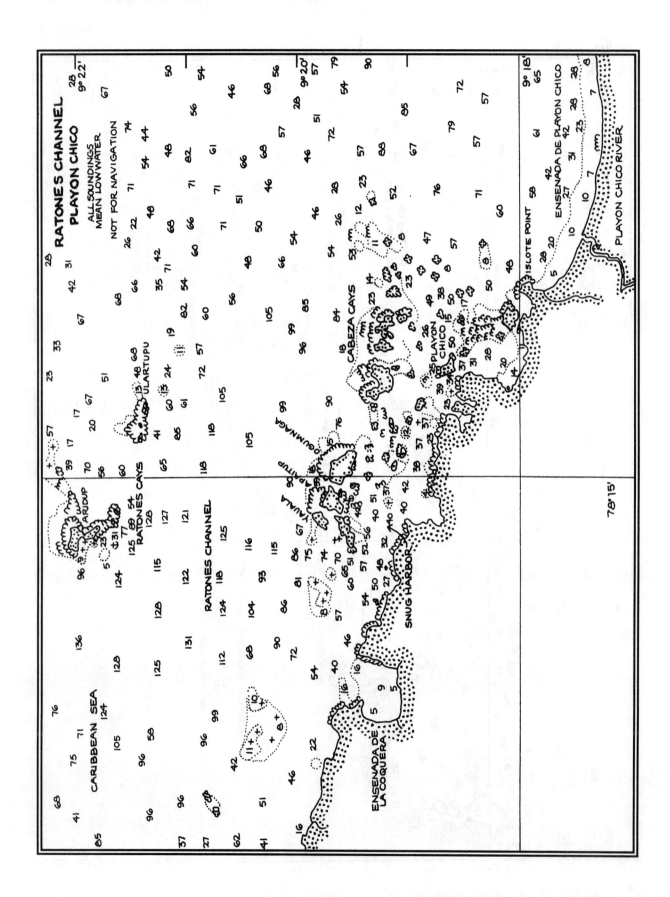

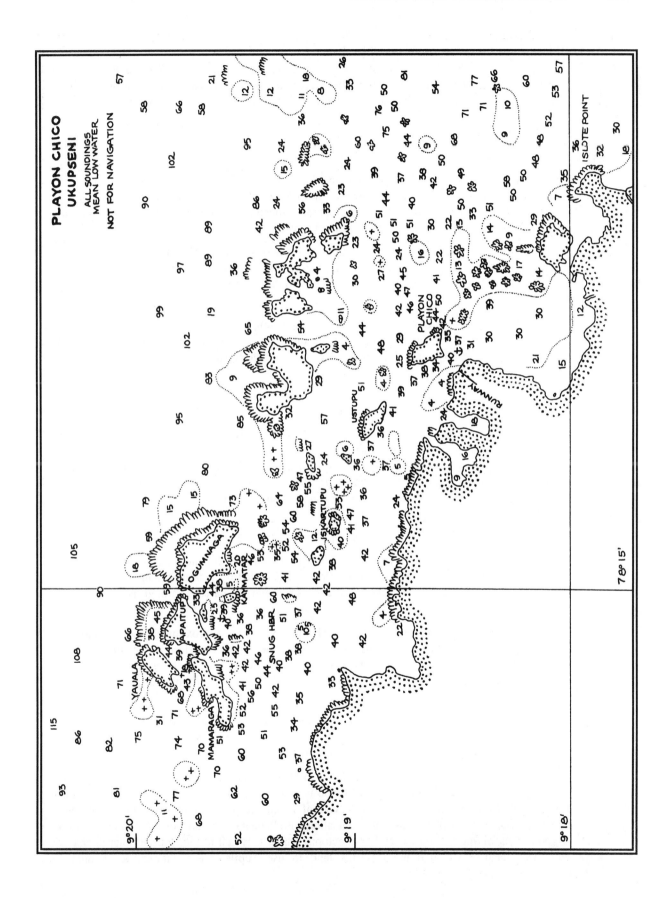

ISKARTUPU

One can anchor off the southwest tip of Iskartupu and visit this Kuna run resort. See the Playon Chico sketch chart. A large bank of solar panels provides all the electricity. Water, which comes from the mainland, goes through a system of filters. Even the waste is treated to keep the environmental impact of the hotel to a minimum.

PLAYON CHICO - UKUPSENI

This densely populated village has several schools including a secondary school and a technical school for agriculture which educate kids from many distant communities. You will find here several stores with widely varying prices, several places which sell Kuna bread, an outboard mechanic and even a cinema next to a large basketball court. The congreso collects a five dollar fee from yachts.

When approaching from Snug Harbor pass close to the south side of Iskartupu and then close to south sides of the islets on the north side of the channel. From Ustupu you should go straight for the west shore of Playon Chico and then parallel it to the anchorage south of the island. Holding is good in mud and 30 feet of water at 09°18.51'N and 078°13.88'W.

There is a channel on the east side of the island and it is considerably easier to leave this way than to arrive from the east. A high sun suitable for eye piloting makes all the difference. The same applies to the channel which runs east and west off the north end of Playon Chico - at its eastern approaches it is littered with coral patches.

PLAYON CHICO TO SAN IGNACIO DE TUPILE

Once out of the maze of reefs off the east side of Playon Chico a clear deep channel starts at Islote Point and goes all the way to Playon Chico Point. When navigating between these two villages one should remember that in the season of strong onshore winds all the shoals break. Local traders treat these breakers as markers and navigate between them but yachts visiting these waters for the first time should sail from the Tupile area northwestward and out into deep water and then enter Snug Harbor from the north and west.

SAN IGNACIO DE TUPILE (MONO VILLAGE ON CHART NO. 26042)

The inshore waters south of Tupile have a vast number of shoals with deep channels between them. One can pilot between them on days with high sun and breeze ruffled waters, aided by polarized sunglasses. However after heavy rains the river outflows completely destroy water clarity and the passage through here turns into a navigator's nightmare.

When approaching from the west one can find the deep channel by steering approximately 095°T on the west point of Tupile. The channel passes between shoals on either side, then continues close to the south side of a small islet with a hut off the west point of Tupile and maintains good depth close to the waterfront of Tupile. About a half mile southeast from the village the shoals start to thicken again. Some of these are marked with sticks and plastic jugs.

One deep channel east of Tupile passes north of Iandu and then close to the south side of Suledup, a tiny islet with four conspicuous palms. Another channel, generally more difficult unless conditions are perfect for eyeballing, goes south of the shoals off Iandu and then south of Ilestu.

One can anchor close to the south shore of Tupile in 40 to 50 foot depths. Of the two anchorages further south from the village the one at 09°17.44'N and 078°09.66'W has good holding in mud 45 feet deep and is within one third of a mile from the village. The busy village of Tupile has a restaurant, several cantinas, stores selling beer and a post office with SSB radio for communication with Panama City and Colón. Young men of the village make a good living diving for lobster, crab and octopus which they sell to the "lobster" planes and you can always buy these fresh. Although the residents tend to use Tupile, the traditional Kuna name is Tannaquetupir.

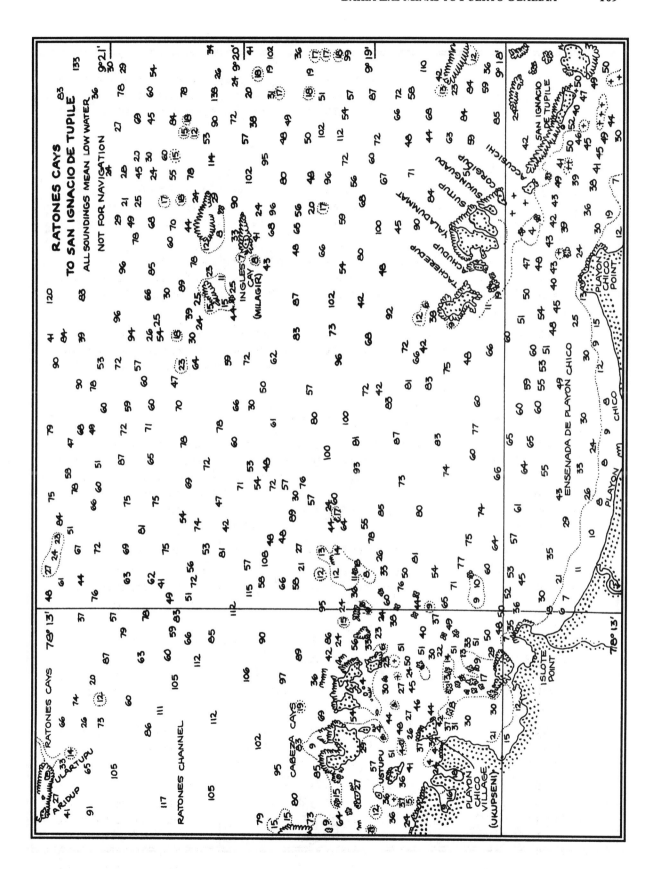

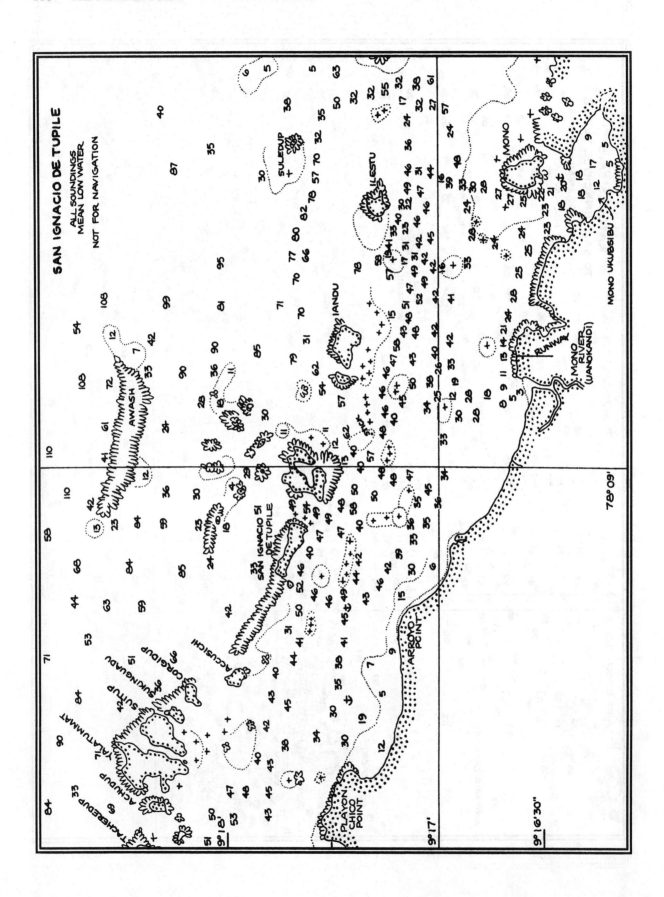

Bahía Las Minas to Puerto Obaldia

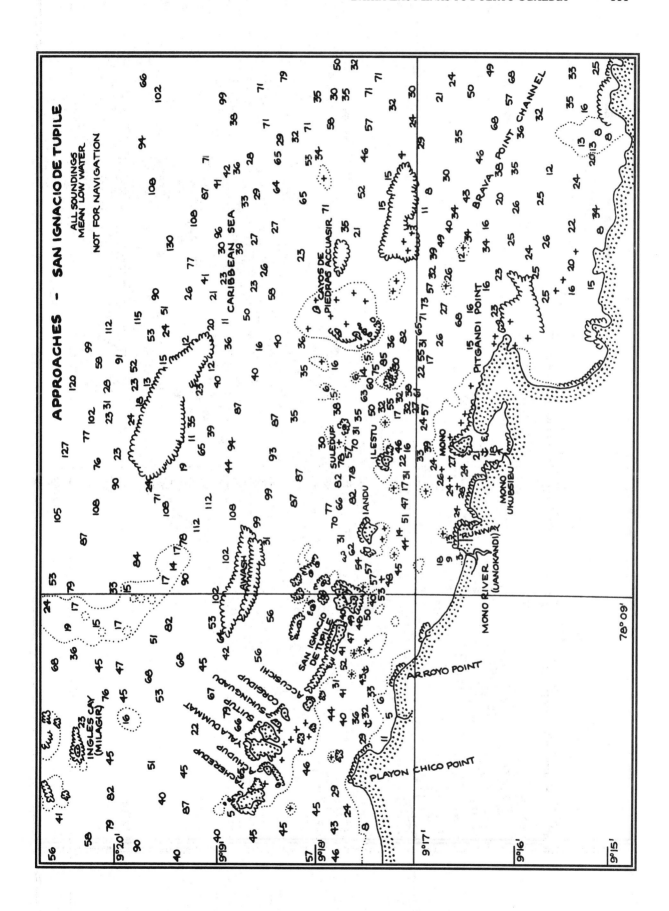

112 THE PANAMA GUIDE

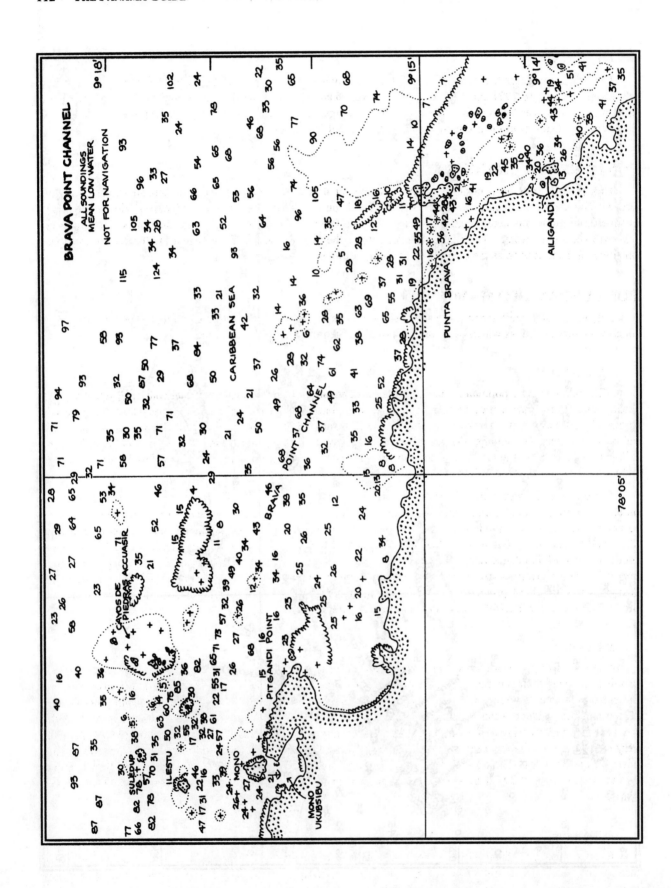

ISLA MONO

Two miles southeast from the village a yacht can anchor in a perfectly sheltered bay off the south shore of Isla Mono. At 09°16.29'N and 078°07.56'W you will have 20 feet of depth with a mud bottom. Mangroves, broken in a few places by small beaches and canoe landings, line the shores of the bay. A deep water approach to the anchorage leads from the north close to the west side of Isla Mono.

PUNTA BRAVA CHANNEL

This channel runs on a northwest-southeast line for 4½ miles from just south of Acuasir shoals to Punta Brava. The shoals of Acuasir are easy to spot and if you pass close to their south edge you will have a clear channel until numerous coral patches just east of Punta Brava. Avoid going right over them as some may have less than six feet of water. The shallow banks outside the northern limits of the channel will have conspicuous breakers on them as soon as the onshore winds bring ocean size swells.

PUNTA BRAVA TO MAMITUPU

Extensive outer reefs smooth out the inshore waters from Punta Brava to Achutupu. Deep channels run along very shallow banks which become very obvious when illuminated by high sun.

AILIGANDI

Ailigandi, a heavily populated island, has the most advanced clinic in this part of San Blas. A Kuna operated resort hotel, Ikusa, has a nice restaurant open to everyone. You will find another restaurant serving baked goodies by the basketball court and the school. A well mannered policeman on duty will check your passport and collect one dollar. The village office, sahilatura, will extract an additional five dollar fee. A small loan bank in Ailigandi was in 1996 the target of a failed bank robbery by Colombians who arrived in a fast launch. A shoot out took place in that corner of the island.

The shady and fragrant Rio Nabsadi will take you far in to where you can walk between stands of bamboo and ancient mango trees. You might even come across the remains of tractors brought here years ago in an effort to entice the Kunas into modern agricultural methods. For many years Ailigandi has been exposed to ardent Christian proselytizing but many villagers have managed to retain their indigenous beliefs and follow both modern and traditional practices when problems occur. During September and October, when the corn crop comes in, freshly ground roasted corn meal, ob tibialeubilet, can be bought. The anchorage off the south shore of Ailigandi has excellent protection and is easily approached from the east. Holding is good in mud but at 09°13.577'N and 078°01.749'W we found a large refrigerator on the bottom.

ISLANDIA

A family from Ailigandi has claimed the northwestern islet as a tourist attraction and charges visitors for the privilege of using their tiny beach. Yachtsmen can land free on the eastern island as well as enjoy snorkeling on the surrounding reefs. From the west one can approach Islandia on 085°T bearing on the south point of the easternmost cay. Deep water runs close to the south shore of the southwestern islet. Another approach leads from the south by steering 013°T on the gap between easternmost and the middle cays. This course will take you very close to a very shallow reef on the starboard hand and then near an 8 foot coral patch on the port side. The basin off the islets has 45 to 53 foot depths and soft sand bottom except a 12 foot patch located by 010°T bearing on the middle cay and 295°T bearing on the southwest cay. The bottom here consists of sand mixed with coral marl.

ACHUTUPU

When approaching from the northwest on the inland route you must locate Wakalatupu, a small islet with three or so palms, lying about 300 yards northwest from Achutupu. A narrow but deep channel passes very close to its south shore. Beware of the submerged reef to the south of this channel. After Wakalatupu steer southeast for a small islet with a hut right off the southwest tip of the village. Close to it swing south, pass east of two reef patches indicated on the sketch chart and anchor south of the village before you get on an extensive shallow sand bank with 4 feet on it. At 09°11.70'N and 077°59.40'W you will have about 20 feet, sand and coral marl with some grass on the bottom.

Deep channels lead into the Achutupu anchorage from the northeast and east. A good deep channel runs from the anchorage suggested above towards the mainland shore. It then goes half way between the mainland and Mantupkwa islet. Trading boats use a very narrow channel that makes a sharp turn between the south side of Achutupu and Uagitupu. The widest and deepest channel enters the inland waters from northeast along the west side of Achutupu and reefs extending from the north shore of that island. The axis of the channel runs 235°/055°T. In boisterous onshore winds the waves break on all reefs on either side of this channel marking its boundaries. When coming from the east one can steer west on Kainora island and turn to 235°T when close to the east edge of the reefs extending from Kainora. In high sun the outer reefs show up very well but the inshore waters become opaque after rains.

Achutupu has been filled to make one island but officially the island has two villages, Achutupu and Murrutuku at the east end. Several stores carry the usual stuff. Mola makers and men carvers keep extra items for sale because the Kuna run resort on Uagitupu (Dolphin Island Resort) brings in a few visitors fairly regularly. Uagitupu sells ice and beer. Women from Achutupu are expert sailors from an early age. In their traditional role as water carriers they always have had to sail their "ulus" up Sankanti Senik (also called Tiwar Dumat or Big River) to fill their containers and wash laundry. It will change soon as a new aqueduct from the hills has already reached the mainland shore and piped fresh water will come to the village soon. That means that yachts should not in future anchor east of the anchorage suggested above to avoid damaging the water pipe on the bottom.

The first sahila of Achutupu (Dog Island) collects a five dollar fee. Two older men, Alfred and Daniel, especially, speak good English. You can do laundry in the big river, Sankanti Senik, which is worth a visit anyhow. By order of the congreso you raise the outboard motor soon after entering the river.

MAMITUPU

Colombian traders call this village En Cuero (Naked) as reputedly the Kunas here did not want to adopt the European style clothing until long after other villages did. The congreso has a traditionally tight grip on the community with "sualipetmar" guys patrolling the village in the evenings with brica mosa nettles in hand and ready to swat any unruly kids. The congreso does not allow the villagers to visit yachts but a brave one or two may come along to sell fish or lobster. Yachts pay the usual five dollars and are informed that no photography is allowed. Also, yachtsmen may not visit the river and the cemetery. Apparently a few years ago some cruisers helped themselves to coconuts there. While visiting the village ask to see Pablo Nuñez Perez who speaks good English and likes visitors. He lived in England for a while after marrying an English girl. Roy Martinez carves very accurate models of Kuna "ulus", or dugouts, and usually has some for sale. Alvariño Lopez makes the gold and silver jewelry that Kuna women typically wear.

The best anchorage is south of the water tower in 28 to 30 feet with a mud bottom. Getting to Mamitupu anchorage from the northwest presents little difficulty. Consult the Achutupu, Mamitupu sketch chart and come south along the west side of Mamitupu and then between the south tip of the island and another reef bank. Trading boats usually come from the north to the two docks and then depart eastward via the channel south of Uastupu. When coming from the east to the anchorage give a wide berth to the indicated coral banks lying southeast and east of Mamitupu. In good eyeballing conditions the area presents little difficulty. In several places the depths diminish to 14 or 12 feet indicating coral outcroppings under the boat - keep a good lookout!

ACHUTUPU TO USTUPU

Coral banks proliferate in this whole area and the deepest area runs about southeast from just north of Achutupu and inside the outer banks. These outer banks break vigorously when strong onshore winds bring Caribbean swells with them. During the calm months a navigator has to keep the eyes open and preferably move when the sunlight is right for reef spotting. Even in the best conditions dark algae growth on coral heads makes them hard to distinguish against deep dark water.

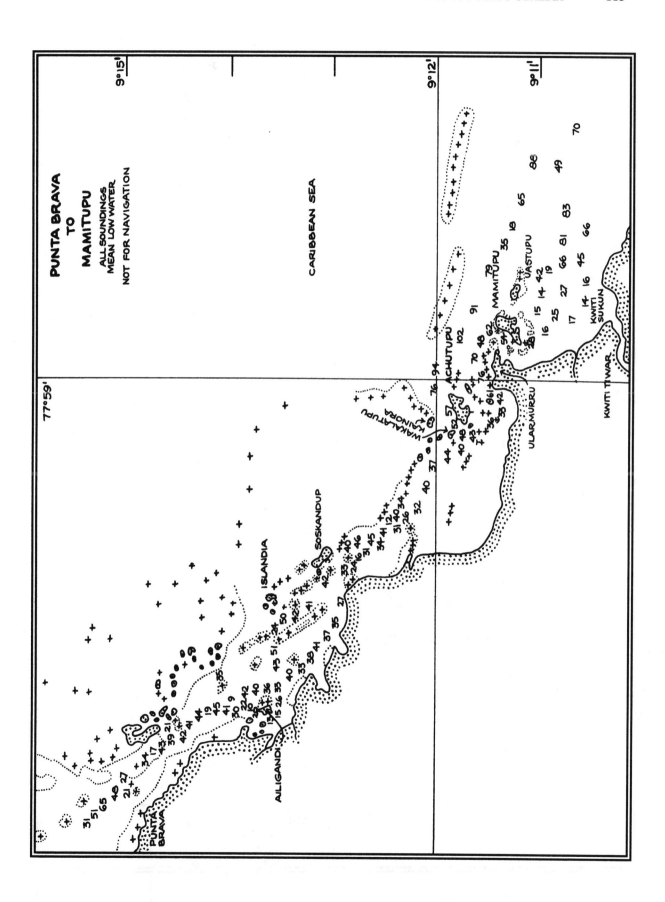

116 **THE PANAMA GUIDE**

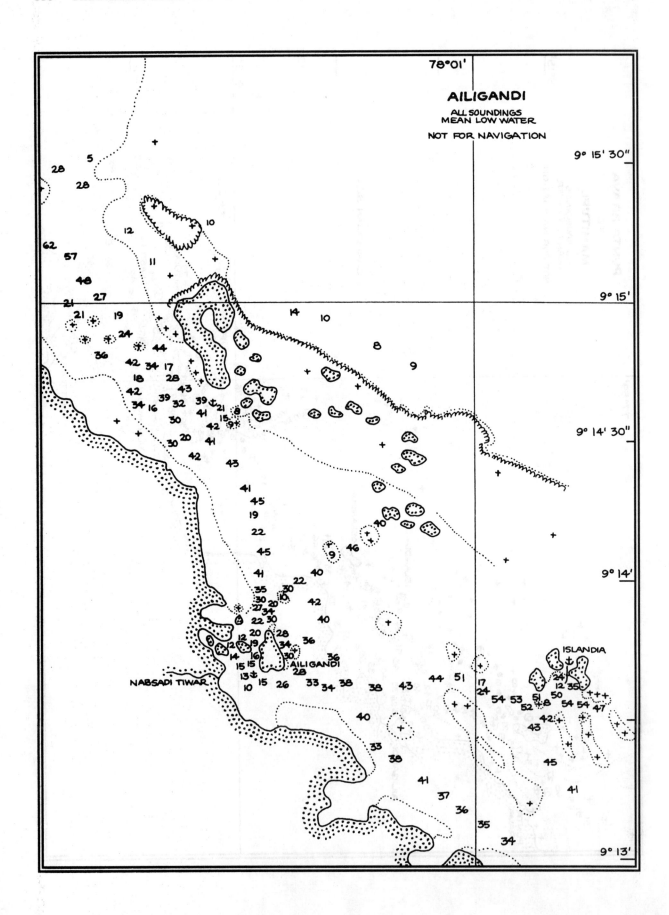

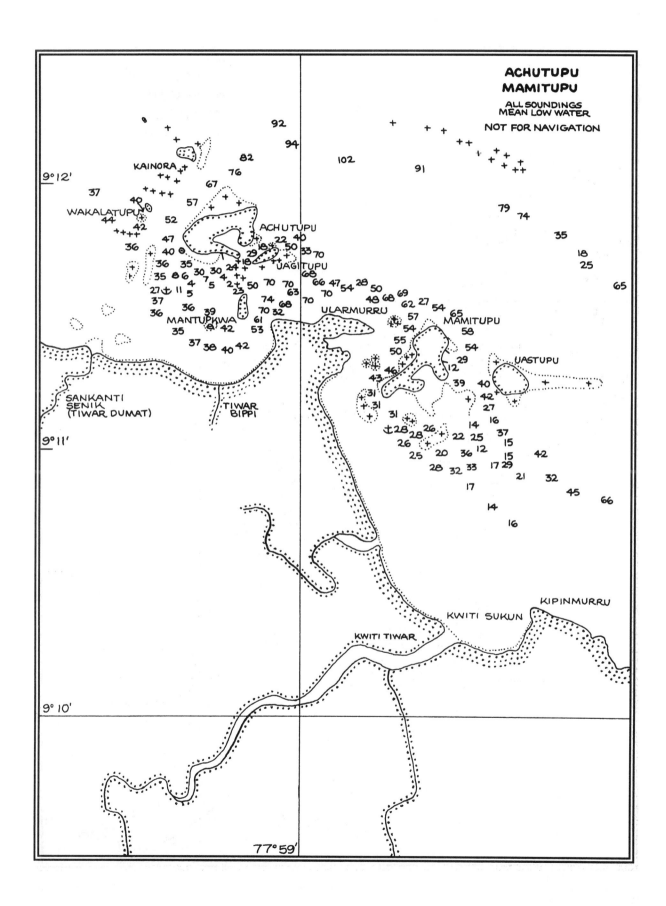

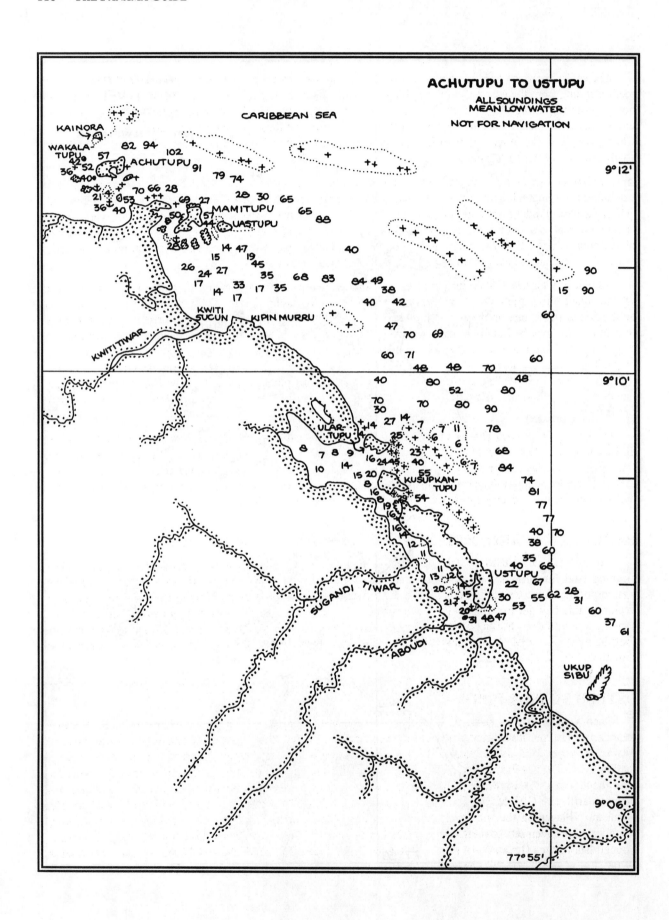

USTUPU

The safest approach to the anchorage off the town dock is from the north and then close to the edge of the reef extending from the east shore of the village. Anchor west of the dock in 18 - 20 feet in a mud bottom. Do not go past the bearing of 190°T on the concrete tombs on Yantupu, an islet south of the anchorage, or you may end up on coral shoals close to the northwest. Most of the time they are marked with sticks and plastic jugs. Clear passages to the inner waters of Ustupu run close to the shore of the village or near the mainland and then south and west of the coral shoals.

Trading boats take that channel along the mainland and then cross to the island side south of the mud bank extending from Sugandi Tiwar river. One can anchor anywhere in those protected waters all the way to the north end of the bay. Trading boats use the northern of the two cuts between the islands north of Ustupu. The channel is deep but makes a sharp turn between shallow reefs. Very good eyeballing conditions would be necessary to pilot through there. When you land in Ustupu you will have to pay 5 dollars in the police station by the dock. Water from the faucet next to the dock costs 2 dollars for ten days of use.

Ustupu, the largest village in San Blas, has some 8,000 people not counting the children. Ogopsukum, a village adjacent to Ustupu and connected by two bridges adds another 2,000 people. Several flights a day land on the two airstrips, one on the island and the other on the mainland. A small hotel and several restaurants cater to visitors. Ice may be bought at the cafeteria by the dock. The policy of the congresos here is against tourism development. No photography of any kind is allowed here unless people invite it and they do not allow drawing or painting either. Villagers do not come to visit yachts. However, the sahilas here will greet you warmly. Sahila Edwin and sahila Tomás both speak English and will be glad to explain Kuna traditions. Nele Kantule, one of the most important spiritual leaders of the Kunas was born here and is buried on Yantupu, the islet south of the dock.

Of the two rivers you should visit Sugandi Tiwar. Its estuary is marked by wrecks of giant trees washed down during the great flood of 1925 which forced the village to move from the mainland to Ustupu. You will find large cemeteries on both sides of the river. Add to it great bird activity during the afternoon hours and you can count on spending at least two hours on this trip. Aboudi Tiwar may necessitate poling the dinghy to cross the entrance bar but is deeper inside and leads a narrow shady course a short distance past many trails.

BAHÍA DE MASARGANDI

No one lives permanently in this bay but people from Ustupu visit daily to carry out communal projects like cleaning land for agricultural purposes or collecting palm fronds from a grove of "soska" palm for making waterproof thatches. One frond costs .25 and a hut may require 1,000 fronds. If you plan to spend a few days exploring this bay get permission from the office in Ustupu - otherwise Kunas may get suspicious about you hanging around there. Sailing down the bay have someone on the bow. Opaque waters do not make it easy to spot the extensive coral shoals. Swell usually penetrates pretty far into the bay but the indicated anchorage is smooth and the bottom is mud.

USTUPU TO ISLA PINOS

Once a yacht arrives north of Ukupsibu, a sandbar surrounded by a large coral shoal located 1½ miles southeast of Ustupu, it will find a deeper water channel running eastward between Kwitupu (Isla Mosquito) and Akwasuit Murru point on the mainland. The channel continues southeastward between this point and a large shallow area 1½ miles further east. You should stay about three quarters of a mile from the mainland steering for a fix about ¼ of a mile northeast of Akwasuit, a shoal breaking the surface off Napakanti. See the Canal de Pinos sketch chart. The GPS of that fix is 09°01.70'N and 077°46.70'W. On the way you will see Mansukum and Napakanti villages on the mainland. Mansukum has a dock for trading boats but the approach to it is very complicated between sets of reefs which protect the dock from swells. Further offshore you will spot the densely wooded Isla Pajaros (Iguana). In calm weather one can anchor off its south shore in 27 feet in a sandy bottom at 09°03.30'N and 077°46.19'W and enjoy diving on the nearby reefs or simply go traipsing on the beach.

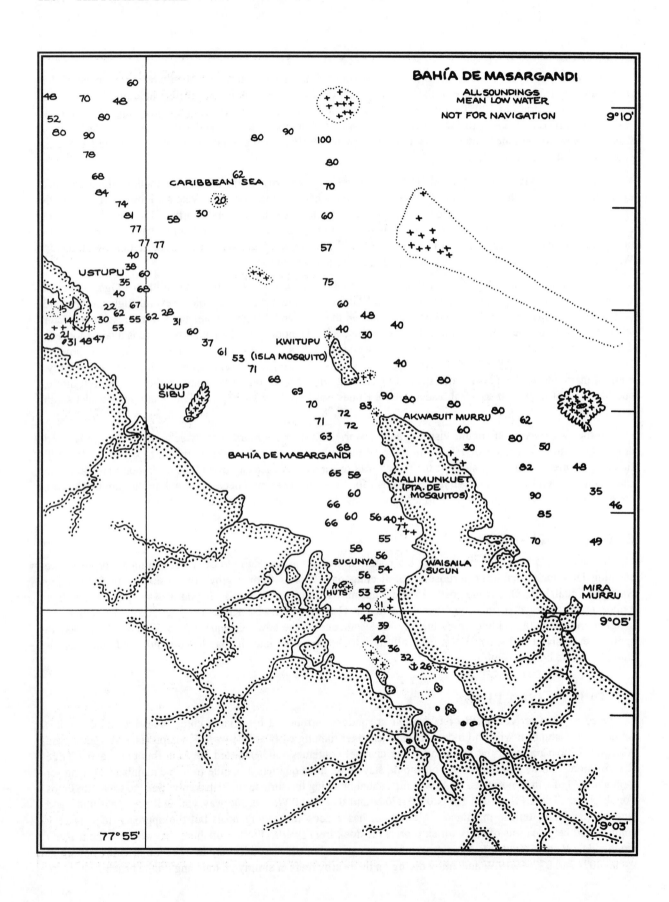

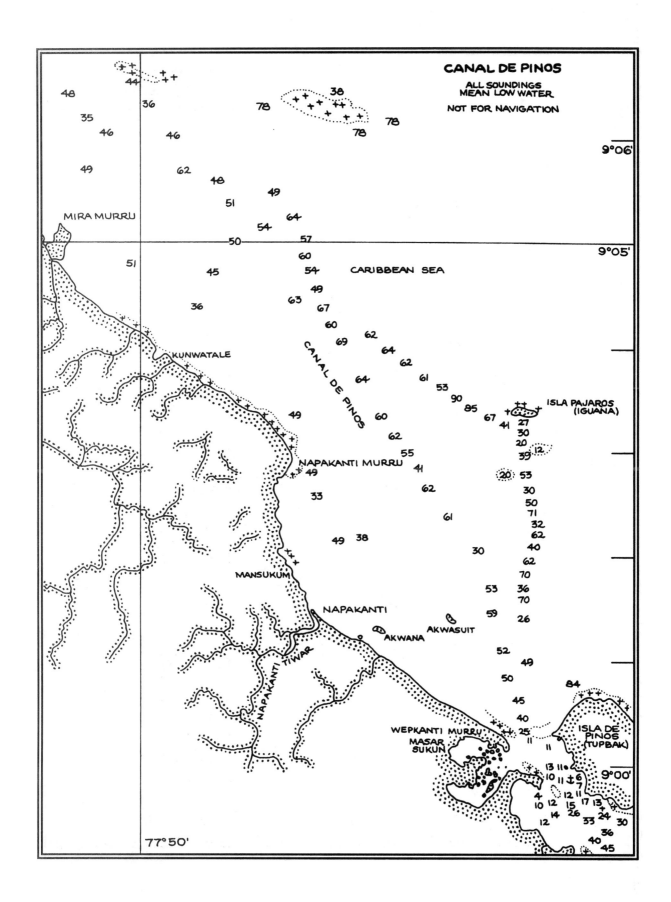

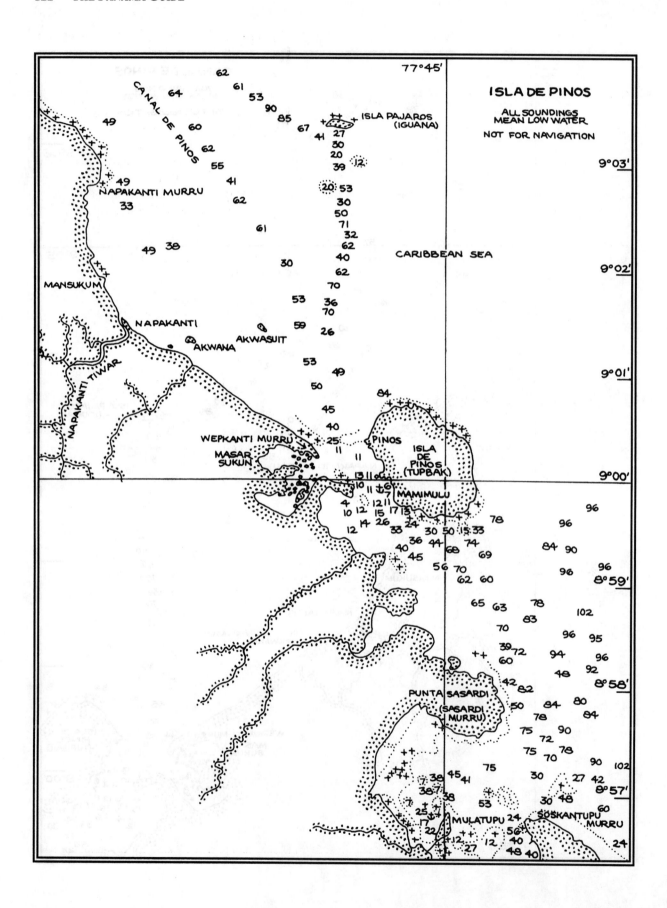

From the point off Akwasuit at 09°01.70'N and 077°46.70'W you should start looking for the breaking reef extending from the west point of Isla Pinos and marking the entrance to the anchorage there.

ISLA PINOS - TUPBAK

The entrance from the west leads between two sets of coral reefs and the channel with a 25 foot bar passes into the inner basin about 11 feet deep. This channel takes you very close to the west tip of the reef extending west from Isla Pinos. It does not always break. However, the reef on the west side of the channel almost always has some conspicuous surf on it. Inside you can anchor off the dock or go further and drop anchor south of a little mangrove islet as the sketch chart shows. At 09°00.0'N and 077°45.7'W you will have 7 feet and a bottom of soft mud and grass. Do not anchor too far west from the island because of the coral ledges on the other side of the channel and trading boats which often pass through the middle of the channel at dusk. The approach from the northeast presents the easiest course free of hazards to navigation. Some charts show a shallow rock half a mile from the southeast point of Tupbak. We and other keen divers have tried to locate this rock and failed, but one should keep it in mind when approaching. You can arrive at GPS point at 08°59.2'N and 077°44.7'W and then steer 310°T into the anchorage.

The Kunas call Isla Pinos Tupbak, or whale, for its resemblance to a giant beached whale. For centuries the 400 foot high island has served as a landfall for mariners of good and bad dispositions. The protected yet easily entered and exited anchorage on the south side of Tupbak made a perfect base for the buccaneers working the Spanish Main, especially the gold transhipment ports. Later, New England schooners would make a landfall here to buy coconuts, a good source of oil for many domestic uses. For several years in recent times Colombian contrabandistas carrying duty free consumer goods from the Colón Free Zone into Colombia stopped here to await clear coast radio calls from their bosses. Due to changed custom regulations they visit Tupbak rarely now, mainly to rest or shelter from weather.

Of the two villages on the island, Isla Pinos at the west end is much bigger. It is home of the cacique elected in 1996 to head this district of Kuna Yala. The police post near the dock will check your passports when you come to visit the village or they may come to the yacht to do this and collect a varying fee. Another fee of five dollars goes to the village kitty. The police have a SSB radio and will alert Ustupu of your arrival, they may ask to borrow your SSB for this. Several families in the village bake bread and the store by the dock has a fair supply of the usual goods. A comfortable path goes along the south shore to the cemetery and then continues south to the tiny village of Mamimulu. You will find a fresh water stream with a clothes washing station a little inland from Mamimulu. You can climb the hill behind Mamimulu through partially cleared growth for an unobstructed view of the islands to southeast. While on that path keep your eyes open for tiny black frogs spotted with bright emerald dots. One can also walk around the whole island in about three and a half hours. Across from Tupbak on the mainland one can walk inland on trails which initially wind through boggy wetlands. Accompanying one of the Kuna men on his way to his plantain plot would make this trip easier. Bring insect repellent, especially during the wet season.

ISLA PINOS TO CALEDONIA

Close to the mainland, an inshore channel with a controlling depth of 11 feet runs in the lee of several islands for a distance of 6 miles between the villages of Mulatupu at the northwestern end and Caledonia at the southeastern outlet.

MULATUPU

With over three thousand souls living there Mulatupu is the second largest village in Kuna Yala. It has a clinic, a post office and radio communications center, water on the dock and several stores. A large building by the main dock houses a restaurant (simple and good) and a hotel upstairs (you sleep in hammocks). The sahilatura by the dock charges yachts US$15 and then the guys in charge of the dock want to charge a few bucks for tying up the dinghy there. The river of Mulatupu, Ibedi Tiwar, has particularly rich bird life and a cemetery. You can use the outboard in the river but the motor noise scares away many bird species.

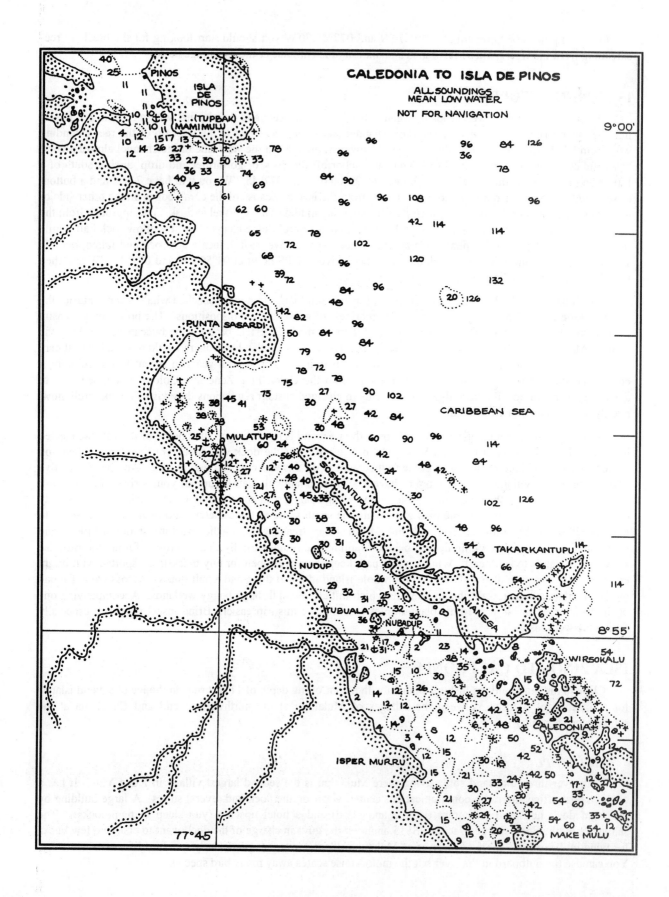

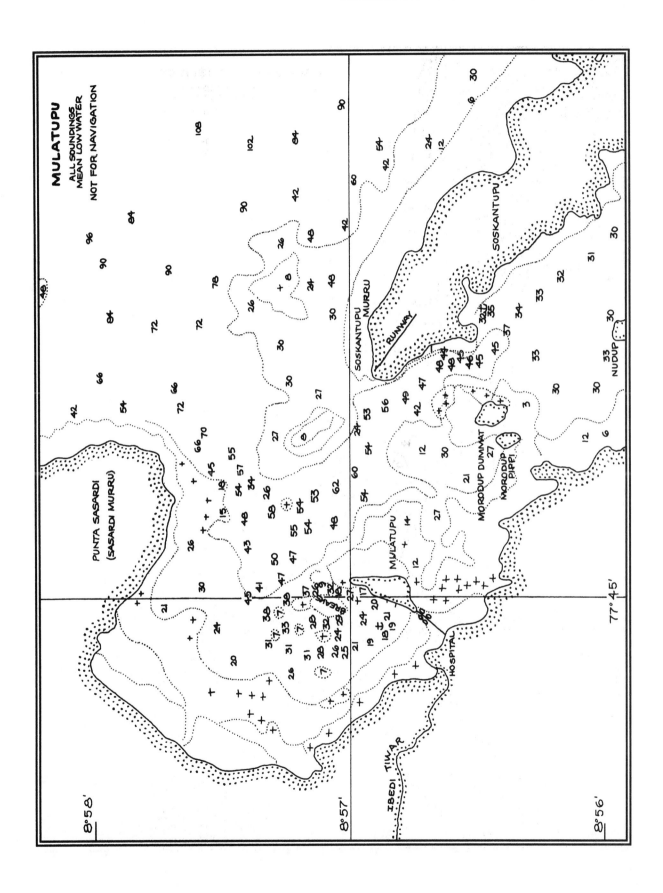

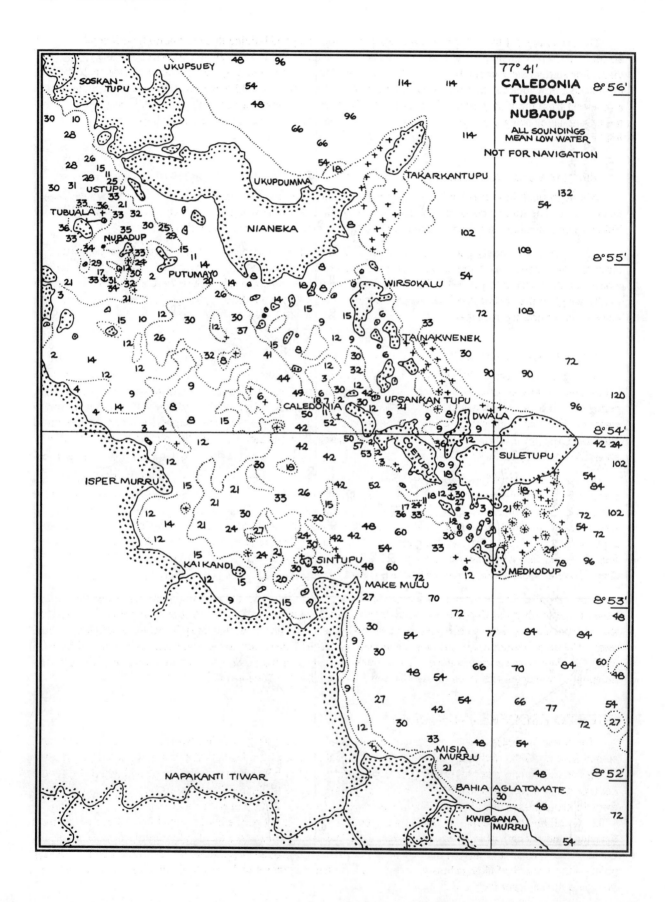

The anchorage off the village has excellent protection and good holding in a mud bottom with depths around 20 feet. The entry channel goes between several very shallow reefs and high sun is essential for the first time visit. For starters steer about 185°T on the school building next to the hospital. When near the reef line you must keep a bow lookout until well south of the shoals. Another good anchorage for visiting Mulatupu lies about a mile east from the village under the shore of Soskantupu off a small bay as marked on the sketch chart. It has the advantage of being close to the airstrip if you are waiting for somebody to arrive from Panama City. Good holding in mud.

TUBUALA AND NUBADUP

Although small in size Tubuala was the home of a late cacique and so has a nice clinic with a concrete bridge leading to it. The trading boats use the dock on the south side of the village where you can find a cantina. Both Tubuala and Nubadup have deep channels around them winding between some shallow banks.

The islands here rarely get any visiting yachts and when we anchored nineteen cayucos carrying between three and nine people each descended upon us. Before we could stow our sailing gear away we had several women on deck trying to get below into the cabin despite our polite refusals. They were so aggressive that we finally weighed the anchor and beat out of there in a hurry. Try your luck there! Nubadup formerly used the name Kuba. Nuba signifies thatch.

CALEDONIA - KANIRDUP

This small and very traditional village has large congreso huts right off the dock. You should stop there to get permission to stay anchored off the village. They sometimes charge the usual five dollar fee. Also ask for permission to visit the mainland rivers Aglatomate and Napakanti. The latter is not only very beautiful but is easier to enter than Aglatomate whose bar often breaks right across. Lately the congreso refused permission to enter the river but their rules often change. You can see their cemetery huts on the mainland just over a mile away and you can visit there.

When anchored off the village remove all the small loose gear from the deck as one bad kid, Elianito, finds pleasure in collecting souvenirs from yachts. Stores in the village sell the basic stuff but you can always get fresh bread and one family makes ice for sale. The village has piped water from the mainland so do not anchor in the area south of the dock or you may damage their PVC tubing. You will have to anchor either in 50 feet plus depths or go to a shallow bank off the west tip of the village which starts at about 11 feet and shoals to less than 6 feet. You can find a spot on the bearing of 060°T on the tip of the island. At 08°54.2'N and 077°41.97'W you should have 8 feet and a firm sand and grass bottom.

You can also find a secluded and very protected anchorage less than a mile southeast from the village between the south tip of Coetupu and the west shore of Suletupu which has a 470 foot high peak. To enter you should steer initially 040° on the west shore of Suletupu and then eyeball your way in between offlying shallow reefs. The coral bottom in the channel has at least 11 feet of water. Inside the protected basin you will have 28 to 30 foot depths and a mud bottom. "Ulus" (dugouts) go by in the mornings when men tend the farm plots on Suletupu. Sometimes kids come to sell fish they have caught - the price is right.

PUERTO ESCOSÉS - SUKUNYA

The name Escosés, which means Scottish in Spanish, comes from a failed Scottish attempt at founding a colony here in 1698. William Paterson, a founder of the Bank of England, financed a 1,200 strong expedition which carried, among other things, English Bibles and wigs as trading items. After a year and a half they could not take it any more. Defeated by starvation and disease they sailed home. Two more groups of reinforcements from Scotland passed them beyond the horizon on the way to Panama. They, too, gave up and returned home in 1702. Of all the 2,800 people involved, two-thousand died. Today only a boat channel hacked out of the coral limestone and a length of moat remain of their Fort Andrew. You can take the dinghy to the north shore west of Punta Escosés, leave it in the old boat channel and roam around often stepping on shards of old pottery. On the point northwest of the Sukunya huts you will find a cement marker set up by Kit Kapp and his Darién expedition. We could not decipher the worn out date.

128 THE PANAMA GUIDE

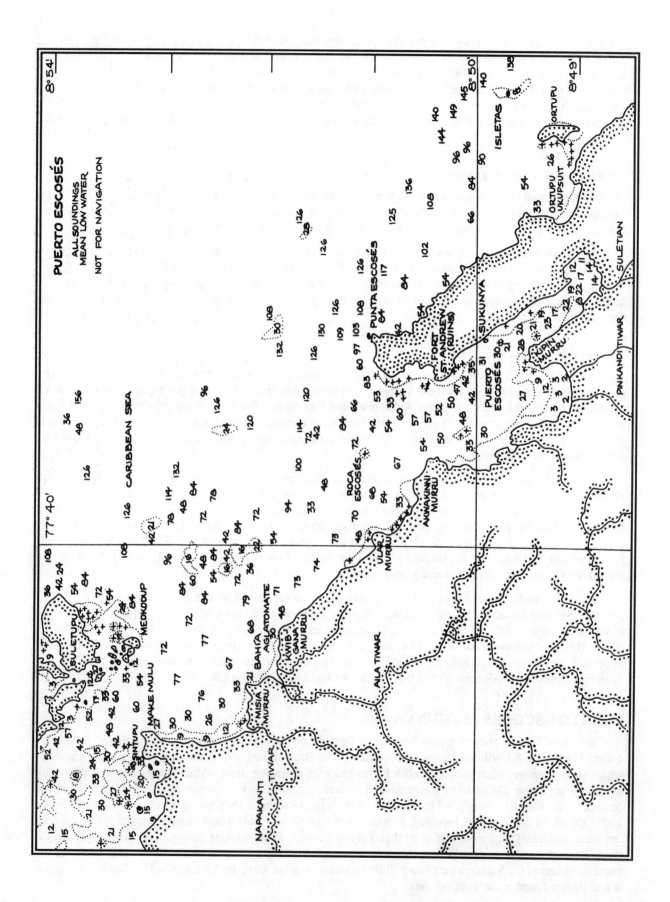

Bahía Las Minas to Puerto Obaldia 129

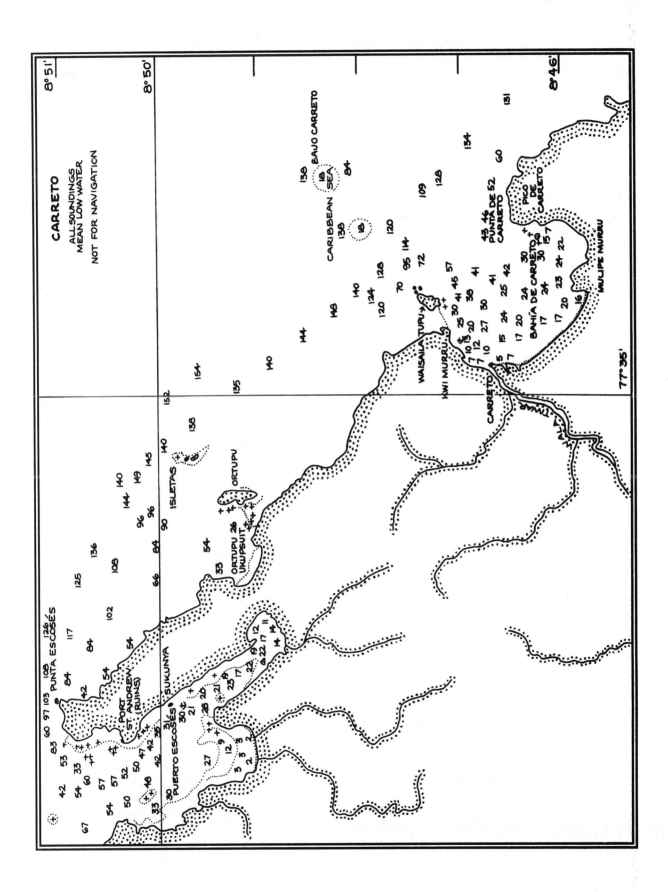

Sukunya and the areas around belong to the people of Mulatupu. The occupants of the huts come here for a few weeks at a time to take care of their farm plots. One of the men always represents the congreso of Mulatupu and comes to visiting yachts with an official printed paper to collect a 20 dollar fee. For this, yachtsmen can stay in a perfectly protected anchorage and explore as long as they please.

To get to Puerto Escosés from Caledonia one should steer close to Makemulu (a point on the mainland southeast of Suletupu) and then sail along the mainland about a quarter of a mile off all the points. Finally steer 115°T on the point St. Andrew and then parallel the shoals lying off the eastern shore to the anchorage near a little island with two huts.

Entering the area from the Atlantic and planning to go to Caledonia one should pass close to Punta Escosés, then steer to a GPS point 08°51.7'N and 077°40.0'W, a course which passes safely north of Roca Escosés (a 3 foot high rock surrounded by breaking waves) and south of the shallow banks to north. The southernmost shoal, 22 feet deep, lies at 08°52.2'N and 077°40.0'W.

When intending to enter Puerto Escosés from the Atlantic pass a quarter of a mile north of Punta Escosés and steer west. Locate Roca Escosés, pass east and south of it and at the longitude by GPS of 077°38.7'W start steering 180°T until abeam of Fort Andrew point when you should steer about 135°T along the shore to the anchorage. Holding is good in mud 30 feet deep.

CARRETO

Carreto, six miles southeast down the coast from Punta Escosés, has a place in the history of the Spanish "entrada" into the isthmus. Vasco Nuñez de Balboa, who in 1513 crossed the isthmus to become the first European to see the Pacific, apparently married a daughter of a cacique of this area. Other sources say it happened in the Spanish settlement in Acla, founded by Balboa or Pedrarias Dávila. Today the Kunas apply the name of Acla or Agla to the point of the mainland across from Fort Andrew. They also mention the existence of stone remains of European origin in that place - there is an open field for research here.

Today Carreto has a village with a congreso which charges yachtsmen the usual five dollars. A couple of stores sell the basics, bread, kerosene and gasoline. The Wala Tiwar river has only 1 to 2 feet on the bar and becomes blocked by shoals about a quarter of a mile in. You should walk up the hill behind the village to their cemetery for the great overall view of the area.

The bay is easy to enter and if you arrive at the GPS point of 08°47'N and 077°33.6'W you can steer directly to the anchorage in the northwest corner of the bay. It has a mud bottom and depths from 12 to 14 feet at 08°47.0'N and 077°34.5'W. The huts ashore close to the anchorage belong to the people of Caledonia who have rights to farming this corner of the woods. Another anchorage lies south of a little islet off the east shore of the bay. The depths range from 14 to 12 feet and closer to the beach rise to 7 feet with scattered coral heads. The winds during the windy season, January to April, blow from between NNE to NNW so one of the anchorages should offer protection. The long beach southeast of the river mouth invites long walks and you can pull the dinghy ashore in a smooth corner on the west side of Mulipe Murru point. On the beach you may find the foot prints of the large Caribbean crocodiles which occur along the coast of Kuna Yala. A path leads along the coast and cuts inland all the way to Anachucuna village.

ANACHUCUNA AND PUERTO PERME

The villagers of Anachucuna follow the traditional Kuna principles. People here will invite you for a visit and serve a cup of plantain drink. Sometimes they have molas for sale but more often they are just curious about visitors. Recently, Eco Tours travel agency from Panama City took their trans-isthmus treks through here so the village has had increased exposure to outsiders. Colombian launches also bring tourists for short visits from Capurgana, a resort village near the border with Panama. As a result the village has opened a cooperative store of artifacts; molas, carvings, straw works and clay figures.

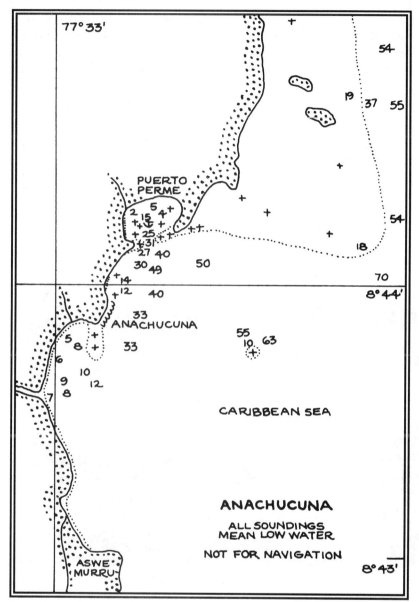

Puerto Perme has excellent protection in all weathers. You should approach it along 08°44.0'N latitude which will take you between the south edge of a large bank growing from the mainland and north of a 10 foot shoal. Have somebody on the bow as the entrance into the basin is flanked by shallow coral patches. Once you spot the opening steer about 330°T, favor the west side of the channel and you should have 25 foot depths.

Anchor about east of the steel girders remaining of an old banana and coconut plantation pier sticking out of the west shore. The GPS position in the basin is 08°44.2'N and 077°32.68'W. The bottom has good holding mud and depths between 16 and 20 feet. Large yachts may want to use two anchors to avoid swinging onto the edges of shoals sticking out from the shores. Trading boats anchor outside, north of the village and near the remains of a concrete sea wall. A wonderful trail leads from Puerto Perme inland and all the way to Carreto Bay about one and a half hours away if you walk smartly.

PUERTO OBALDIA

The town of Obaldia has a mixed population of Panamanians, many of whom work in the government offices in this border town. Friendly police come to inspect all yachts whether they come from foreign ports or from Panamanian waters. The Immigration office stamps passports to exit or enter the Republic of Panama. The Port Captain issues clearances to other countries or cruising permits for Panama. The Colombian consulate will stamp, free of charge, a permit in a passport so yachtsmen can enter ports in Colombia before formally clearing in at Cartagena. The town stores have better supplies than the villages in San Blas and better prices. These are also better prices than around the corner in Sapzurro or Capurgana, Colombia. Restaurants serve tasty meals and pensiones take in visitors who fly in three times a week on a plane from Panama City.

You should anchor when the dock bears 035°T in 17 to 18 feet of water. At 08°39.84'N and 077°25.32'W you will find a firm sand bottom. During the calm months of the rainy season a barely detectable swell enters the bay but it may be very different during the persistent onshore winds of the dry season.

LA MIEL

In the northwest corner of Puerto La Miel, just short of the border with Colombia, you will find a village from which a path goes over a hill through the marked but unguarded border and downhill into Sapzurro village in Colombia. Swell enters the bay except along the east shore which has depths over 60 feet. Only in a small bay with a beach and shelters for tourists can one find a fair weather anchorage in 32 feet with a sandy bottom.

SAPZURRO - COLOMBIA

One can enter or exit Colombian waters without any hassles in Sapzurro on the east side of Cabo Tiburon. Anchor in 25 to 30 feet of water and sandy bottom off the town dock which is surrounded by shallow reefs. Extensive coral shoals block the northern part of the bay while further south the bottom is generally sandy and 28 to 20 feet deep. However, swell enters that part of the bay.

The mainland village of Carreto.

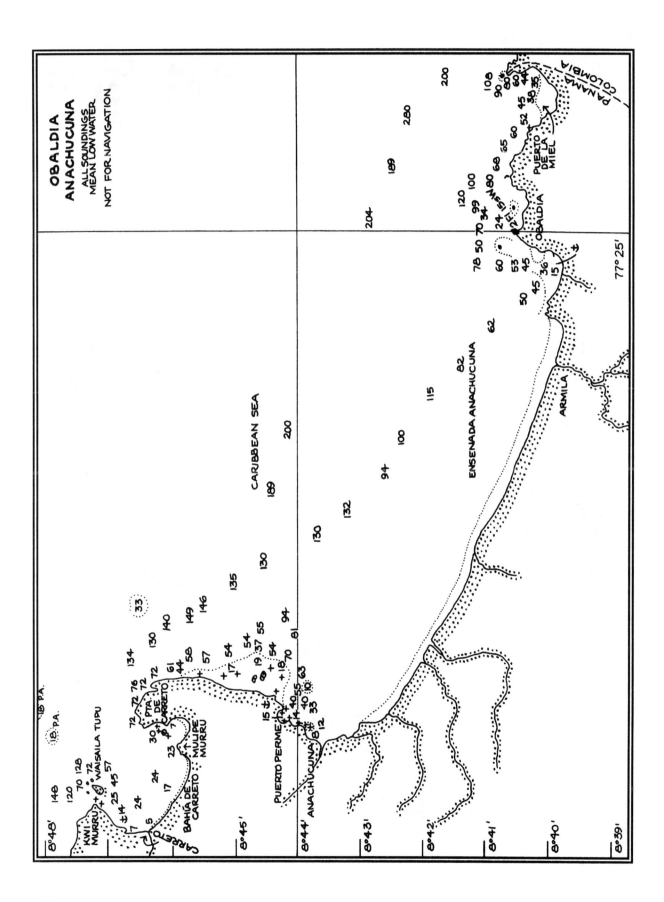

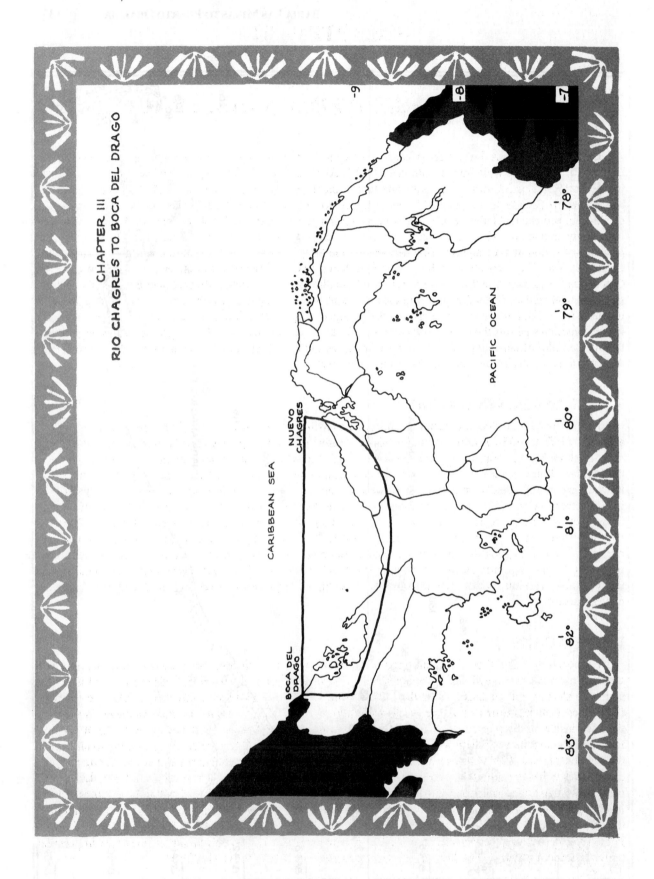

CHAPTER III
RIO CHAGRES TO BOCA DEL DRAGO

CHAPTER III

RIO CHAGRES TO BOCA DEL DRAGO

Chapter III describes the Caribbean coast of Panama from Rio Chagres (7 miles west from Cristobal harbor) to Boca del Drago, the westernmost entrance to Bahía Almirante. After Rio Chagres the first stretch of 130 miles in the Golfo de Los Mosquitos has only one totally protected anchorage, Tobobe Creek, and one good island anchorage, off Escudo de Veraguas. However, further westward two almost landlocked bodies of water, Laguna de Chiriquí and Bahía Almirante offer superb cruising in pristine waters against a backdrop of forested mountains with many indigenous villages to visit. Should one bypass the harborless shoreline of Costa Abajo, in the province of Colón and Veraguas? That depends on the time of the year and the swell conditions in the western Caribbean Sea. We encountered calm seas in March and again in May and the natives consider September and October as the calmest months. During these good months yachts can anchor offshore and take their tenders into many tropical verdant rivers flowing from the mountains of the continental divide. The dry season dirt road used by buses from Colón to Costa Abajo ends in the village of Miguel de la Borda, the location of the police outpost which sometimes patrols the coastal settlements as far as Belén. Further west the craggy mountains begin to rise behind the miles of coconut palm lined deserted beaches and only a few small settlements of subsistence farmers and fishermen cluster around the mouths of the major rivers.

WINDS, CURRENTS and TIDES

Regular trade winds do not reach the Golfo de Los Mosquitos and winds depend on localized systems which are greatly influenced by nearby mountains. Good weather dry months produce regular onshore day breezes and night offshore breezes, especially when the sky is clear. Frequent overcast skies diminish or delay the arrival of the breezes. Rainy weather often brings a westerly slant to the winds and well developed cumulonimbus clouds release very strong squalls from about northwest to northeast. Heavy violent rainfalls often accompany these intense storm cells. Tide ranges average about one foot with nearly two feet at the height of springs. Consequently, tidal currents are negligible. The most significant water movement results from the Caribbean countercurrent which flows along the coast of Golfo de Los Mosquitos eventually running east and later northeast. Inside Laguna de Chiriquí and Bahía Almirante only heavy rains cause noticeable currents. The entrances to the lagoons, Boca del Drago, Boca del Toro and Canal del Tigre may occasionally have unpredictable currents which result from the meeting of tidal flows, river outflows and the Caribbean countercurrent.

RIO CHAGRES

Approach on 090°T on the south edge of the bluff crowned with Fort San Lorenzo. Locate Lajas Reef which in calm weather may break only occasionally, then pass close to the south side of the reef in 11 to 14 feet and keep steering for the south tip of the bluff staying in 25 feet. There are some deep pools here but if the fathometer reads less than 15 feet you are probably too far south. Keep close to the shore on the north side until the dock inside on the river's north bank bears 148°T when you should steer for it staying in depths of about 20 feet and avoiding the very shallow water in the bight on the port side. When the sandy spit on the south bank of the river bears about 180°T steer for the middle of the river entrance. One should remember that during the years of particularly heavy rainfall the Panama Canal Commission has to release excess water from Gatun Lake. This causes a tremendously rapid torrent through the river which can wash away the sand spit at the entrance as it did in 1996 making the river mouth much wider. In the drier months that follow, the sand will gradually build up to the shape drawn on the sketch chart of Rio Chagres. The well fendered dock has 23 feet on the face and further in the river depths vary between 25 and 60 feet for the next 5½ miles. One can anchor anywhere in peaceful, perfectly smooth waters and be surrounded by a forest resounding with the calls of birds.

136 THE PANAMA GUIDE

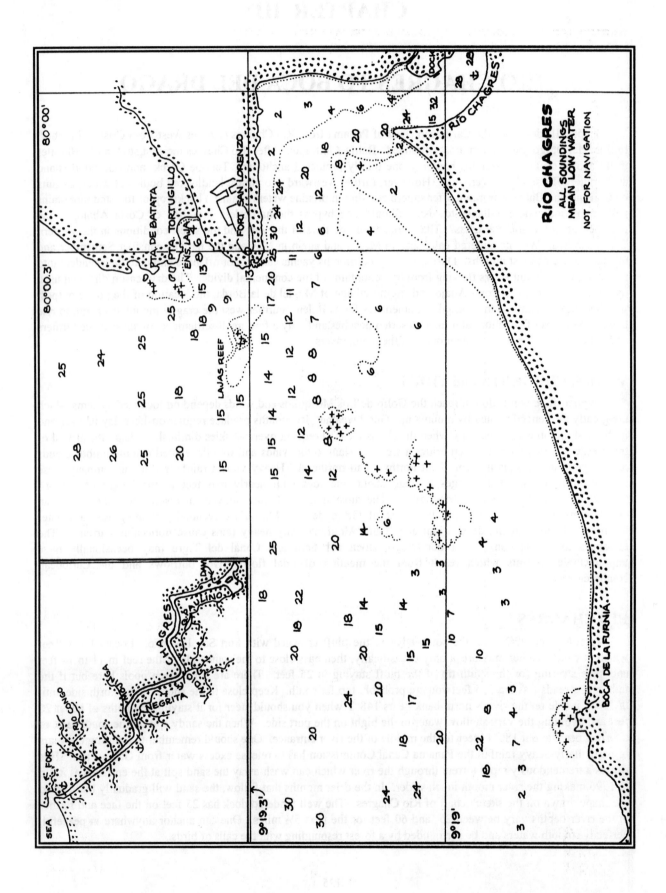

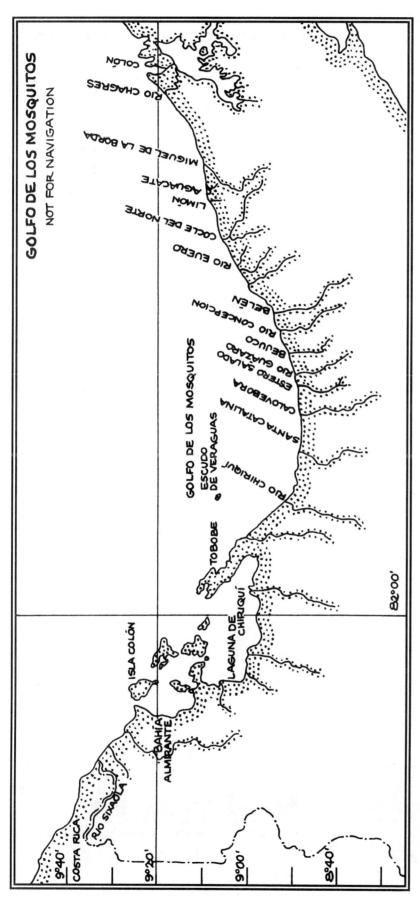

There is an attractive anchorage up the river at 09°16.88'N and 079°57.82'W under a high hillside. American swallow tail kites regularly feed near this part of the river. The multitude of trails through the forests on both sides of the river are part of the U.S. military's jungle training area. Rio Indio leads to a small bridge and a path. Across the river a cleared area serves as a helicopter pad. Further upstream Quebrada Paulino runs into a small, swampy lake and further, up by the dam a rocky reef blocks the lagoon. A small boat launching ramp is located on the east side of the dam spill. Good fishing led to the founding of the Tarpon Club located on the west end of the dam. The restaurant in the Club has a phone and one can climb the earthwork of the dam to reach it. Only dinghies can make the trip to the dam as shoals and rocks block the last half mile of the river in many places.

During rainy Novembers and Decembers water from Late Gatun may be released from the dam into Rio Chagres. A patrol boat will alert visiting craft to leave the river.

RIO CHAGRES TO TOBOBE CREEK, GOLFO DE LOS MOSQUITOS

After leaving Rio Chagres and going westward along the coast for the next 130 miles one can find only one protected harbor, Tobobe, and one island anchorage, in the lee of Escudo de Veraguas. By sailing a mile offshore or in depths of no less than 25 feet a boat will clear most of the offlying rocks. We indicate places with extensive rocky shelves in the following text. We managed two trips to explore this coast before being chased away each time by the sudden arrival of threatening swells and pummeling squalls with driving rains. We made dinghy forays into some of the rivers and in addition to enjoying the unspoiled scenery we had the satisfaction of doing something usually unattainable. Here are some of the places to explore.

AGUACATE

The anchorage has good holding in a sandy bottom, 20 feet deep at GPS Long. 080°26'W, Lat. 09°08'N, or as shown on the sketch chart. The dinghy had no problems entering the smooth shallow bar of Rio Aguacate. In this very small village several fishermen catch sharks using large outboard powered dugout canoes. Shark liver oil, fins, backbones and dried meat are all sold to Chinese buyers in Colón, 6 hours away in a fast dugout.

LIMÓN

The village of Limón, 1½ nautical miles west from Rio Aguacate, has an easy landing on a beach protected by Punta Limón. Approach from the northwest giving a good berth to the shoals extending from Punta Limón and anchor in 12 feet.

RIO EUÉRO

This anchorage in 16 feet with a sandy bottom at GPS 080°45.8'W and 08°57.9'N, or as shown on the sketch chart, is the most comfortable on all of this coast because of the protection of Punta del Copé. A temporary shelter hut for the fishermen who tend their nets in the bay stands on the south bank of Rio Euéro. We had to drag our dinghy over the shallow bar of Rio Euéro, but further in this shady stream has a profusion of vines, flowers and epiphytes while on the beach at the river entrance we found thousands of tiny frogs, the first time we have seen seagoing beach frogs!

BELÉN

Anchor three tenths of a mile from shore off the orange bluff promontory in 21 feet, mud and sand bottom, at Long. 080°52.2'W, Lat. 08°53.3'N. The river pouring out of the craggy mountains was named Belén by Columbus on his fourth voyage when he brought his ships over the 7 foot bar. The native name of Yebra now persists only in history books. We optimistically hoped to find the same depth Columbus had but in the course of nearly five centuries the bar has silted to 3 feet, easily passable for the large outboard motor dugouts used on this coast for travel. Somewhere in the mud under 20 feet of water inside the river mouth lies the wreck of GALLEGA, an abandoned caravel from the explorer's fleet. When asked if he had any bananas to sell, the mayor (alcalde) of Belén replied no, they had only gold to sell! The surrounding mountains have been a lure to gold prospectors since man arrived on the isthmus.

Mollymawk *on Rio Chagres.*

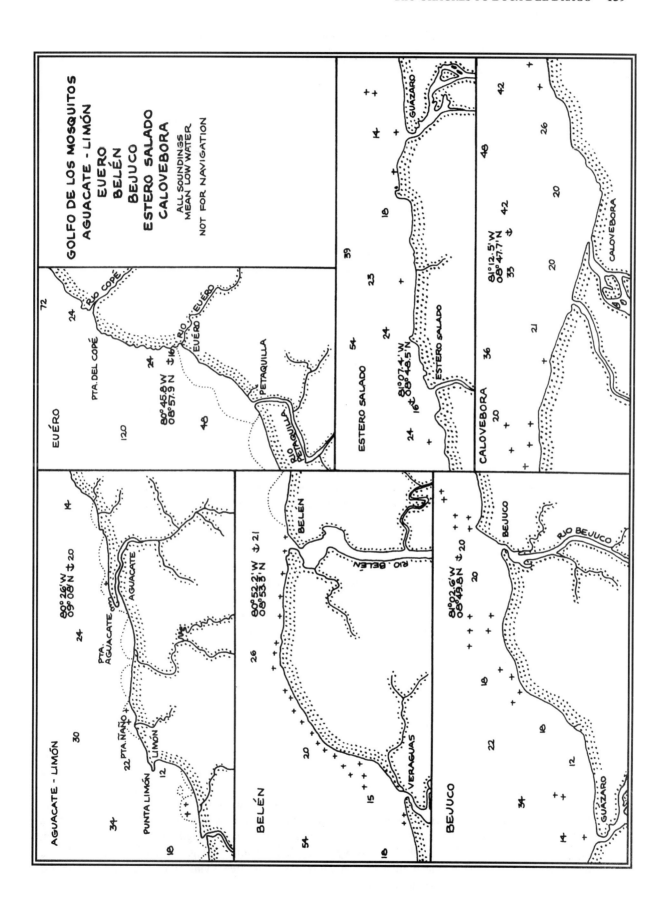

The small village has potable water, a clinic with two doctors, a school and is in radio contact with the other settlements along the coast. It takes two days to hike to the nearest real road. According to local fishermen, the northwest wind here brings bad squally weather.

BEJUCO

Anchor in 20 feet on a mud bottom at Long. 081°02.6'W, Lat. 08°49.8'N, or as indicated on the sketch chart, between two sets of shallow reefs which extend four tenths of a mile from shore. In the evening we watched dugouts surfing into the river on breaking waves which had increased in size towards dusk. By morning the sea turned rough, the shoals on our flanks roared with breakers and we had to leave.

The fishermen of Bejuco use balsa turtle decoys to net sea turtles.

ESTERO SALADO

At GPS 081°07.4'W, 08°48.5'N, or as indicated on the sketch chart, anchor on a firm sandy bottom in 16 feet of water off the cliffy entrance to the small Estero Salado. The dinghy ride brought us over easy, small breaking waves and into a calm shady river winding far inland. On the sandy west bank overlooking the sweeping beach lives one indigenous family whose older daughter has to cross the river and then walk over two miles on a coastal path to reach the school in Guázaro, a village to the east. The entrance to the cool, shady Estero Salado is at the eastern end of the beach. Unusual orchids with green blossoms (phragmipedilum longifolium) grow on the rock wall that overhangs the east river bank.

CALOVÉBORA

Anchor three quarters of a mile offshore in 20 feet with good holding mud and sand at Long. 081°12.5'W, Lat. 08°47.7'N, or as indicated on the sketch chart. We took the dinghy towards the mouth of the river which appeared to be breaking continuously with waves three to four feet high. One of the young men fishing offshore in a tiny dugout offered to lead us in or to bring out his larger boat with a 15 HP motor to carry us over the bar. We watched as he caught the right wave and surfed in a boat so tiny and tipsy that it seemed merely an extension of his body. He brought out a 24 foot dugout with a 40 inch beam which we gingerly boarded and zoomed right into the river on top of a wave. In the tiny clean village we found a good tienda, gasoline sales, and unexpectedly bought a sack of quality oranges then in season. Further up the river we found about two foot depths with a gravel bottom of perfectly round stones covered by clear water. The shallowness of the river made us wonder about a concrete pier jutting into the river off the village. It was about the right height for a small freighter and too high for dugouts. The locals explained that some rich man from Panama had it built. Can ships get in the river from the sea? Never, emphatically. After forging through the breakers on the way out we realized that an inflatable like our 12 foot Avon could make the entrance if equipped with a motor strong enough to make it plane. It was a question of waiting for the right low series of waves and then quickly getting out before the rough ones arrived. The local arrow thin dugouts cut through the breaking waves perfectly although they lack form stability.

ESCUDO DE VERAGUAS

This 2½ mile long densely wooded island situated 10 miles from the nearest point on the mainland has a smooth anchorage on the west side of West Point in about 20 feet of water with a sandy bottom. GPS 09°05.6'N and 081°34.4'W. There isn't any protection from a westerly wind but in a northwesterly one can move to the south of West Point where there is good holding in a sandy bottom at GPS 09°05.2'N and 081°34.0'W. In the prevailing conditions some swell sweeps into the second anchorage from around Booby Cay. The light on Booby Cay worked during our visits. The north shore of the island has an extensive coral shelf dotted with islets of varying size. Winding passages among them make a circumnavigation by dinghy fun as well as an extraordinarily beautiful adventure. Boobies nest on the tiny cays and long lianas hang down to the sea surface. In Cotton Bay live the only permanent residents, a family headed by a Guaymi (Ngöbe) man, Señor Anderson. The Andersons are very friendly people who always welcome visitors. Otherwise, only lobster divers, indigenous young men from the mainland villages, visit the island. After free diving all day down to 14 fathoms they spend the night in thatched huts on the west shore.

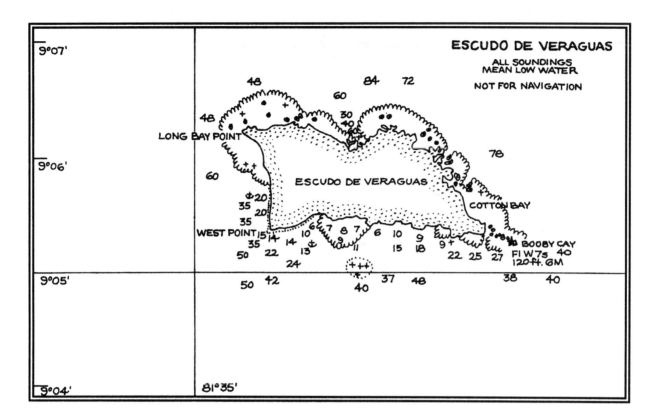

TOBOBE CREEK

From Escudo de Veraguas one can see towards the west 14 miles distant Big Plantain Cay (230 feet high) and Small Plantain Cay (150 feet high) which mark the entrance to the best harbor on this coast, Tobobe Creek. To enter follow the edge of the coral reefs which extend south from Plantain Cays and continue in the deep channel between them and the coral shoal about one mile south of Tobobe Point. After this bank (marked by breakers) head for the north shore and favor that side watching the depth sounder to avoid the sudden shoaling indicated on the sketch chart. Pass close to the thatched tienda at the end of a short dock, pass the broken remains of the westernmost pier ruins and anchor anywhere off a little bay on the north shore. Do not enter too far into this north bay as a hard to spot coral shelf sticks out into it from the mangrove shore. The deep water continues west slowly narrowing and shoaling as one gets closer to the Tobobe Creek entrance. The tienda on the dock sells gasoline (no diesel) and basics; cookies, tomato paste, sugar, salt. Ask for fresh fruit and roots. There is no telephone. One can walk eastward along the shore through the village and eventually end up on a classic ocean beach that constitutes the major thoroughfare for people walking between Tobobe and the village of Cusapin on the ocean side of Punta Valiente. Several families of indigenous Guaymi (Ngöbe) people, like those in Tobobe, live across the bay in Pueblo Nuevo surrounded by pastureland and they welcome visitors.

LAGUNA DE CHIRIQUÍ

Over 40 rivers flow into this 30 mile long bay, Laguna de Chiriquí, from the highlands of the continental divide rising close to the south shores. The mountainous mainland contributes to the mostly overcast sky here. The rivers bring mud which darkens the waters and makes reef spotting by eye difficult. The large size of the bay allows stronger winds to build up a considerable chop so yachts should anchor in well protected bays. While choosing a place to anchor one should recognize that in Laguna de Chiriquí most places with less than 20 feet of water probably have coral reefs on the bottom. You will find the exceptions to this rule near the outflows of large muddy rivers where suspended matter in the water stops coral growth. The villages around Laguna de Chiriquí differ ethnically. Indigenous Guaymi (Ngöbe) people tend to live on the remote fringes while the Latinos of Spanish or Antillian descent make up most of the population in the town of Chiriquí Grande and in the small hamlets on the mainland.

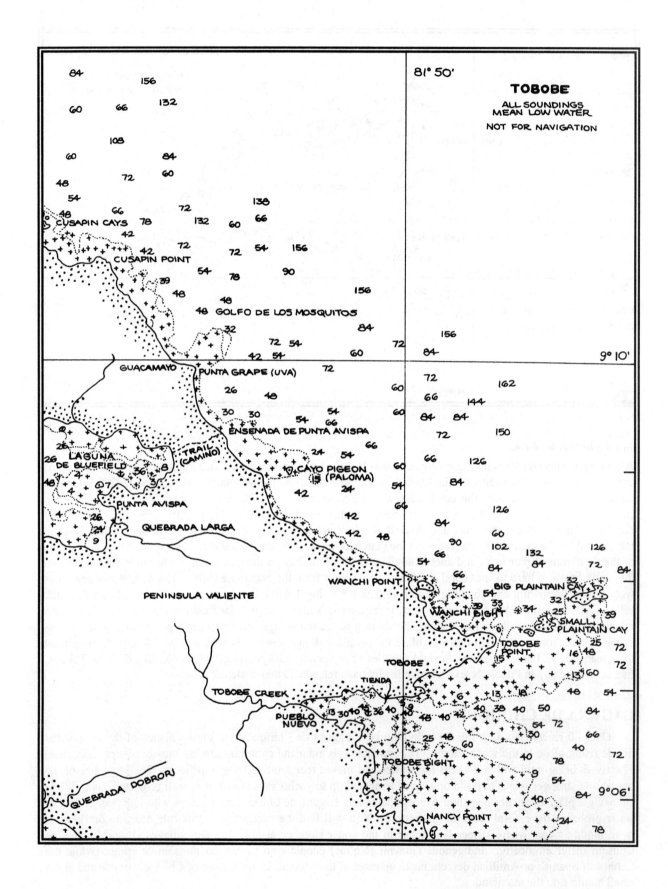

ENTRANCE INTO LAGUNA DE CHIRIQUÍ

The easiest courses through Canal Valiente when coming from the east lead close to the 20 foot high Barren Rock just north of Punta Valiente or close to the south side of Cayos Tigre. Either course avoids the 18 foot shoal, Revantazones Valiente, plumb in the middle of Canal Valiente. This shoal could conceivably break when extremely high swells occur. From Barren Rock or from Cayos Tigre one can steer straight for Cayos Valiente which are very conspicuous due to palms growing out of them. When bound for Laguna de Bluefield (locally known as Bahía Azul) skirt the edge of a rocky coral area by going outside Virginia Rocks, which are low and almost awash, and then outside the 30 foot high Bluefield Rock, also topped by high palms. All sources indicate depths over one fathom in the area contained inside these outer islets but we have not personally examined the area and generally in Laguna de Chiriquí coral growth flourishes in depths under 20 feet. Large ships use Canal del Tigre entering west of Revantazones Tigre and then head south to pick up the buoyed deep water channel that passes close to Cayo de Agua and points the way to the oil tanker terminal in Chiriquí Grande port.

LAGUNA DE BLUEFIELD

Many local people call this place Bahía Azul, Blue Bay, a derivative translation of Bluefield. Laguna de Bluefield was originally named after a Dutch born pirate, Blauvelt, who worked the western Caribbean shores in the seventeenth century.

PUNTA ALLEGRE

A yacht can find several anchorages in this deep and spacious bay. On the east side of Punta Allegre the water is deep quite close to the little sandy spit. Anchor in 40 feet along the northeast side of the spit. There is about 12 feet within 25 feet of the beach. Further north towards the mangroves it shoals abruptly from 25 feet to 4 feet. The village of Punta Allegre has a Guaymi (Ngöbe) population. The tienda is extremely basic. A trail from the village goes along the shore then across the peninsula to the village of Cusapin. You may hike there and back in the same day.

PUNTA AVISPA

Another anchorage at the very end of the bay just north of Punta Avispa, has 38 to 40 feet, mud bottom, but make sure you will not swing on the shoals south and north of the anchorage. Anchoring here makes it easy to get to the short trail which cuts across the peninsula to the ocean beach. You can walk on the beautiful sandy shore backed by palms and flowers either towards Tobobe or towards Cusapin. The Cusapin trip has the advantage of being able to get a soda in the tiendas in Guacamayo and Cusapin.

BAHÍA AZUL

The best stocked tienda, which also sells gasoline, is in the village of Bahía Azul on the south shore. The owner, Señor Robinson, speaks English and knows the area perfectly. The access to the shore there is complicated by many outlying coral shoals and unless the sun is high for eye piloting leave your boat further outside and use the dinghy.

Shelter behind Punta Rio Silico is good, Laguna de Chiriquí.

144 THE PANAMA GUIDE

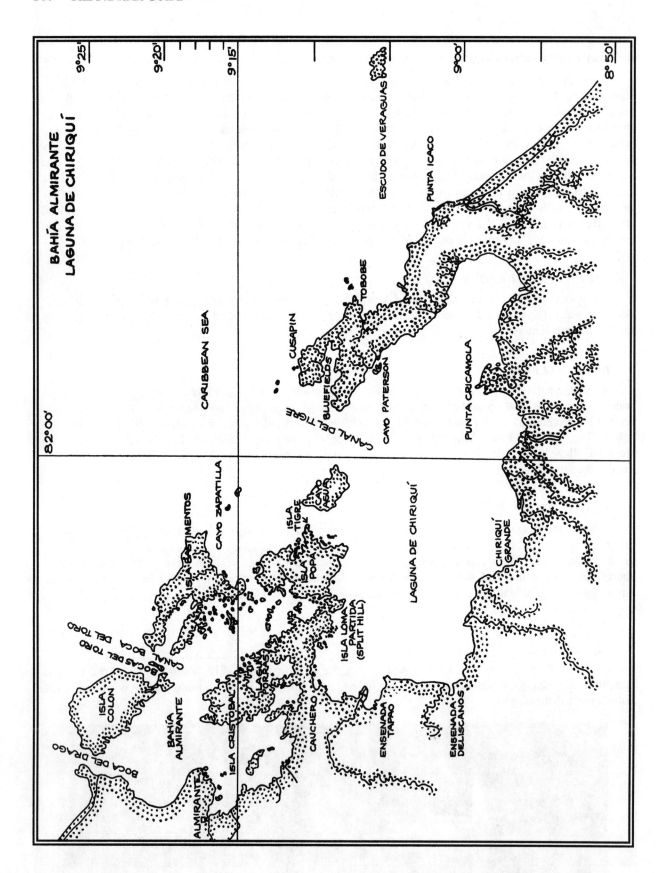

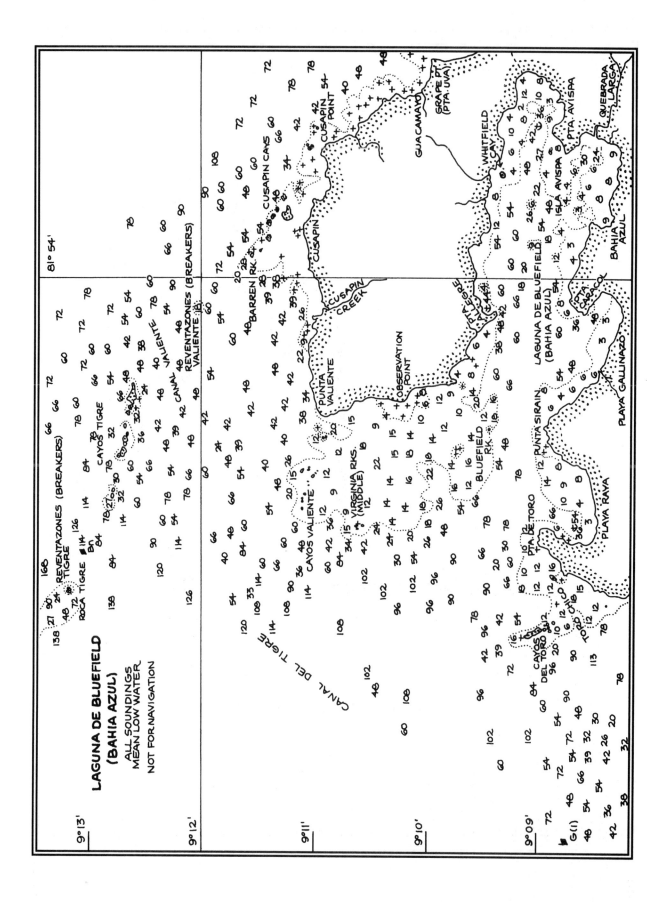

146 THE PANAMA GUIDE

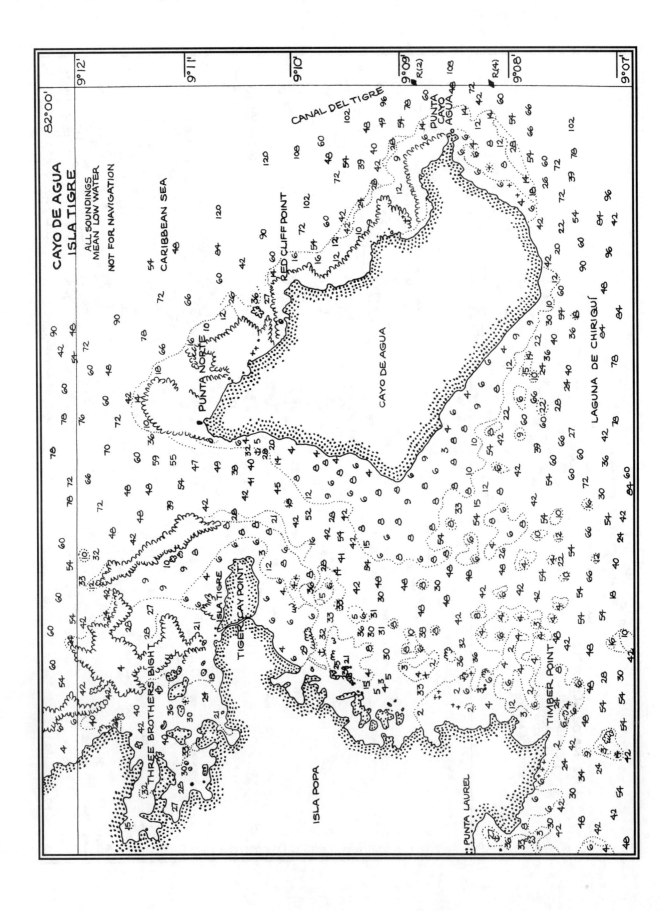

RIO CHAGRES TO BOCA DEL DRAGO 147

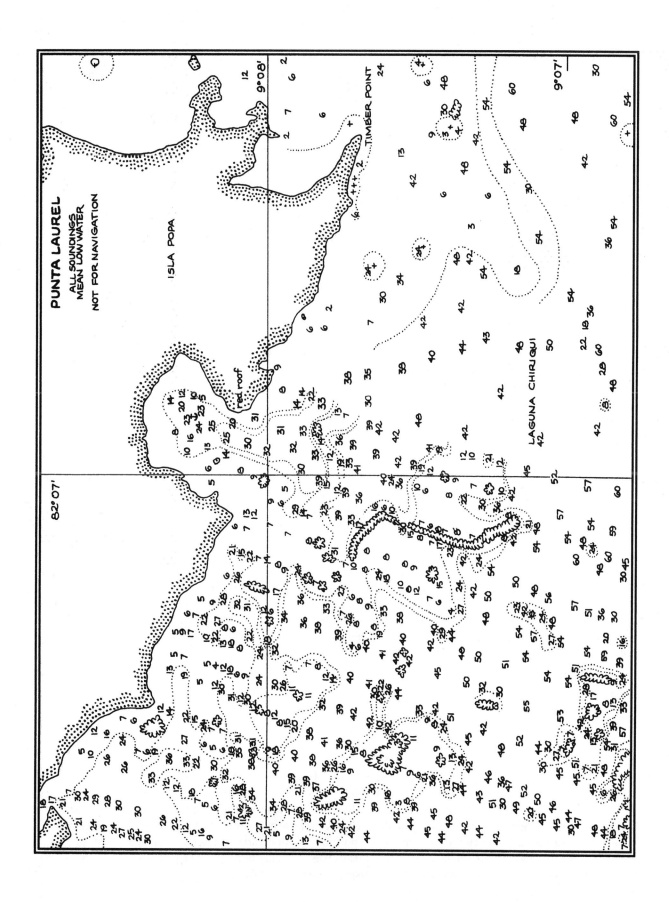

PLAYA RAYA

Off Playa Raya on the south shore of Laguna de Bluefield one can find a good but very deep anchorage which makes a good departure point.

EASTERN AND SOUTHERN ISLA POPA AND CAYO DE AGUA

Across Canal del Tigre from Laguna de Bluefield looms the large Cayo de Agua fringed by breaking waves on its shallow north and east shores. The channel between Isla Popa and Cayo de Agua abounds in coral shoals in its southern portion and should only be negotiated in the best conditions for eye piloting, that is high sun and blue sky. The northern part is straightforward. The anchorage off the northwestern shore of Cayo de Agua receives good protection from the outer shoals and stays smooth despite sizable swells less than a mile north. Several families of the indigenous Guaymi (Ngöbe) make their homes along the shore and there are several trails ashore. One can also dinghy to the shallows off Punta Norte for some shallow snorkeling or simply white beach traipsing.

ISLA TIGRE

With a good high sun and polarized glasses one can pilot between many shoals that front the southeastern shore of Isla Popa. The anchorage has very good holding in a mud bottom in depths between 27 and 29 feet. Half a mile to the north on the west side of the narrow dinghy navigable canal between Isla Tigre and Isla Popa stands a small indigenous village of Guaymi (Ngöbe) people who live mostly by lobster diving. They have a nice school, a nurse and a basic clinic, a relatively good tienda which also sells gasoline. Fresh bread is available. One can carry on in a dinghy through the canal and enter Three Brothers Bight to explore this vast area of mangrove islets and deep channels mingled with very shoal flats.

PUNTA LAUREL BAY

This very well protected bay on the south shore of Isla Popa has good holding mud and nice surroundings with usually at least one Latino family living there. However, several very shallow coral reefs lie scattered in the approaches. The safest initial course is to line up the southeast point of Isla Popa (Punta Timber) with the north point (Punta Norte) of Cayo de Agua. Another safe initial course is on the transit of Punta Timber with the easternmost point of Isla Popa on Isla Tigre. Follow these leads until the east headland of Punta Laurel Bay bears 340°T. The red roof on this point is visible from 025°T to 360°T and can help identify the place. Carry on 340°T until a small wooded islet in Punta Laurel Bay bears about 330°T. Turn onto that heading. By now you should be seeing the edge of a shallow bank to the northeast and north. Skirt the edge of this shoal until you positively see the reef on the west side of the channel. Pass east of it. When about half a mile from the islet in the bay the shoals appear to overlap so follow the edge of the one to the east until you can steer about 360°T and then about 012°T into the anchorage where you can anchor in 22 feet in good holding mud. A good high sun and polarized sunglasses will help to pilot among the reefs lurking in the somewhat murky waters.

CAYO PATTERSON

A very deep channel runs along the south shores of Peninsula Valiente until the shallow water extending from Yellowtail Cay. Skirt the edge of this shoal, avoiding the bank west of Cayo Patterson, as it is hard to detect coral heads in the unclear water. Do not go too far into the bight of Cayo Patterson and anchor in about 30 feet of water. Patterson, a long gone pastor, left the legacy of the name along with some English language knowledge which has passed down the generations even to the little kids in a few of the families on the islet. Across the channel you will see the larger village of Bugori which has a clinic, a store with cold drinks and a great supply of fish and lobster, the main quarry of the divers who live there. To leave Cayo Patterson going southeast one should have good light because, although a deep channel winds between shoals, the lack of distinguishing landmarks makes it hard to keep track of one's exact position. With polarized sunglasses on and a high sun it is possible to see the edges of the shoals. The shoals themselves generally have 10 to 12 feet of water on them but there is a good chance of encountering a coral head rising closer to the surface.

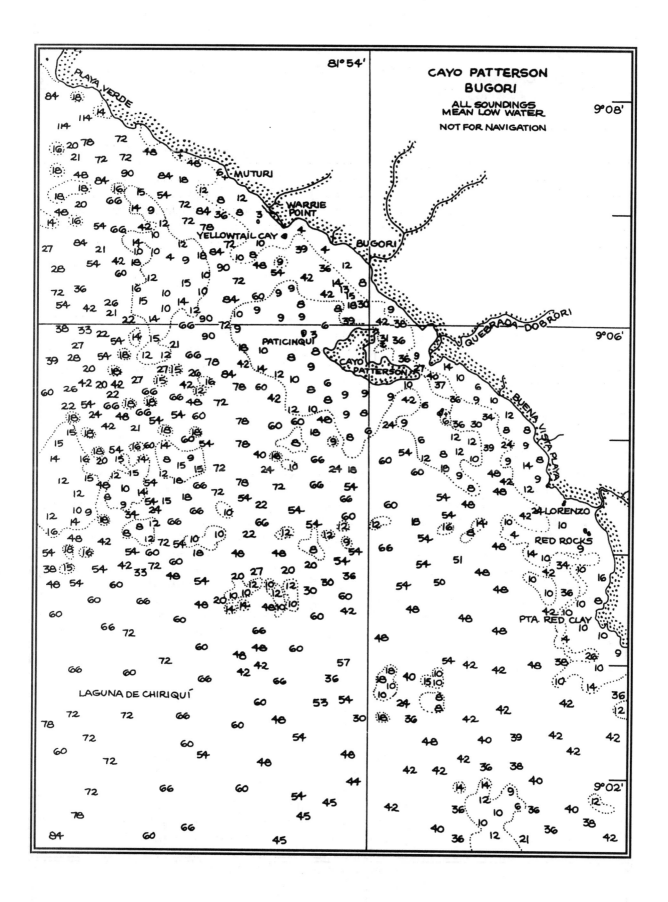

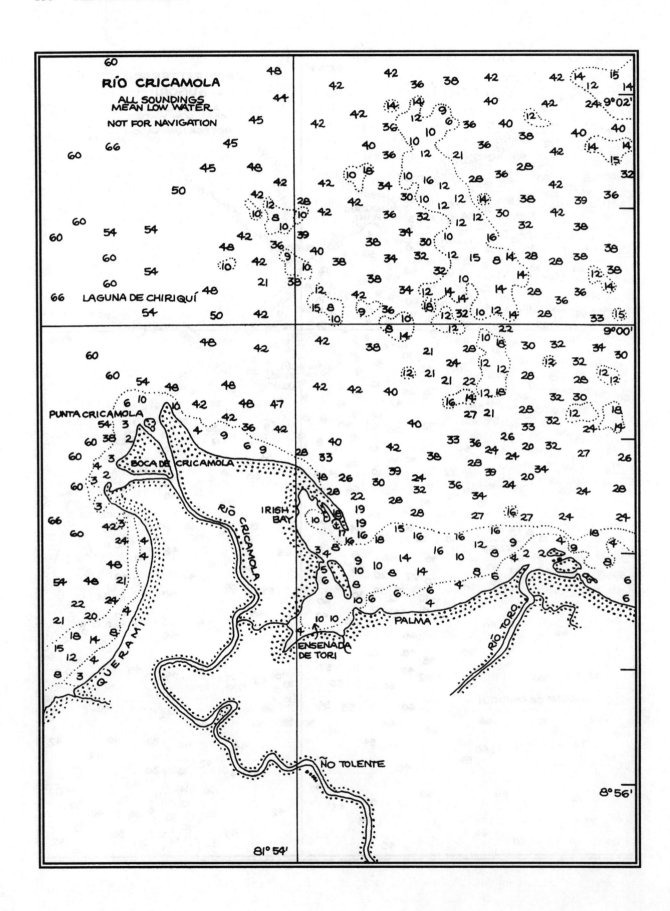

IRISH BAY AND RIO CRICAMOLA

You can follow the shore east of the mouth of Rio Cricamola quite close to the strip of land which gives total protection to Irish Bay and then anchor anywhere inside in a mud bottom. This is a very peaceful, calm anchorage. Friendly people paddle by occasionally and you can leave the boat unattended if you lock it securely and hide all loose gas cans and deck gear. In order to visit Rio Cricamola go by dinghy to Ensenada de Tori and follow the west shore until you come to the entrance to a tiny creek. Putter down this tiny waterway until you pass a homestead of thatched huts at the corner of the mighty Cricamola and then turn left. The current can be strong and it takes about one and a half hours from Irish Bay to the first Guaymi (Ngöbe) village on the river called Ñotolente - several huts on stilts along the bank. The people there will be happy to sell you all kinds of bananas, roots, like yucca or dasheen, plantains, etc. The best time for shopping would be in the afternoon after the men have paddled back home from their farms on the river banks. The women and children can be shy and may at first hide from you.

CHIRIQUÍ GRANDE

Chiriquí Grande port was created as the Atlantic terminal for an oil pipeline which crosses the Isthmus from Puerto Armuelles on the Pacific coast. Two large orange buoys mark the ends of pipeline connections used by large tankers which nowadays rarely visit this facility. The deep channel, marked by lit buoys with radar reflectors leads between large shallow areas from the main entrance to Chiriquí Lagoon off the Valiente Peninsula. A lit range on 212°T stands above the town to aid approaching ships. A breakwater and a pier combined have deep water alongside and can serve freighters. In 1995 the Panamanian government allotted funds to extend the pier and develop more shipping facilities. Unfortunately, yachts must anchor outside the area protected by the breakwater arm and also out of the way of the Almirante ferry ships which come to the short town dock. The closest place for a yacht is off the mouth of the small river, Rio Margarita, in water between 18 and 12 feet deep with a very good holding mud bottom. The place becomes choppy when the afternoon breeze blows from the northeast. The port captain, who speaks English, advised that it would be possible for a yacht to pick a mooring or to anchor in the inner harbor, 7 foot depths, after contacting him on the VHF in the event of bad weather. Normally, the petroleum company does not allow yachts to enter there.

The town has two public phones, one by the bus stop near the foot of the ferry dock and another down the road along the coast in the southern part of town beyond the small river. Several stores offer a variety of household goods, clothing, hardware, bakery items and groceries. There is a dental clinic and a pharmacy. Several restaurants specialize in seafood. There is no post office. Buses from Chiriquí Grande maintain a regular connection with David, a large city on the Pacific side of Panama. The bus takes about two hours and ascends to the continental divide, mountains covered with virgin forests, and then descends through pasture land on the Pacific slope. In David one can find banks which give cash advances, Jetex and DHL offices (the international couriers), faxes and good shopping. Two gasolineras on the waterfront of Chiriquí Grande sell gasoline and diesel is available in town. It will have to be ferried aboard by jerry jugs. The gasolineras have water from tap but sometimes the pressure drops hopelessly low.

A yacht can clear into the country here as well as clear out. For the route between here and Bocas del Toro the port captains in either harbor, and also in Almirante, will insist on issuing zarpe clearances even though yachts must also buy a cruising permit which officially eliminates the need for zarpes between Panamanian ports.

ENSENADA DELISCANOS

About 10 miles further north from Chiriquí Grande along the west coast of Laguna de Chiriquí a yacht can find perfect protection in Ensenada Deliscanos. By keeping in the middle on a course of 275°T between the two points one will pass over a 9 foot bar and into a deeper pool of water surrounded by mangrove covered shores with some high hills in the background. A short dinghy ride up the Rio Molejones will take one to a fairly large very traditional indigenous village. The women occasionally have chacaras (colorful hand woven net bags made from "pita," a plant similar to the century plant) to sell, and the men make fish nets with a similar weave. The village has a tiny tienda with few items. To obtain homemade ice, gasoline, and diesel, one has to go outside the bay and about half a mile south to Miramar village.

152 THE PANAMA GUIDE

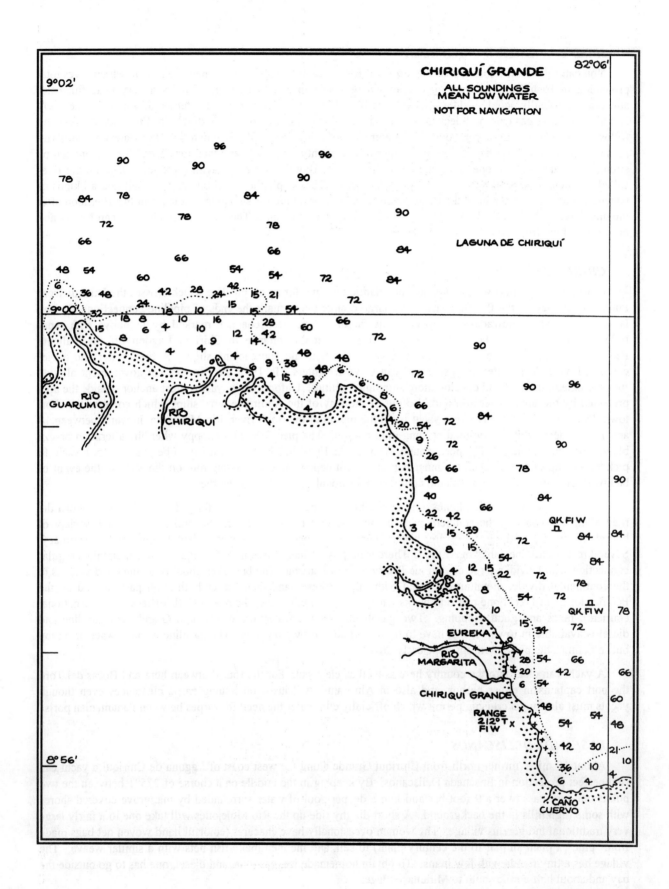

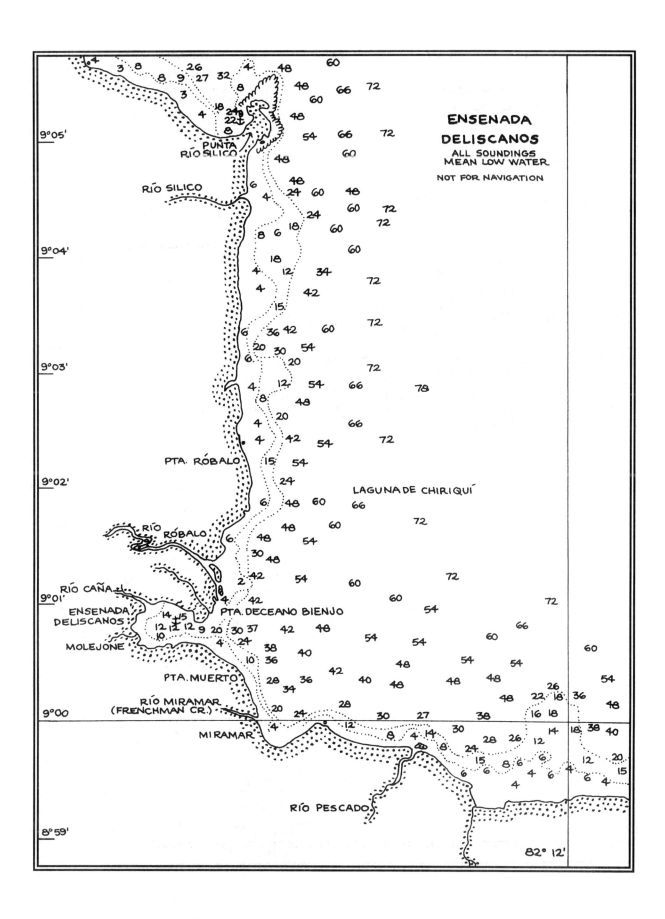

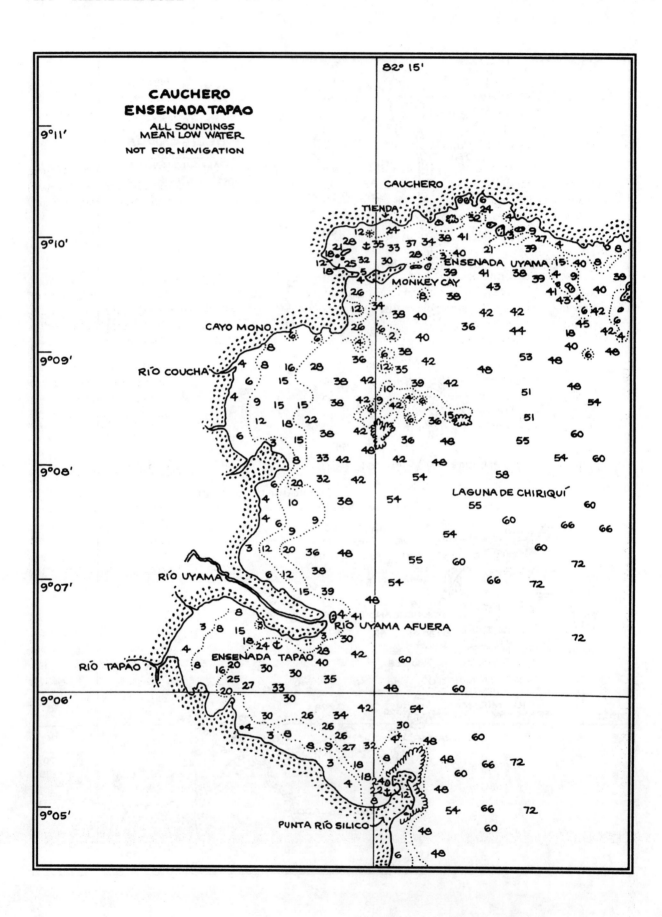

ENSENADA TAPAO AND ITS ANCHORAGES

Five miles north from Punta Deceano Bienjo, a yacht should swing wide around Punta Rio Silico on account of far reaching shoals, before turning south to enter a small perfectly protected cove on the west side of Punta Rio Silico. Steer about 150°T on the west edge of the small mangrove islet, then skirt the shallow shelf off it by keeping in about 18 to 20 feet of water, and heading about southeastwards. When the small islet bears about north one can anchor in 18 feet of water with good holding in a mud bottom.

One can also anchor in the north part of Ensenada Tapao. Take a dinghy for a long ride up Rio Uyama, which goes on for miles shaded by trees and winding through more or less abandoned cacao (chocolate) plantations. The easiest entrance into the river leads from the south and west of the outermost islet. We saw caimans in the lower reaches of this river.

CAUCHERO

The northwest corner of Laguna de Chiriquí, protected from the south by Monkey Cay, is locally known as Cauchero. Enter from the southeast, and after rounding the shoals and islets east of Monkey Cay, turn west into the anchorage. Green hills surround this excellent anchorage about 35 feet deep with good holding mud. Three very friendly families of Latinos live here, and the tienda on the north shore offers the typical basics. Often available is fresh Bocatoreño bread, yeasty large heavy buns with a slight delicious coconut flavor.

Between Cauchero and Split Hill Island, the shore has several coves with deep water approaches which wind through a multitude of reefs. Among them Acuacate Bay, rimmed with a few Latino houses, is relatively easy to enter. In sunny weather with the sun high the reefs become obvious particularly through polarized sunglasses. Overcast calm windless weather hides them completely. In such conditions when bound from Cauchero for the channels into Bahía Almirante give this tricky area a wide berth.

THE PASSAGES FROM LAGUNA DE CHIRIQUÍ INTO BAHÍA ALMIRANTE

Two large car carrying ferries maintain a daily connection between the town of Almirante and Chiriquí Grande. They use the channels on the west and east sides of Isla Split Hill, and the ship owners have marked the reefs. These markers describe the waterway in a somewhat peculiar way. Inverted 55 gallon drums stuck on mangrove poles positioned in the shallow parts of the reefs have a variety of colors, stripes and designs on them, none of them indicating the way to go if you are new to the area. Bear in mind that the markers are not very durable either. A high sun and blue sky reveal the reefs and help you negotiate the channels.

SPLIT HILL CHANNEL - LOMA PARTIDA

When approaching Split Hill Channel (Loma Partida) from the south, disregard a highly visible large steel buoy located close to Isla Split Hill, and steer for the two southernmost channel entrance markers. One should approach these quite close, and should pass to the east of them before negotiating the rest of the channel. After the narrows on the west side of Isla Split Hill the deep channel runs close to the west side of a house on a reef, then cuts across the shallowest area on a roughly northerly heading, comes close to the west side of a mangrove islet, takes a sharp turn to the east along the north side of it and goes north again to join the main waterway from Sumwood Channel.

SPLIT HILL - LOMA PARTIDA

Several brightly painted houses with small landings line the narrows on both sides. Most of them sell a good variety of typical tienda basics and gasoline. To visit them anchor north of the community in 8 feet on a grassy bottom as indicated on the sketch chart and use your dinghy. The shop keepers are very friendly and it is fun to shop by puttering from one dock to the other.

156 THE PANAMA GUIDE

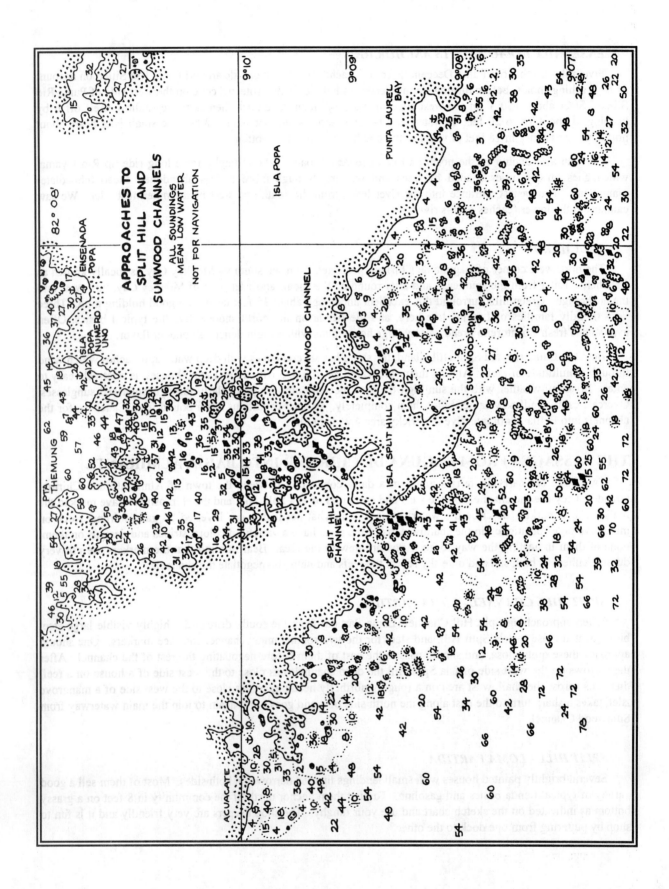

RIO CHAGRES TO BOCA DEL DRAGO 157

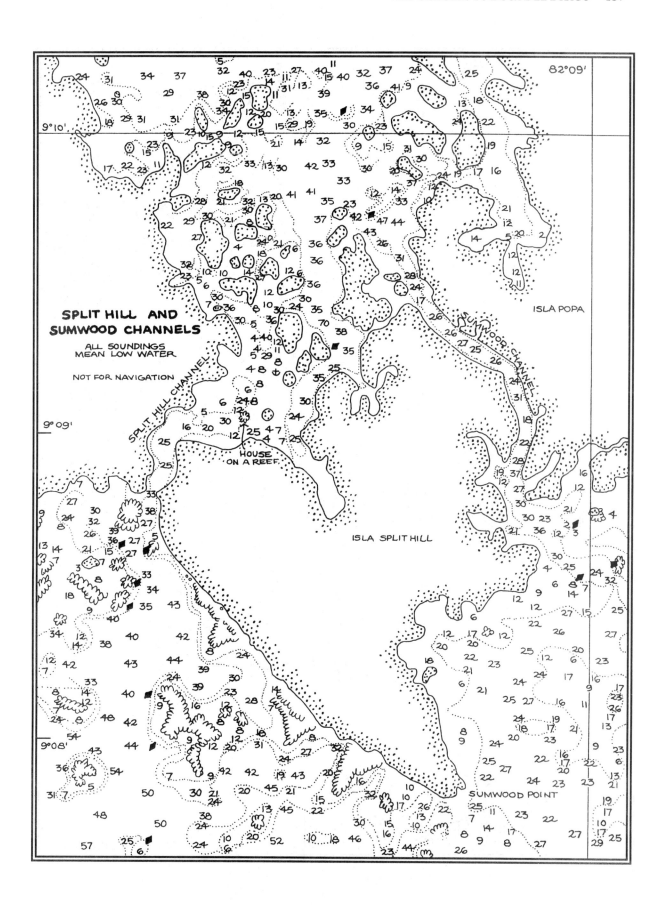

158 THE PANAMA GUIDE

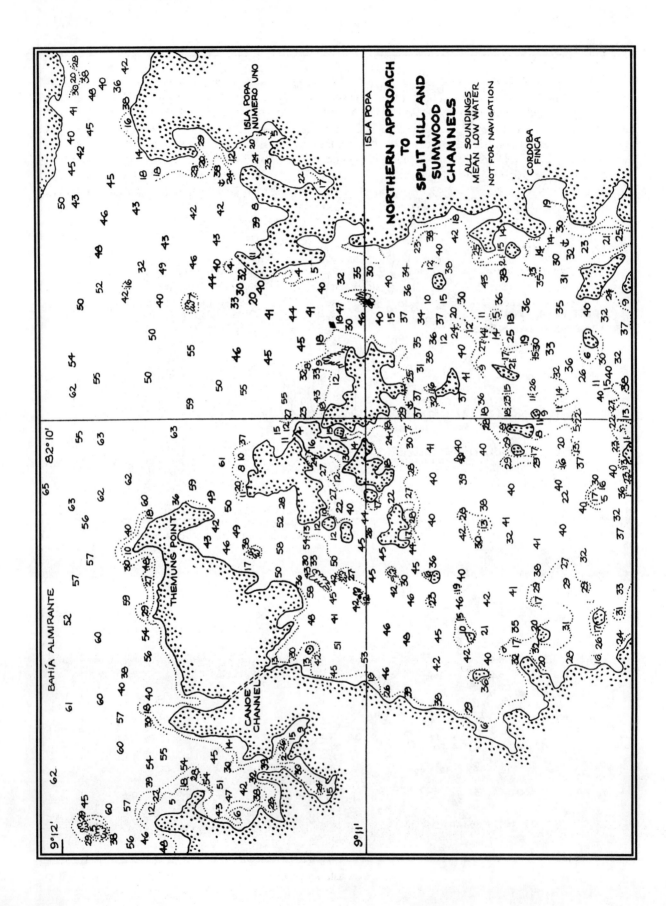

SUMWOOD CHANNEL

Sumwood Channel is the preferred channel for the ferries and indeed seems more straightforward to use. Initially a yacht must pass between two pairs of markers. The southernmost stood at Lat. 09°06.6'N and Long. 082°08.1'W in 1995. Sumwood Channel trends a bit west of north and the trickiest part comes when it nears the eastern part of Isla Split Hill. Pass between the last paired markers and take a sharp westward turn to pass close to the mangrove point on Isla Split Hill as indicated on the Split Hill and Sumwood Channels sketch chart. Stay well west away from the last marker which sits in the middle of an extensive shoal to the east. After that, keep in the middle of the waterway winding through low mangroves until it emerges north of Isla Split Hill. More scattered markers show the worst of the reefs along the way to Punta Themung. One can anchor in several places off the main channel some of which are indicated on the sketch chart.

BAHÍA ALMIRANTE

Bahía Almirante, about one third the size of Laguna de Chiriquí, has clearer waters, more sunny weather and a multitude of protected anchorages. Parts of Isla Bastimentos and Cayos Zapatillas have become National Park areas. The town of Bocas del Toro on Isla Colón makes a good base for a yacht cruising this body of water. On the other hand Almirante, the banana company town on the west shore, lacks attractions.

A population of Antillean descent concentrates in Bocas del Toro although a growing number of Latinos are moving in as the town has become the area's tourist center. The people in small hamlets on sparsely populated islets and fringes of Bahía Almirante are either of Antillean origins or the indigenous Guaymi (Ngöbe).

ANCHORAGES NORTH OF SPLIT HILL

ISLETS SOUTHEAST OF THEMUNG POINT

There is a good anchorage south of the islets southeast of Themung Point on the west side of the channel. Anchor in water deeper than 20 feet on a sandy bottom. Anything less than 20 feet deep will have coral which makes for uncertain holding and should be protected anyhow. The anchorage keeps you out of the traffic. The ferries and deeper draft vessels will pass to the east and shallow draft outboard powered water taxis between Almirante and Chiriquí Grande use the waters to the west. See the Northern Approach to Split Hill and Sumwood Channels sketch chart.

FINCA CORDOBA

The anchorage off Finca Cordoba in 30 feet, mud bottom, is easy to enter and leave. Further in, a narrow canoe channel through the mangroves leads to a landing where Señor Cordoba builds dugout canoes. You can see his large thatched houses from the main channel.

ISLA POPA NUMERO UNO

Further north on the west shore of Isla Popa you will spot several thatched huts in the Guaymi (Ngöbe) village unimaginatively called Isla Popa Numero Uno. Anchor off in 24 feet, mud bottom. You can take the dinghy to their dock and village kids will probably take you for a tour between the widely scattered houses. This village is a stronghold of Mama Chi followers and many women wear long brightly colored gowns sewn like nun's habits which advertise their faith. Mama Chi is a Guaymi religious movement which emerged in 1961. There are good views of the islets all around from the slopes of the village. Fresh bread is available.

ENSENADA POPA

Around the corner from Isla Popa Numero Uno a bight called Ensenada Popa runs east and branches into many secluded anchorages. Only one indigenous man, Señor Stonestreet (who is looking for a gringo wife), lives in the southernmost bay. Courtesy requires that you ask his permission to walk around his pastureland and the paths through the trees, but he welcomes visitors. The views from the hills are great. A few reefs lie scattered in the bight most of the time marked with mangrove sticks. Waters deeper than 20 feet have good holding mud bottoms.

ISLA POPA NUMERO DOS

Further northward along the west coast of Isla Popa lies the village of Isla Popa Numero Dos, a lot smaller place than Numero Uno. The anchorage off the east side of Ferro Cay has total protection. The shallower 21 foot spot in the middle of the area has a hard coral bottom surrounded by a slightly deeper mud bottom. By all means visit the village where you can tie the dinghy to their wooden dock. You can get fresh water from a well equipped with an old fashioned iron hand pump. One of the two tiendas sells freshly baked bread, nicely carved canoe paddles and chacaras (hand woven colorfully patterned bags of various sizes) are also available.

One should ask to see chacaras for sale in all these indigenous settlements as they are reasonably priced attractive examples of indigenous utilitarian art.

A useable channel runs eastward along the north coast of Isla Popa and then out into the ocean. However, navigating through it would require the best of eye piloting conditions as several shoals of complex shape sit plop in the middle of the passage. The northern part of this passage called Crawl Cay Channel is easier to go through and you can find it described later in this chapter.

Cruising in rain forest, Laguna Almirante.

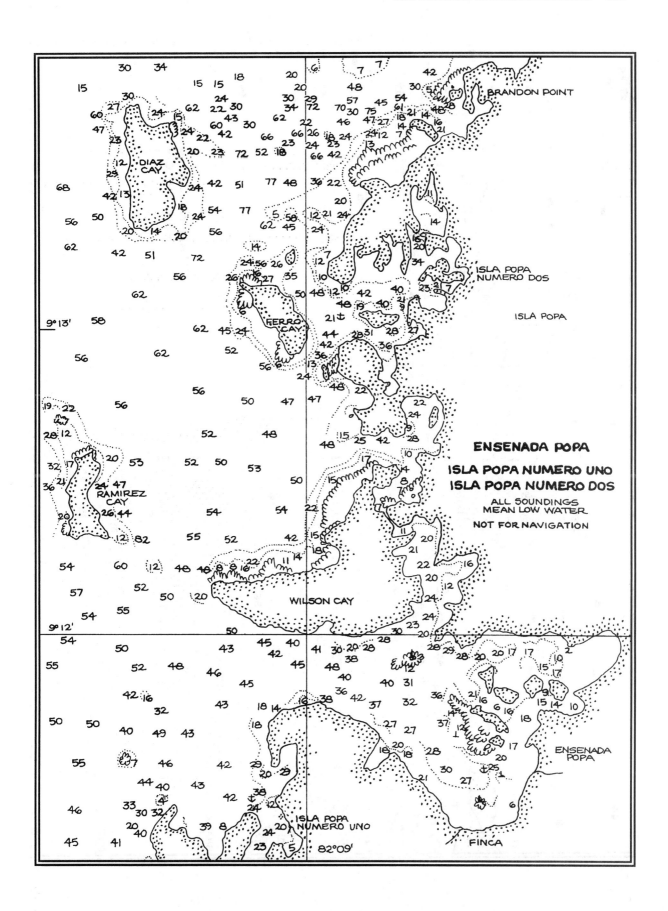

162 THE PANAMA GUIDE

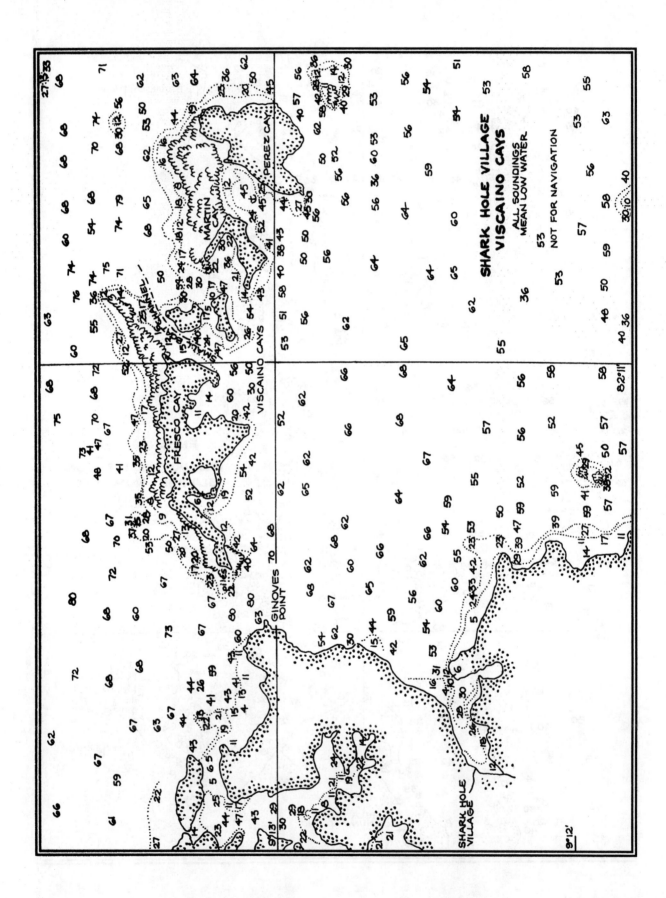

Beautiful Kuna woman photographed in San Blas.

*Above: Punta de Cocos, Isla Del Rey, Las Perlas Islands.
Below: Morodup, Holandes Cays, San Blas Islands.*

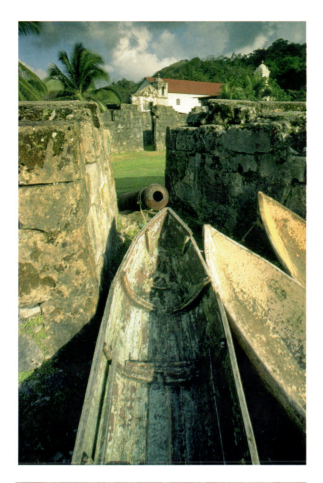

Photos by Tom Zydler

Top left: Canons of Portobello make handy bollards for local boats. Top right: Kuna girl holding pet bird. Bottom left: Yachts entering Portobello sail past Spanish colonial forts. Bottom Right: Tigre Village in San Blas.

Photos by Tom Zydler

Top left: Kuanidup, San Blas Islands. Top right: View from Isla Ensenada over Isla Guarume, and Bahia de Chamé. Bottom: Ensenada Bejuco (from Chapter 4).

Mollymawk, anchored peacefully in Rio Chagres.

Top: Nuinidup anchorage, San Blas Islands. Bottom: Deep Channels run between mangrove islands in Laguna Almirante.

Top: Playa San Bernardo, Isla Pedro Gonzales, Las Perlas Islands. Bottom: Fishing boats dry out for repairs in La Palma, Rio Tuira, Darien.

Photos by Tom Zydler

Sunset over Boca Chica Channel (from Chapter 4).

RIO CHAGRES TO BOCA DEL DRAGO 171

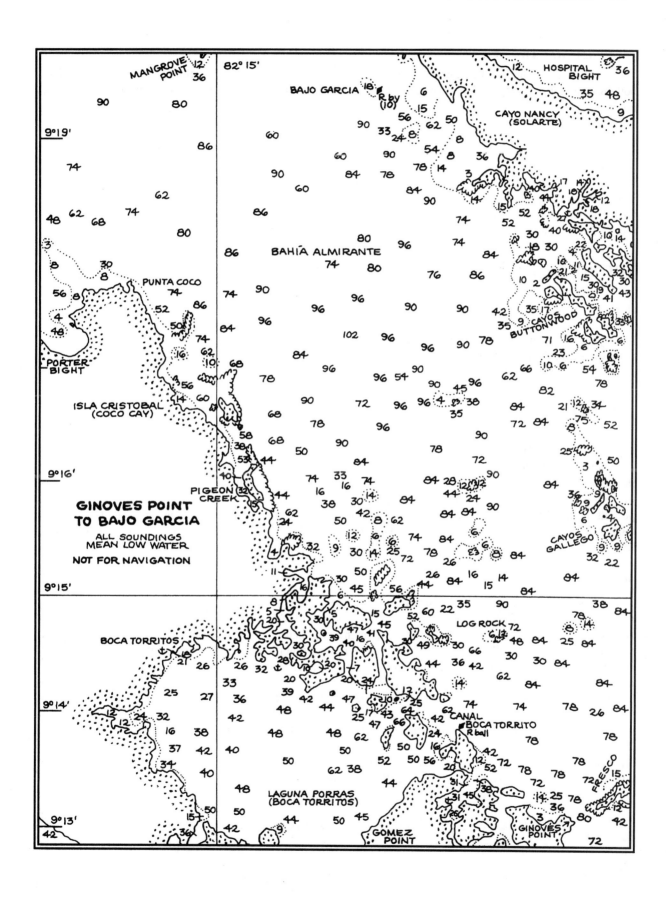

VISCAINO CAYS

Viscaino Cays, uninhabited mangrove islets, have an anchorage between Perez and Martin Cays. The bottom is mud and while the shallow water at the northern edge cuts out any waves it does not stop the cooling breeze.

SHARK HOLE

Across from Viscaino Cays a long indentation in the mainland forms a bay and the approach to the indigenous village of Shark Hole. A narrow 10 foot deep opening over a hard reef bar leads to a deeper pool inside. Anchoring outside of the lagoon may be preferable because of insects. Going by dinghy into the creek in the westernmost corner you will find a good tie-up at a concrete dock. A path from it leads to the largest Guaymi (Ngöbe) village in the area.

THE ROUTE TO BOCAS DEL TORO

After passing west of Isla Popa between the two northernmost markers on the waterway from Isla Split Hill steer northwestward towards Themung Point when heading towards Bocas del Toro. Next, pass through the channel between Ginoves Point and Fresco Cay, the westernmost island in the Viscaino Cays. After Ginoves Point you will encounter a few scattered shoals separated by plenty of deep water. Approaching Bocas del Toro town waterfront you will see a large yellow and black steel buoy. which marks a 15 foot deep shoal. After it the shallowest places will have 11 feet of water.

BOCAS DEL TORO

A large concrete dock with 16 feet of water alongside at the southeastern corner of the town of Bocas del Toro serves the Almirante ferry ships and an occasional small freighter. Yachts arriving from foreign destinations usually have to tie up along its well fendered face and report to the Port Captain office at the foot of the dock. The Port Captain monitors Channel 16 VHF during working hours. Bocas del Toro being the capital of the province of the same name has an immigration officer and a Consular y Naves office which issues cruising permits. The port captain in Bocas follows the old policy of issuing a clearance, "zarpe", between the ports of Panama even if the destination is as close as Almirante or Chiriquí Grande. Cruising permits are handled in the Ministerio de Hacienda y Tesoro building near the main dock. The immigration office is in the "Palacio," the administration building by the plaza. Visa extensions are issued in Changuinola, an inland town reached by way of Almirante.

The best anchorage for yachts lies on the north side of the town and the channel, with a least depth of 12 feet, runs close to the waterfront. Anchor in a good holding mud and sand bottom when you reach the area off Hotel Brisas which has a balustraded deck and hanging banana stalks. Further west the deep channel narrows considerably and eventually shoals. The drying shoal on the north side of the anchorage makes this a very smooth anchorage. A yacht can be brought stern-to at Hotel Brisas and use their power supply for a negotiable charge. It is safe to leave the boat for extended absences. If you prefer to stay anchored find another place to leave the dinghy while in town as Brisa's management wants $10 a day for dinghy tie-up. A very large percentage of the town's population of Antillean descent still speak English. The first black people arrived here with Scottish settlers from Isla Providencia and San Andres in 1826 and their numbers increased as more West Indians came to Panama as workers on the construction of the trans-isthmus railway and then on the building of the Panama Canal. The gingerbread Georgian housing which appears so much like the architecture of the Antilles suffered a lot of damage in the April, 1991 earthquake.

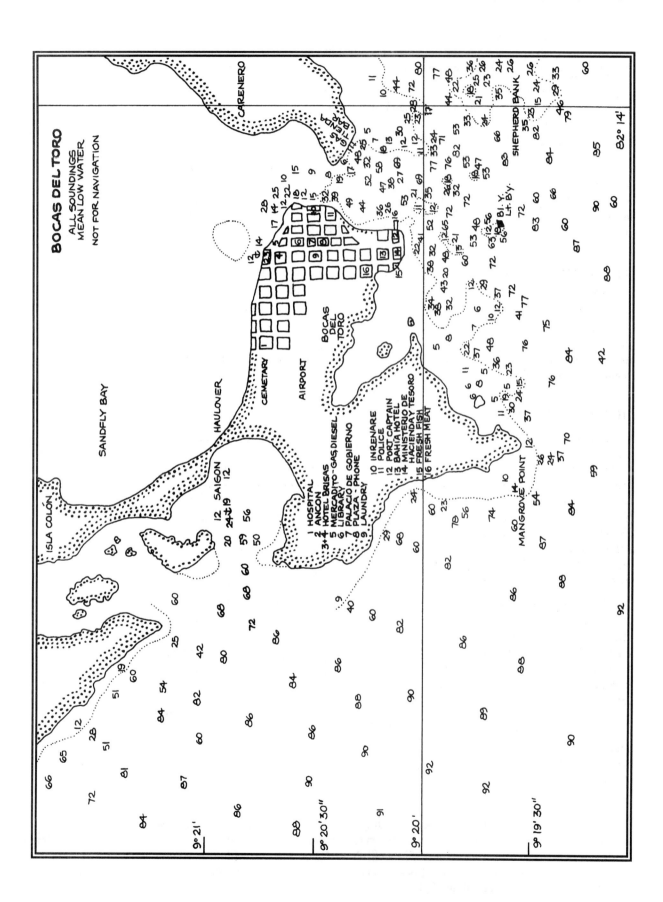

However, the earthquake also brought some help from the government in the form of new paved roads as well as the total revamping and enlarging of the air strip. The town has become a low key tourist destination and a couple of dive shops offer full services. The largest festival of the year, Fiesta del Mar, which includes boat races, is held in September. The exact date changes annually.

The shops in Bocas have limited merchandise and most people take small boat taxis, which leave from the dock in front of Hotel Bahía, for the half an hour trip to Almirante on the mainland. For an even better choice of shops one can take an hour long bus ride from Almirante to Changuinola. This is the way to go when you have to extend your initial tourist visa as the main immigration office for the region is in Changuinola.

On the north shore of Bocas near the yacht anchorage you will see the short concrete dock of the local mercado; local produce, gasoline and diesel sales are located here. One can get good drinking water from a tap inside the mercado. Ice is always available from one house or another - ask around. The lady in Restaurante Don Chico does laundry using a washing machine and an electric dryer. The only way to get propane is to carry the Panamanian exchange bottles. The bank in town cannot give cash advances with any credit card. One can reach international phone operators (109 for ATT) from a pay phone in Hotel Bahía, another in the main plaza by the government "Palacio," the town administration building, and a phone booth outside of the fire station at the north end of town.

CARENERO - CAREENING ISLAND

The little island right across the channel from Bocas del Toro has in recent years sprouted a row of tiendas, a restaurant and a gasolinera along its southwest shore. A new facility, Marina Carenero, has opened just across from the north end of the town of Bocas del Toro. Yachts up to 60 feet long will find ample slip space equipped with 120volts/30Amps and 240volts/50Amps 60 Hz of power and pressurized potable water. The marina offers showers and laundry as well as cabin rentals. Marina Carenero hopes to attract people escaping the hurricane season further north as this section of Central America lies below the hurricane belt. The Marina will arrange permits for unlimited stays for yachts – their owners will, however, still be subject to immigration regulations. The telephone and fax number is: 507-757-9242, the email address is: marcar@cwp.net.pa. Mail should be addressed to: Marina Carenero, Bocas del Toro, Rep. de Panama.

OCEAN ENTRANCES TO BAHÍA ALMIRANTE

BOCA DEL TORO

Two deep channels lead into Bahía Almirante from the Caribbean. Of these Boca del Toro is wider and deeper as well as buoyed for use by the banana carriers which go to the Almirante loading pier. The outermost buoy lies about a mile and a half from Punta Bastimentos at Lat. 09°22.2'N, Long. 82°12.7'W. This channel is so wide and deep that yachts can go through in any sea conditions with the exception of prolonged rain squalls which may blot out all visibility.

BOCA DEL DRAGO

Boca del Drago, the channel which leads into Bahía Almirante through an opening by the northwest point of Isla Colón will require more vigilance and can possibly turn somewhat wild when large swells arrive from the northeast. To enter from the north first identify Sail Rock, shaped like a pillar, the low lying Wreck Rocks and the large bulky Swan Cay. The correct course leads close to Punta Cauro but from a distance you will probably spot Lime Point first because of the conspicuous tall coconut palms rising over the low ground. The reefs extending far east from Punta Sarabeta and those from Punta Cauro will have breaking waves only when a good size ocean swell exists. It helps to steer about 197°T on Lime Point until Sail Rock bears 035°T when one should steer 215°T until the rocks of Punta Cauro line up with Punta Norte on Isla Colón. Then change to 250°T until you get close to the shore of Punta Antón, a low lying sandy point with coconut palms. If you rely on a GPS for some assistance, note that at Lat. 09°25.5'N, Long. 082°19.8'W you should steer 215°T.

To exit Bahía Almirante through Boca del Drago pass about half a mile off Punta Rancho and steer about northwest towards the shore just south of Punta Antón. When the depth sounder reads about 48 feet parallel the shore staying in 60 to 70 feet of water and steering about 025°T until Punta Cauro lines up with Punta Norte at 070°T. Stay on this new heading towards Punta Cauro until Sail Rock bears 035°T. Change to that heading until Punta Cauro bears about 135°T when you can head out on a heading of 360°T.

Rio Chagres to Boca Del Drago

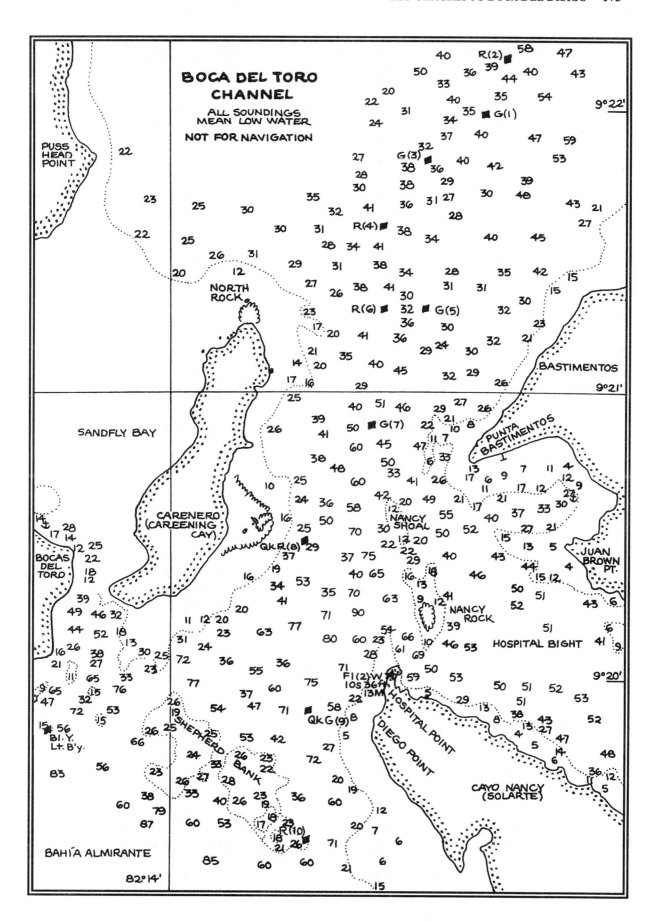

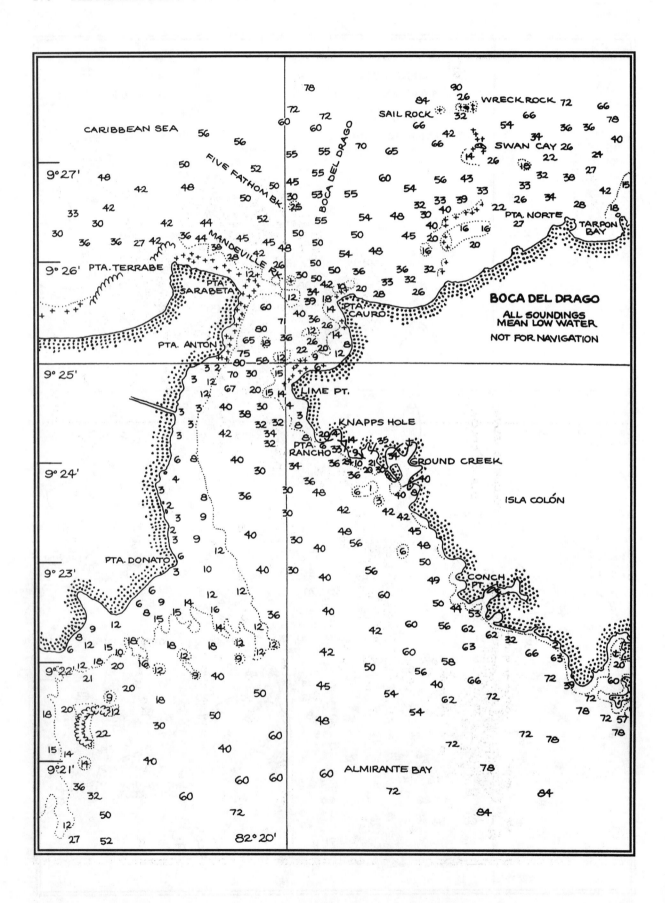

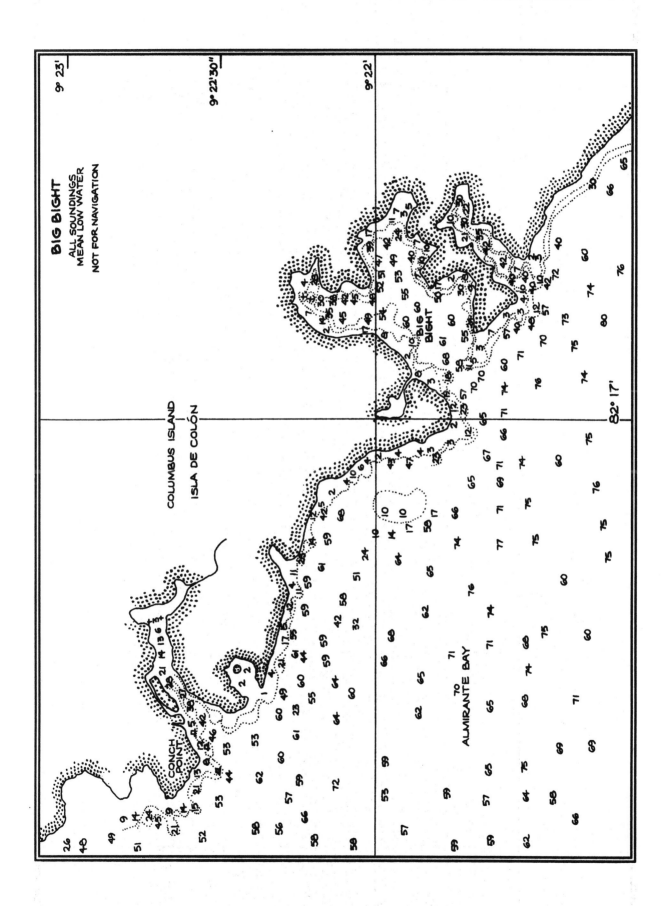

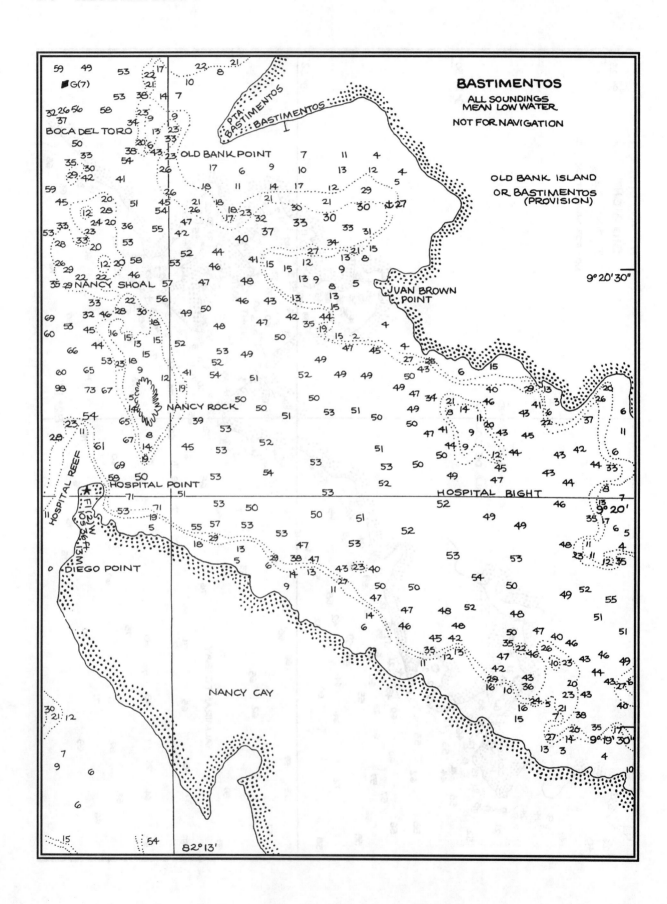

RIO CHAGRES TO BOCA DEL DRAGO 179

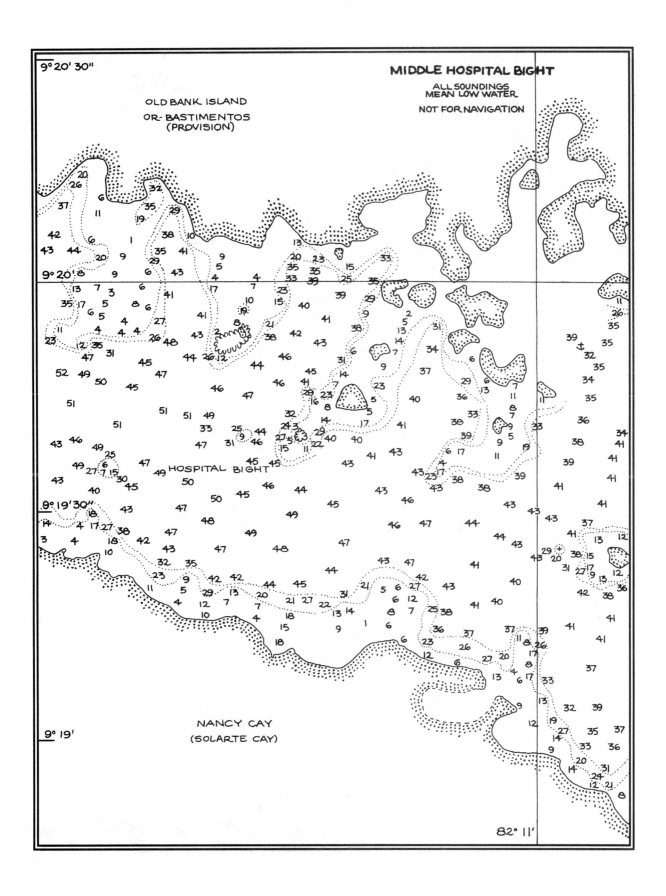

180 THE PANAMA GUIDE

RIO CHAGRES TO BOCA DEL DRAGO 181

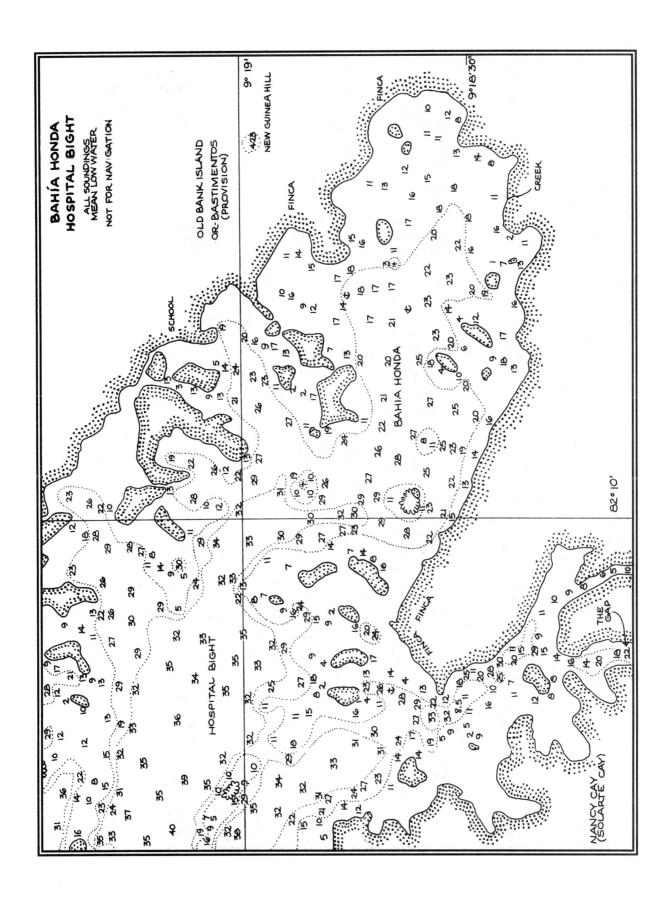

ISLA COLÓN ANCHORAGES

SAIGON

The southwest shore of Isla Colón (Columbus Island) has several bays with secluded well protected bays. On the west side of the causeway which joins Bocas del Toro town to the rest of Isla Colón lies a bay whose southern part bears the local nickname of Saigon. See the Bocas del Toro sketch chart. Several plank houses line the east shore and some rickety docks jut out into the narrow shallow shelf in this generally very deep bay. One can anchor in an area under 20 feet deep with a coarse sand bottom when the mangrove islet in the northwestern part bears northwest. Tie up the dinghy at one of the docks after getting a readily granted permission from whoever is hanging around the household and you can step onto the causeway road. Turn right and you will reach the town in a few minutes of walking. Turn left and you can walk for miles along the shore of Sandfly Bay.

BIG BIGHT

Big Bight, about a mile further northwest along the southwestern coast of Isla Colón, has a good anchorage in 30 feet, mud bottom, in its northwestern corner. You may anchor in either arm of the bight. The shallower water has a coral bottom. No one but the birds will disturb your tranquility here. There is another anchorage in the narrow bay to the east of Big Bight, keep in the center of the channel when entering and anchor at the head of the bay.

CONCH POINT

A narrow bay cutting into Isla Colón on the south side of Conch Point has no inhabitants other than birds and fish frequenting the mangroves. There are good depths until the head of the bay. It is possible to go far enough in to close the gap of the entrance. Private buoys (55 gallon drums) mark the western shoal. Conch Point has a nicely wooded forest.

GROUND CREEK

Further to the northwest one can enter Ground Creek bay with the best anchorage in the northwestern corner in 30 feet with a mud bottom and good holding. See the Boca del Drago sketch chart. A long creek there enters the mangrove lined shores and leads past several landings that belong to large family size huts. The northeastern arm has 37 feet between the entrance points and shoals to 18 feet further in. The easternmost arm with 25 feet in the entrance and shoaling rapidly further in ends in a pretty winding creek which leads to a Ngöbe household. It shoals rapidly further in. Notice that coral shoals extend from all of the points within Ground Creek Bay. This anchorage is better than Knapp's Hole - better holding and better protection.

ISLA BASTIMENTOS

The National Marine Park in this area comprises about one third of the eastern end of Bastimentos Island (also called Old Bank or Provision Island), includes a multitude of mangrove islets in the southwestern bay formed by Bastimentos and Nancy Cay as well as Zapatillos Cays, close to the eastern end of Isla Bastimentos. The INRENARE office in Bocas del Toro has full time wardens on eastern Zapatilla (Cayo Zapatilla Numero Dos) and others patrol the remaining areas. To visit the Zapatillas Cays, described later in this chapter, one has to obtain a permit, free of charge, from INRENARE in Bocas. Yachts may anchor in the other places within the park but they must do no fishing of any kind or take anything other than photos.

BASTIMENTOS VILLAGE

A smooth anchorage in 25 to 30 feet, mud bottom, can be found at the eastern end of the bay protected from the ocean swell by Punta Bastimentos. The town, populated mostly by criollos of Antillean descent, has two active cantinas and a restaurant in a small hotel marked "Pension" on the main plaza. There is a pay phone on the plaza which can connect one with the rest of Panama when it works. Many of the friendly people here speak English but their main means of communication is guari-guari, a linguistic mixture of Afro-Antillean English, indigenous Ngöbe dialect and Spanish. The town pier serves the banana company ferry boat that carries workers from Bastimentos and Bocas del Toro. Drinking water is available from taps in town.

Among the fallen fronds in the coconut grove on Punta Bastimentos one can see many endemic tiny bright orange and yellow frogs splotched with black.

HOSPITAL BIGHT

The long body of water between Bastimentos and Nancy Cay bears the name of Hospital Bight because of a hospital operated in the early 1900's by a banana company on Hospital Point on Nancy Cay. One can find secluded anchorages in many mangrove coves along the Bastimentos shore.

SHORT CUT

The first anchorage from the west marked on the sketch chart is close to a place known as Short Cut. Anchor in 32 feet, good holding. The landing is a loose collection of logs so wearing sea boots is a good idea. From there, a path, very slippery when it rains leads over a small hill, past a farm with cattle to an ocean beach with a great view.

BAHÍA HONDA

Hospital Bight ends in Bahía Honda, a totally peaceful retreat. A few Guaymi (Ngöbe) family huts hide along the shores and during the week school children dressed in white and blue paddle their dugouts past the anchored yacht on the way to school, which is visible on Isla Bastimentos from the anchorage. The salt water creek shown on the sketch chart leads to a trail. One must negotiate a boggy wet section before getting onto dry land. Many smaller trails branch off here into a coastal humid forest which harbors colonies of loud Montezuma oronpendolas and other birds which one can hear all the time but only occasionally see, as well as interesting and fragrant plants and trees.

THE GAP

There is an anchorage in 26 feet in gray sand with mud at the entrance to the Gap. This is a good place to stop to check the passage through the Gap first in the dinghy or to wait for good light.

The channel between Cayo Nancy and Isla Bastimentos has a least depth of 7 feet and allows one to take a short cut through an amazing maze of mangrove islets. The islets south of the Gap are totally unpopulated and well endowed with deep passages between and around shoals which in sunny weather and high sun become very obvious to the eye especially when wearing polarized sunglasses. In dull overcast weather one has to go very slowly with an eye on the depth sounder. Anchor anywhere and expect a smooth anchorage. There are more cays than the government charts, and this sketch chart, indicate. We have counted more than 90. To reach the Crawl Cay area from the Gap, steer generally southward. Pass east of Cayos Gallego and carry on southward to pass between Johnson and Manx Cays after which one can turn east for the Crawl Cay Channel.

NANCY CAY - SOLARTE

Off the south shore of the very little populated Nancy Cay one encounters such a proliferation of mangrove islets that even the topographical surveys from aircraft somehow missed several smaller cays which exist between the largest southernmost Buttonwood Cays and the shore of Nancy Cay.

NORTHEAST OF BUTTONWOOD CAY

Northeast of Buttonwood Cay several anchorages may be found amid the mangroves. The two marked on the sketch chart have good holding mud in depths deeper than 24 feet and have perfect all weather protection. From these anchorages one can take a dinghy to the south shore of Nancy Cay and try to enter the real jungle - a tropical lowland boggy forest of twisted roots, limbs and rotting substrata which makes for slow going. Note that all this area is within the National Park limits.

NORTH OF BUTTONWOOD CAY

Further on northwestward along the Nancy Cay shore an anchorage can be found in a nameless bay with two long fingers. Only one indigenous family lives in the northern branch. Enter the bay on the centerline between the obvious reefs off the points on either side. Anchor at the bay mouth in a mud bottom at 27 feet. There is also a pool 30 feet deep at the meeting of the two branches.

CRAWL CAY CHANNEL

This channel has an abundance of coral reefs that will delight a marine biologist but will speed up the heartbeat of a navigator going through in any craft deeper than about 4 feet. However, the deep water channels are very deep and with a good high sun the shoals become obvious. The easiest passage leads close to the south shore of Auree Cay, also called German Soldier Cay on some charts. When south of the east tip of Auree avoid a shoal that runs south from the small mangrove islet there. After Cayo Auree steer about eastward to go close to the south of Cayo Crawl and maintain a good lookout for reefs. After Cayo Crawl follow along the southern edge of a large area of very shallow reefs extending to the east and north. Even when out in what seems like deep water with ocean swells the depths tend to jump between 50 and 24 feet and vigilance is advised.

The reefs within Crawl Cay Channel attract indigenous divers who chase lobsters free diving with wire snares to retrieve the crustaceans alive. There are lobster buyers in a small village at the south tip of Isla Bastimentos and on Cayo Crawl. Both places have small well supplied tiendas which also sell cold drinks and gasoline.

They usually have good fresh coconut bread (Bocatoreño bread). Anchor off the southwest tip of Cayo Crawl in good holding sand 35 to 50 feet deep. One can cross Crawl Cay Channel in a dinghy and enter the channel around Isla Deer. The area has good bird and plant life as only three indigenous families live on the shores of this tiny waterway.

RIO CHAGRES TO BOCA DEL DRAGO 185

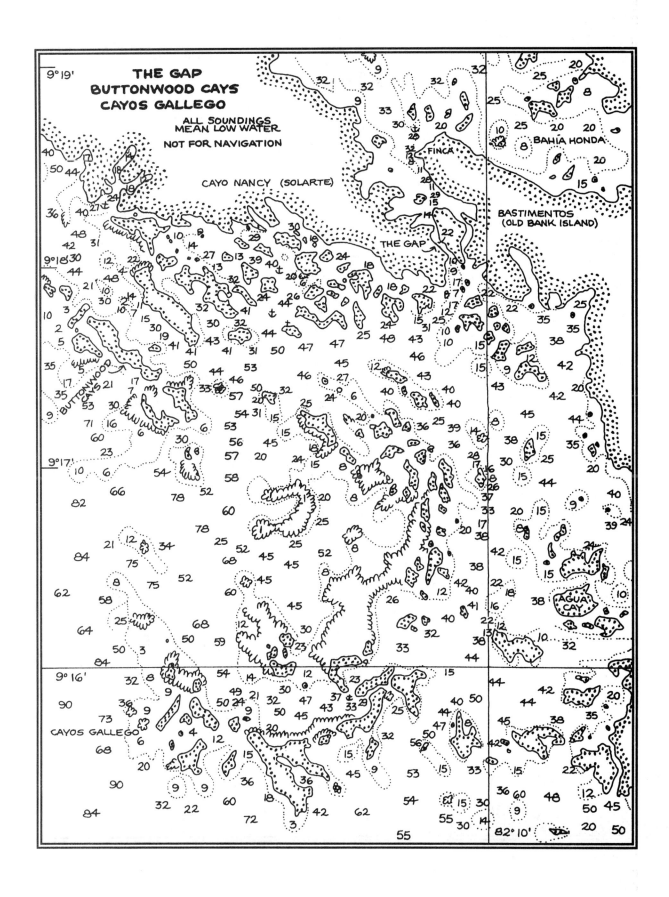

186 THE PANAMA GUIDE

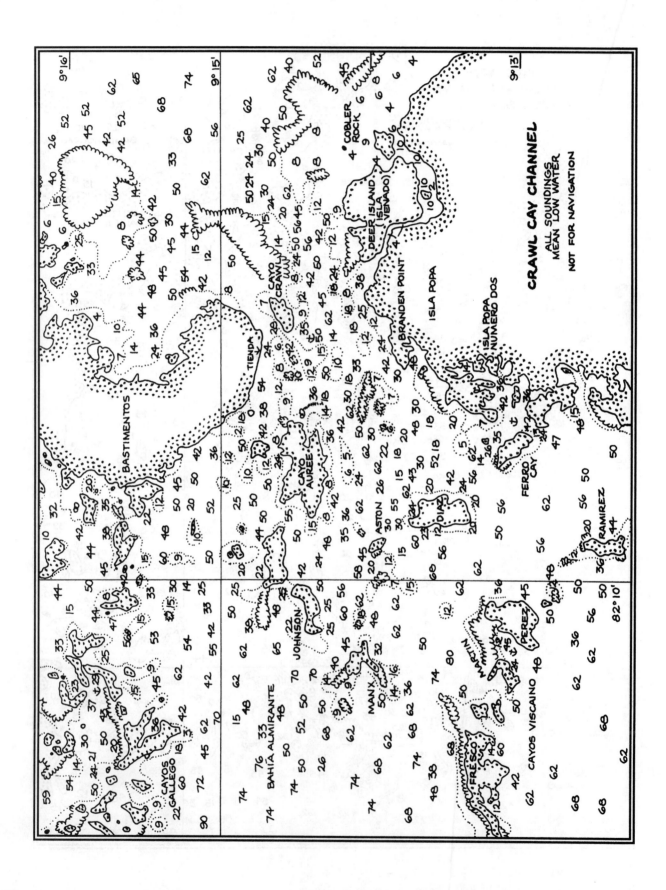

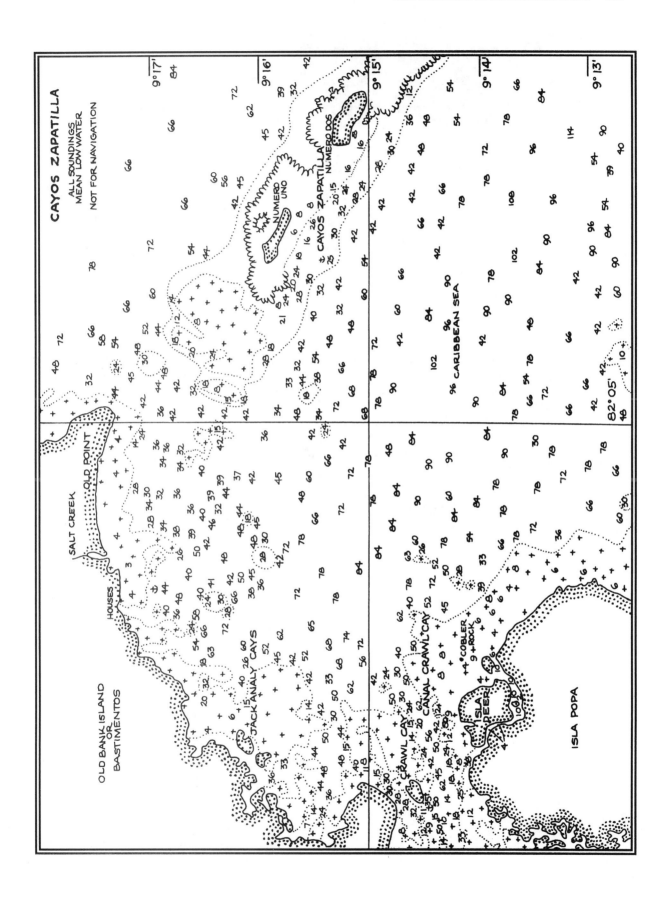

Boat Landing of Salt Creek village.

SALT CREEK

When coming to anchor off Salt Creek pick your way carefully between the offlying reefs, as the one to the east of the anchorage breaks now and then but the rest are shallow enough to damage a yacht yet deep enough not to reveal their presence by breakers. The spot about ½ mile southwest from the river has good holding mud about 35 feet deep. Unless a very large swell exists in the Caribbean this anchorage stays comfortable.

The entrance to Salt Creek, which is hard to spot, lies just west of a single planked house with a metal roof. Further to the west of the river mouth one can see a group of several thatched huts. Up the short narrow river a cluster of dugouts marks the village landing - a muddy affair at low tide. From here the path climbs a small bluff and winds across a boggy lowland to the village which has about 400 indigenous people living in huts scattered on low hilly pasture land. There is a school, a tienda and one of the huts sells freshly baked Bocatoreño bread. From the village one can pick up a path to a long ocean beach. As the long established nesting site for hawksbill sea turtles it has been included in the Bastimentos National Marine Park.

CAYOS ZAPATILLA

The National Marine Park of Bastimentos also includes the two small islands east of Isla Bastimentos known as the Zapatilla Cays. Dense coconut groves cover both islands and the indigenous people from Valiente peninsula who own them still come to tend the trees. INRENARE has its headquarters on the eastern cay, Cayo Zapatilla Numero Dos, and if you acquired a permit to visit here at the Bocas office hand it to the warden on duty. Yachts coming from other places without the permit may be visited by the wardens who can also issue a free of charge permit to stay here.

The best anchorage, almost entirely free from rolling, lies on a bearing of 50°T on the east point of the western islet, Cayo Zapatilla Numero Uno. Do not come closer than depths of 21 to 22 feet, over a sandy bottom, as extensive reefs lie off the shore. You will find dinghy landing with the least amount of surge in about the middle of the shoreline on Cayo Zapatilla Numero Uno and towards the eastern end of the beach on Numero Dos. On Cayo Zapatilla Numero Uno in the woods close to the northwestern point INRENARE has constructed a refuge hut with a supply of water.

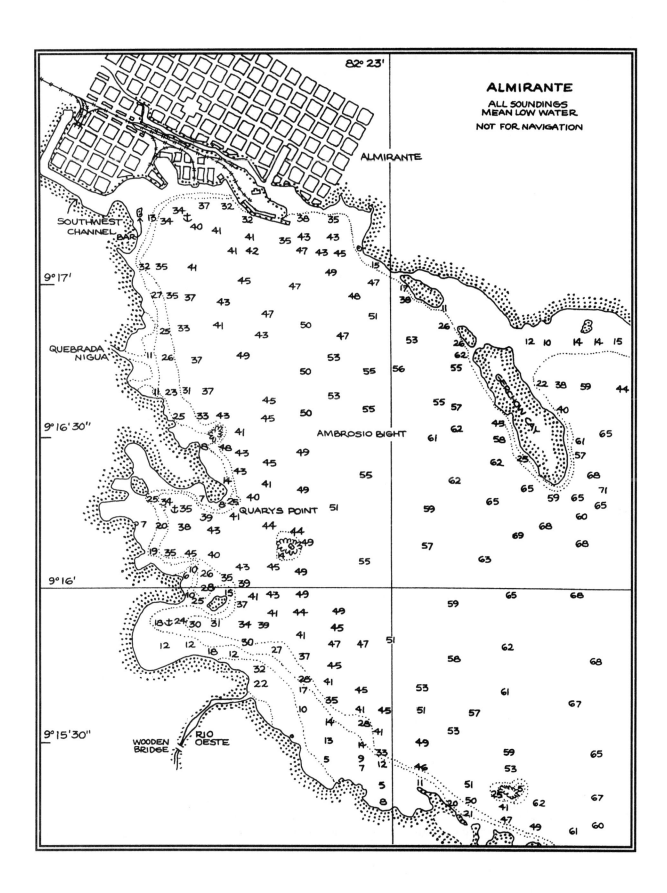

WESTERN PORTION OF BAHÍA ALMIRANTE

ALMIRANTE

Most yachtsmen visit Almirante using a fast taxi dugout or launch from Bocas del Toro. Apart from better inventories in the tiendas in Almirante the town has a good bus connection to Changuinola where the immigration office can extend tourist visas. In turn, Changuinola has bus connections to Costa Rica. Almirante lacks many attractions as a town and though the town wharf can serve only one banana ship at a time there is room for the ferries coming from Chiriquí Grande and Bocas del Toro. However, all fuels are available in several tiendas along the shore of Southwest Channel. One can usually find home made ice after asking around on the river north of the banana dock. When coming from Bocas del Toro a yacht drawing more than two feet must make sure to go north of the green beacon number 11 off Punta Juan on Isla Cristobal and give a wide berth to the red beacon on Pondsock Reef. (See the Isla Shepard sketch chart.) It stands in the middle of the reef. The anchorage in Almirante off the mouth of Southwest Channel and close to the entrance to a small basin has good holding mud in 34 feet. The locals say that one can also anchor safely inside the small basin between some private docks. You can leave the dinghy at the dock at the northeastern corner of this basin after it has been securely padlocked to the dock, motor and all.

AMBROSIO BIGHT ANCHORAGES

QUARY'S POINT

Although Almirante is no beauty spot, just to the south are a couple of very attractive and quiet anchorages. You will find a good holding mud bottom in 30ish foot depths just southwest of Quary's Point. Similarly, the next bay south has a good anchorage in about 20 feet. The large white house belongs to the owner of the huge finca, Don Bosco, which stretches from the shore inland to Rio Oeste. From either anchorage one can easily dinghy to Rio Oeste, a tree lined river that eventually passes under the wooden bridge connecting the dirt road from the small inland villages to Almirante. Buses pass this way several times a day.

ENSENADA SHEPHERD - PUNTA DE GALLINAZO

The perfectly calm sheltered waters of this bay backed by high dark hills suffer from being almost too deep to anchor. One can find depths between 50 and 60 feet with a good soft holding mud under Punta de Gallinazo, also known on some sources as John Crow Point or Iguana Point. Only a couple of indigenous families make their homes here. This is a convenient anchorage when going to or from Almirante.

ISLA SHEPHERD

The steep wooded hills of Isla Shepherd continue their sharp decline under water although a few spots on a narrow shelf allow anchoring in 40 or so feet on a mud bottom, good holding. A few people of Afro-Antillean descent live and farm on the island. The locals consider Shepherd and Garcia as one cay named Isla Pastores. Roldan Cay is Pastores Pequeño. Originally named Guana Key, the island's name changed in the 1880's when three brothers, Samuel, Julián and Pedro Shepherd from San Andrés colonized the island with their slaves. These three men produced a great quantity of children with the slaves and with the indigenous women, so many that they opened a school and a drug store for them. Benji Richard, an English speaking outboard motor repairman, lives on Cayo Garcia where it almost joins Shepherd Island in a house perched partly on firm land and partly on stilts driven into the shallow water - a typical arrangement for the area. Señor Richard's shop sits beside a large mango orchard. At the south end of Cayo Garcia a cement dock juts out and one can drop an anchor near it in about 40 feet, mud bottom. The cement dock leads to a tiny cemetery surrounded by dense vegetation. The English names on the majority of gravestones reflect the influx of the first European settlers to the area - most of them Scots or Englishmen driven away from San Andrés and Isla Providencia, west Caribbean islands claimed by Colombia.

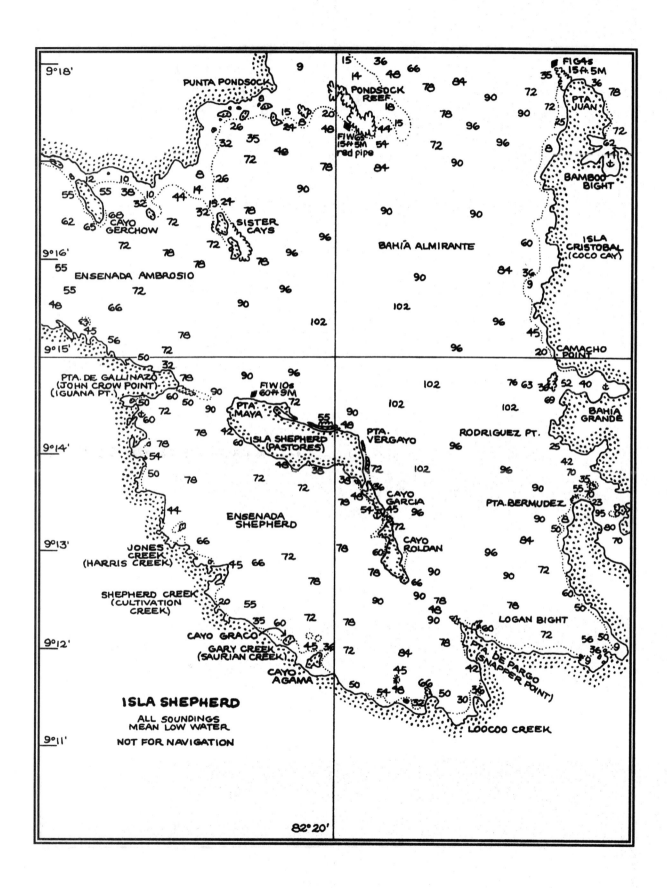

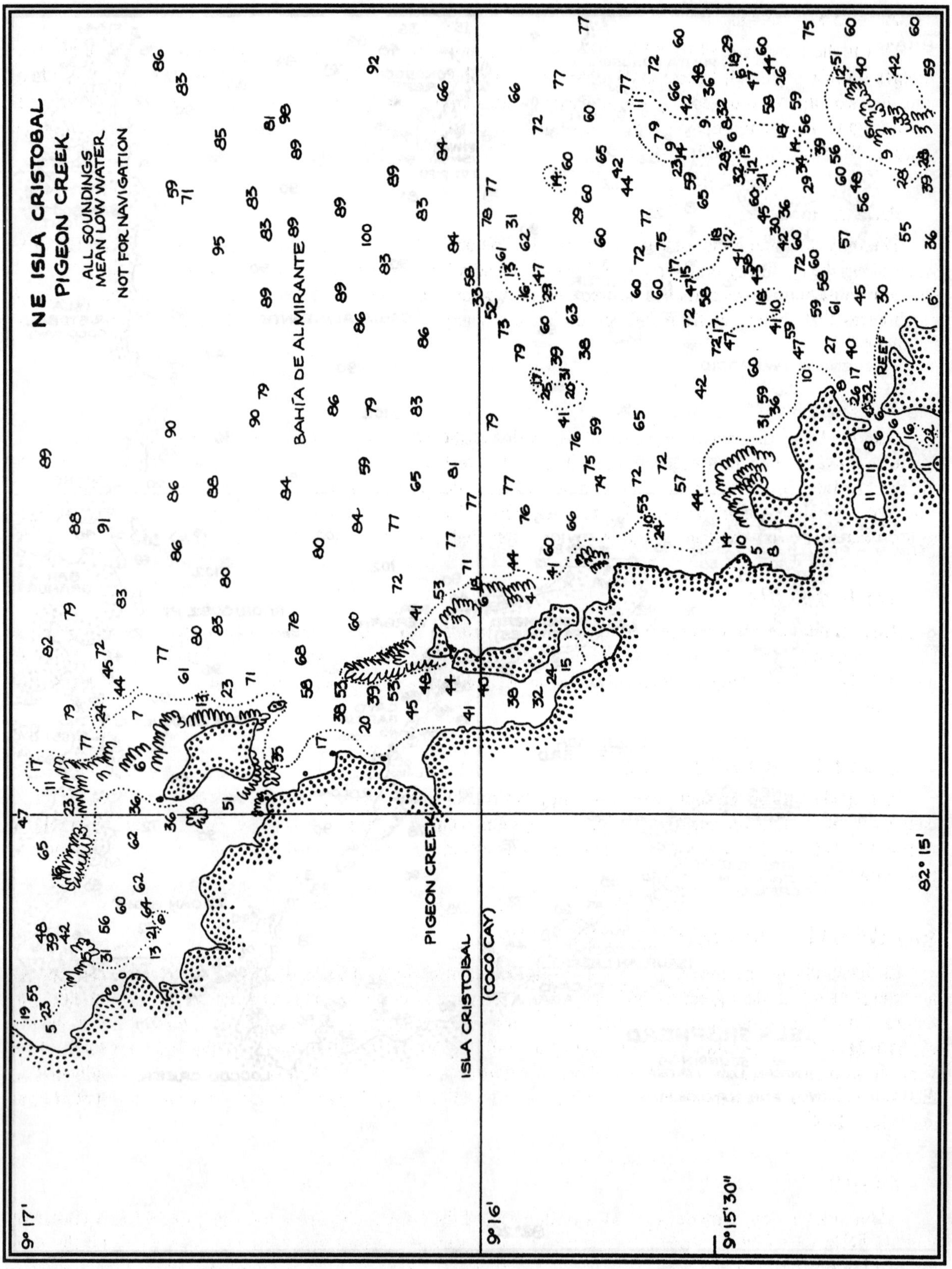

NE ISLA CRISTOBAL PIGEON CREEK

ALL SOUNDINGS
MEAN LOW WATER
NOT FOR NAVIGATION

BAHÍA DE ALMIRANTE

PIGEON CREEK

ISLA CRISTOBAL
(COCO CAY)

ISLA CRISTOBAL

This is the most farmed island in the area with many hectares devoted to cattle ranching. There are four villages on Isla Cristobal; Puerto Escondido, San Cristobal, Bahía Grande and Boca Torritos. Off its southern sides lie two large landlocked bays. The eastern one is known locally as Boca Torritos, although many sources call it Laguna Porras and the western bay, locally called Dark Land or Tierra Oscura, is Laguna Palos on some sources. Black people who live in Dark Land know Isla Cristobal as Coco Cay.

PIGEON CREEK

The only anchorage on the east shore of Isla Cristobal, Pigeon Creek, has an easy entrance with the deep water along the small cay on the starboard hand. Avoid a long and easily discernible reef to the south. The low cay with some mangroves and coconut trees which protects the anchorage from the east lets in a good amount of the breezes that spring up from the sea during the sunny afternoons. There are several landings along the mainland.

BAMBOO BIGHT

Bamboo Bight has several branches of which the southeastern has the most space as well as the most breeze. There is good holding in a mud bottom. The small creek in the southeast corner leads to Puerto Escondido village. Leave the dinghy at the long landing and walk the well maintained path to the village where seasonal fruit and vegetables are often available. Friendly people live in the well organized hilly village. There is a path to San Cristobal, a large village on the shores of Porter Bight, the open bay to the east.

BAHÍA GRANDE

This commodious bay on the west shore of Isla Cristobal has a deep entrance south of the long reef growing from Camacho Point. The middle of the bay has good holding in mud although coral shoals extend from all points of land. The village of Bahía Grande has an indigenous population scattered in houses on the east and south shores.

BERMUDEZ POINT CHANNEL

A deep channel on the southwest corner of Isla Cristobal leads into Laguna Palos (Dark Land). The principal dangers to navigation are marked by fifty five gallon drums inverted on mangrove poles as the Almirante to Chiriquí ferries pass this way. A good tienda sits on stilts in a little bight called Bellevue. They sell gasoline and basic goods.

PALOS LAGOON - DARK LAND

In the southwestern corner of Dark Land (also known as Laguna Palos or Tierra Oscura) one can find an anchorage near high dark green wooded hills that echo roaring howler monkeys early in the morning, at dusk and before rain. A lot of bird species live here and a fairly good trail beginning in an old cacao grove leads to the top of the ridge. A few families of mixed Antillean and indigenous ancestry live around the area and some speak very old fashioned English. The entrance channel runs on the south side of three mangrove cays as indicated on the sketch chart and the anchorage in 22 feet has good holding mud. The shallower places have a mixture of sand and bits of coral.

LAGUNA PALOS CUT

Almirante-Chiriquí Grande ferry boats routinely use the narrow cut which joins the northeastern corner of Laguna Palos with Laguna Porras, locally known as Bocatoritos. This waterway has deep water all the way through but one has to avoid going too close to the shore of Isla Cristobal in Laguna Palos where there are three shoals. A rusty buoy at the Laguna Porras end serves to mark the location of the channel for the vessel approaching from the east. Tienda Abramares sitting on stilts half way through the channel sells gasoline and other basics.

BOCA TORRITOS

One can anchor in several places along the northern shore of Laguna Porras and the village of Boca Torritos is only one of them. There is a good anchorage in 21 feet, mud bottom off a little hook of mangrove peninsula shaped like a miniature Italy. The tienda here has very few items and only warm sodas but the people are extremely friendly and ready to chat. This area must have been occupied by people of European descent in the long forgotten past as the cemetery here is a treasure-trove of old clay beer bottles.

A little bit further eastward one can anchor off or among an archipelago of mangrove islands and islets. The reefs on the east side of the area can be easily reached by dinghy and are quite spectacular.

CANAL BOCA TORRITO

A deep water channel, Canal Boca Torrito makes a good connection with the rest of Bahía Almirante. Ferry boats use this route routinely which explains the existence of a rusty buoy at the southeastern end of the canal. See the Canal Boca Torrito sketch chart for details.

SHARK HOLE LAGOON

Immediately south of the eastern end of Canal Boca Torrito lies another mangrove archipelago with an excellent anchorage in its western portion. Good dinghy exploring opportunities here wind through a maze of mangrove islets and narrow channels. The shallow pass in the northwestern part of Shark Hole Lagoon serves as a short cut for cayucos traveling between Bahía Almirante and Boca Torrito. See the Canal Boca Torrito sketch chart for details. The village of Shark Hole is located south of Ginoves Point, about a 30 minute dinghy ride.

The morning sun will vanish as afternoon clouds build up over Laguna Almirante and Darkland Bay.

RIO CHAGRES TO BOCA DEL DRAGO 195

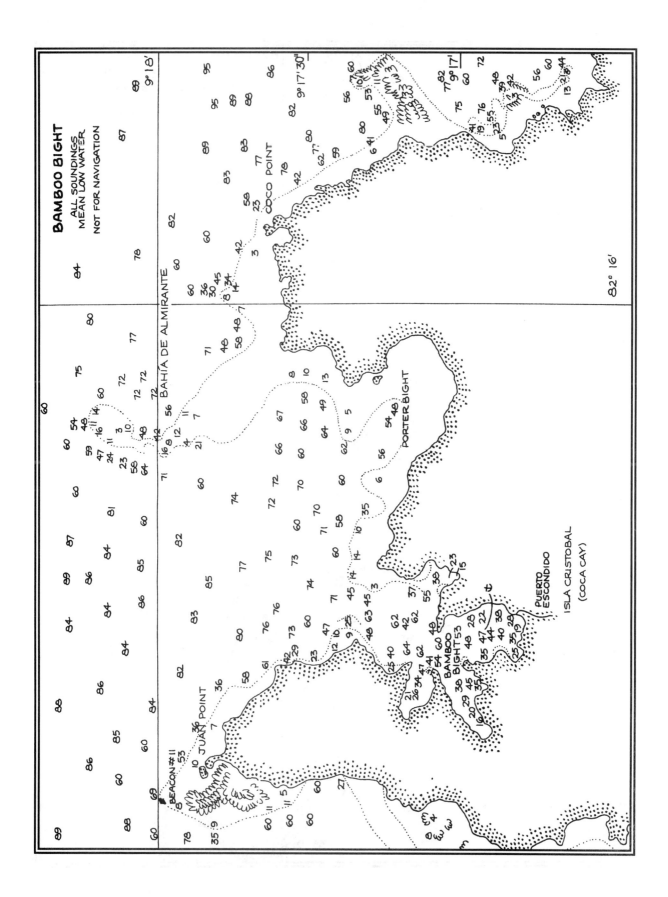

196 THE PANAMA GUIDE

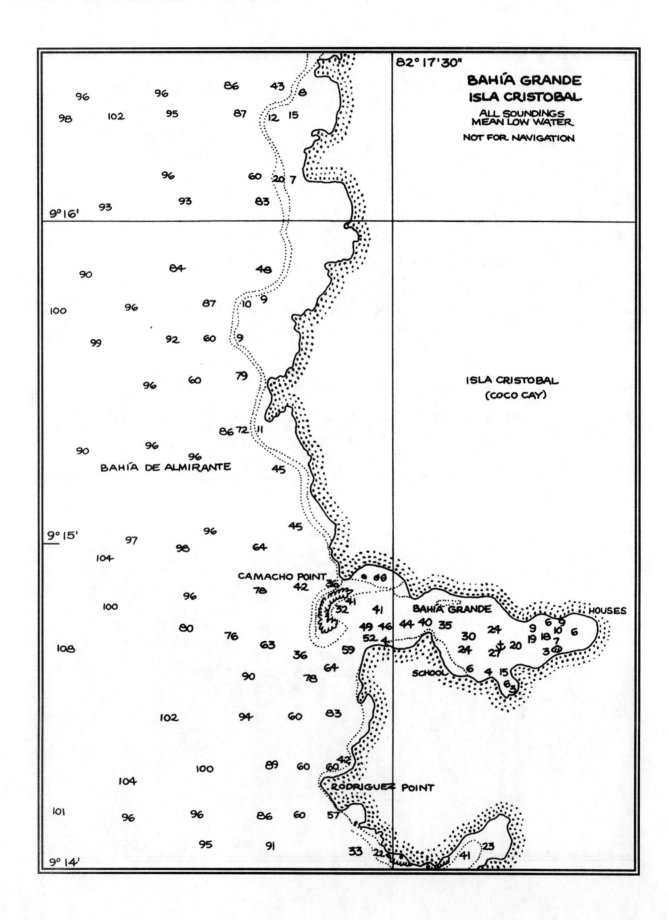

RIO CHAGRES TO BOCA DEL DRAGO 197

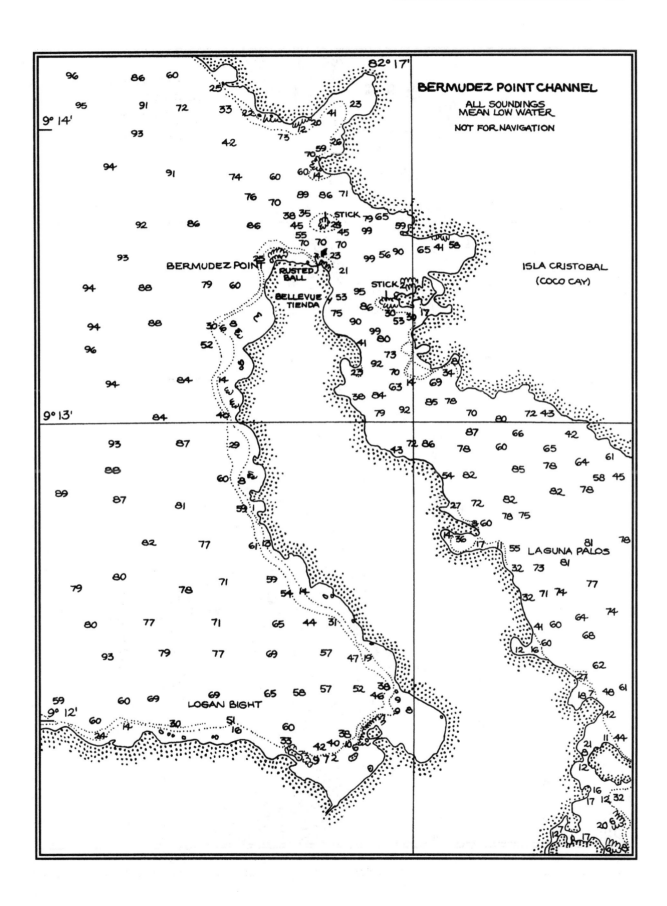

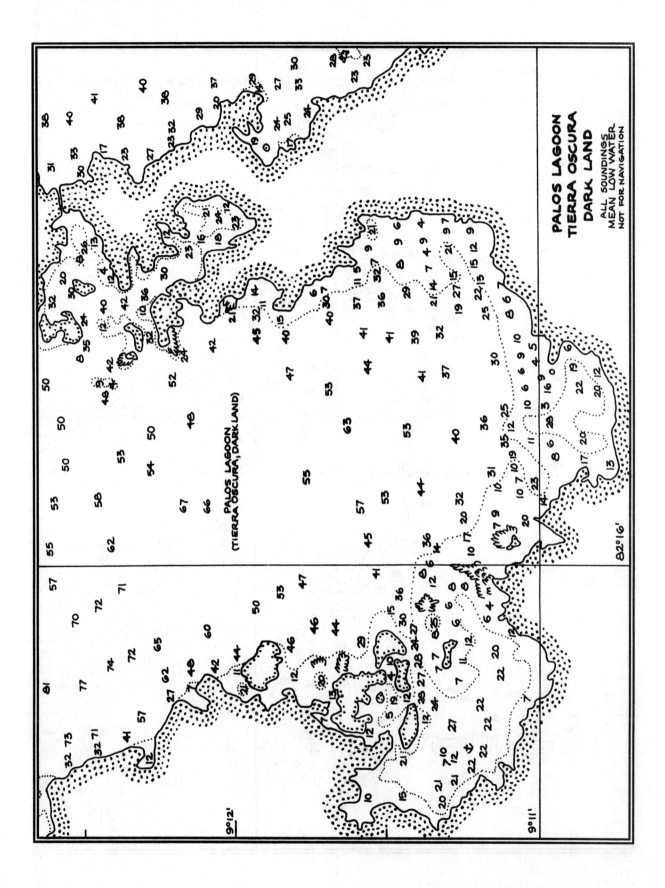

Rio Chagres to Boca Del Drago

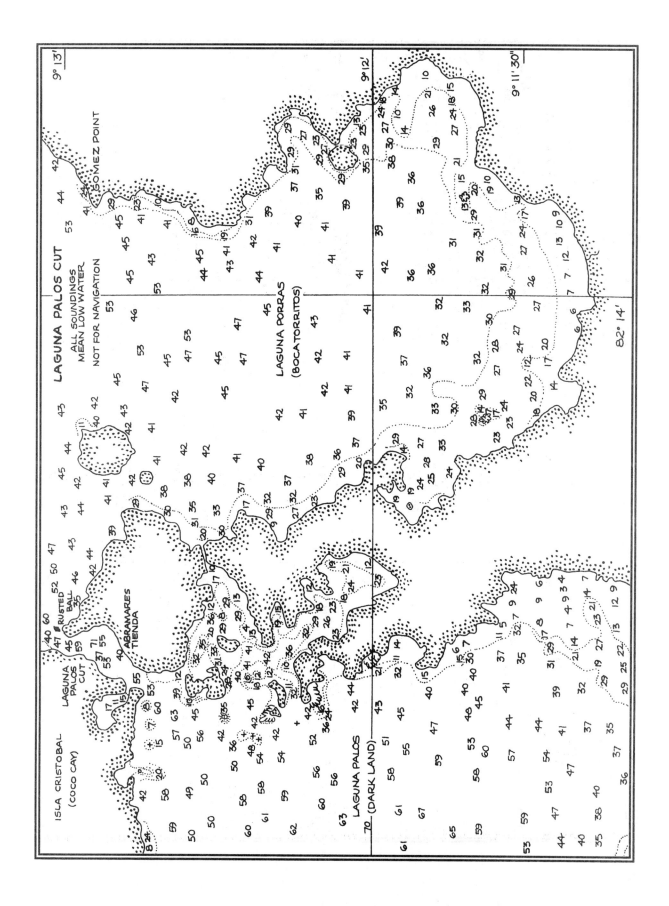

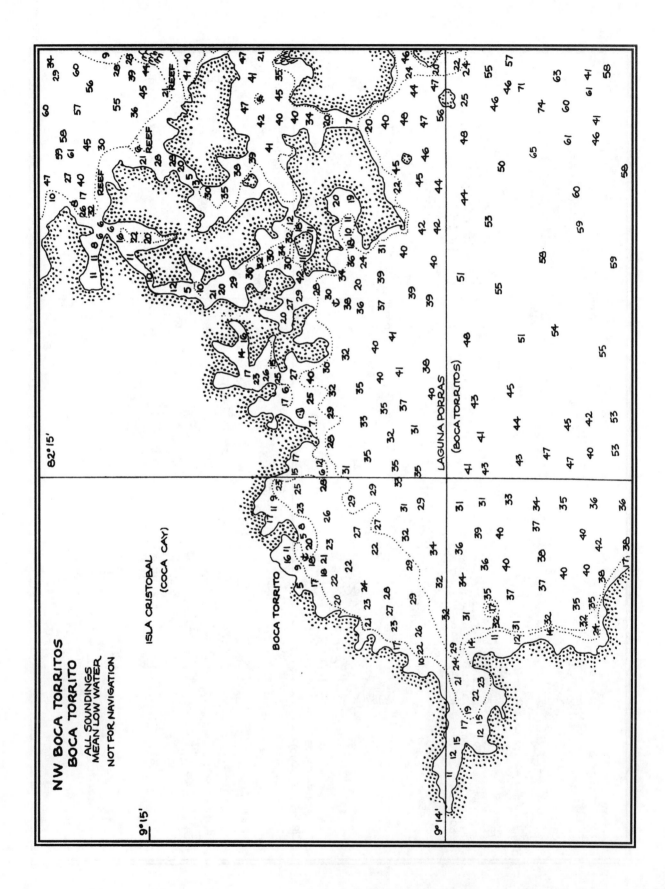

RIO CHAGRES TO BOCA DEL DRAGO 201

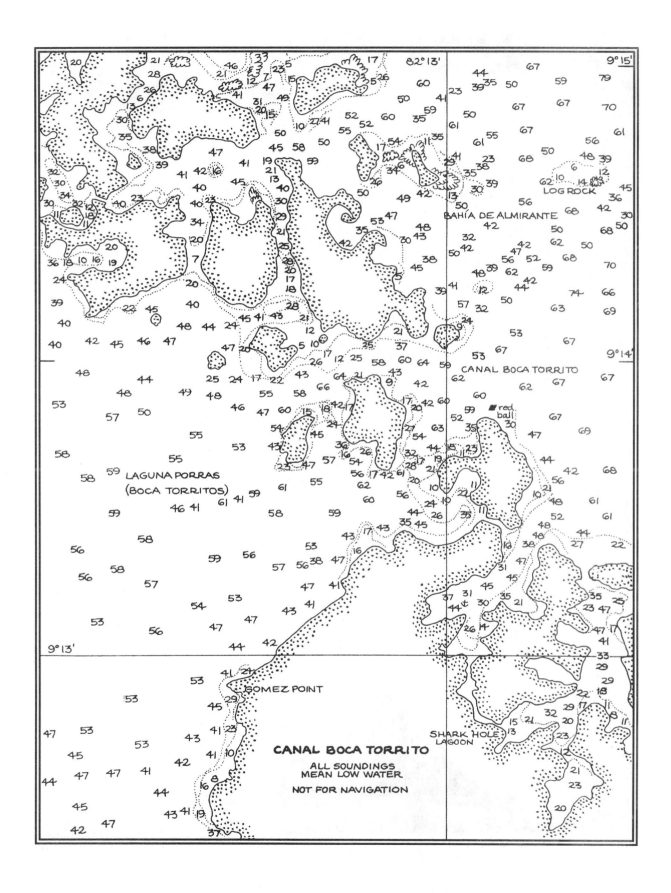

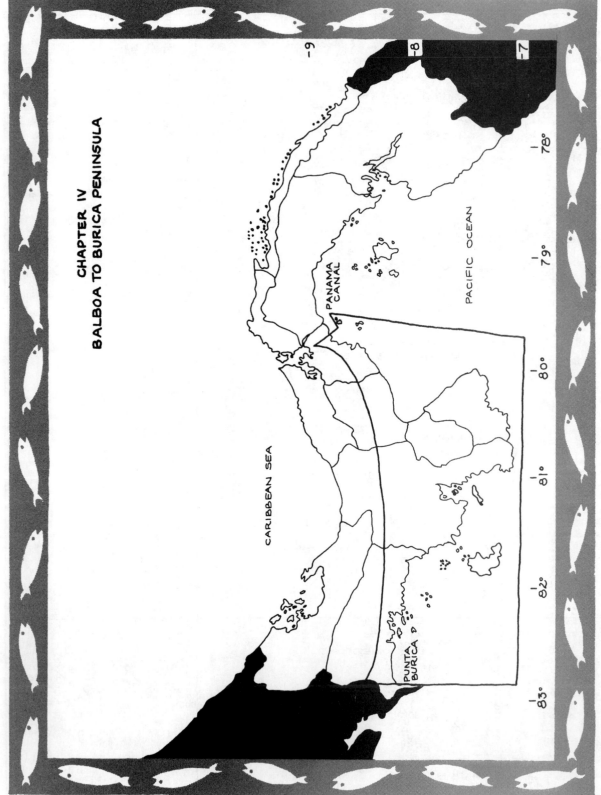

CHAPTER IV
BALBOA TO BURICA PENINSULA

CHAPTER IV

BALBOA TO PUNTA BURICA

The distances between major landmarks along this route are small, 90 miles from Balboa to Punta Mala, 60 miles from Punta Mala to Punta Mariato and 135 miles from Punta Mariato to Punta Burica or Puerto Armuelles. Yet the route runs through areas with distinct characteristics of winds, currents and tides. An interesting cruise along this coast would combine the often rolly island anchorages with some tranquil river visits. Generally moderate weather, much kinder than that encountered on the Atlantic coast, prevails and in the distant past must have helped the first migration of people move south from the Bering Strait along this Pacific coast.

WINDS

In a narrow belt paralleling the western shores of the Gulf of Panama northerly winds prevail all year. In some locations during the dry season of December, January and February these winds can often reach 20 to 25 knots. The rest of the year the northerlies occur with less strength and duration until September, only to reappear with strength in November. The frequency of these north winds drops significantly at the height of the rainy season in July and August.

West of Punta Mala and especially west of Morro de Puercos a vessel will encounter variables and onshore and offshore breezes closer to shore. Between Punta Mariato and Punta Burica variable winds in direction and strength occur in all months except for strong northerlies during January and February.

CURRENTS

Significant ocean currents enter the Gulf of Panama along the eastern shores, parallel the Darién coast and follow the sweep of the Bay of Panama towards the west. This oceanic current gathers speed on the way south along the western coast of the Gulf. The southern flow is augmented by the ebbing tide and strong northerly winds in the upper Gulf. Near Punta Mala northbound yachts often report a 3 knot current screaming south.

When heading north a yacht should time the rounding of Punta Mala on the rising tide which slows down the southerly flow. During daylight hours a yacht can stay very close to the shore of Punta Mala keeping in 18 to 25 feet of water (low tide depths) to avoid the strong current further offshore. If a fresh northerly blows out of the Gulf a northbound yacht should follow the western coast until the land along the north shore of Bahia Parita smoothes out the sea and the course can be altered directly for the islands, such as Otoque or Taboga. In the case of a very strong northerly with bad seas a sailing vessel should go on the port tack and try to work her way towards Las Perlas where relatively smooth waters await. In the middle of the Gulf the southerly current diminishes and further eastward near the shores of Darién a vessel will encounter current moving north.

TIDES

The northernmost part of the Gulf of Panama has the most extreme tidal ranges, sometimes reaching 21 feet. Further south, at Punta Mala, the tide at high water rises about five feet less than at Balboa. To the west, at Cébaco Island, you must multiply the Balboa high tide value by 0.7 to find the local high tide rise. The correction for low water is 0.6. For example, a 14.5 foot HW in Balboa will only rise 10 feet at Cébaco and the Balboa 2.1 foot LW will be 1.2 feet at Cébaco. The same correcting factors, 0.7 HW and 0.6 LW, apply in Bahia Honda. Around Isla Parida and Puerto Armuelles the correction ratios are 0.6 for HW and 0.5 for LW. The time corrections are negligible as they never exceed 10 minutes. See the Tide section in Chapter Five for a simplified method of finding levels of tide between HW and LW.

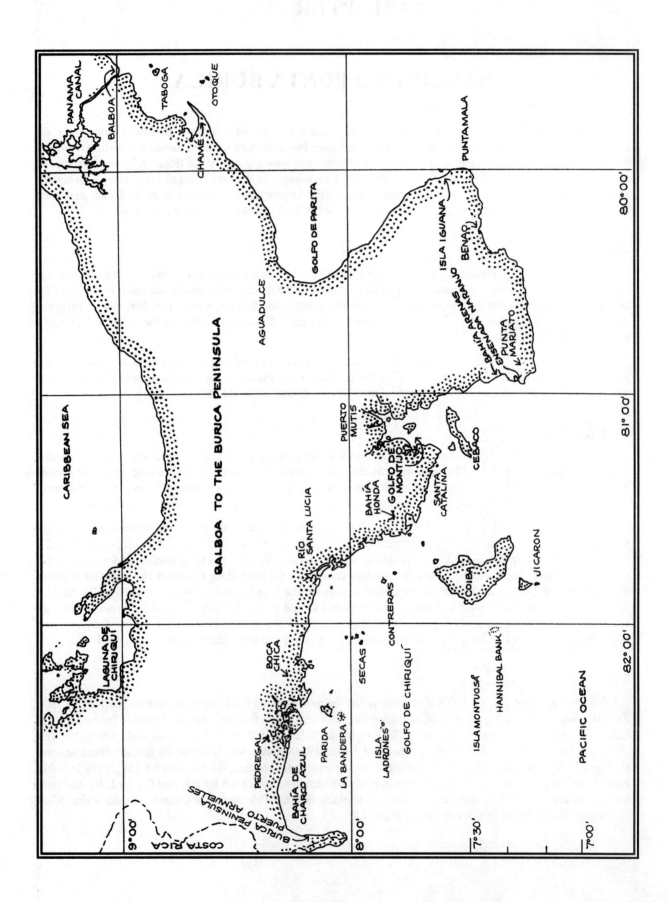

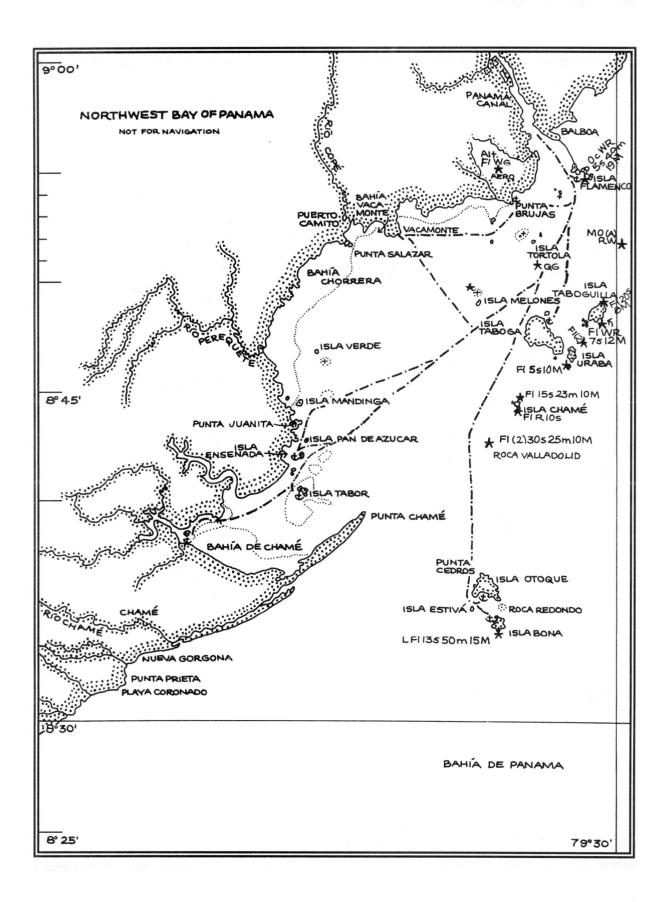

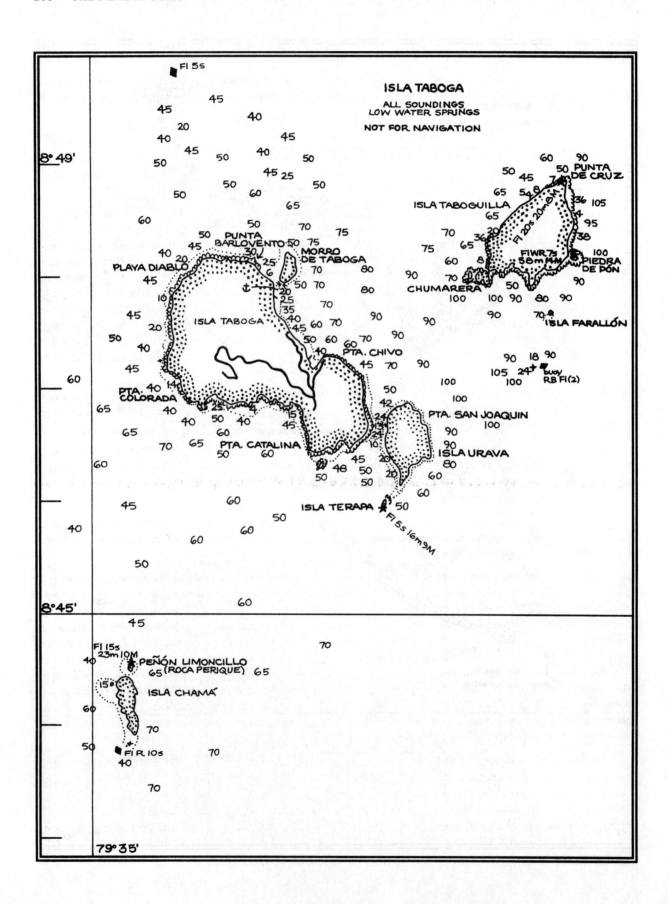

AIDS TO NAVIGATION

Many of the lights marked on navigation charts do not exist any more while others that are working have not been indicated at all. Refer to the list of lights in this guide. For a list of available charts for this chapter see the Chart section.

ANCHORAGES AND HARBORS IN THE GULF OF PANAMA

TABOGA

Located 8 miles south from Balboa Yacht Club Taboga, the Island of Flowers, has long served yachts as a popular stop. The least rolly anchorage, on the south side of Morro de Taboga and to the east of the ferry dock, suffers from overcrowding on weekends when yachts from Panama arrive to pick up their moorings. Transient yachts must then anchor outside the line of moorings in 50 to 60 feet of water. Do not come closer to the ferry floating dock than the bearing of 345°T on a white pole on the ruins of a stone wall on the west end of Morro de Taboga because further west the wreck of a small sailboat lies on its side in about 21 feet. Also keep your yacht anchored north of 240°T bearing on the ferry dock to allow the ferry a clear approach. If crowded out from there you will have to anchor further south, off the town beach and also in deep water since local boat moorings occupy the shallower areas. On weekdays visiting yachts may pick up the moorings off Morro de Taboga, but remember there may be only the weight of a small engine block at the other end of the mooring rope you cleat on the bow of your yacht.

In the cove at the south end of Taboga harbor lies the wreck of a large ferrocement sailboat. Sometimes yachts that have to dry out for bottom maintenance lean against the high side of the wreck. Survey the area beforehand as pieces of small wreckage are strewn off its stern.

Occasionally yachts anchor north of the sandbar connecting Morro de Taboga with Taboga. The sandy bottom rises gradually and there is 6 feet of water at low tide about two hundred feet from the sandbar. It is a good anchorage during the rare storm that arrives from the south. Otherwise, treat it as a day stop since the northerly winds raise a good size chop here.

Morro de Taboga itself was once the headquarters of the Pacific Steamship Navigation Company whose twelve vessels ran to Valparaiso, Chile in the 1840's. The coal pier ruins and pieces of machinery on the south side of Morro de Taboga are all that remains.

In the pretty, flowery town ashore a yachtsman will find phones with connections to overseas operators, a couple of tiendas with basics, a bakery (near the church), a post office and a few restaurants. Gasoline may be obtained in a pinch by inquiring at the boat ramp next to Hotel Chu. Ask for water at the INRENARE station beside the pier. If you follow the main town drag to the south where it changes into a dirt road and go right at the fork further on, you will start walking upwards towards the highest point on the island (1010 feet). Along the way look for lime green striped black frogs and giant hairy spiders crossing the road. From the hill top and an old US military search light facility you will have good views of the pelican colony on the west side of Taboga, the islands of the northern Bay of Panama and the mainland. On the other hand, if you take a sharp left at the fork you will end up walking down along a fence towards the water and the cove with the ferrocement wreck. Soon after the sharp turn, though, on your right you may spot a rough path going up into the hills - it leads to the white cross that overlooks the harbor, another scenic stop.

Following the traditions of Francisco Pizarro and Diego de Almongo, who plotted the subjugation and pillaging of Peru from Taboga, many pirates planned their devious deeds here. However, when the inhabitants of Panama City expected a siege by land they would flee to Taboga with their most prized possessions. By the 1880's life on Taboga had calmed down enough for the French, who were making a canal building attempt, to choose it for the site of a sanatorium for malaria and yellow fever stricken workers. The French Impressionist, Paul Gauguin, recovered on Taboga from illnesses he contracted while working as a laborer on the canal. (He worked on Culebra Cut and was paid $150 a month.)

Declared a wildlife refuge, today Taboga might be called the island of hummingbirds as well as flowers, bird life on the island is prolific. A large part of Taboga's western coast has been set aside as a brown pelican reserve.

On July 16th, the day of the Virgen del Carmen, an image of the Virgin Mary is transported by sea around the island followed by processions of local and visiting vessels.

ISLA OTOQUE

Otoque is a striking island, high and verdant with farming plots scattered about under coconut palms. Otoque Oriental, the village on the east shore, has a busy fishing fleet of open boats but numerous dangerous rocks make it impossible to anchor a deeper boat there. Outside the rock line you will find 50 feet. The erratic behavior of the depth sounder suggests the bottom may be foul with rocks. Otoque Occidental on the west shore has a harbor very well protected from the south. The village pier dries at low water but you will find 15 to 20 feet fairly close to it. Unfortunately, this nice place gets very choppy in the usual afternoon northerly.

Ensenada de Pata, the bay on the south shore has excellent protection from the north but landing on the beach gets rough when swell from the south is present. There are patches of rocks on the sand bottom, check that the anchor is holding.

ISLA BONA

This uninhabited island belongs now to birds like boobies, ospreys and cormorants. Some abandoned equipment on Punta del Morro indicates exploitation in the past. The anchorage in Ensenada del Corral is generally free from southerly swell.

BAHIA CHAMÉ, ISLA ENSENADA AND ISLA TABOR

Just 20 miles southwest from Balboa, Bahia Chamé offers anchorages under the hilly mainland in an area of islets and sand banks inhabited by more birds than humans. The only town, La Punta on Punta Chamé peninsula, is a popular vacation retreat for Panamanians. The access by boat is easy yet the anchorage off the town is extremely choppy most of the year because of the full exposure to the north. However, a smooth anchorage off the southwest side of Isla Tabor can be approached from Punta Chamé by utilizing a rising tide to get over some very shallow spots. The deep channel can be seen between the drying banks only during spring low tides. At that time use the very beginning of the rising tide to get through.

The usual approach into the area is possible for moderate draft yachts at all times except extreme spring low tides. The course leads from Balboa towards Taboga, passes close to and south of the buoys marking Commissioner's Rock, then south of Isla Melones. From Isla Melones a course of 250°T for Isla Pan de Azucar, a conical island usually visible from far away, will bring the yacht close to the passage across the shoals and then to the deeper water inside. If you have a GPS it should read 08°43'N and 079°42.6W when close to the shallow bar. Continue for the gap between Pan de Azucar and Isla Ensenada on a heading of 250°T. You will cross an area which has only 5 feet at spring low tides but depths begin to increase close to Isla Ensenada. Next you can pass between Isla Ensenada and Pan de Azucar in 12 to 14 feet and turn south to anchor off the west shore of Isla Ensenada when the north point of this island bears about 025°T. You can climb the steep Ensenada hills for an overall view of Bahia Chamé and pick up old indigenous pottery pieces which lie scattered on the saddle of the ridge between the two higher points.

From the anchorage off Isla Ensenada a vessel may continue as far as Rio Sajalices. If you want to go specifically to Isla Tabor instead of passing between Isla Ensenada and Isla Pan de Azucar keep close to the eastern shores of Isla Ensenada and Isla Sapé on a southwesterly heading until you can turn southeast and drop the hook off Isla Tabor. Close to Tabor's southwestern shores the silty soft mud can be a foot and half deep on top of a good holding bottom so dig your anchor in well. During the dry season the place becomes a wind tunnel with 20 to 25 knots blasting from the northerly semicircle. Fortunately, the water stays smooth. Keep a good light on at night as motorized sand barges from Panama City pass through here often in the dark and then stop to suck up sand on the banks southeast of Isla Tabor. The barge owners have set up markers on the shoals to the east of Isla Ensenada but they often drift from position and are unreliable.

Isla Tabor is all beaches with some low bushes and scattered trees. At the east end of the island, sea birds and shore birds set up a raucous rookery during April, May and June. Across the deep channel to the south, a vast area of sand banks bares at each low tide and becomes really extensive during spring tides. The firm sand there makes for good walking while the tide is out.

Anchorage between mainland and Isla Ensenada, Bahia de Chamé.

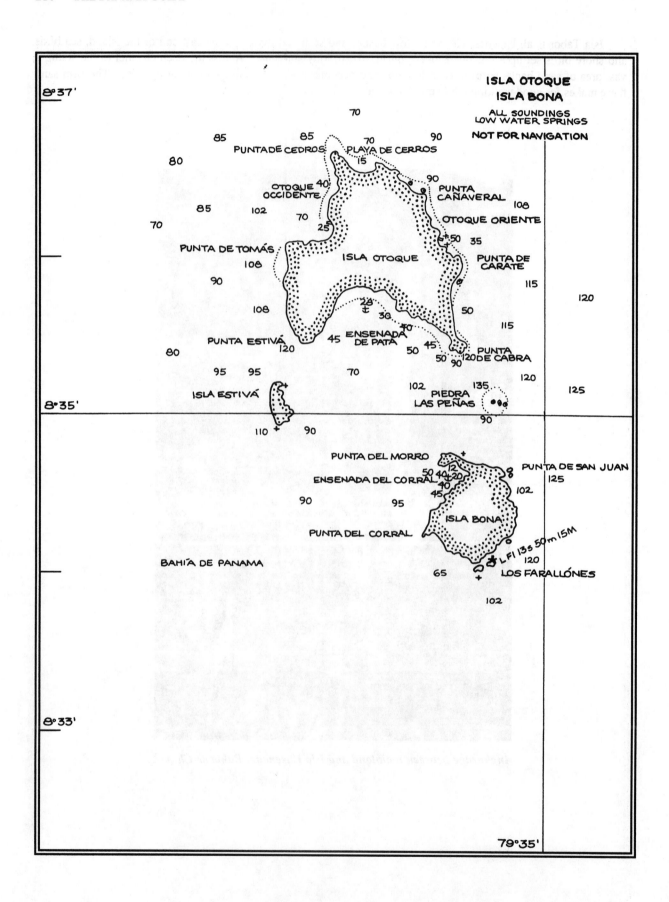

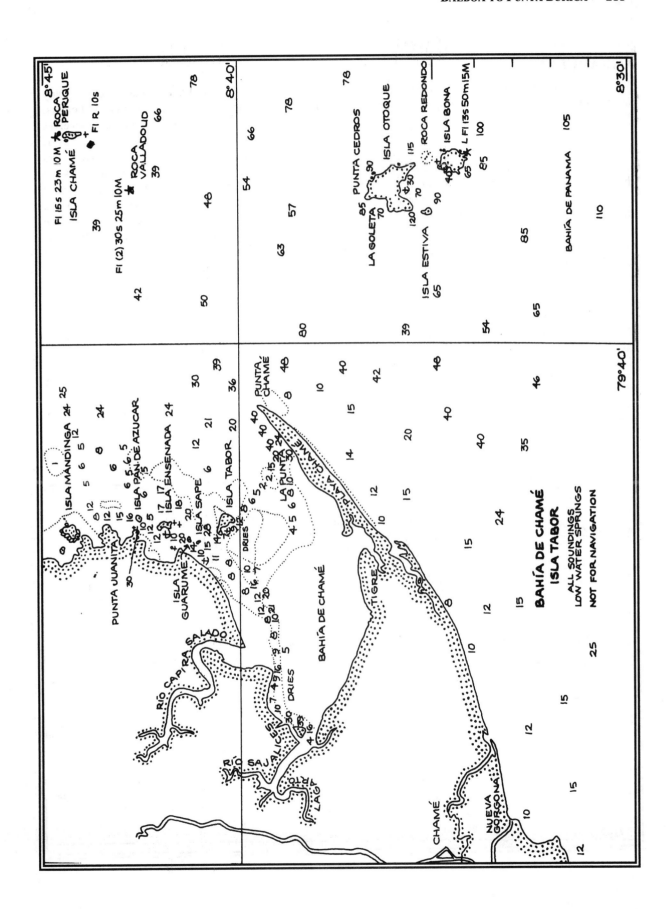

AGUADULCE

The 55 mile stretch of coastline of sandy beaches between Punta Chamé and Bahia Parita does not offer any real harbors but only anchorages in open roadsteads off weekend resort beaches like Playa Coronado and others. They should be discounted when a heavy swell from the south appears. The north shore in Bahia Parita receives a lot less swell and here a passage making yacht can anchor a couple of miles offshore to get a rest. However, only Estero Pablo Blanco with its buoyed channel leading into the river, and its port of Aguadulce offers opportunities to find a completely sheltered anchorage. From further offshore the buoys appear to mark several channels but after locating the first pair things fall into place neatly. A large white buoy equipped with a radar reflector and a light flashing every 3 seconds marks the roadstead off Aguadulce and the entrance to the marked channel. You will need a few feet of rising tide over low water as the channel passes over patches that will have only 3 to 4 feet at spring tides. After negotiating the estuary we sailed up this fairly narrow river which has numbered markers at several points on the shores until we finally came upon a concrete dock with a 250 foot freighter drawing 15 feet which was loading scrap iron. After the dock the river narrows considerably and we found an anchorage at the next river curve in about 10 feet at spring low tides.

The port may have only one small pier but its offices, run by some formidably efficient ladies, treated our yacht with attentions due to a larger commercial ship. Despite our cruising permit which relieves yachts of having to obtain clearances between ports in Panama, we had to get a "zarpe" for the next destination, get a Customs clearance and the blessing of the Ministry of Agriculture, all at under US$20.

About a 45 minute walk or 5 minute taxi ride down a decent road will get one to Aguadulce, a nice medium size town centered around agricultural enterprises, plastics production, fertilizer factories and salt making. Several modern stores line the main streets, including well supplied supermarkets, hardware stores and clothes stores.

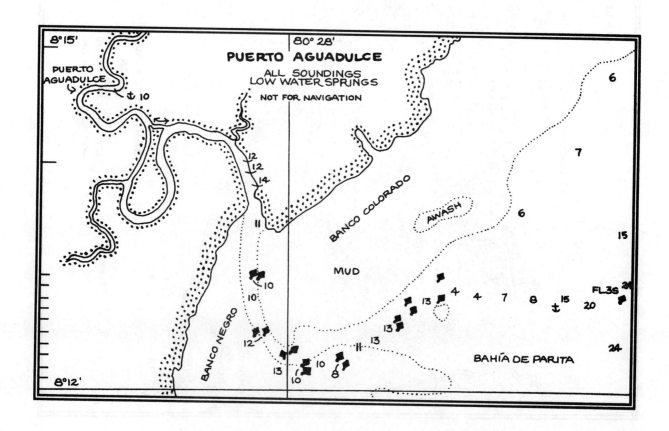

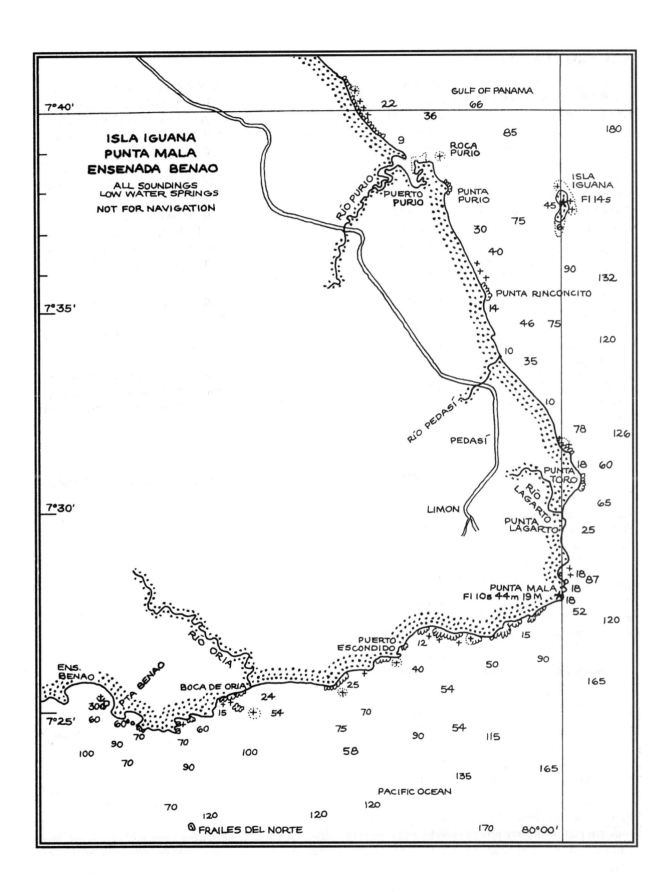

AZUERO PENINSULA

BAHIA PARITA TO PUNTA MALA

Along this 50 mile long stretch of the coast only Isla Iguana, distant 43 miles from the Aguadulce sea buoy, occasionally serves yachts as a stop over. However, in our experience the anchorage off Isla Iguana is only seldom feasible. A yacht has to anchor in water deeper than 50 feet as the shallower depths closer to shore are strewn with rocks, boulders and coral in which an anchor can easily foul for good. This deeper position brings the vessel outside any protection afforded by the island unless one is lucky to encounter very mild conditions or moderate winds from the easterly semicircle. We planned to anchor there twice and were foiled by strong northerly winds and waves. However, we have spoken to yachts which did find good enough conditions to spend a pleasant time off Isla Iguana.

A southbound yacht will have a swift passage around Punta Mala since a strong current usually flows south in its vicinity. A northbound yacht should follow tactics suggested in the currents section at the beginning of this chapter.

ENSENADA BENAO

Wave surfing aficionados go to Ensenada Benao to sample its famous rollers which seems poor recommendation for a yacht anchorage. However, most of the time the anchorage in the northeast corner of the bay just north of the islet is reasonably comfortable and holding is excellent in 11 feet (springs, extreme low water). The bottom is mud mixed with sand. The only dinghy landing is in the east corner of the bay. The mooring buoys north of the islet belong to a marine laboratory located in the bay around the corner to the southeast. Ashore, there are a couple of farms and further to the west are cabins and a restaurant which cater to the surfing crowd and welcome other visitors as well. A road connects Ensenada Benao to the rest of Panama.

PUNTA GUANICO

Should an exceptionally high southerly swell make the anchorage in Ensenada Benao untenable, Punta Guanico, only 10 miles further to the southwest offers a sheltered anchorage. A yacht will find the smoothest water in the southern part of Ensenada Bucaro where in depths between 11 and 20 feet the holding is excellent in mud mixed with sand.

A short walk along the beach will take you to the village of Bucaro where one can get some basic supplies, fresh fish, water, gasoline and ice. A road from there joins the network of main roads in the interior of the country. A fleet of open fishing boats operates from here and they dry out at the mouth of Rio Tonosí. The anchorage off the village, although it has 8 to 12 feet, is subject to breaking rollers if any swell from the south is running outside. The anchorage off Punta Guanico becomes very choppy in strong northeasterly winds.

PUNTA GUANICO TO PUNTA MARIATO

The 40 mile stretch between Punta Guanico and Punta Mariato to the west lacks harbors. The coastline of mostly high cliff shores backed by high mountains has only a few slight indentations which could possibly serve as roadsteads in the absence of ocean swells and that means very rarely. However, better anchorages are available around the corner north of Punta Naranjas.

ENSENADA NARANJO

An almost swell free anchorage inside this bay northeast of Islote Roncador and at 07°16.4N and 080°55.5W by GPS has excellent holding in firm fine sand in 18 feet of water at low tides. Two sandy beaches at the southern part of the bay provide good dinghy landings. Hills backing the anchorage have all been turned into pasture land and cows come down to the trees on the beaches to seek shade. Two households stand behind the beach in the middle.

BAHIA ARENAS

Located 3 miles north from Naranjo, Bahia Arenas has good protection from a southerly swell but would become wind swept in the season of the strong northerlies, late December, January and February. Holding is very good in fine sand mixed with mud but do not approach too closely to the shores as many rocky outcroppings disappear as the tide rises. Only at low water should one attempt to get nearer to shore. Ashore a little stream runs down from the hills by a small abandoned concrete house.

Hiding in perfect tranquility in Rio Caté, Bahia Montijo.

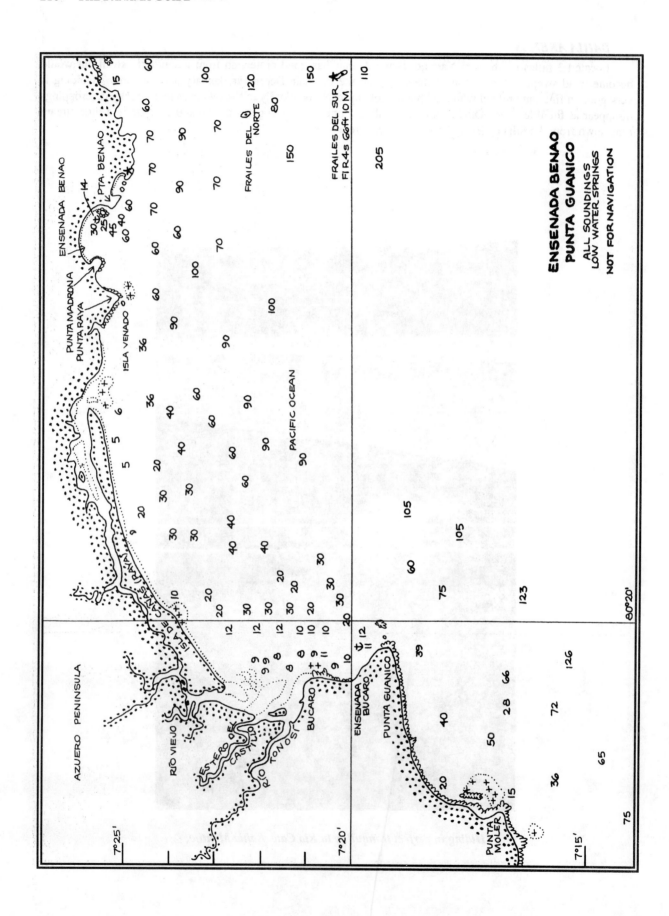

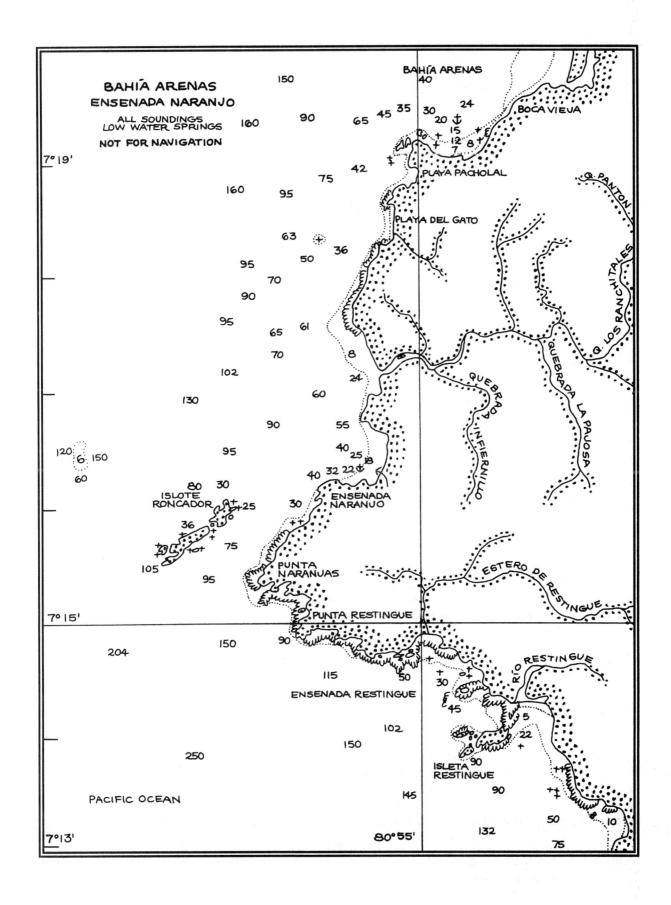

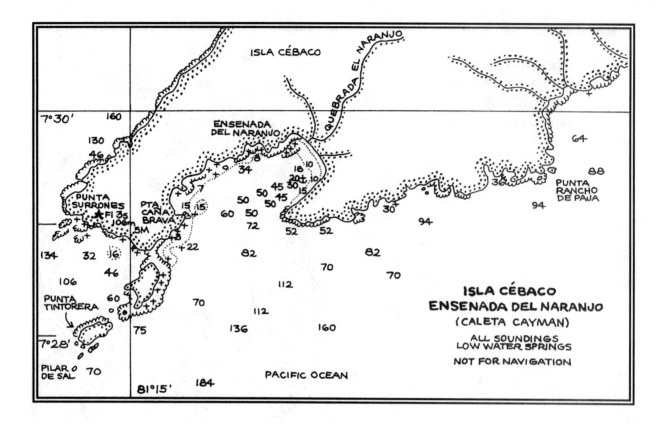

CÉBACO

SOUTH COAST OF CÉBACO

Transient yachts usually stop in Ensenada del Naranjo (Caleta Cayman) at the southwestern corner of the island. Nearly one mile wide at the entrance, Naranjo lays exposed to swells from the south and southwest. The smoothest water lies in the east corner of the bay in about 20 feet of water in soft sand, a good holding bottom. Fresh water runs from the hills in a creek, Quebrada El Naranjo, behind the thatched hut in the middle of the beach. Walking up the shallow stream opens a world of fragrant plants and beautiful flowers to any one willing to make the trip. Local fishermen sometimes stop to rest in this bay at night as do the shrimp trawlers. The islands to the southwest from the bay show beautiful beaches but they have teeth - sharp rocks bare at low tide along most of them.

NORTH COAST OF CÉBACO

The north coast of the island enjoys good protection from the ocean swell normally persistent along the south shores during most of the year. Starting from the west the first anchorage lies off El Jobo, a village on the long beach in the bight west of Punta del Campamento. As in many places along the north Cébaco coast the deep water runs close to the shore but you can find a shallower shelf near El Jobo - just make sure the anchor digs in. The tienda here sells cold sodas, very basic dry goods and gasoline. The generous and welcoming people who live in a very narrow zone between the sea and the hills grow their own food on the fertile land and earn cash by fishing from boats they build on the spot in their settlements. The beaches here are great for walking and one can easily reach the next settlement to the east, Manzanillo on foot. However, a yacht can find there about 20 foot depths with a sandy bottom close to the west of a little point of land dividing Manzanillo in two.

Further eastward lies the village El Roble, then Almacigos which has 18 foot depths with good holding near a little church. People are friendly and the view is great over the coconut palms from the school on the hill above the church. Platanal, the easternmost village on this coast is also the largest and the most organized. The best anchorage is off the school situated on the hill overlooking the long bight. Here, the holding is excellent in sand mixed with shells about 20 feet deep. West from there lie extensive drying mud flats. The eastern part of the bight has the funny name of El Divorcio whose origin no one here could explain. In the village one can buy fresh oranges, mangoes and other fruit in season as well as papaya, plantains, bananas and several kinds of roots. Put your order in and you can collect the stuff the next day at very reasonable prices. According to the local fishermen Platanal is the only tenable anchorage on the north coast when strong winds come from the northeast during late December, January and February. When leaving Divorcio and bound for the open ocean around Punta Campana, avoid the submerged rock located one mile east of the point, which, incidentally, has deep water close in.

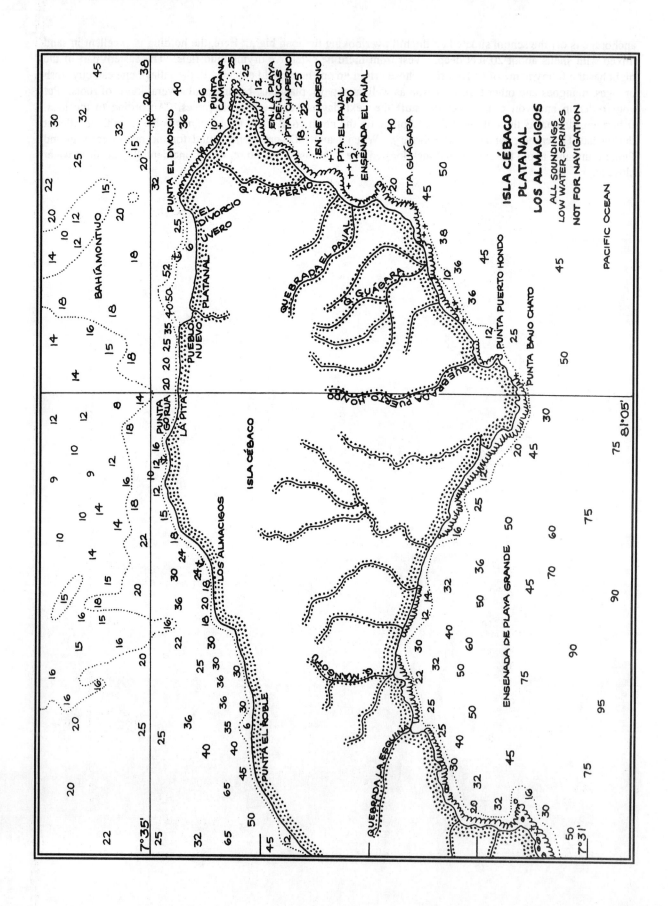

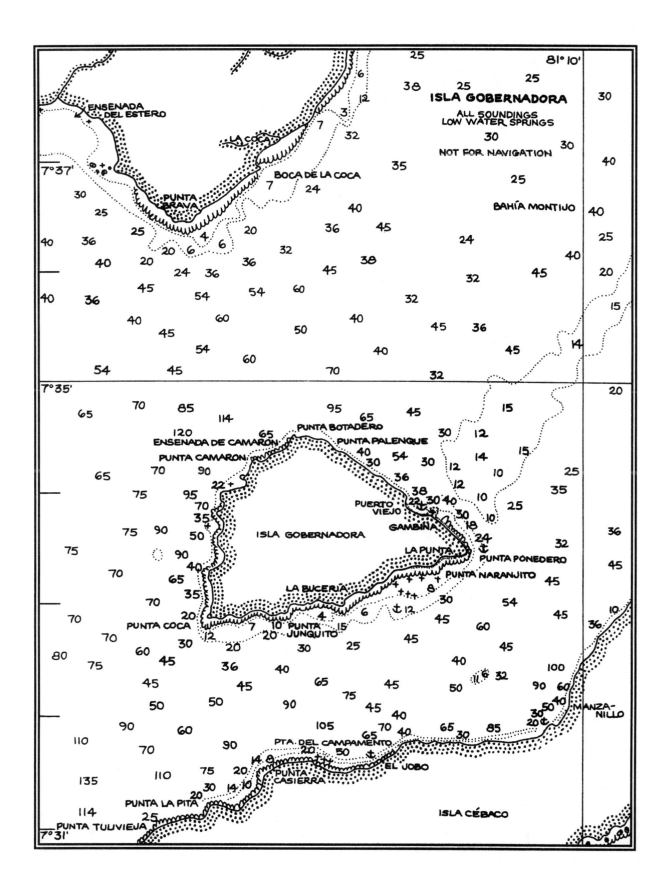

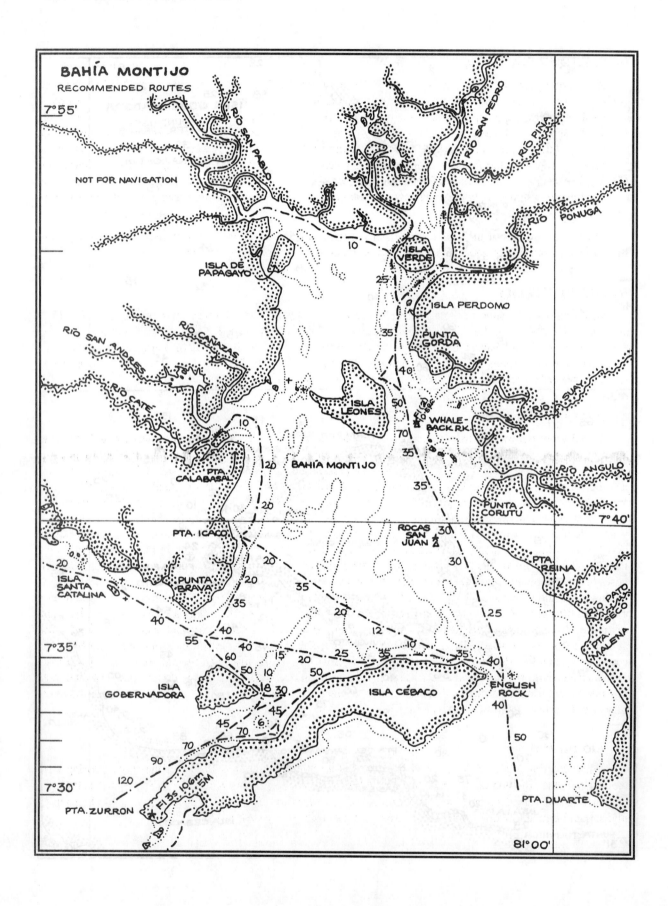

ISLA GOBERNADORA

Isla Gobernadora lies approximately 1½ miles north of Isla Cébaco. Although the 1,163 foot peak on Cébaco towers over all, Isla Gobernadora is no midget as its peak rises to 734 feet. At the bottom of the green and fertile hillsides is a prosperous settlement of active fishermen and part time farmers. They keep their boats on either side of Punta Ponedero. Yachts can anchor comfortably in Puerto Viejo, a cove on the east coast, which has a gooey mud bottom and depths that gradually diminish from about 40 feet offshore to about 20 feet on the line between the points forming this indentation in the coast. During the season of strong northerlies, December, January, February everybody anchors off the south coast of Gobernadora. Be careful not to come too close to the rocky ledges near shore. A white cross mounted on one of the rocks gives some warning at high tide when all dangers are covered.

Most of the houses of the settlement cluster along the southeastern shore. The store here has the best, but still limited, assortment of goods and will sell small quantities of gasoline for outboards.

BAHIA MONTIJO

Counting from the shores of Isla Cébaco, which acts as a gigantic natural breakwater, Bahia Montijo cuts 15 miles inland and even further if you throw in several miles of the shallow, but navigable on the tide, Rio San Pedro. The bay is the estuary of the major water courses draining the highlands of Veraguas province. The mangrove tree lined rivers are navigable and can substitute for heaven for somebody who likes remote places, solitude and birds. Needless to say fishing here can be very rewarding, too.

PUERTO MUTIS

The channel northwards from the east end of Isla Cébaco has wide and deep water until a couple of miles north of Isla Leones. The two dangerous places, Rocas San Juan and Whale Back Rock are marked by beacons equipped with lights. Note that sometimes the iron pipe of the San Juan beacon is hard to see against the dark land beyond. When northbound make sure to go to the east of Isla Verde and continue along the east shores of Rio San Pedro. Off Rio Piña the channel has a few shallow spots and past Puerto Mutis the depths diminish to 5 feet. Remember that these minimum depths will only occur during extreme spring low tides just a few times a year. The high tide arrives in Puerto Mutis about an hour after times tabulated for Balboa. As the major supply port for the settlements along the coast as far as Bahia Honda, Puerto Mutis has a good road connecting to the Pan-American Highway, the main transportation artery of the country. An hour long ride on one of the regular buses brings people to Santiago de Veraguas, the largest town of the province. The port caters to a large fleet of fishing boats and so ice and all fuels including diesel are available from the pier. The pier might be occupied by a large landing craft, COIBA, which travels often to the island of Coiba. The small bay closest to the pier is full of moored fishing boats so visiting craft have to anchor a little further upstream in shallower water (about 5 feet at extreme low spring tides). Deeper craft may have to anchor about ¼ mile south of Mutis in Rio de Jesus and commute by dinghy. Puerto Mutis has a phone, an outboard motor mechanic and several restaurants specializing in fish and shrimp, but the tiendas here have only the most basic supplies. To get groceries go on the 20 minute bus ride to the town of Montijo. The policemen in the station overlooking the river will ask to see the boat's papers and a cruising permit or a zarpe from a previous port.

RIO DE JESUS

When entering Rio de Jesus from Puerto Mutis make sure to go south of the tip of the shoal growing from the north shore. The end of the shoal has grown bushes and appears as an islet. The river near the entrance is deep with a few very deep holes, but at the bend after the second creek on the north shore a large rocky shoal in mid stream bares at low tide. A deep but narrow channel follows the north bank.

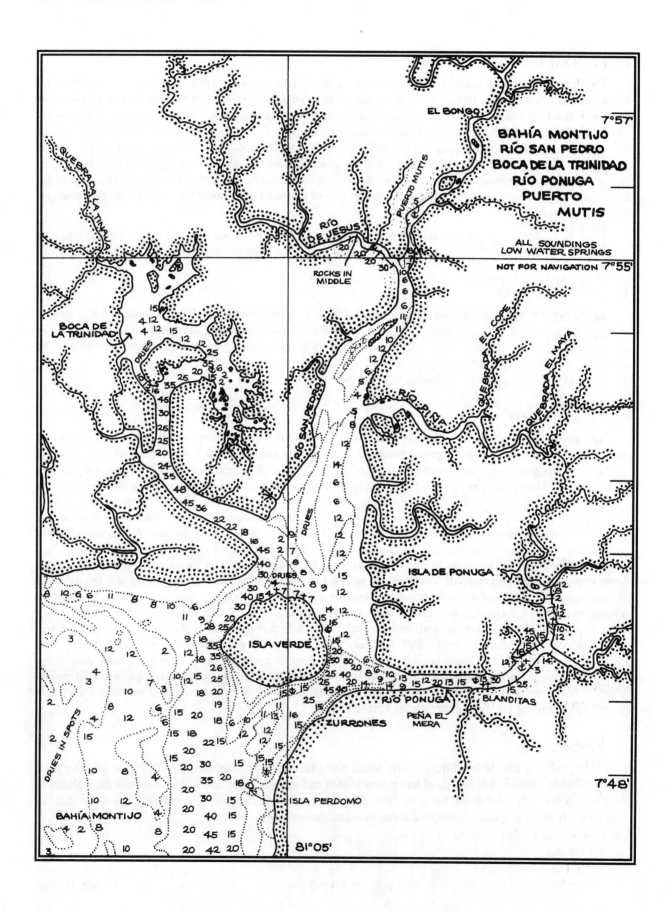

RIO PONUGA

The depths along the south shore vary between 12 and 30 feet until a rocky shoal growing from the south shore just before Blanditas. The channel goes north of the shoal, then the river stays deep until another shoal as the sketch chart indicates. The channel again turns towards the north shore. After the major tributary creek on the east shore the river shoals and the bottom becomes rocky.

Mangrove lined Rio Ponuga has good bird life and from Blanditas, a village of a few thatched and planked houses, a clay road climbs up the hill. From there one can see this hilly country of pasture land mixed with pockets of trees and ribbons of rivers.

ISLA VERDE

No one lives on Isla Verde which, except at the northwest end is mostly composed of mangroves and creeks perfect for good dinghy trips. A yacht can anchor off the northeast shore or the southeast shore in mud. Use an anchor light at night, Puerto Mutis traffic runs around the clock.

BOCA DE LA TRINIDAD

By following the west shore of Isla Verde a yacht can pick up the channel into a deep river which flows into a wide expanse of lagoon called Boca de la Trinidad. A lack of shoals until the bend to the east makes this one of the easiest rivers to navigate. A few households stand on the firm land behind mangrove creeks which drain into the lagoon. The river itself remains quiet in the shade of tall mangrove trees, roseate spoonbills feed along the shore and only flocks of shrieking parrots break the absolute peace here.

RIO SAN PABLO

After clearing the southern tip of the shoal growing southward from Isla Verde one can sail into the unpopulated Rio San Pablo which goes far inland to the town of Soná. Mangrove tree lined, winding and filled with bird song this river has plenty of fish and solitude. Currents seem to run faster here than in the other rivers and many shoals extend from the shores as indicated on the sketch chart. The river is wide enough for maneuvering, but beware of being swept by a fair current onto a bar.

ISLA LEONES

To leave the northern section of Bahia Montijo one must drop south towards Isla Leones and follow its eastern shores. The waters between Rio San Pablo and the rock filled passage west of Isla Leones are full of shifting, ill-defined mud and sand banks used by only shallow draft cayucos.

Isla Leones has a small population of farmers and fishermen whose houses dot the shores from Leones Arriba to La Pluma. You can find gasoline and hard candy in the only tienda which is located on the shore a bit west of Punta Quita Pampanillo. The owner loves meeting foreign travelers. The walk from the anchorage marked on the sketch chart at Leones Arriba to the tienda passes through beautiful thickets of moist forest, and takes about an hour. The tienda does not sell sodas so carry your own water to quench your thirst.

HICACO

To reach Hicaco, an important village on the west shore of Bahia Montijo, a yacht must drop south of Isla Leones and during high tide can go across the bay north of Rocas San Juan. At low water or falling tide one should go well south of Rocas San Juan beacon before heading west.

A set of bad rocks extends from Punta Hicaco eastwards. They are visible near low tide but disappear as the water rises. Even north of these rocks one cannot go too close towards shore as shoals run out far. A deeper channel lies just east of the rocks so when they are visible you can anchor near them when Punta Hicaco bears about 210°T in an area which should have 10 feet at low water springs. Good holding in mud. When arriving after the rocks have disappeared, anchor ½ mile out sounding carefully. High tide occurs in Hicaco at Balboa times, but low water lags about 1 hour. Hicaco has a telephone, a tienda with fresh baked goods and gasoline and diesel sales. Fuels must be transported in your containers down a bluff to your dinghy. If a lot of diesel is needed, a trip to the fuel dock at Puerto Mutis would be worth the extra time. A mechanic near the tienda takes care of the outboard motors used by the large fleet of open cayuco type of fishing boats. A road which connects the village to the rest of Panama continues along the coast to Santa Catalina village.

RIO CATÉ

Rio Caté, to the north of Hicaco, is used by canoes from Los Amarillos, a village up river on the south shore. A good anchorage lies in 12 feet, good holding in mud, off the red cliff on Isla La Muerta. Several kingfishers use holes in the cliff for nest sites. One can reach the main road by taking the dinghy to Amarillos or to a landing in the westernmost corner of a mangrove islet filled bight southwest from the suggested anchorage. Most of the cayucos there belong to the Cruz family who own a lot of the land nearby and who may pay you a friendly visit under the pretext of selling bananas or yucca.

BALBOA TO PUNTA BURICA 227

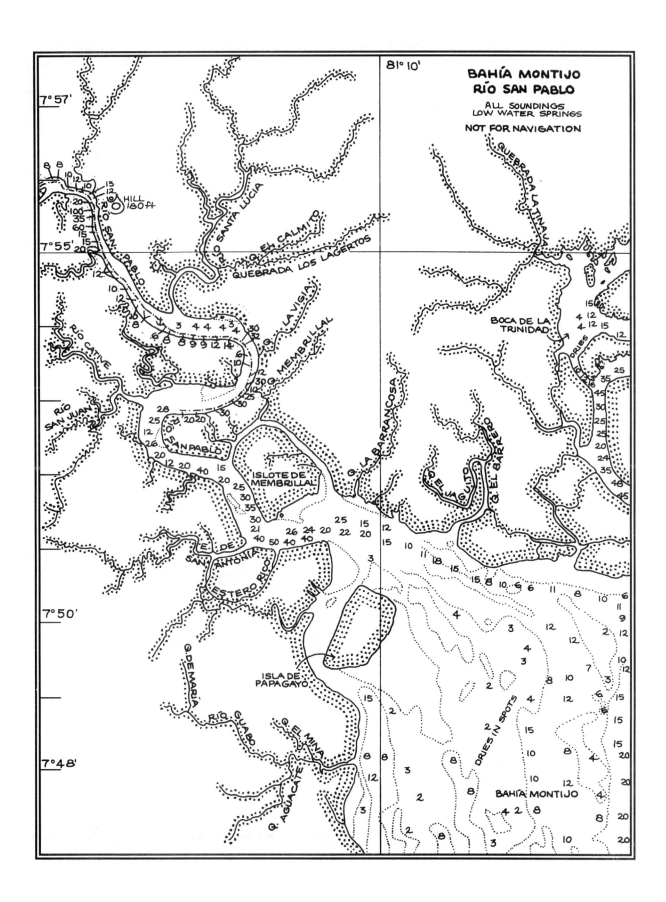

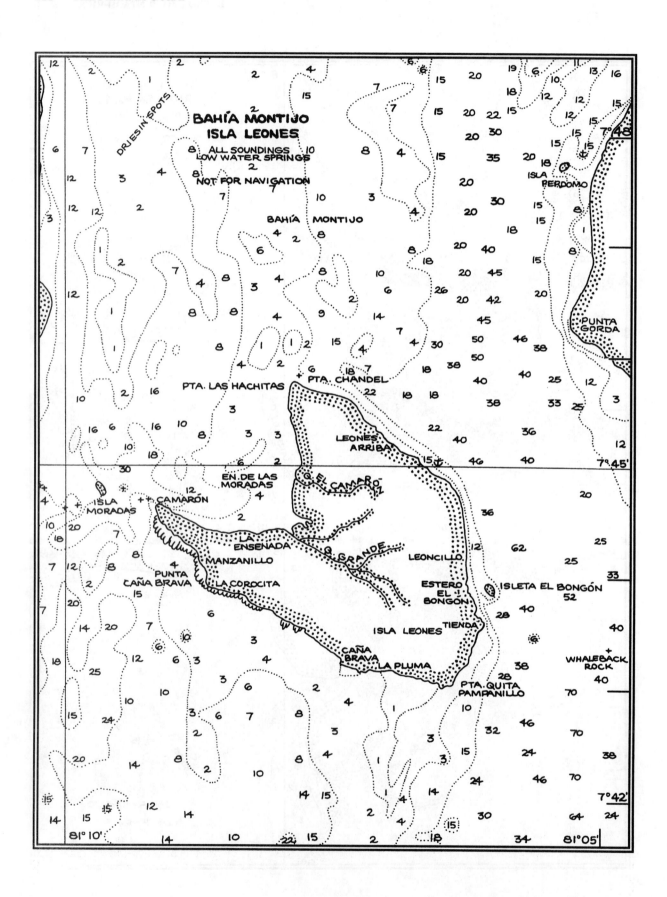

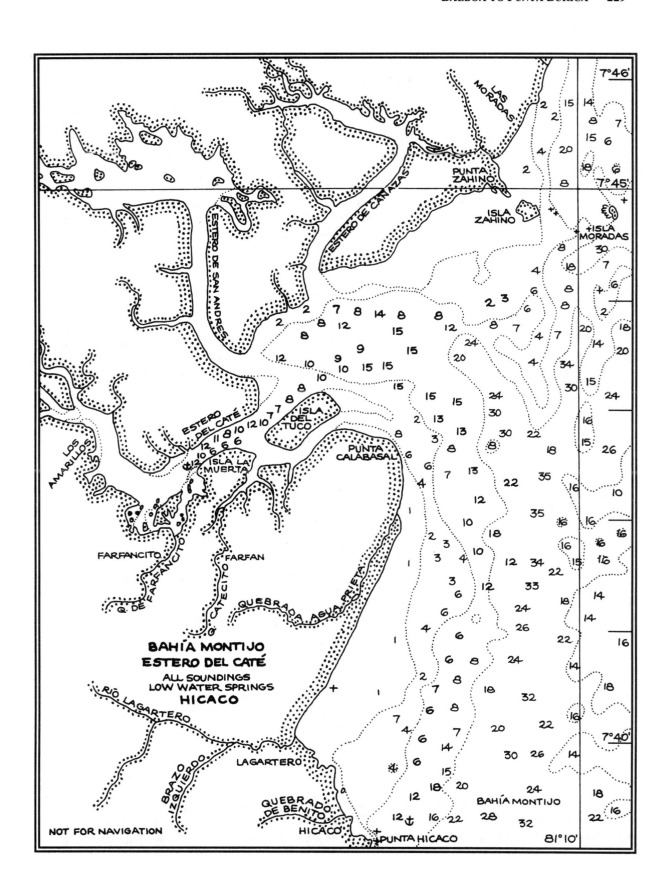

SANTA CATALINA TO BAHIA HONDA

ISLA SANTA CATALINA

About 7 miles west from Hicaco lies Isla Santa Catalina behind which yachts can find a good anchorage. The holding is good in 18 feet, mud and shells, off a white beach with a white house on the north shore. This anchorage, although perfectly safe, can be rolly at the change of tide. Ashore, on the mainland, Santa Catalina bay attracts surfers as this part of the coast has some impressive rollers. Many surfers have been injured by coral here, so if you surf, beware! Landing a dinghy off the village is only possible in January and February when the ocean swell goes down. The same applies to Ensenada San Lorenzo further to the northwest. Every time we sailed by we looked longingly at its beautiful beach lined with coconut palms but high ocean swells roaring on the shoals fringing the entrance to San Lorenzo precluded any dreams of landing there.

FROM SANTA CATALINA TO PUNTA CATIVO

Sailing this stretch of 10 miles you will look at bulky hills rising about a thousand feet to pasture land and small farms and then dropping steeply through wooded valleys to beaches of all colors, white, orange and black, which are lined with coconut palms. In rainy season ribbons of waterfalls shine on the cliff sides. Deep water runs close to the shore so one can admire this particularly beautiful coastline from a short distance. However, you must sail outside an islet marked as Bajo San Pedrillo and follow the deep channel inside Isla Los Octavios whose rocky sides drop sheer into the sea.

ISLAS CIMARRONES

In conditions of mild swell a yacht can anchor in the bay northwest of Islas Cimarrones off the mouth of Rio Ballena. There is also room on the north side of Cimarrones in about 23 feet. The view is spectacular with a choice of beaches to play on. All yours if the swell outside disappears, but keep in mind that you may have to leave quickly.

ENSENADA DE CATIVON

A small settlement hides along the shores of Ensenada de Cativon. No roads connect this part of Panama to the main network and people use canoes or take hill trails on horseback. As in all of the remote villages in Panama, the inhabitants smile readily and willingly sell what they grow, bananas, plantains, papayas, all kinds of roots and fruits in season. Good holding mud covers the bottom and a yacht will find 20 plus to 30 feet in the southern part of the bay. The anchorage may roll - it all depends on the direction and height of the swell outside and the state of tide.

PUERTO ESCONDIDO

When Cativon is rolly Puerto Escondido will be smoother. The entrance from the southeast is deep and straightforward but mind the rock which covers at high tide located about ½ mile off the shore. The anchorage has a backing of hilly farmed land and a nice beach slopes down into the sea allowing a yacht to anchor in 12 to 15 feet when the larger islet at the entrance bears about southwest.

HACHA

Further west from Puerto Escondido, on the north side of Punta de Hacha, a small cove has a vivid orange beach backed by palms. Off the beach a yacht will find about 20 feet while the best dinghy landing is in the southeast corner. Ocean surge sweeps in around the point so the anchorage is best left for those days without swell.

BAHIA HONDA

Bahia Honda offers several protected smooth anchorages within its large area. The deep almost mile wide entrance lets some swell in and this affects the southern and southeastern shores of the bay. However, yachts can find pond like calm anchorages anywhere along the western and northern shores. To make things more interesting a few very shallow spots dot the otherwise deep waters. Most yachts these days make a bee line to anchor off a cluster of cabins along the northern shore about ¾ of a mile from Isla Bahia Honda and just west of Islote la Mona. Watch out for a submerged rock with 1½ feet of water over it at a low tide about ¼ mile directly south of the cabins. The property ashore is private and landing is by invitation only.

Local farmers come and offer produce for sale. Isla Bahia Honda, populated by friendly Latinos, has a couple of tiendas, which sell freshly baked bread and other basics. An outboard motor mechanic takes care of the local ailing motors with varying success. As yet no road connects Bahia Honda to the rest of Panama and people use trails on horseback to travel over land. Very occasionally the swell outside gets high enough to affect the anchorage off the club. Yachts can then move to the west or go east of Isla Bahia Honda using the narrow but deep channel north of the island.

CAUTIONARY NOTE

The nearby island of Coiba has a large penitentiary colony. In 1991, pro-environment activists close to the Panama government realized that primary growth virgin forest covers 82% of the island area. Through their efforts Coiba was declared Coiba National Park and the penal colony scheduled to be removed in the course of the following five years. In 1995, the Minister of Government and Justice announced that relocating all Coiba prisoners into new institutions on the mainland would be completed in two and a half years. Meanwhile, prisoners try their best to remove themselves from the confinement by paddling away on makeshift rafts under the cover of night. Until the prison closes a yacht should never pick up people swimming or drifting on rafts. Some of the inmates have committed murder to get to the mainland and freedom. These voluntary castaways often end up on the islands between Coiba and the mainland. Local fishermen who routinely refuse to help them know which islands should be avoided until police round up the starved fugitives. At present yachts should keep night watches if anchored for the night at Isla Medidor, Isla Canal de Afuera, Islas Contreras and the bays on the mainland between Bahia Honda and Ensenada Punta Muerto. Ask fishermen for recent information.

ISLA MEDIDOR (on some charts, Isla Canal de Tierra)

This uninhabited island has a dogleg shaped bay on the west shore where yachts can find a smooth anchorage. Initially the bay has prodigious depths until it turns south when suddenly it shoals to 30 and very abruptly to 9 feet. The southern pocket has a beautiful palm lined beach. Along the north coast of Isla Medidor yachts will find a deep channel used when traveling to or from Bahia Honda.

ISLA CANAL DE AFUERA

Small and uninhabited this gem of an island has a couple of places shallow enough to anchor along the north shore off small sandy beaches. Waterfalls spill onto the beaches and the clear sea water invites snorkeling or diving. There would not be any protection in a northerly wind. Also, see the note on fugitives from Coiba. We have personally seen escaped prisoners here.

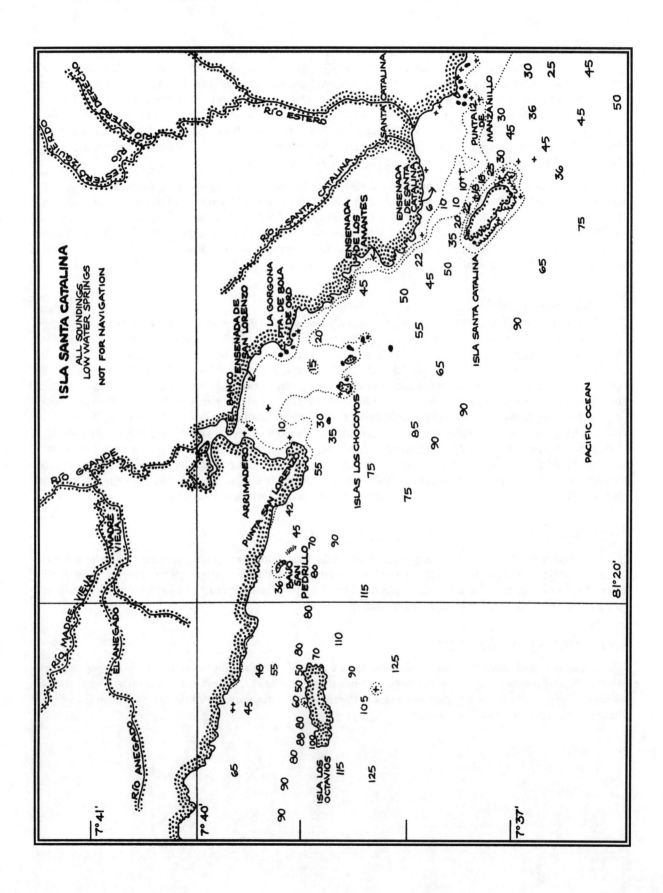

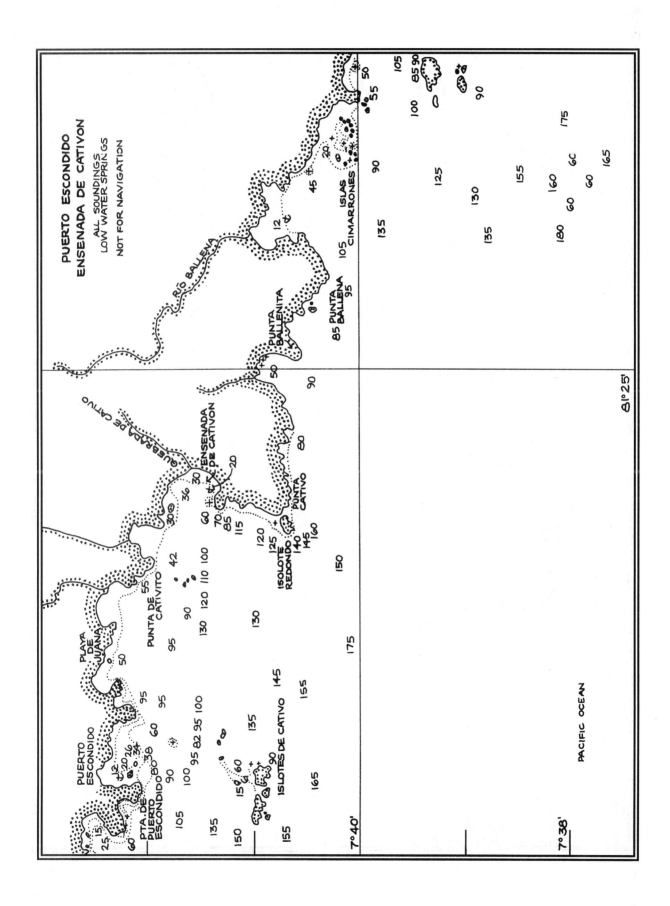

234 THE PANAMA GUIDE

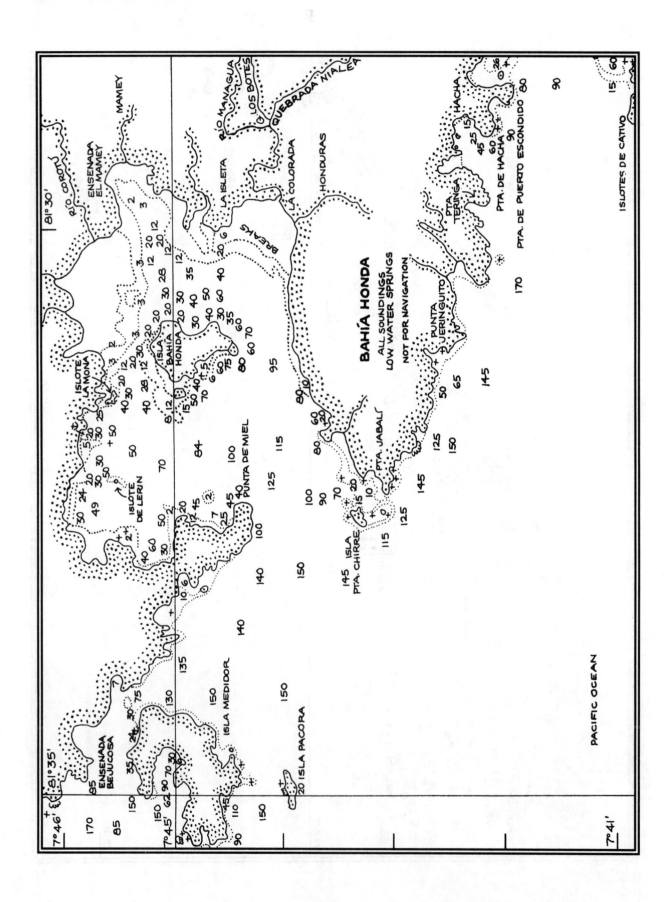

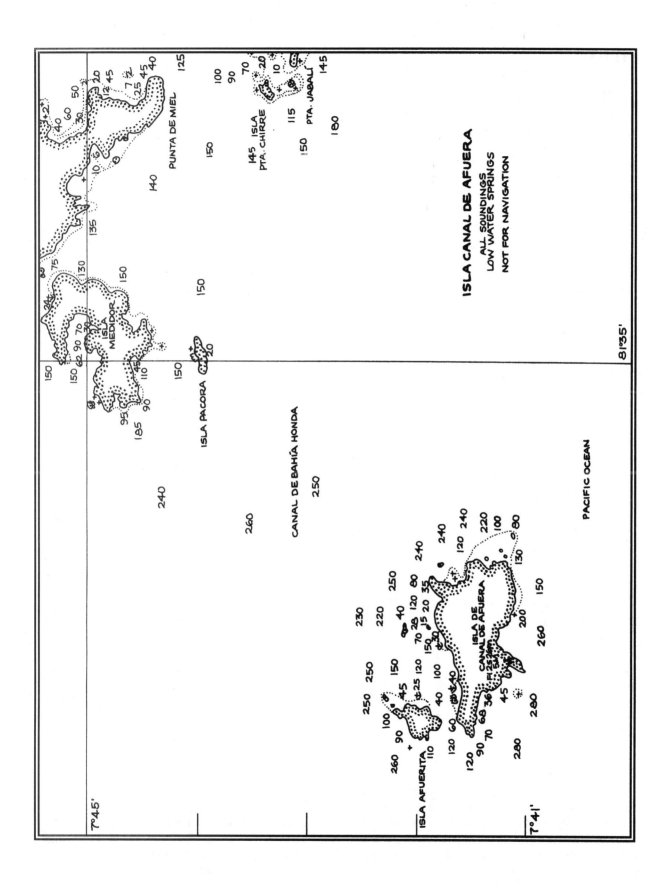

COIBA

PUNTA MACHETE

Due to the continuing presence of the penal colony the safest place to anchor is off the biological station located on Punta Machete on the northeast tip of Coiba. Yachts can find about 10 feet at low tide on the line between the north point of the little bay and the islet off the south point. Good holding in sand. The anchorage remains reasonably smooth most of the time. Further in the bay becomes very shallow. After arriving report ashore where the chief of the police detachment will check the boat's papers and issue a free of charge permit to stay in the park waters. The police are very friendly and if you want to go on any island trails one of them, equipped with weapons, will go as a guide and protector. We recommend the climb to Cerro Equi to sample the untouched forest growth, see the howler monkeys and some interesting birds, perhaps the scarlet macaws which have become extremely rare on the mainland but have a breeding colony on Coiba. Wear long pants and rubber boots, part of the trail is up a running creek bed. The personnel of INRENARE, the government environmental agency, will explain the most interesting aspects of the island ecology and show you a film on Coiba. You will probably meet a researcher or two who come here to carry out scientific work. Coiba National Park has been divided into red and green sectors. Red is open only to research and green is open to ecotourism. Yachts are allowed to visit the red areas as long as they leave only footprints and take only photographs as the saying goes. We used the biological station bay as a base to spend the nights and went to several bays for day trips.

RANCHERIA - COIBITA

Rancheria island, which is privately owned, has two places to anchor, off the south shore and in a beautiful cove on the east side. To go ashore one has to talk to the caretaker who has a house on the south beach. Anchor in a sandy bottom off the beach according to your depth. You will see here the 115-foot *Coiba Explorer II* at anchor as a base for sportfishing and diving guests. Fishing season runs November through May and divers take over from June through September. For reservations call in the U.S. number 1-800-733-4742.

GRANITO DE ORO

We highly recommend a trip to Granito de Oro off the northeast coast of Coiba and close to the station. Anchor northwest of the island. The holding is poor on a hard rocky bottom. We encountered more species of colorful, plentiful and tame fish in one snorkeling session than seemed possible to see without spending an evening with a fish guide book to the area.

PLAYA ROSARIO and ENSENADA SANTA CRUZ

Several beautiful bays on the east coast are worth visiting as day destinations. The lovely small beaches at Playa Rosario are backed by a dense green forest. Natural piles of rocks here and there create canoe size coves. Playa Rosario has an easy, straightforward entrance and is protected from the southwesterly swell. Small islands mark the entrance to Ensenada Santa Cruz. The depth does not become shallower until the bay narrows. There is good holding in sand and mud but the southwesterly swell moves into the anchorage. Check with the police before visiting these anchorages. Some of the other bays have prison camps which we marked on the sketch chart. Occasionally one can join the station boat which takes scientists to some particularly interesting parts of the Coiba coast.

JICARON

This island, separated from Coiba by a wide channel has strong currents which make it safe from any lurking fugitives. No one lives here and the beauty of the lush landscape can take your breath away. We rated Jicaron as the most wildly beautiful stop in Pacific Panama. The anchorage off a cove towards the eastern part of the north shore of Jicaron has very good holding in sand and mud. Ashore, two rivers discharge on the beach and sometimes fishermen land here to fill their water jugs. The personnel at the bio station told us that during calm seas we could find excellent diving off Punta Ursula. Phil Wade, a very experienced diver and captain of the maxi yacht *Timoneer,* considered it among the best he has seen.

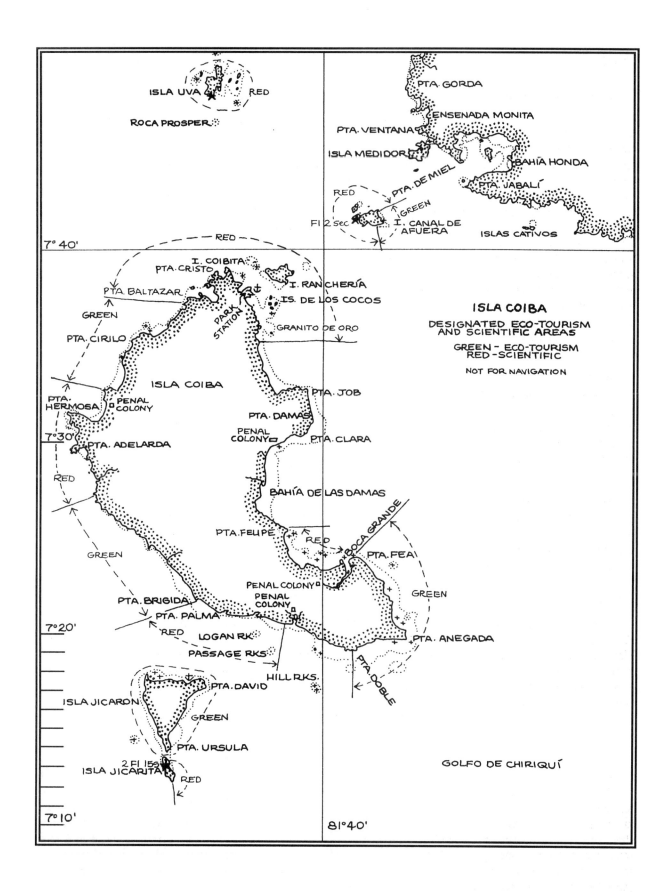

238 THE PANAMA GUIDE

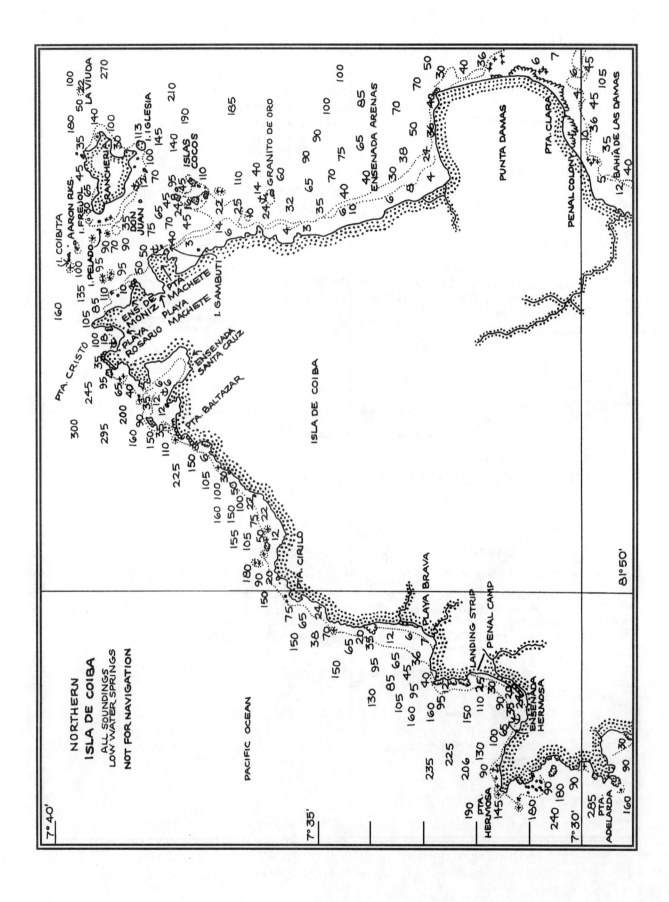

ISLAS DE CONTRERAS

Although 10 miles from Coiba, officially Islas de Contreras are part of the Coiba National Park. No one lives on the two islands and only fishermen use them regularly as a resting stop. Isla Uva has a good, although very small, anchorage in its northern part. The depths in the bay suddenly jump from about 80 feet to 30 and then 6 feet near the beach with palms. Isla Brincanco also has an anchorage on the northern shore with lesser depths in the southwest corner. There is good holding in a sandy bottom. A rocky ledge which covers at high tide extends from a point in the middle of the bay. The beaches here also shrink to almost nothing at high tides but the southeast corner has a small stream of fresh water running to the beach.

MAINLAND BAYS BETWEEN PUNTA ROBLE AND ENSENADA MUERTO

PUNTA ROBLE and ISLA MONA

The bay just north of Punta Roble is very deep and indeed a yacht would have to anchor very close to shore in the southeastern corner of the bay. Swell enters this bay even on a day of low ocean swell outside. The northern part of the bay had worse swell and many rocks off the point in the middle. The bay just north of Isla Mona has a spot 18 to 20 feet deep near the cut between Isla Mona and the mainland. This would be a rolly anchorage even on a good day.

ENSENADA DE PIXVAE

Ensenada de Pixvae is a shallower bay than the ones to the south. You can find 30 feet shoaling to 20 and 15 feet along the southern shore. Pixvae settlement is the largest for miles with a school, telephone and tiendas. Dinghy landing may turn out pretty wet - try the southeastern corner of the beach.

ENSENADA DE ROSARIO

We found the smoothest water in the bay just to the southeast of Mogote de Doña Juana where even near shore the depths stay at about 20 feet. Swell enters the main bay which shoals very rapidly in the southeast corner.

ENSENADA DE MUERTO

The bay has good holding in mud at around 30 feet of depth. Shallower spots have a hard bottom and a few rocky ledges run out from the points along the shores. Not much wind enters this miniature fjord and only rarely any waves. Rio Muerto, although not long, is worth exploring in the dinghy at high tide to see the tropical shady swamp with flooded trees covered in epiphytes. At the east corner of the bay you will see some roaming pigs and a hut that is obviously used on occasion. Many orange and mango trees around the bay will provide fruit in season.

ENSENADA DE PLAYA BRAVA

Ensenada de Playa Brava, of which Ensenada de Muerto is a part, seems to receive the full run of the swell, hence the name Playa Brava which means a rough, wild, beach. Punta Pajaron, the northeast point of Playa Brava has a white concrete cross on it probably signaling to local fishermen the location of the entrance to Rio Lovaina. At the time of our visit waves were breaking across the river bar.

RIO SANTA LUCIA AND SURROUNDINGS

The river channel close to Punta Entrada is deep and can be easily negotiated in any weather. The shoals on the north side of the entrance break most of the time and the breakers serve instead of navigational markers. The first bay in has a wonderful beach with a couple of households but the anchorage lies fairly far off and is rolly. Less swell reaches the next bight to the east. Here the bottom is hard so check that the anchor holds well.

240 The Panama Guide

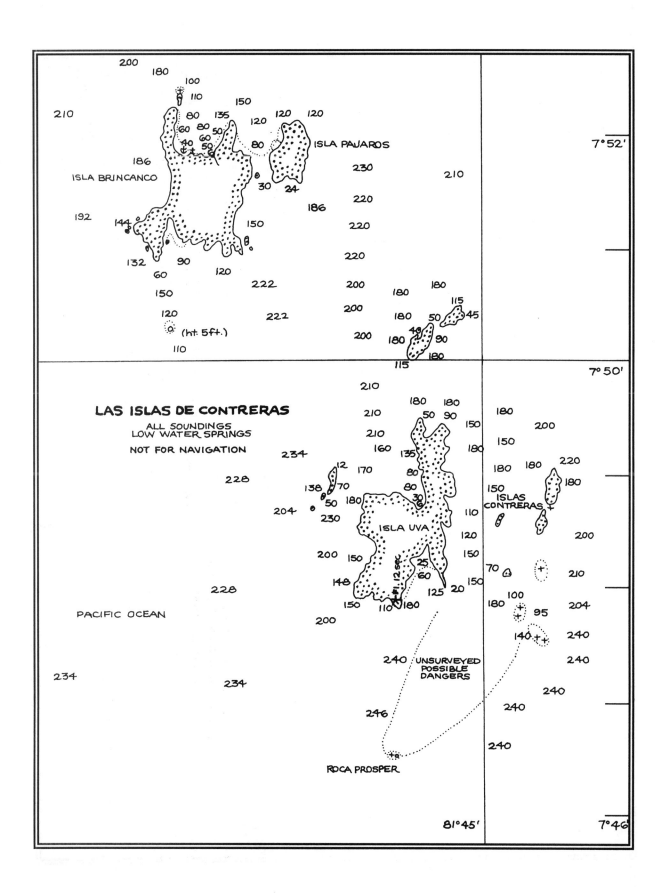

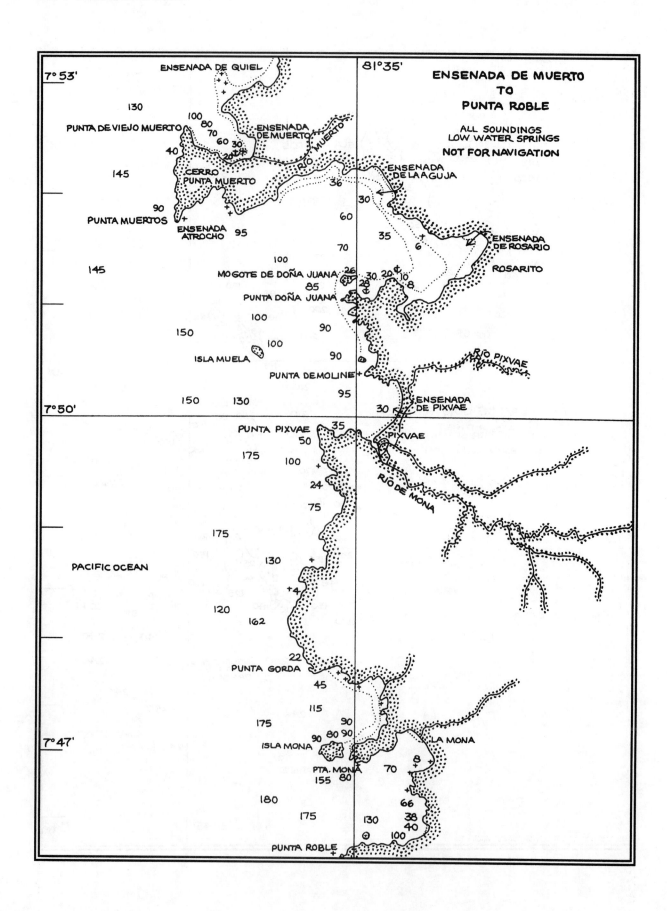

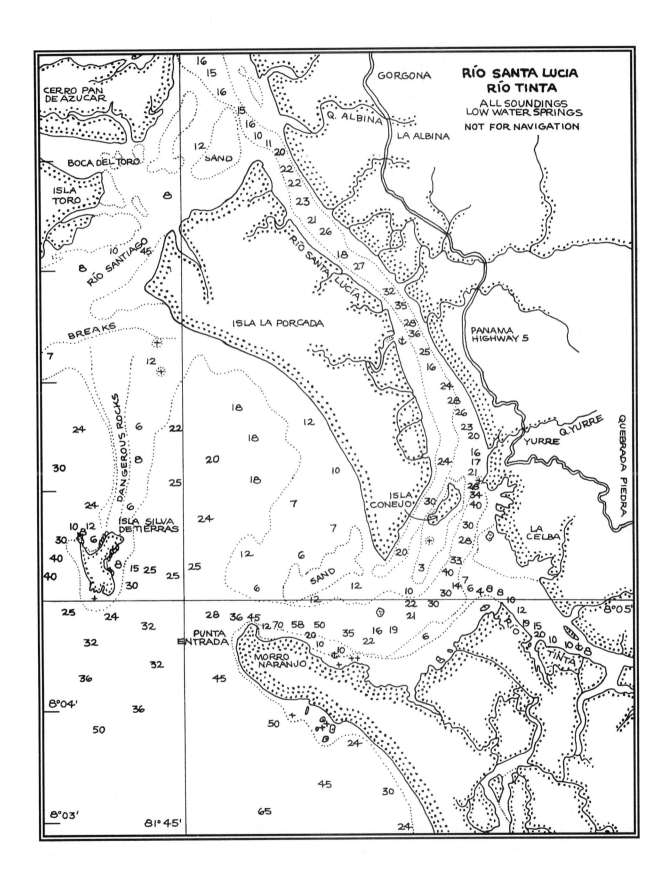

244 THE PANAMA GUIDE

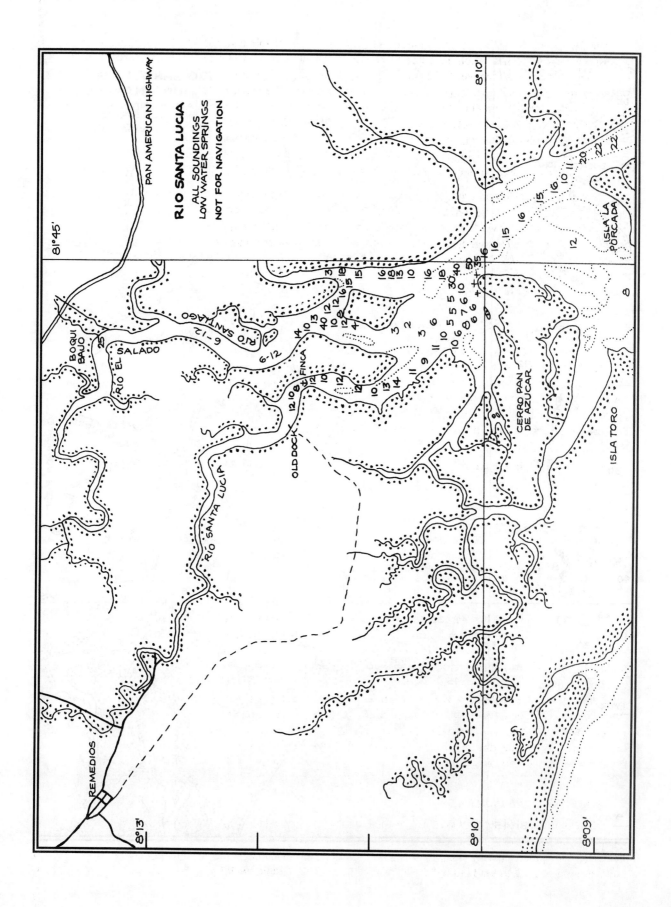

The few people who live here will gladly sell any produce available and will let visitors climb to the top of the hillside for a full view of the hills and the estuary. Yachts with considerable draft can venture far up Rio Santa Lucia. The easiest channel follows the east side of the river. The tributary, Rio Tinta, can also be entered to find perfect quiet and peace along the mangrove south shore. The creek northeast of Isla Conejo on the east shore of Santa Lucia allows a dinghy access to Yurre, a settlement of three households on the edge of Highway 5 which eventually joins the Pan-American Highway. A phone may be found down the road to the right (east) at the village of Quebrada Piedra. Many charts persist in showing Puerto Nuevo at about this area. However, according to our research and a record by the buccaneer writer Basil Ringrose, the last known visit to such a port was by an English raiding party on May 22nd, 1679. And even that Puerto Nuevo was further upstream.

From Yurre a yacht can proceed up river for 6 to 7 miles. Nowadays, the cattle town of Remedios at the very end of Santa Lucia is the only town around and only a shallow draft boat and dinghies can get through the last two miles below town. Remedios has a telephone, several tiendas, ice, gasoline, a clinic and small restaurants. A good anchorage lies just north of the mud bank off Cerro Pan de Azucar, an unmistakable pointed mount on an island. With the help of a rising tide yachts can continue from there up Rio Santa Lucia and anchor in the nice wide reach between the finca on one side of the river and the dock remains on the other. Keep the anchor light on, small fishing boats commute to and from Remedios at night.

RIO SANTIAGO

From the northeast point of Cerro Pan de Azucar there is also a channel up Rio Santiago. The depths vary between 6 and 12 feet but the anchorage on the river bend, off the collapsed pier at Boqui Bajo, has deep water. From here a short dirt road goes to the Pan-American Highway. At this intersection buses stop and one can go to Tolé, a small inland town in the low hills where the majority of traffic is on horseback and Guaymis come from the mountains to shop. Just before the dirt road joins the highway lives Mario Castrellon with whom vacationing Panamanians leave cars and runabouts. For a small fee he will send somebody to watch your dinghy for you.

ISLA SILVA DE TIERRA

This islet lying at the entrance to Rio Santa Lucia has two beautiful beaches. We found the anchorage off the east side of the islet quite rolly but the bay on the north shore was almost roll free at depths of 12 feet just outside the line between the two points forming the bay. Nevertheless treat it as a day anchorage only.

ISLAS SECAS

ISLA CAVADA

From the entrance to Rio Santa Lucia one can see Islas Secas only 18 miles distant. Isla Cavada, the largest island, has a few huts on it and fishermen from Boca Chica often come to rest here after fishing all night. The main, most popular anchorage with good holding in sand and shells lies west of a point and the islets in the middle of the northeast shore. A narrow vee of deeper water penetrates somewhat into the bay, but the shores and the bay proper are very shallow. (On the sketch chart this anchorage shows 4, 6, 4 feet). In conditions of little ocean swell the next bay to the east is quite acceptable, but do not venture further in than the line between the outer points. The coves along the shore between the main anchorage and the islet off the north point have reasonable shelter, too. We found the cove on the east shore, where the sketch chart shows 20 feet, the smoothest of all on that particular day but the place would only accommodate one yacht of about 45 feet. In case of a northerly wind this is the anchorage to try.

SOUTHERN ISLAS SECAS

The small island to the southeast of Cavada has a cove with a pebbly beach. The ocean swell sweeps into the anchorage on some days. The north shore of the large island to the southwest of Cavada has two lovely beaches complete with palms and tiny streams during rainy season. The anchorage may be entered between the two islets and has good holding in sand but will be rolly on days of large oceanic swell from the south.

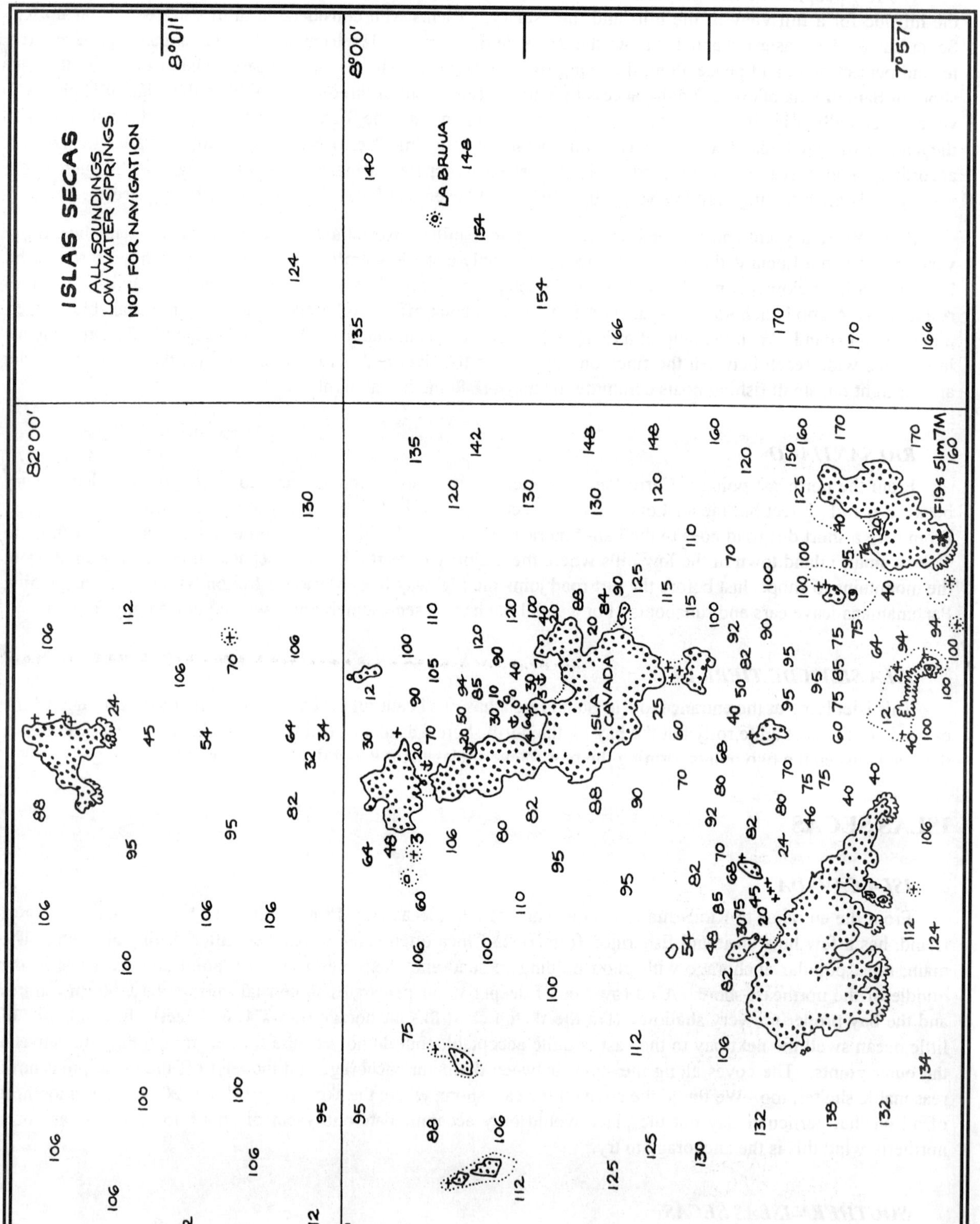

ISLAS SECAS
ALL SOUNDINGS
LOW WATER SPRINGS
NOT FOR NAVIGATION
LA BRUJA
ISLA CAVADA
Fl 9s 51m 7M
82°00'
8°01'
8°00'
7°57'

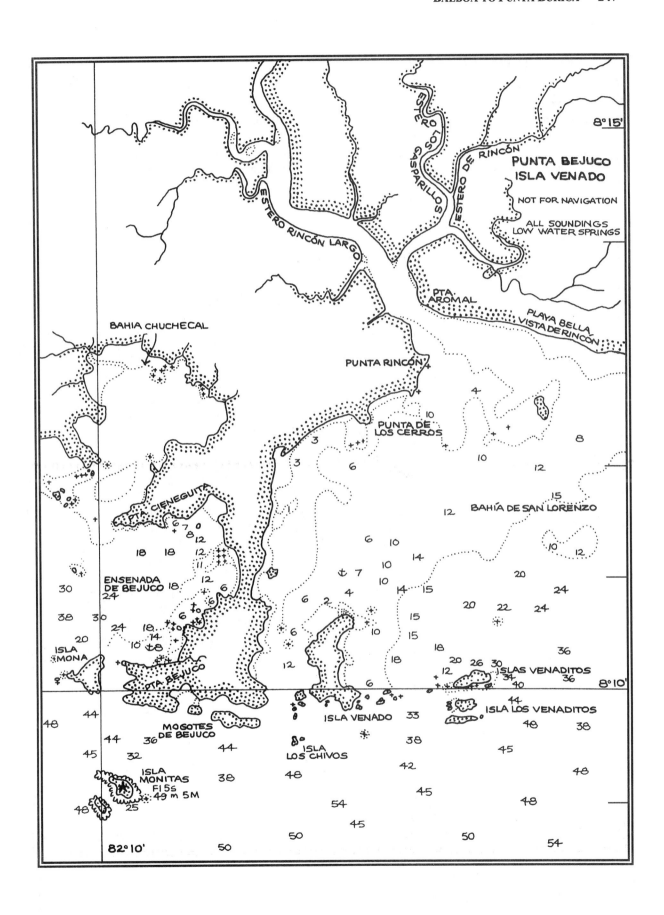

ISLA VENADO TO PEDREGAL

ISLA VENADO

About 12 miles north from Islas Secas several islands protect Bahia de San Lorenzo from most of the ocean swell. We found a good anchorage, at 08°11'N and 082°07.6'W, in mud with depths of 7 to 8 feet a little less than ½ mile north of Isla Venado. At the time no one lived on the island. The best dinghy landing, on the sand spit on the north point, lies right under posted signs banning the cutting of trees and hunting on the island. The paths lead into a forested dark interior with a tremendous variety of large trees and plants and easy walking on a leaf littered ground. We judged it as one of the coolest, most shaded, beautiful trails in this chapter.

ENSENADA DE BEJUCO

Only a narrow strip of land separates Ensenada de San Lorenzo from Ensenada de Bejuco but one must sail about 9 miles around many rocks to get there. The anchorage, close to the north side of Punta Bejuco, has a mud bottom with good holding in about 10 to 12 feet. Closer in the bottom changes to firm sand at about 8 feet deep but by then the boat may swing too close to rocks which cover at mid tide.

A nice little stream runs out onto the beach and at low water one can walk comfortably along the shore to the northeast. In the trees overhanging the first point we encountered the troop of howler monkeys who had chorused us the previous night. From above, and plainly visible, they threw sticks to keep us from moving onto their trees.

The depths would allow anchoring further in Ensenada de Bejuco but at spring low tides a whole mess of rocks emerges which requires great care when moving a boat in this area.

BOCA CHICA

By counting islands as one sails westward from Ensenada Bejuco it is easy to find the channel leading into Boca Chica. Turn north after the third set of islets and pass east of Isla Saino with its outlying rocks and then favor the east shore until you can identify the rocks one third of a mile north of Isla Linarte. Even at high tide there is an occasional lazy breaker over them. See chartlet LA VENTANA, ISLAS SAN JOSE, page 258. Pass to the east of these rocks then turn west towards the southern side of the channel leading to Boca Chica. When the passage between Isla Boca Brava and Punta San Lorenzo opens up and bears about 285°T, turn west and steer for the north shore of Isla Boca Brava. Follow that side of the channel until close to the narrowest part when you must change course for the point on the north shore and keep on the northern side until you arrive off the village. Anchor outside the moored local boats in depths between 8 and 12 feet. If you time your passage into Boca channel at low tide you should see the tops of all rocky shoals. The tidal currents run fast here and reverse directions at the change of tides. A lot of boats use this passage at all hours so show a good anchor light at night.

There are more channels to the ocean through Boca Chica. Some shrimp trawlers go out from the east end of Isla Boca Brava straight for the west end of Isla Saino. However, we have not sounded that passage and instead we used the channel which goes along the north side of Isla La Ventana and hugs the west end of it to avoid the rocky shelf further west. The anchorage off the house on the north shore of Isla La Ventana is quite comfortable.

Boca Chica, a small village of fishermen, has a couple of tiendas, gasoline and ice. A dirt road leads to the town of Horconcitos and the Pan-American Highway on which one can go to the large town of David. This road out of Boca Chica is wonderful for walking or running.

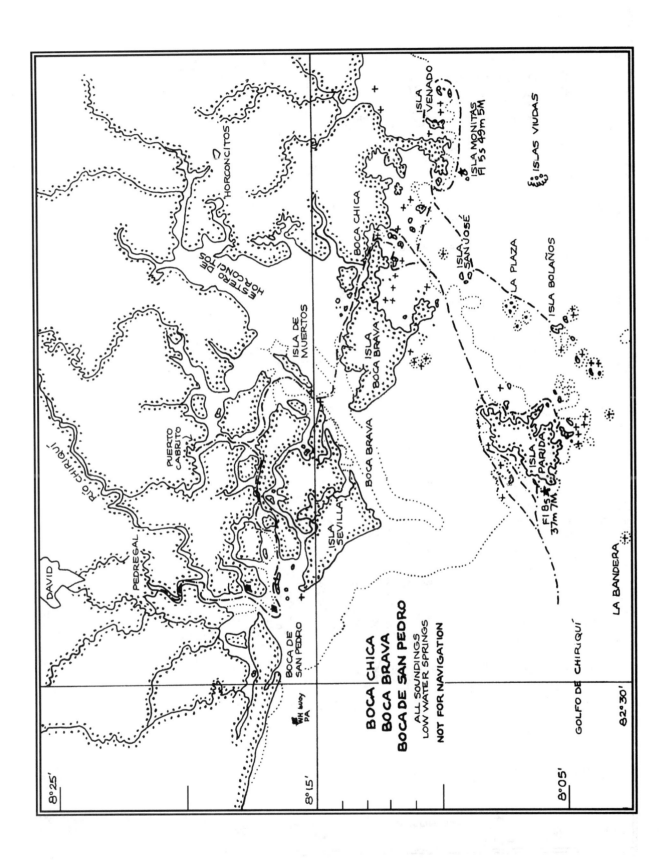

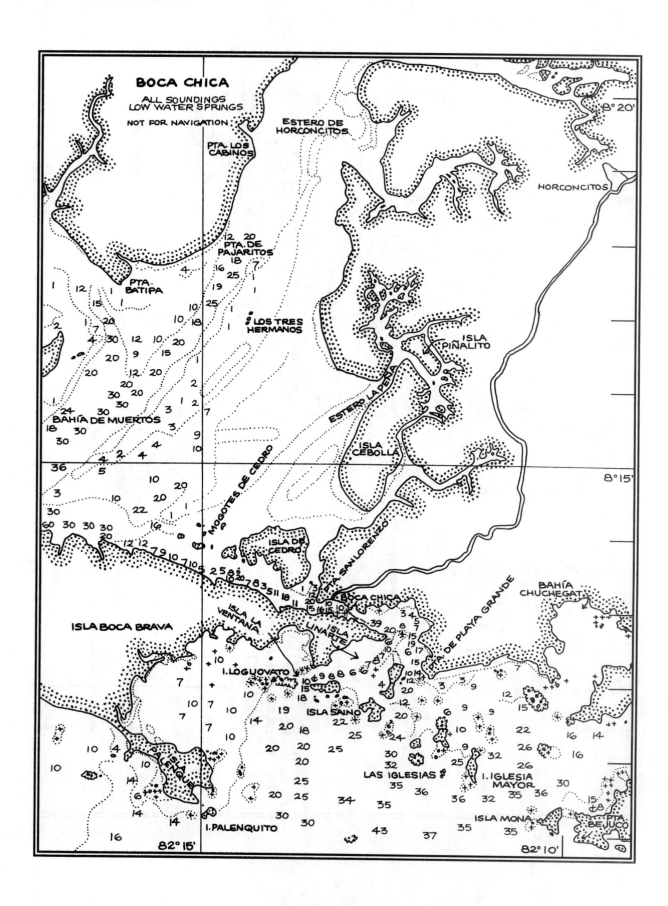

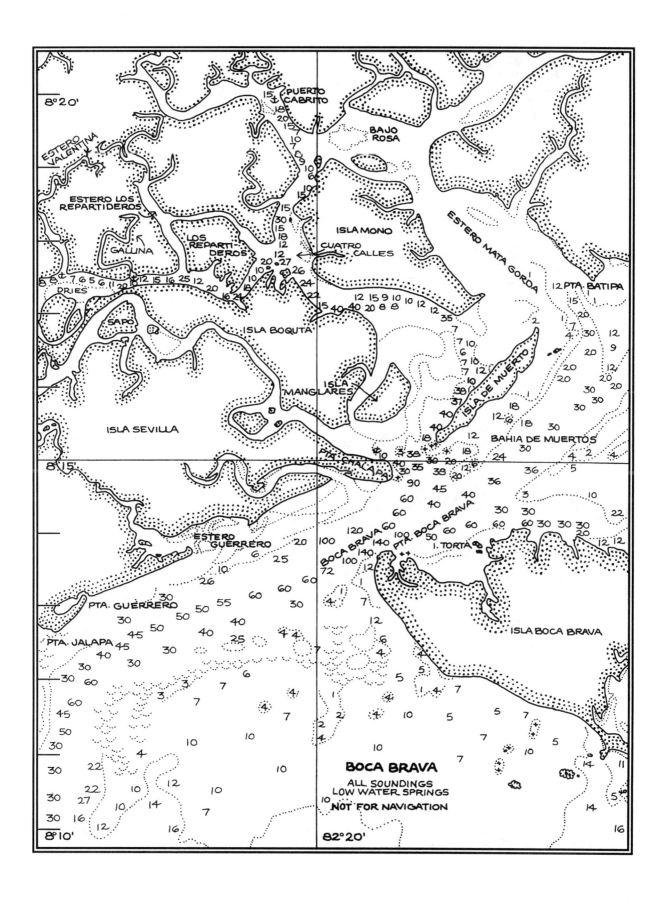

PEDREGAL AND THE CHANNELS TO THAT PORT, INCLUDING PUERTO CABRITO

A channel leading westward from Boca Chica opens a huge area to cruising yachts and it leads to the port of Pedregal in protected waters. It does have several very shallow spots until a yacht gets abeam of the islets Mogotes de Cedro. Any vessel with a draft over 2 feet will have to plan going through on the rising tide at about half tide. When south of the west end of Isla de Cedro one should steer close to Isla Boca Brava's north shore (Boca Chica sketch chart) and carry on in deep water to a point about half way between Punta Chalapa (see PUNTA CHALAPA heading) and Isla de Muerto (Boca Brava sketch chart). After the shoals off the southwest point of Isla de Muerto very deep water runs close to this island. From about the middle of Isla de Muerto the channel leads between very shallow banks towards the southeast point of Isla Mono and then close to its south shore. As the sketch chart Boca Brava indicates one should steer towards Isla Boquita and Mono. Continue along the shore of Isla Boquita and some islets off its north tip and turn southwest to go between Isla Boquita and Los Repartideros. At this point called Cuatro Calles one can take the channel north to Puerto Cabrito. No real port exists there, just a nice wide reach of the river with many creeks and good bird life. A dirt road cuts to a landing at the bottom of the red cliffs off Puerto Cabrito. The road eventually joins the Pan-American Highway.

Boca Chica Channel

Going west from Cuatro Calles presents no tricky spots until the southeast point of Isla Higueros (Pedregal sketch chart). Steer close to the point and then take a sharp turn to the south and run close to the shore on the south side of the channel. From Punta Sabino steer slightly north of west until you spot the red buoy marking the west edge of Banco de Las Matitas. The GPS position of the buoy is 08°17.4'N and 082°26.4'W. You should have about 20 feet until almost due west of the buoy, but beware of the 7 feet close to the west side of the buoy. The buoy itself is moored in 5 feet. When abeam of the buoy steer 020°T for the red marker No.1 on the shore. It has a white cross installed on top. The depths which diminish after the buoy will increase again when close to the shore. The marker is on the shore just south of the river north of Punta Las Matitas. Off the river mouth the depth suddenly plummets to 100 feet and then goes up to about 18 feet. After the next creek the channel shoals to about 7 feet and one should steer as indicated on the sketch chart. Markers on the shore usually indicate the deeper side of the river but thick vegetation often hides them from view until one is right abeam.

The port authorities would like new arrivals to anchor in the bay on the east side of the commercial wharf which often receives a fertilizer ship drawing 15 feet.

A deep channel by the south end of the dock goes into the creek where Chiriquí Marina has its docks. Close to their docks visiting yachts will find an 8 to 10 foot deep area also recommended as an anchorage. After some arrangements it is possible to dock the boat to fuel up from a truck which will come when a vessel buys a considerable quantity of diesel. Otherwise, a few minutes down the road a large tank farm sells smaller quantities of all fuels and lubricating oils.

Right off the commercial wharf one can find the customs office and a little further the port authorities who will clear in a vessel arriving from foreign ports. They can also issue cruising permits as well as clearances or zarpes to other countries. To deal with immigration matters one should take a taxi to David which will cost about $2.00 for the five minute ride to the immigration office.

The port captain's office will phone the immigration people to come and clear arriving yachts but the immigration officer will then charge a fee for the trip to the port. Explain to the port authorities you will do it yourself. They are very helpful and understanding. The only questionable character we encountered was the customs officer who wanted $20.00 (and got it) for some unspecified services. In Panama the Customs office should not charge yachts any fees.

The main reason yachts visit Pedregal is to attend to official business, refuel, resupply or to use communication facilities in David. David, the second largest town in Panama, has good stores of all kinds, courier shipping companies, fax possibilities and the like. The town is very clean and safe for foreigners. However, the profusion of uninhabited, quiet rivers and anchorages makes the whole area between Pedregal and Boca Chica a desirable cruising destination in itself. Boca Chica channel is the main and safest entrance into these inland waters and is used mostly by local small boat fishermen and large shrimp trawlers.

BOCA BRAVA

Boca Brava, a deep channel which on the chart appears fairly straightforward has well defined shallows along the edges on which waves break almost always. We started out of Boca Brava one day using the remains of the outgoing current to give us some help. This way we avoided the fastest rate of the outgoing tide when the current undercuts the swell from the ocean and causes the channel to get pretty rough if not downright dangerous. We got past Punta Guerro when the incoming tide started and slowed down our progress while the chop actually got worse. In the end we turned around and went back in. Possibly a larger yacht (ours is a 38 footer) with a powerful engine would have faired much better. The ocean swell conditions are the deciding factor in Boca Brava and some days later we were sailing outside the ocean end of Boca Brava and could see breaking waves on areas charted as 12 feet deep.

PUNTA CHALAPA

Right off the inland end of Boca Brava, on the north side of Punta Chalapa, yachts can anchor in a very protected spot with good holding in depths between 10 and 40 feet. Those speaking some Spanish should visit the friendly elderly couple who live on Punta Chalapa. One can order fresh produce from them (what kind depends on the season) and if they have fresh corn ask for "bollos" from the lady, they will melt in your mouth!

OFFSHORE ISLANDS SOUTH OF ISLA BOCA BRAVA (or south of BOCA CHICA)

Many yachts passing through Panamanian waters stop in this group of islands to rest, enjoy the pretty anchorages or even do some diving. Isla Parida, the largest, naturally has the greatest choice of anchorages to give protection in whatever wind or waves the weather gods visit upon the seafarers. However, several uninhabited smaller islands have even more beauty and more fish to admire and are close enough to day visit from a more permanent anchorage at Isla Parida.

ISLAS SAN JOSE

This group of four islets about 3 miles south from Boca Chica channel has a place to anchor just north of the southernmost islet and in the lee of a long reef. Unfortunately, the reef disappears at high tide under several feet of water and if a strong wind from the southwest builds up it will send a short chop into this anchorage. The large ocean swell does not penetrate here and one can take a dinghy ashore to the sandy beach on the largest island. The gap between this large island and the ones to the south is blocked by some toothy rocks which may disappear altogether at high tide.

ISLA BOLAÑOS

Isla Bolaños, which lies 4 miles south-southeast from San Jose and 3 miles east from Parida, has a good anchorage on its east side and receives some protection from the swell from Isla Berraco. The anchorage off the sandy beach there has good holding in sand about 15 to 20 feet deep. Coconut palms back the beach as well as other trees, many festooned with orchids and interesting bromiliads. During rainy season the rock faces turn red with hundreds of blooming plants. Should the swell direction make this anchorage too rolly one may try anchoring off the north side of the island. There are two white beaches and the best day anchorage is off the one between the gravel beach to the west and the sandy beach to the east. Shallow ledges extend from the points of land so pick your spot carefully. The west point of the beach in the middle runs out far to the north-northeast and is very shallow. The bank, 7 to 8 feet deep, growing off the northeast point of Bolaños also merits some attention. Both shallow points have a good amount of coral and fish to view while snorkeling.

ISLA PARIDA - PUNTA JUREL

The most popular anchorages on Isla Parida cluster around the northeastern point in the bay between Punta Jurel and Punta del Pozo.

When entering from the west beware of a rock lurking under the surface just to the east of Punta Jurel. The bay has ample space to anchor in depths between 12 and 18 feet. This anchorage may become choppy during the season of northerly winds (January and February). Visiting yachts can move west of Punta Jurel and anchor off the west side of the narrow neck of land at the back of the resort during strong easterlies.

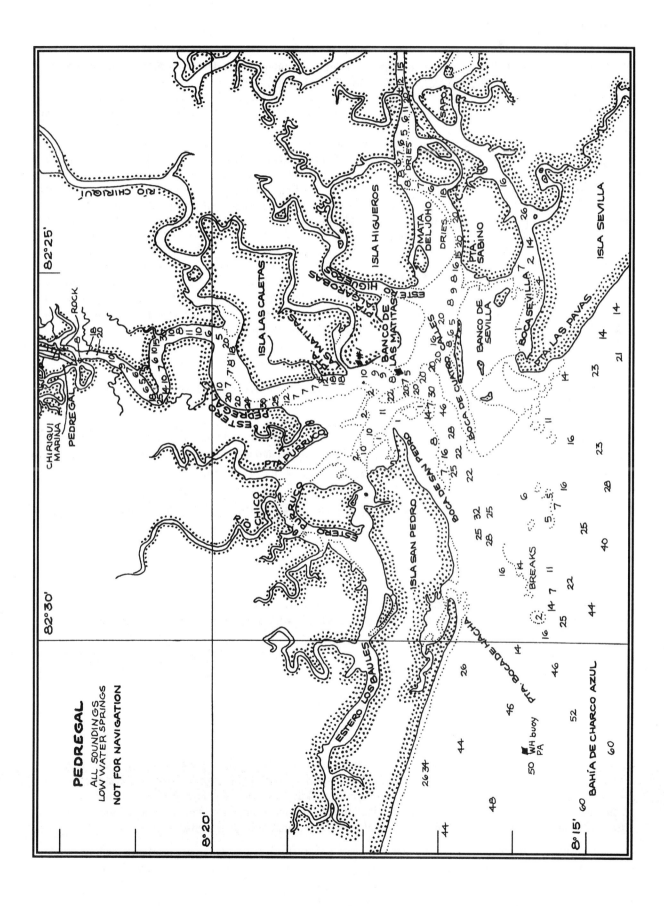

PLAYA DEL SOCORRO

A pretty and good anchorage also lies off Playa del Socorro south of Punta del Pozo. From there a trail goes all the way to the resort bay and also along the coast towards the south.

ISLA GAMEZ

The first time we anchored off Isla Gamez we noticed a conspicuous sign. I swam ashore to read it expecting a "no trespassing" kind of message. It said, "This beach is for everybody." A nice thing to say to visitors even though it merely reflects the Panamanian law (all beaches are public). During the weekends families from David take their boats from the Pedregal club and marina and zoom down here for a weekend of play. A cruising yachtsman will find an anchorage in sand with good holding off the beach on the north side. Should the wind come strongly from the north one can move to the south side of the island. Do not come too close to this shore as many rocky shelves run out fairly far.

NORTHWEST OF MOGOTE DE SEPULCRO

A deep water channel runs along the east side of Parida giving access to more anchorages, some limited to the times when the ocean swell dies down. We found the anchorage off the beach on Parida to the northwest of a rock called Mogote de Sepulcro only slightly rolly when the southerly swell was quite heavy out in the ocean.

ENSENADA DEL VAREDERO

The approach to this bay, on the southeast corner of Parida, should be made only from the east coast. Isla Paridita protects the bay from the worst of the swell. However, on some days the rollers which break on the shoals visible through the gap to the west of Isla Paridita cause a pretty uncomfortable scend in this bay. During northerly winds the protection is perfect, anchor holding is very good in a sandy bottom and the surroundings are very pleasing. Several thatched homes nestling under coconut palms and mango trees lie behind the beaches.

ENSENADA SANTA CRUZ

Offlying Hijo Mocha and another islet cut off enough ocean swell to make this bay quite smooth. The calmest southern part of the bay has good holding in sand. On the other hand, the northern part of the bay ends up in a mess of rocks and shoals.

ENSENADA LOS NEGROS

The spacious cove can be remarkably smooth on a day with large oceanic swell outside. A few huts hide in the greenery behind the white sandy beach. During the northerly wind season yachts should find good protection here as well.

PUERTO ARMUELLES

Distant 35 miles from Parida and located almost on the border with Costa Rica, this port is convenient for obtaining clearances to or from Panama. Take notice that foreign nationals arriving here without a visa into the Republic of Panama will be asked to go to the Immigration Office on the border in Fronteras to obtain the tourist visa. One can make the 30 kilometer trip by bus for US$1.50 one way or take a taxi which may cost up to US$60.00 round trip. By the way, visas issued in Panamanian consulates abroad are free. All the other clearing procedures happen right in Armuelles. The Port Captain speaks some English, works in an office at the base of the banana pier, and is very helpful. Try to arrive on a weekday to avoid overtime charges. Coming into the anchorage becomes difficult at night as no navigational lights, including the Punta Burica lighthouse, work. After anchoring call Autoridad Portuaria on channel 16 VHF and announce your arrival.

The best place to anchor is when the pier end bears about 015°T at a distance of about one tenth of a mile from it. You should be able to locate a shelf 16 to 30 feet deep which then drops suddenly to about 70 feet.

Holding is good in sand, swell in our experience was negligible but be prepared to leave if rollers arrive from the southeast. Dinghy landing on the south side of the pier is best by the steps which start under the pier buildings. One can safely leave the dinghy tied here. Most of the beaches nearby cover at high tide and suffer from surge. The only conceivable beach dinghy landing is on the north side of the base of the pier.

The largest supermarket in town has an excellent selection of dry groceries - a relief after trying to stock in Costa Rica or dealing with the small coastal tiendas in Panama. One can find fruit and vegetables in a covered market in the center of the town. Telephones have direct access to overseas operators (109 for ATT, 106 for international), the INTEL office will send and receive faxes and there is a reliable courier service office (Expreso National SKYNET). You may find banks, film developing, all kinds of stores and good restaurants. All fuels and water must be carried in your containers.

Drying Banks on the way to Pedregal.

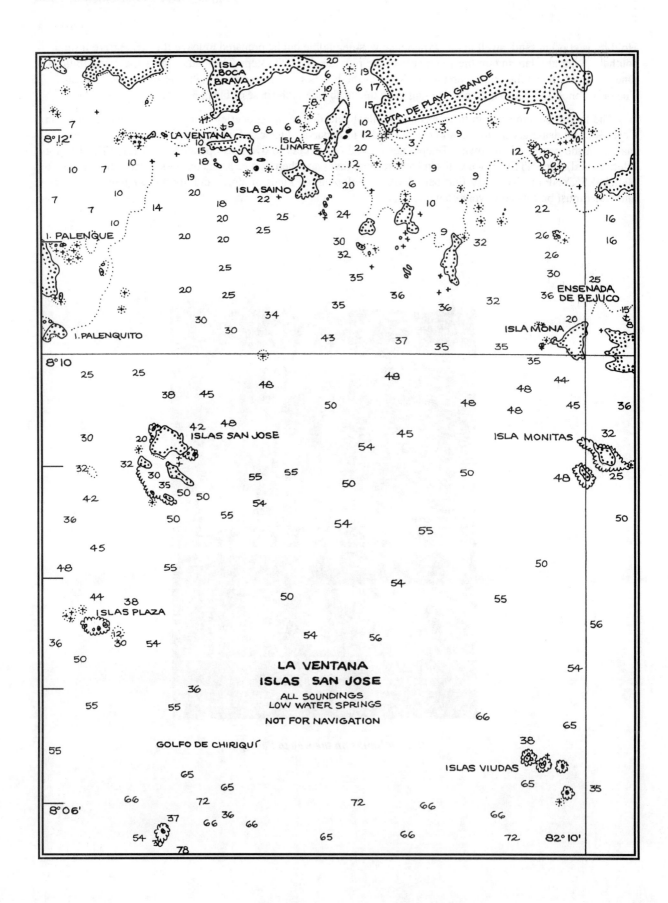

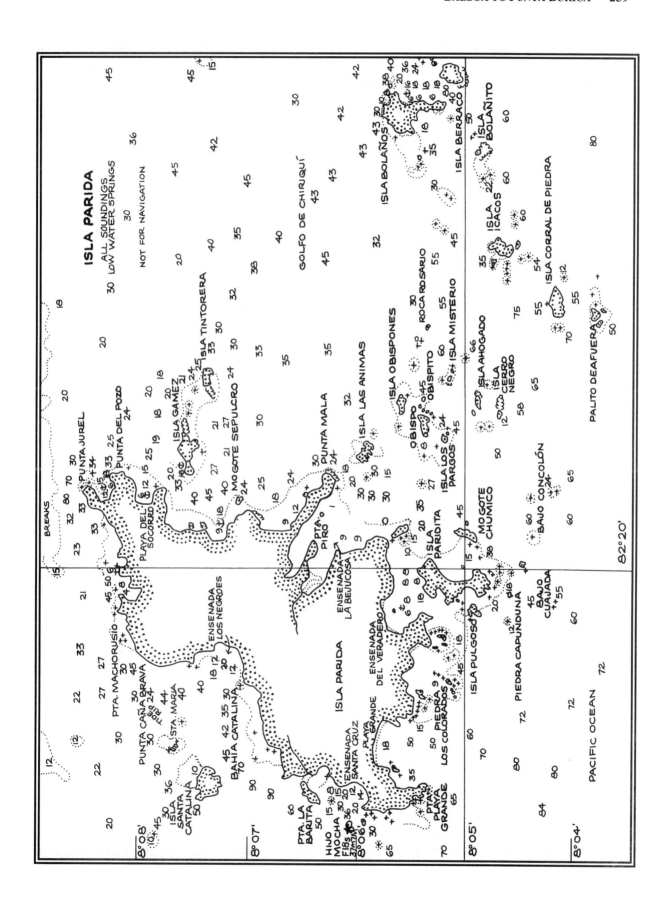

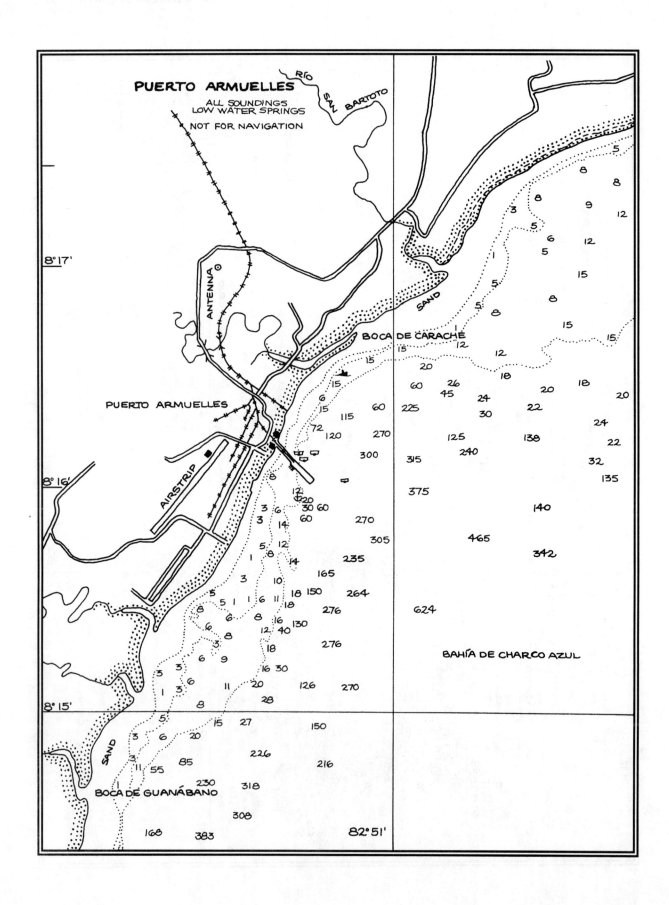

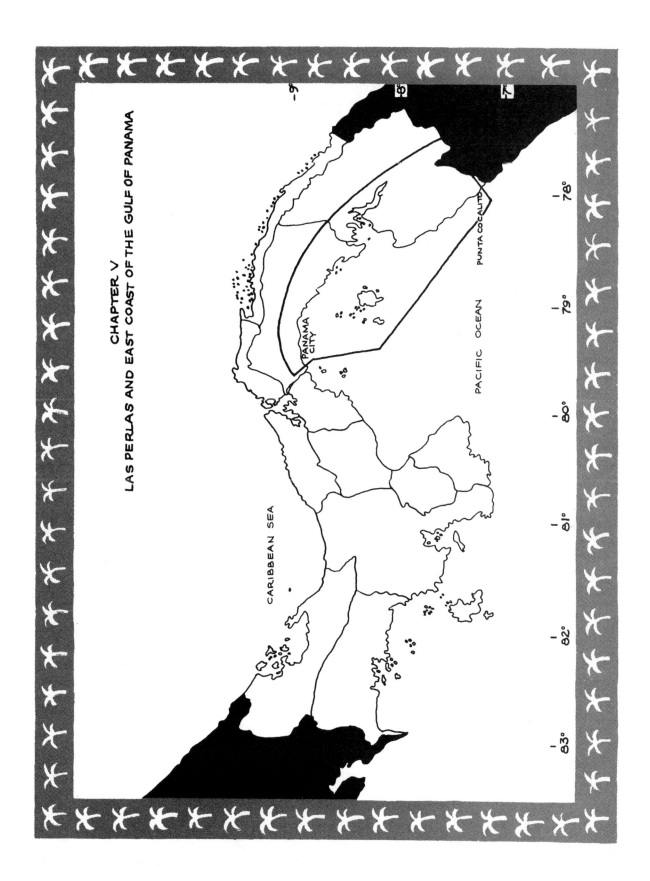

CHAPTER V
LAS PERLAS AND EAST COAST OF THE GULF OF PANAMA

CHAPTER V

LAS PERLAS

AND

EAST COAST OF THE GULF OF PANAMA

This chapter covers the Pacific mainland coast of Panama from the entrance to the Panama Canal to the border with Colombia 160 nautical miles to the east including Las Perlas Islands which lie 38 nautical miles south of the Panama Canal. The best cruising time for the whole area falls between the beginning of January and the middle of April - the driest months there. About the middle of May showers start and will continue with varying intensity until December.

The fairly clear seas of Las Perlas Archipelago attract diving enthusiasts. Snorkelers can find plentiful spiny lobsters and cambombias, large edible mollusks that closely resemble the Caribbean Queen conch when naked, but live in drab rounded shells. Innumerable sandy beaches glow in the sun against the green wooded islands and carpets of orange and purple shells often cover their shores.

The Gulf of San Miguel, east of the Perlas, leads into the heart of Darién and receives several rivers coming from the mountain ranges in the central land mass of Panama. The brown, muddy, swirling waters of these rivers discourage any desires to dive but a cruising sailor will find opportunities to anchor in uninhabited waterways shaded by dense forests along the shores. The awe inspiring roars of howler monkeys roll through the woods, parrots screech in tree tops above the mast head, black mangrove hawks silently patrol the world below, peeping ospreys cruise over mud flats peppered with feeding shorebirds. Occasionally an odd looking mammal of prey will chase crabs among the arching prop roots that bare as the tide falls. The indigenous people, the Embera and Wounaan, live along the rivers in small groupings of thatched huts on stilts. The interiors of the huts, dark with use and smoke from cooking fires, hide astonishing treasures. The women will shyly show the baskets they make, tightly woven, exquisitely shaped and adorned with traditional patterns. The men will pull out a piece of rag wrapped around delicately carved animals cut in tagua, a palm fruit sometimes called ivory nut for its resemblance to polished horn material. These people, gentle and friendly, live off subsistence farming, fishing and hunting, very often with bow and arrows.

Darién forests represent five ecological zones of tropical forests from the high elevations to lowlands, with a flora of about 10,000 known species of plants. Out of 800 resident species of Panamanian land birds, the majority occur in Darién. Sailing in the Gulf of Panama presents a traveler with a display of marine species from giant tentacled jellyfish to marlins jumping out of the sea as if trying to stab the sky. One day when ghosting between Las Perlas and the Darién coast we passed over and among nine whale sharks while two tentatively identified blue whales puffed in the background.

NAVIGATIONAL LIGHTS

Some lighthouses have been printed in incorrect positions on the US DMA marine charts, for example, on Punta Brujas and Punta Garachiné. Refer to the light list in the guide for the correct locations.

SOUNDINGS

On the chartlets for Chapter V all soundings are in feet and have been reduced to extreme Low Water Springs. The US DMA charts use Mean Low Water Springs as datum, however, the tide may fall 2.7 feet below that level at certain times of the year. Consequently, our soundings will show less depth than government charts.

TIDES

A current issue of tide tables should accompany a navigator cruising this area since the tidal range at springs may exceed the already considerable tidal range at neaps by an additional 10 feet. For example, on March 29, 1994 the difference between low tide and high tide was 20.7 feet while on March 21, 1994 the difference between LW and HW was only 7.1 feet. The Port Captain offices in Colón and Balboa give away tide table booklets which tabulate times and heights of the tides for the standard reference ports of Colón and Balboa and the tide differences for a few chosen ports along each coast. Tide tables for Balboa are also printed in a booklet called "Tabla de Mareas" which can be found at the marine stores as well as at Gran Morrison and Novey stores.

The so called "twelves" rule serves to establish the height of the tide at times between LW and HW. According to the rule the tide changes 1/12 of the range during the first hour from LW or HW, whichever the navigator chooses, 2/12 during the 2nd hour, 3/12 during the 3rd hour, 3/12 during the 4th hour, 2/12 during the 5th and 1/12 at the last, 6th hour. To apply the 1,2,3,3,2,1 rule the navigator has to find the tide range for the particular time he needs by finding the difference between the heights of the closest high water and low water. Then, after establishing the value of 1/12 of this particular range he has to add the appropriate number of "twelves" to the nearest LW if the tide is rising or subtract these "twelves" from the nearest HW if the tide is falling. For example: You want to cross a river bar on February 12, 1994 at 0700. The chart shows 4 feet and you want to know the actual depth at the time.

The tide tables show:	12 Feb.	HW 0502	15.2 ft.
	Saturday	LW 1104	-0.8 ft.
	Range	16.0ft.	1/12 = 1.3 ft.

Applying the 1,2,3,3,2,1 rule, the correction for two hours (since you will cross at 0700, 2 hours after HW), that is 1+2 equals 3 which means you need 3 of the twelves you just calculated. Thus, you arrive at 3x1.3 = 3.9 which has to be subtracted from the HW of 15.2 since the tide is falling. The height of the tide at 0700 is 11.3 ft. After adding this to the charted depth of 4 ft. you find the actual depth of the water at 0700 will be 15.3 ft. The rule assumes 6 hour duration of rise or fall. While the duration actually varies either way, the rule works well when applied with a little safety factor as all tidal predictions should be.

TIDAL TERMS ILLUSTRATED

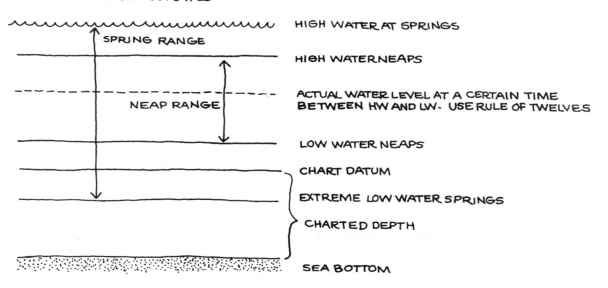

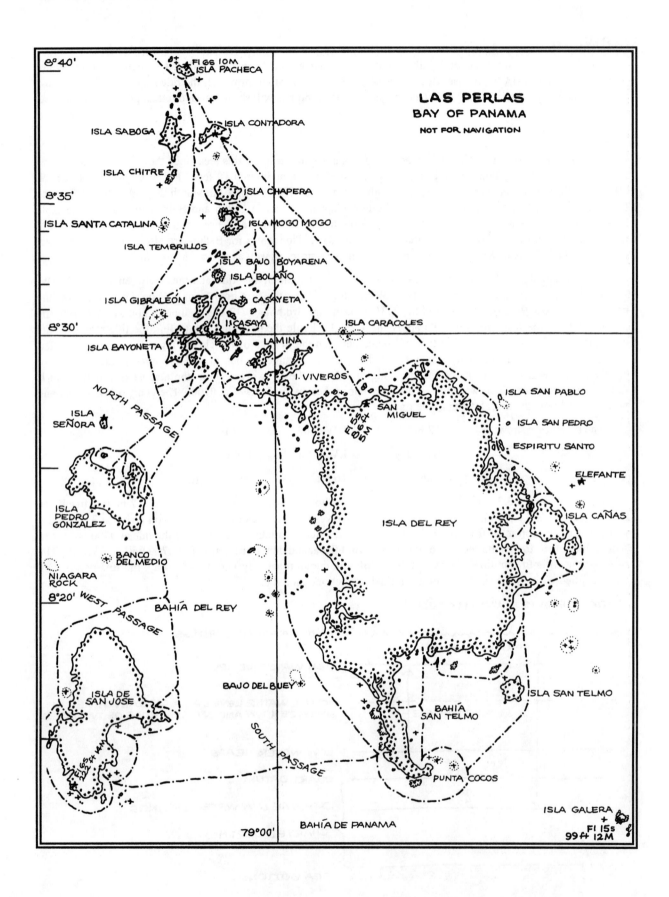

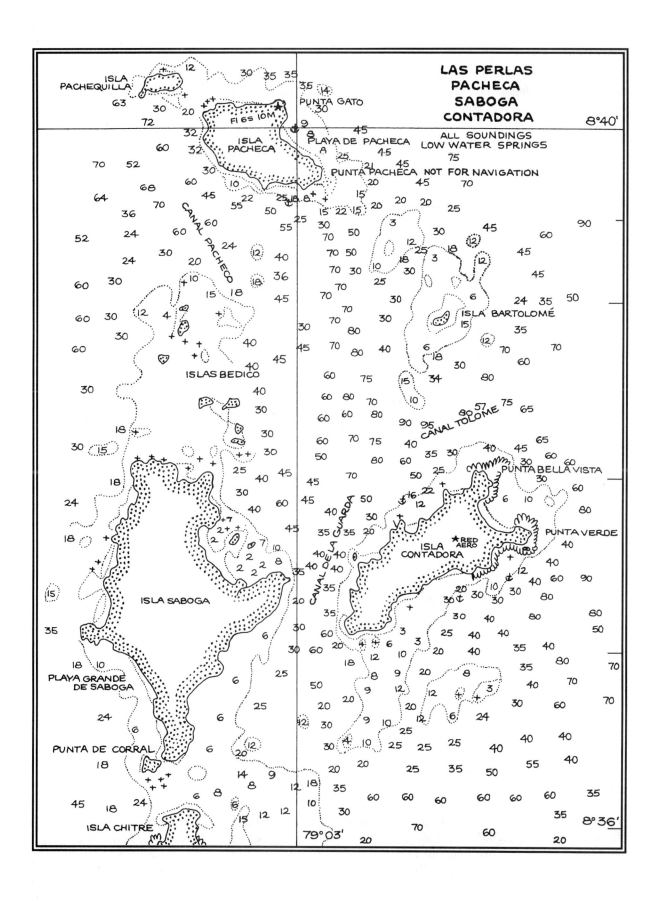

LAS PERLAS

The best cruising time for this archipelago falls during the dry months from the middle of December to about the end of April. Northerly winds prevail then, sometimes reaching 20 to 25 knots, while the otherwise persistent southerly swell diminishes considerably opening many beaches to visiting dinghies and many diving spots to divers. However, Las Perlas with uninhabited islands and untrodden shores make a desirable cruising destination all through the year. In the rainy season and especially during July, August and September an anchorage must always be chosen with an eye to the possible arrival of very large southerly swells. From the navigational point of view, many isolated rocks in unexpected places force a yachtsman to pay attention to charts and chartlets when planning a passage.

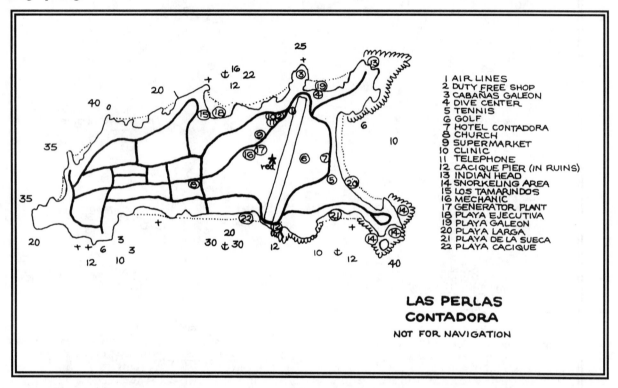

CONTADORA, PACHECA, SABOGA

The name of Contadora will ring familiar to anyone who has followed South American politics. The distance of 38 miles from Balboa and 16 miles from the nearest mainland makes it easy to provide the island with security during meetings of foreign statesmen who often ponder Latin American affairs there as guests of the government of Panama or the wealthy Panamanians who own vacation homes on Contadora. A network of paved roads covers the island and daily scheduled air connections bring it close to Panama City. Contadora Resort Hotel has just expanded to 470 rooms and all modern water sports are available to visitors. The only grocery store also sells gasoline and close to it a large mechanical shop which takes care of the island's generator and resident's cars will also repair outboards or do other work for visiting yachtsmen. Fresh water is very scarce during the dry months.

Depending on the wind direction, yachts anchor off the north or south shores. The best anchorage off the north shore is in the area northeast of the large white pier. Dinghies may land at Playa Ejecutiva (#18) or Playa Galeon (#19). On the south shore one can land on the nudist beach, Playa de la Sueca (#21), or dinghies from yachts which anchor west of the rusty pier can land under the white and blue mill above the beach, Playa Cacique (#22). A path along the side of private property leads to a bigger road. Should the sudden arrival of a strong wind force a yacht to move from one side of the island to the other it should travel around the east point of Contadora in clear deep water, especially at night. All anchorages have good holding in sand and marl.

LAS PERLAS AND THE EAST GULF OF PANAMA

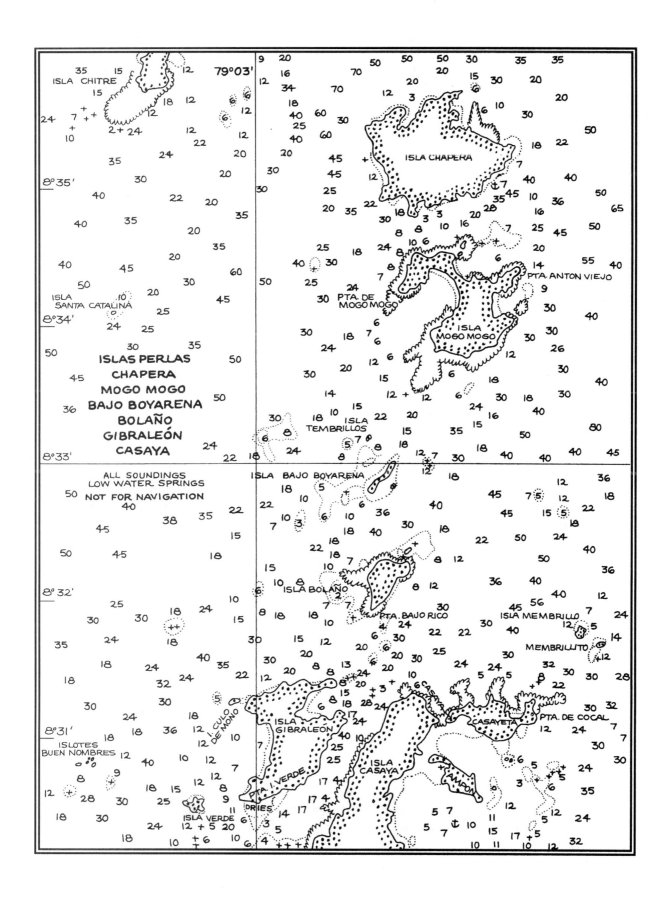

A yacht can also seek protection from winds and waves off the southeastern point of Pacheca where the anchorage in 15 to 28 feet of water has a good holding bottom in sand. Pacheca serves thousands of cormorants, frigates and pelicans as a giant rookery. The owner of the island prohibits bothering the birds although short term visitors can land on the sandy spit off the southeastern point. A strong guano smell may permeate a boat anchored downwind of the rookery!

Saboga has a small clean settlement whose inhabitants mainly work on Contadora. The anchorage off Saboga has a very rocky bottom with poor holding in depths less than 30 to 40 feet. The best method of visiting Saboga may be by dinghy from Contadora.

ISLA CHAPERA AND MOGO MOGO

The channel between these two islands has good protection but the bottom is very uneven and rocky. The best anchorage over a sandy bottom lies off the small white beach at the southeastern side of Chapera. Panamanian vacationers often come here from Contadora, including teams of jet skiers. Mogo Mogo beaches invite dinghy trips and rarely have visitors. Both islands are densely wooded and uninhabited.

BAJO BOYARENA

South of Mogo Mogo a large heap of sand bordered with volcanic rocks makes a good day trip during low tides when this bank, Bajo Boyarena, grows into an island. Big old cowries, limpets and cambombia shells lay strewn over the bar. Only during spring high tides does the bank disappear totally under water. Anchor off the south edge where holding is poor on a rocky bottom covered by a thin layer of sand.

Countless islets fringe the main islands of Las Perlas Islands.

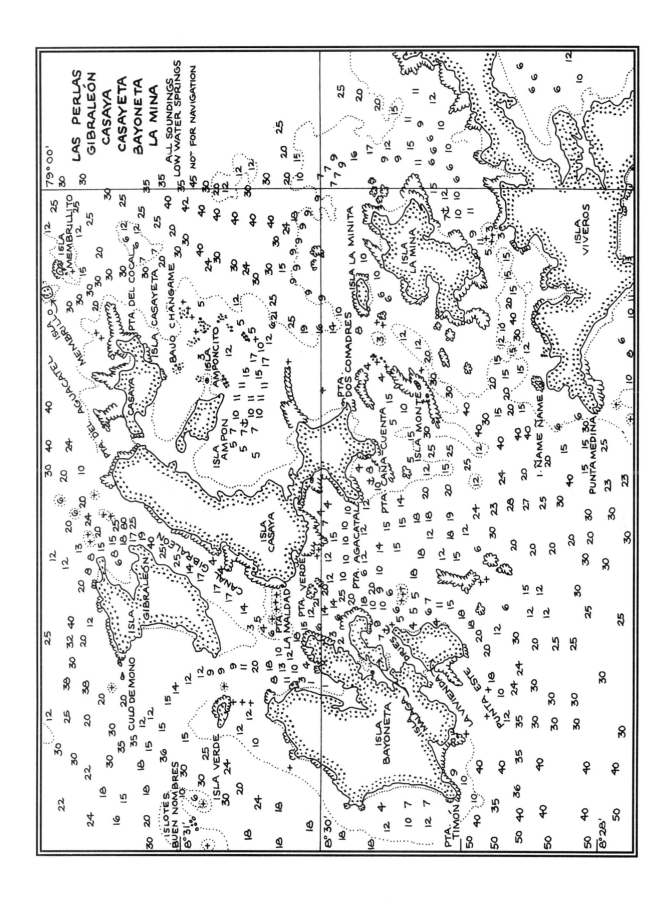

CANAL GIBRALEON

The channel between the island of Gibraleon (privately owned) and Casaya stays smooth no matter what direction the winds and waves come from outside. The easiest entrance is from the northeast. Pass ¼ of a mile north of Isla Membrillo, then steer for the northeast point of Gibraleon. The depths vary between 20 and 30 feet. This course takes a boat close to and north of a large rocky heap which may disappear in very high spring tides. For the sake of your nervous system, plan the entrance soon after low tide when the sea level starts rising and while the rocks are easily visible. Anchor any place in the channel between the islands. From here you may want to dinghy to Isla Casayeta and visit the tiny village of Casaya. People there sell oyster pearls, nowadays quite small, but a reminder that the famous 31 carat Peregrina pearl worn by the English Queen Mary Tudor came from these islands. You can exit Canal Gibraleon by the southern opening which has only 3 feet at spring low tides. Many rocks extend from the south west point of Casaya at Punta La Maldad while a wide sandy shoal runs south from Gibraleon, so favor the Gibraleon side of center.

ISLA CASAYA

The southwest coast of Casaya between Punta Agacatal and Punta Caña Cuenta has a nice anchorage off a small cozy beach. On the other, east side of Casaya lies Isla Ampon with an anchorage off its south shore. To enter you must negotiate a channel between two sets of rocky shoals. A back bearing of 112°T on the obvious white beach on the northeast point of Isla Viveros leads between these dangers which become visible only at low tide. South of Isla Amponcito the bottom tends to be sandy and changes to mud as you go further in. The village of Casaya on Casayeta is an easy dinghy trip from here. One of the homes sells cold sodas and children sell shiny dark cowries the size of eggs.

ISLA BAYONETA

Isla Bayoneta with its satellite islets of Malaga and La Vivienda, abounding with shore birds and an untrodden beach on the west coast makes a miniature cruising ground. A good anchorage midway between the east points of Malaga and La Vivienda has good holding in a mud and sand bottom. Rocky spurs run out from all the points around so do not venture too close to the shore. A bright purple and orange beach off the south coast of the northeastern arm of Bayoneta lured us into believing the beach lay covered with fallen flowers, instead we found layers of bright scallop shells. This is a low tide person's dream anchorage, beaches and explorable bars are prolific.

ISLA MINA

An anchorage off a cove on the southeastern shore of Isla Mina has mediocre holding in a bottom of small rocks and sand. Do not go too close to the tempting little cove as rock spurs reach from the shore far into the channel. This anchorage, apart from good protection, places a yacht within a short dinghy ride to several sandy beaches on the north shore of Isla Viveros. Sometimes yachts anchor southwest of the west point of Isla Mina but the turbulent currents there make it an uneasy anchorage.

ISLA VIVEROS

The anchorage in firm sand off Playa Brava on the south shore of the uninhabited Isla Viveros can be entered from the south through a deep channel which leads between Platania and Quiros islets. This easily accessible anchorage can accommodate a small fleet. The beaches to visit by dinghy, Playa Brava and Playa Ensenada, are long interesting strands good for stretching your legs. At low tide the beautiful, well wooded Platania and others around it swarming with sea birds make good shore explorations. Leave via the safe route you used when entering. Although the waters along the shore westward to Punta Medina are deep we found a few scattered rocks making it necessary to move this way only at low tide when dangers can be seen.

Las Perlas and the East Gulf of Panama

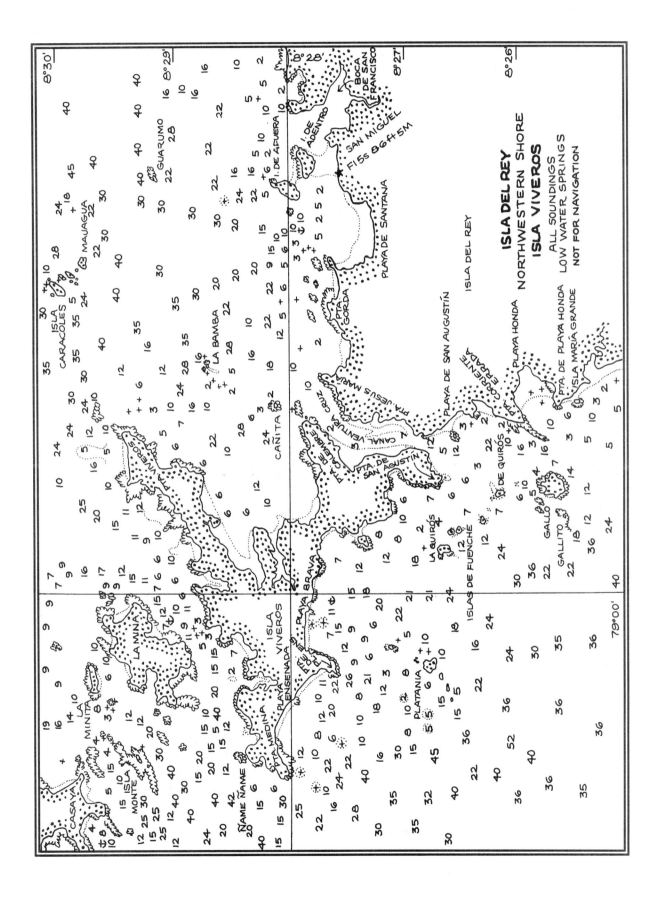

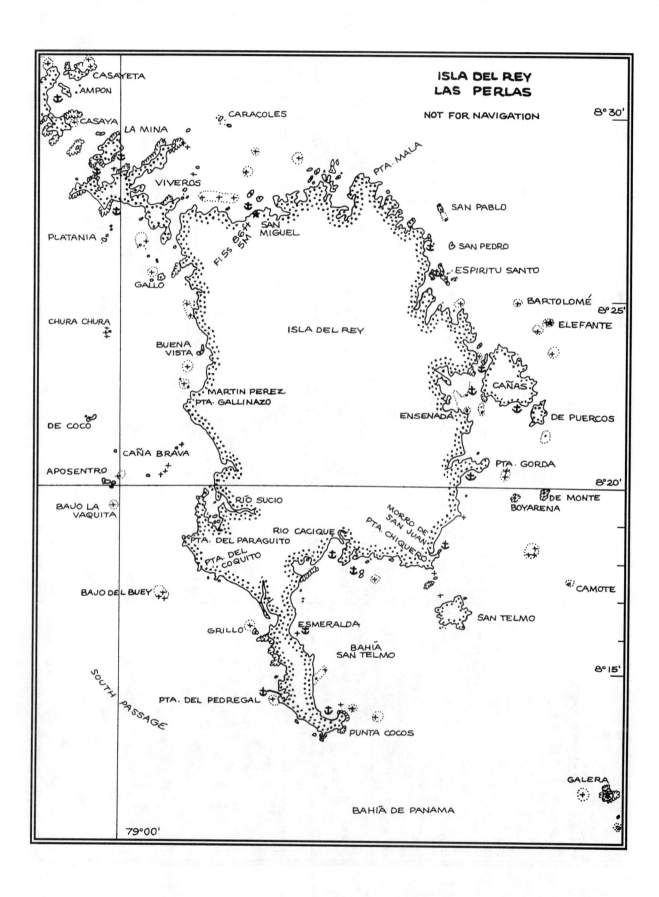

Las Perlas and the East Gulf of Panama 273

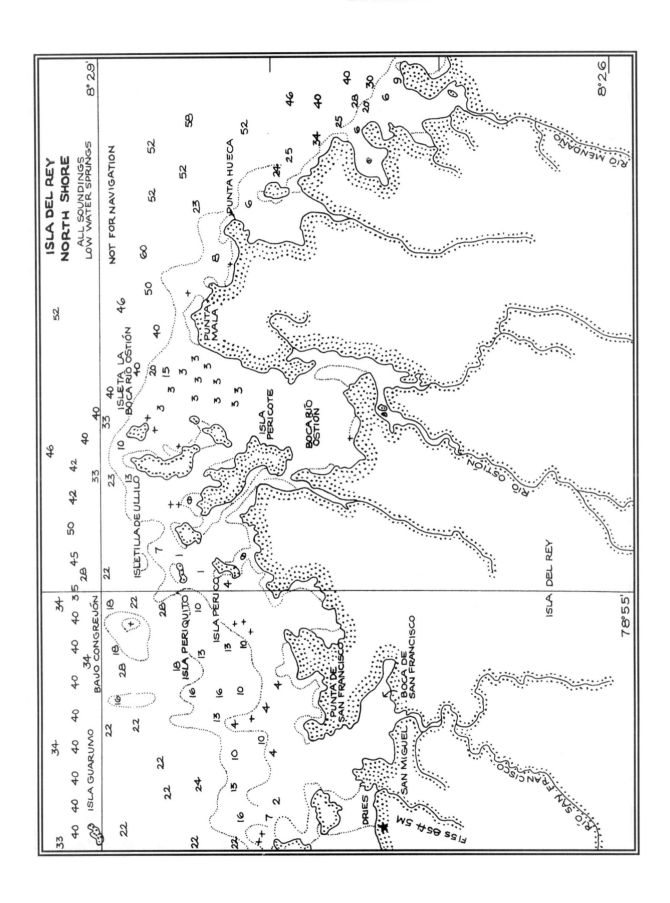

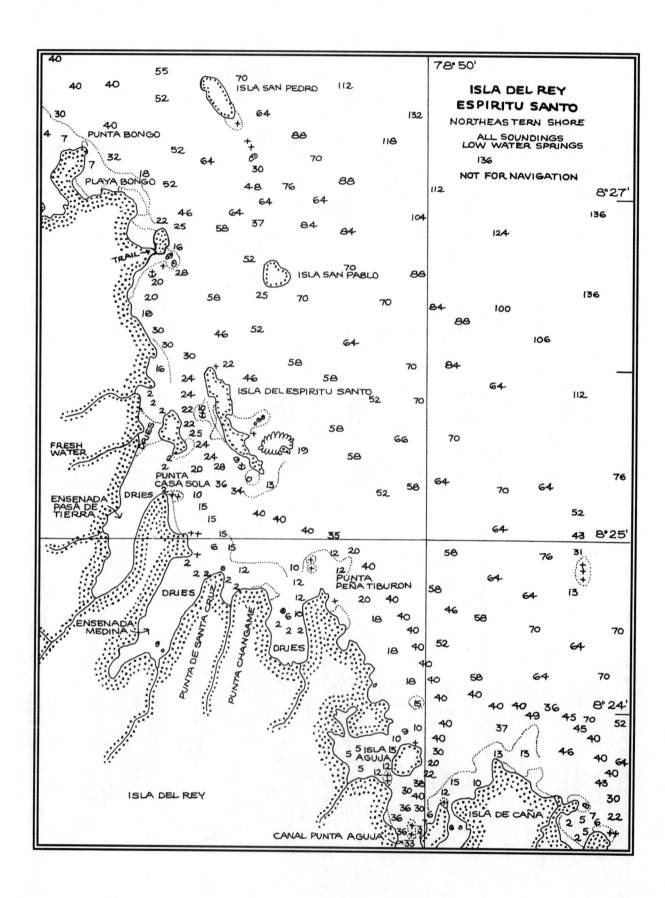

LAS PERLAS AND THE EAST GULF OF PANAMA 275

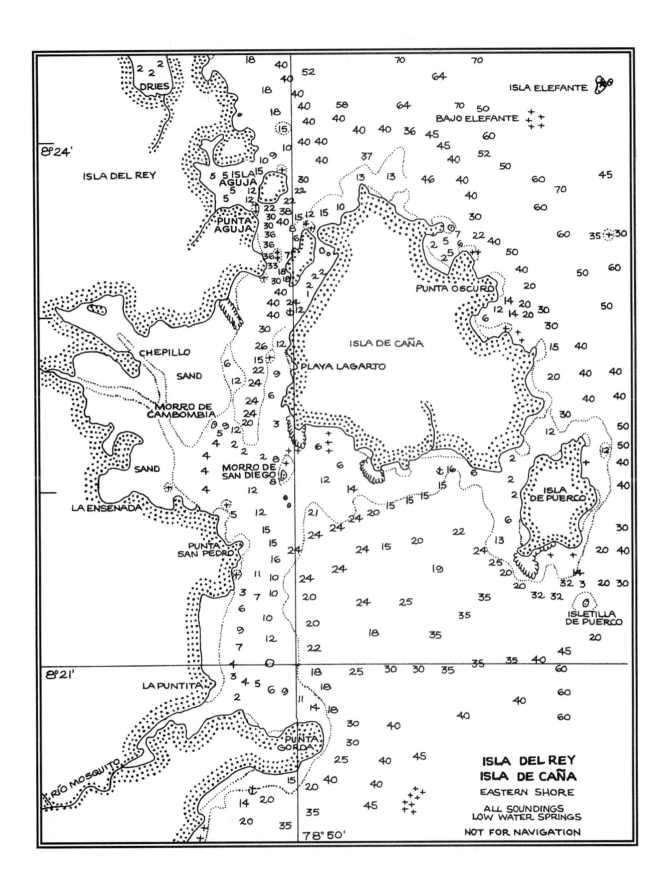

276 THE PANAMA GUIDE

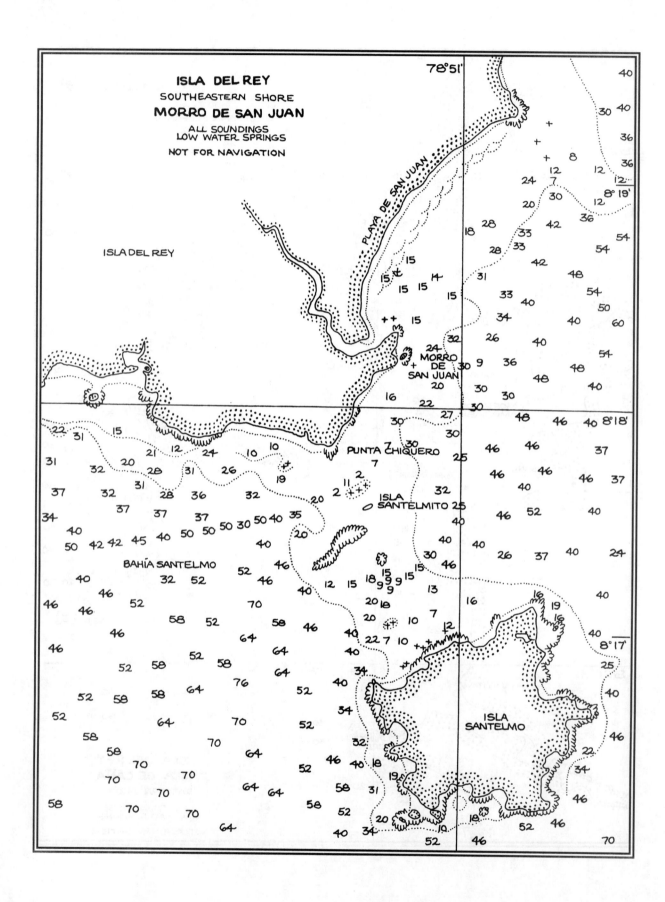

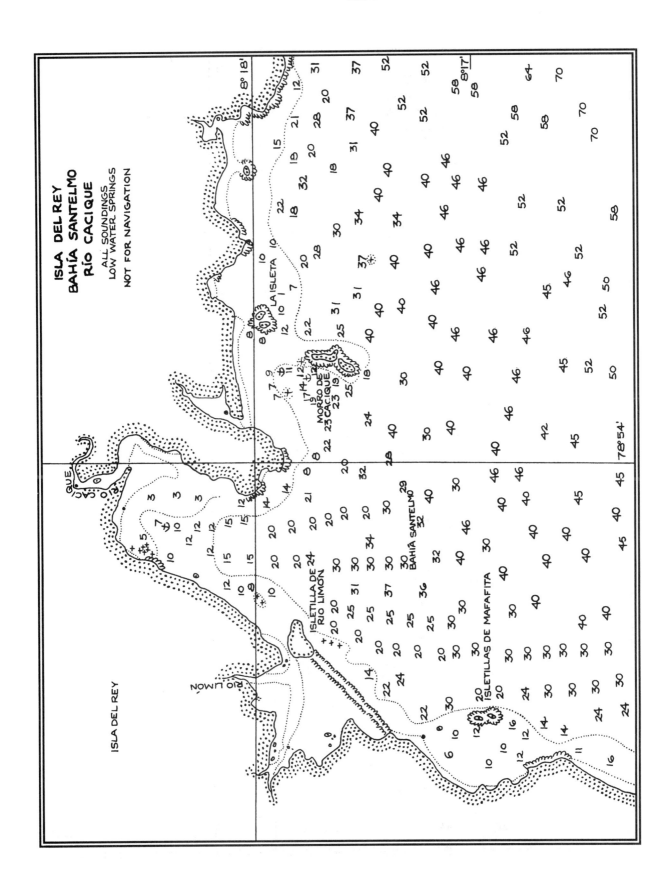

278   THE PANAMA GUIDE

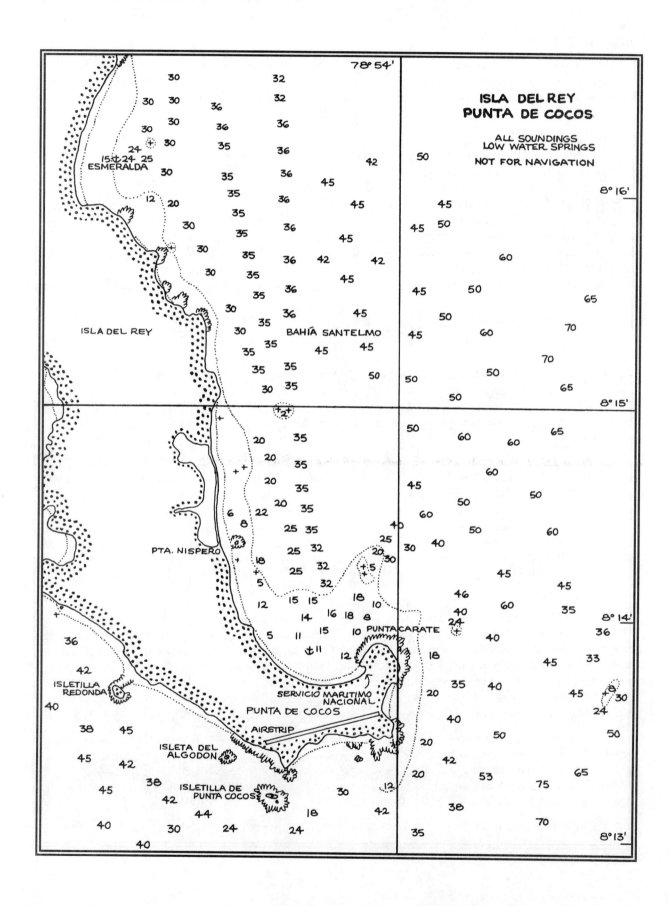

ISLA DEL REY

This largest island in Las Perlas has four villages, San Miguel, Ensenada, Esmeralda and Martín Perez, but you will see only an occasional dugout canoe going by. By far the most noticeable aspect around here is the profusion of wild beaches, the most accessible ones situated along the eastern shores.

SAN MIGUEL

A yacht coming from the north will soon spot the houses of San Miguel, the most populated settlement in Las Perlas, on the north shore of the island. The community has a phone, several stores, bakery, outboard motor and generator mechanic, while potable water and fuels are also available. The runway has scheduled weekly flights. It is best to time your arrival at the anchorage off Isla de Afuera at low water in order to see the rocky shoal close to it. At other times anchor further out in 15 feet or so. The best and safest dinghy landing lies right under the front door of the office of the Servicio Maritimo Nacional (the coast guard of Panama). Scout the beach for sharp debris that may damage your dinghy and remember the considerable tides since a large bar in front of San Miguel dries. A yacht eastbound from San Miguel should keep outside numerous islets and shoal banks until Punta Bongo after which deep water runs close along the shore as far as Isla Espiritu Santo.

ISLA ESPIRITU SANTO

The channel along the west side of Espiritu Santo creates a perfect anchorage area over a sandy bottom. In strong northerly conditions some gentle swell enters with the incoming current and then a yacht can move a little further south. The white beach in the middle of the island extends fairly far south, so sound your way in carefully if arriving at high tide after the beach has disappeared. At night keep an anchor light on as fishermen anchor in this area, too, sometimes arriving in the dark. Another anchorage, more comfortable than it appears on the chart, lies under the prominent point of Isla del Rey north of Espiritu Santo. A little path cuts across the point to another bay.

To explore all the coves, beaches and to do all the diving this area offers would take a long time. One can walk across Espiritu Santo on an overgrown path which starts at the south end of the beach. The east side of the island has a small beach from where a short swim will take a snorkeler to a group of rocks. On Isla del Rey behind an offlying islet a small stream of fresh water comes down from the hills during the better part of the year. Another pretty beach and a stream lie around Punta Casa Sola. The remains of two houses there are surrounded by annato, mango, lime and coconut trees all now very overgrown so wear long pants and rubber boots when tackling the bush.

ISLA DE CAÑA

A channel, Canal Punta Aguja, separates Isla de Caña from Isla del Rey and it can be navigated with caution. The deep water runs close to Isla Aguja and Punta Aguja west of the rocky shoal in mid channel. The shoal disappears with the rising tide. A smooth anchorage off the west shore of Isla de Caña has good holding in a sandy bottom. In the early mornings and late afternoons local cayucos pass this way going to and from farming plots. You can also anchor close to the little Morro de Cambombia and visit La Ensenada, a tiny village of less than a hundred very friendly people who have pearls to sell as well as fruit in season. To go further south inside Isla de Caña you will have to wait for the tide to come up to take you over the 2 foot bar.

The hilly east coast of Isla de Caña has two coves with enticing white beaches, orange bluffs and shiny black bouldered outcroppings. One cove lies north and one south of Punta Oscuro. Anchoring in the northern bay, with large trees shading the sand and sparkling bottle green water, could be a disaster if the wind came from the northeast. The cove south of Punta Oscuro does not penetrate the island as much and has less protection. There are scattered rocks near the beach. Treat both bays as day anchorages.

A good anchorage lies off the long beach backed by farmed hills on the southeastern shore of Isla de Caña. Although protected from the north the southerly swell may find its way in.

PUNTA GORDA

The anchorage on the south side of Punta Gorda has excellent holding in sand and very good protection in the dry season. It stays fairly comfortable in the other months although between May and December a swell may arrive from the south. A spectacular long beach is the main attraction. Shoals and islets to the east, de Monte and Boyarena, are visited by a dive boat from Contadora. Because of strong currents and variable visibility under water only experienced open water divers should venture there.

NOTE: The chartlets of the east coast of Isla del Rey between Punta Gorda and Morro de San Juan do not overlap.

PLAYA DE SAN JUAN

Sailing southward from Punta Gorda give a wide berth to the vast rocky shoals which extend southeastward from the northeast point of Playa de San Juan. The chartlets do not overlap in this area. After rounding this navigational hazard, a day anchorage ¼ mile north of the prominent Morro de San Juan will give you easy access to another long classic white untamed beach. You can also dinghy at high tide into the creek which flanks the northwest side on Morro de San Juan. A tiny cove with a beach for two lies under the hill of Morro de San Juan.

SANTELMITO CHANNEL

A prominent islet, Santelmito, stands in the middle of the wide channel between San Telmo and Isla del Rey. There are rocks in here but the passage on the south side of Santelmito has the widest clear channel. Still, it should be negotiated at low tide when the rocky shoals close to Santelmito break the surface. The rocky patch charted closer to San Telmo will remain unseen. Once you have located the Santelmito shoals pass south of them steering 245°T for the deep waters of Bahía San Telmo. If you missed the low tide for this passage take the safe route and go east and south of Isla San Telmo, a beautiful, densely wooded island protected by ANCON.

BAHÍA SAN TELMO

Three widely spaced isolated rocks, one east of Morro de Cacique, one northeast of Punta Nispero and another east of Punta de Cocos, demand careful navigation in this otherwise quite deep area. Also, avoid rocks north and east of Punta de Cocos and east of Esmeralda as well as others close to the shore.

MORRO DE CACIQUE

The islands of Morro de Cacique make this a smooth anchorage with good holding on a sandy bottom. Ashore a nice beach beckons but the tiny lagoon at its western end almost dries out at mid tide. The word "cacique," which means a native chief, may refer to King Toe after whom Isla del Rey (the King Island) was named. We speculated that perhaps he lived in this area when the Spanish arrived in 1515 to defeat and enslave the indigenous inhabitants who were at that time skilled pearl divers. Two conquistadors, Gaspar de Morales and Francisco Pizarro, seized masses of pearls from Toe thus bringing the islands to the attention of the Spanish conquerors.

RIO CACIQUE

The excellent anchorage in the bay off Rio Cacique allows explorers the chance to dinghy into this stream around high tide. Between tides make sure to avoid some rocks at the mouth of the creek after which the bottom consists mostly of sand and deep channels may be found close to the shores. The trees grow higher as the stream narrows and many birds feed on the banks. Occasionally yachts dry out on the gently shelving beach at the head of the bay to scrub their bottoms and apply antifouling.

ESMERALDA

Previously known as Mafafa, the village of Esmeralda changed its name about 20 years ago although the old name persists on some charts. Drinking water is available here throughout the year along with some produce, depending on what is in season. Young men who fish daily always have fish, shrimp or lobsters for sale. The anchorage lies off the village beach south of the submerged rock. At times of southerly swell the steep beach can cause a wet landing. Small shops with limited dry goods may have cold sodas. We do not recommend anchoring here overnight.

PUNTA DE COCOS

Punta de Cocos and its shoals protect the anchorage here from any southerly swell, a feature appreciated especially during the rainy months. During the dry season a chop may enter when the wind tends to the northeast. Ashore, a Panamanian flag flutters above the station of the Servicio Maritimo Nacional (the coast guard of Panama) and the friendly, courteous men on duty will come in their boat to take the name of your vessel and the names of the crew, they do not inspect any other papers like "zarpes" or cruising permits. To us, the reason to anchor here is the access to the spectacular beach and shore along the south side of Punta de Cocos. To get there, leave the dinghy at the Servicio beach and take the path that leads to the old World War II landing strip which is still in excellent condition. Walk west on the runway until you see a tarmac side road on your left. Take that and you will eventually walk along a grassy trail to a point overlooking the ocean. A few abandoned remains of houses stand under the coconut palms and a set of stairs leads to the eastern beach by the side of the easternmost house. At high tide a rocky headland will stop you from walking far to the west, but you can descend to the shore on a faint path at the west end of the runway. The walk from Punta de Cocos to Punta del Concholon is nearly two nautical miles long on a deserted untrodden beach.

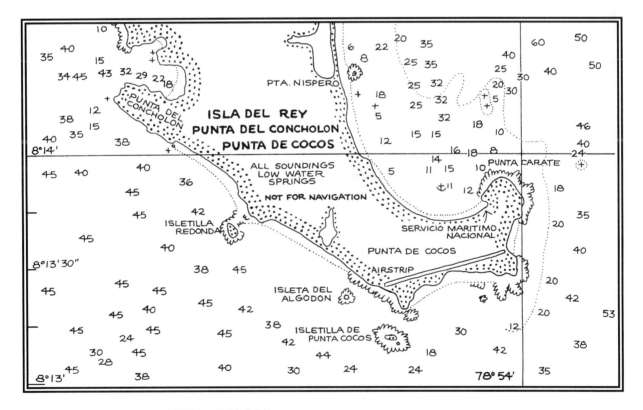

THE WEST SHORE OF ISLA DEL REY

The bay on the north side of Punta Concholon, sometimes called Punta Pedregal, makes a good anchorage during the dry season. When entering, favor the southern side of the center of the bay entrance since rocky spurs extend from the north point. Proceed into the southern bay and anchor off the beach. A deep water channel leads northwards between Isla del Rey and the outlying navigational hazards. Spectacular beaches flank this coast but the size of the swell discouraged us from attempting to land a dinghy on any of them. Martín Perez, a small village, stands on the north side of Punta Gallinazo and small local fishing boats anchor between the rocks in front of the settlement in an area probably only accessible to a shallow draft multihull.

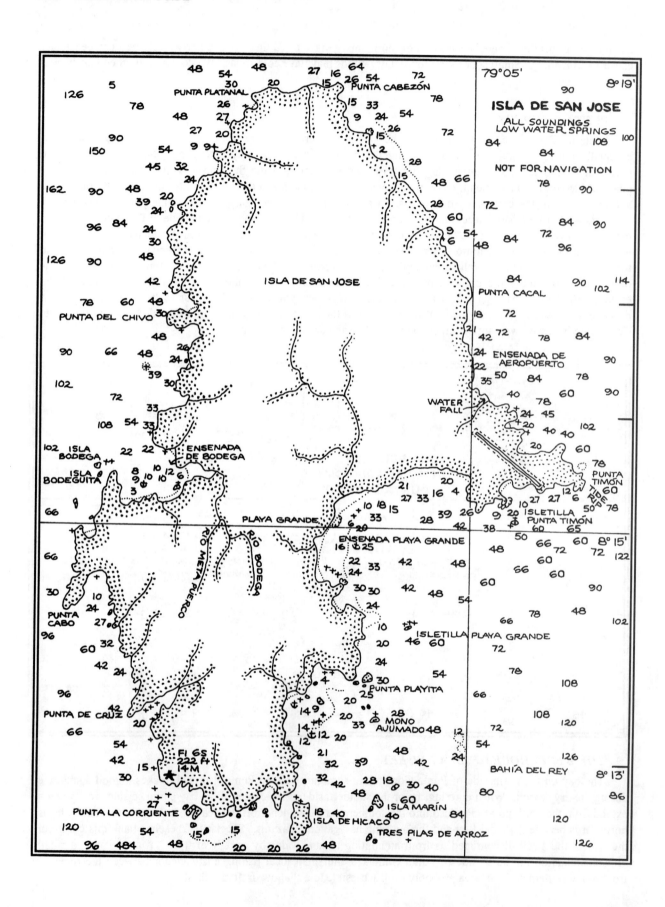

ISLA DE SAN JOSE

The owners of Isla de San Jose have put up several no trespassing and no hunting signs. While originally these were aimed at Panamanian hunters, the instances of yachtsmen dumping their garbage and used engine oil ashore has somewhat soured owner-visitor relations. Dieter (see later in the text) has a place for used oil and garbage so dispose of them with him.

Roads crisscross the island and if you venture ashore walk with an eye open for snakes and wild pig traps. One of the island's owners often flies in and stays in his camper which he moves around the island on the superb roads his highway construction company has built.

After more than a decade of camping ashore with their tiny ketch hanging on a mooring nearby, Dieter Ziesler and Gerda Leve from Hamburg have become the reason why most cruising yachts visit this island. They live in a bay to the southwest of Punta Playita and welcome yachts, even though Dieter maintains a busy work schedule to keep their farm going. During December and January he has citrus fruit for sale.

The bottom in this anchorage alternates between rock and sand. The closer you get to Dieter's SEEPFERDEN the rockier it gets. Further out towards Mono Ajumado (smoked monkey) rock you will find better bottom, but make sure the anchor holds. Some swell always enters here and it can get rolly. In July, August and September large breaking rollers may suddenly appear, too.

ENSENADA PLAYA GRANDE

Just to the north, around Punta Playita, Ensenada Playa Grande makes a lot smoother anchorage with good holding in mud and sand. At low tide the beach here becomes quite large. Enjoy it but remember that San Jose is a private island.

NORTH OF PUNTA TIMON

North of Punta Timon several bays invite day stops. The second white beach from Punta Timon has a nice small bay, a stream of fresh water and a cleared grassy track that connects it to the roads on the island. The bottom is hard rock with pockets of sand, so double check that your anchor holds.

ENSENADA BODEGA

On the west coast the large Ensenada de Bodega has less protection than the chart suggests because the bay becomes very shallow further in. In the dry months, December, January, February, it will serve much better as long as the wind does not come to blow from the northwest with some strength. The bottom is sand mixed with pieces of pumice and some flat rocks - make sure the anchor holds.

A few maintenance workers live in two homes situated above the anchorage which has everything a cruising enthusiast may desire in terms of scenery. Coconut palms line the peach colored beaches, rocks of obviously recent volcanic origin have frozen in intricate patterns and a winding but extremely shallow creek runs inland. You may see crocodiles, they live in many creeks around the island.

SOUTH TIP OF SAN JOSE

The German yacht, SOUL MASSAGE, with a draft of 4½ feet anchored in the bay northwest of Isla de Hicaco. In December and January, the season of northerlies, the anchorage remained smooth. The skipper, Frank, entered passing close to the west side of a small islet in the middle of the bay and reported 10 feet further in. A short path from this bay leads across the island to Dieter and Gerda's.

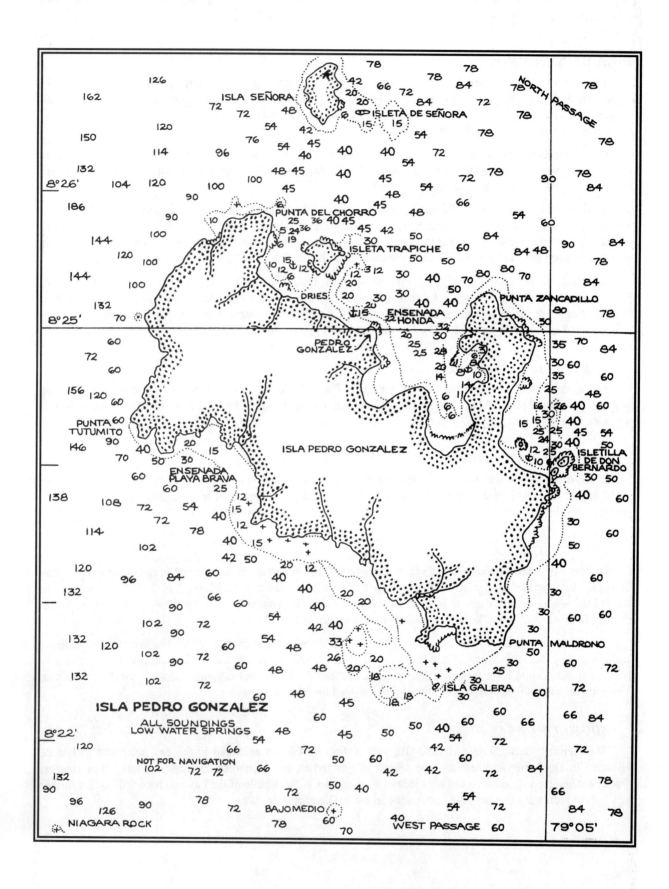

ISLA PEDRO GONZALES

The West Passage, the channel between Pedro Gonzales and San Jose, has two isolated submerged dangers, Roca Niagara and Banco del Medio - navigate carefully when crossing this body of water.

PEDRO GONZALES

The 450 friendly people in the small village on the north shore of Pedro Gonzales welcome visitors and always have some products from their farms to sell. The tienda has a few dry goods, eggs and cold sodas. Gasoline is available near the beach landing. However, the frequent occurrence of strong northerlies from the end of November until the end of May make the anchorage off the village only good for a few hours. If your draft allows you can find a well protected anchorage in the northeast corner of Ensenada Honda. Beware of the long rocky spur marked on the sketch chart - it disappears under the rising tide. The anchorage in the bight west of Isleta Trapiche is also good according to local fishermen, but although we have sailed into the bay we have not spent any time there during the northerlies. Pelicans nest on the shores.

ISLA SEÑORA

Isla Señora, ½ mile north of Punta del Chorro, has a large breeding colony of pelicans. Young birds learn to fly during May and June and many die in the process. Their corpses floating around show how much a wild species has to compensate for the normally large mortality rate of their offspring.

DON BERNARDO

A good anchorage with excellent holding in sand on the east cost of Pedro Gonzales lies between Isletilla de Don Bernardo and a little islet with a white cross. The clear approach presents no problem and there is plenty of room to maneuver. The pretty coconut palm lined beach, which makes this one of the most beautiful anchorages in the Perlas, has several trails leading into the hills beyond.

Playa Don Bernardo, Isla Pedro Gonzales, Las Perlas Islands.

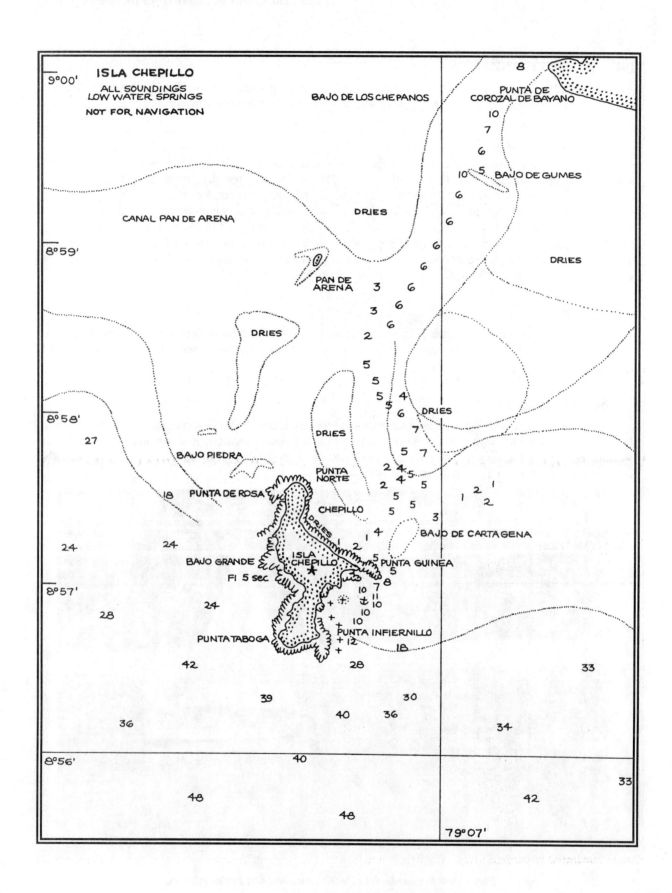

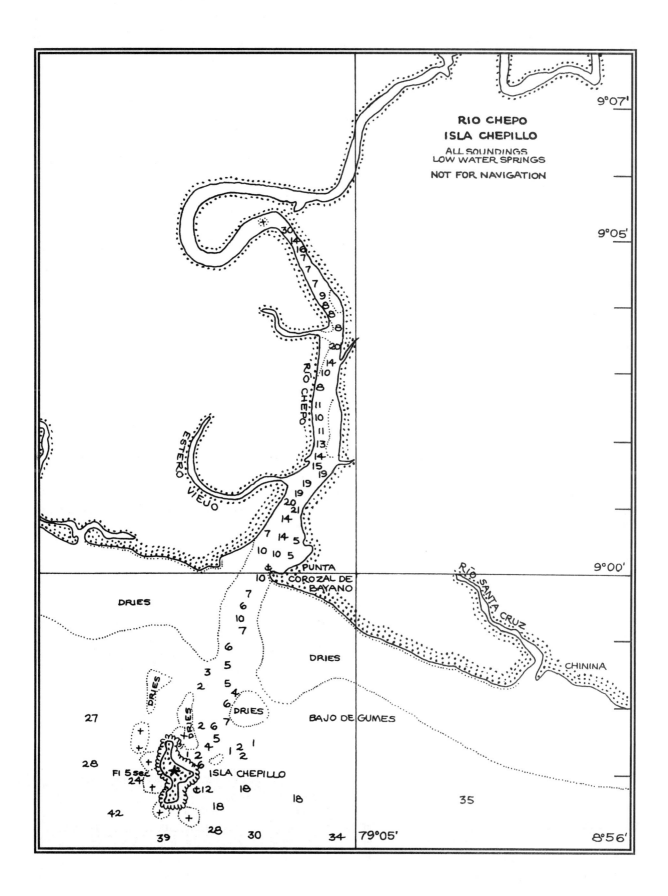

EAST COAST OF THE GULF OF PANAMA

ISLA CHEPILLO

A mere 25 nautical miles from Balboa a conspicuous wooded island guards the entrance to the Chepo River which flows for over 24 nautical miles from Bayano Lake Dam.

Chepillo has a permanent population of about a hundred people who are engaged in fishing and subsistence farming. Their prosperous village on the northeastern shore of the island has a plentiful supply of good fresh water and a few small stores which sell basic goods and cold sodas. No fuels are available. A pay phone near the church can connect you to the international operators to call direct (109 and 106). A small police building stands next to the white Catholic church and the friendly men on duty may ask the purpose of your visit or to see your papers.

Isla Chepillo has an impressive array of rocky arms jutting far into the sea. The southeastern point ends in a long string of rocks which vanish as the tide rises. Give this shoal a wide berth as it causes the impressive breakers which often attract cruising surfers. The best anchorage, just south of Punta Guinea, has a firm mud mixed with sand bottom - excellent holding in 10 to 12 feet. Punta Guinea ends in a long rocky spur which also disappears under a rising tide. Do no venture past the transit line formed by the high rocks of Punta Guinea and trees on Punta Norte. A bearing of 300°T on the white lighthouse high on the hill designates the southern limit of the anchorage. The latticed structure of the light drops behind foliage as the boat nears shore so take bearings early enough. At low tide all dangers become clearly visible. Also, at low tide one can walk, or rather bolder hop around the island and admire the colors and formations of the rocks along the western shores.

The village overlooks drying mud flats flanking the river estuary. Shrimp trawlers often dry out here or anchor in 5 to 6 feet of water on the north side of Punta Guinea and close to the rocks.

RIO CHEPO

If you contemplate going up the Rio Chepo you should walk to the southeast end of the paved walkway in the village and look out over the pattern of shoals at low tide. The depth in the shallow channel between the drying banks can change considerably within a year and where we once had 7 to 8 feet we later encountered 4 to 5 feet. Hence, always venture into Rio Chepo on the rising tide. The river gets deeper near its mouth and we have tacked as far as the first tight loop to the west where a thumb like large bolder sticking out above the narrowing water of the river convinced us to turn back. At this point the dense coastal forest full of birds and howler monkeys gives way to pasture land and we felt that progressing further at the risk of bouncing on rocks was not worth it. However, small freighters from Panama City go with the high tide all the way to the cattle town of Chepo. In the lower forested parts of the river a yacht can anchor almost anywhere. The two small rivers that join Chepo along its western shore invite dinghy exploring and watching blue herons, white herons and ospreys. Flocks of ibis frequent the river in the mornings and evenings and formations of cormorants commute up and down all day. A 10 to 12 foot deep anchorage may be found close to the shore northwest of Punta Corozal de Bayano. From here walking enthusiasts can follow the beach which continues to the southeast for many miles. One family lives on the point permanently and fishermen frequently occupy the thatched shelters nearby.

PUNTA BRUJAS

Punta Brujas, an arm of craggy forested land terminating in a lighthouse 63 nautical miles from Balboa, cuts off the ocean swell and protects the anchorage off the fishing village. To enter bring the point of Brujas to bear 090° True and distant about 2 miles, then locate Roca Shag, visible against the low wooded land, and steer 020°True for the rock. To enter by GPS first arrive at 08°34.8'N, 078°34.7'W and steer 020°T for Roca Shag. When the village bears 110°T steer for it and anchor off the beach according to your draft. The villagers advised that the deepest and smoothest anchorage is further east along the south bank at the mouth of Rio Trinidad - sound your way in carefully. Well water, gasoline and very basic supplies are available in this settlement of hard working fishermen. An experienced boat builder lives here capable of constructing 40 to 50 foot long fishing vessels. A seafood buyer's plane occasionally comes from Panama City and lands on the beach at low tide.

On his first expedition across the isthmus the conquistador Balboa on a clear day sighted the Las Perlas archipelago from Brujas. This first trans-isthmian journey by a European took him out of the Gulf of San Miguel, west along the coast to Brujas, then inland again at Chimán.

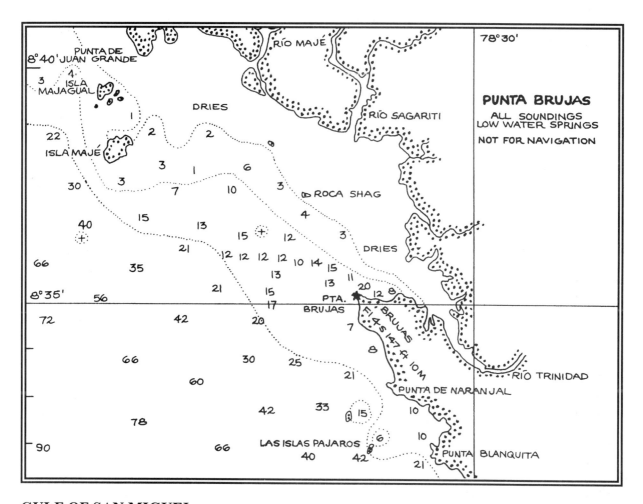

GULF OF SAN MIGUEL

Scarcely 18 nautical miles southeast of Brujas (or 80 nautical miles from Balboa) lies the fabulous San Miguel Gulf. The easiest and deepest passage into the Gulf leads through the middle of the six mile wide entrance marked by a lighthouse on Isla Batatilla to the north and a lighthouse on Punta Patiña to the south. It is also possible to sail in close to the north shore along Punta Brava and Punta San Lorenzo passing north of the breaking shoals of **Banco del Buey** and then turning south close to the western shore of Isla Batatilla before heading east again into the Gulf. In the mouth of the Gulf great swirls of brown muddy water mixing with greener ocean waters may cause unnecessary alarm. Actually, these are only a prelude to the totally brown thick water further in.

Several rivers empty into the Gulf of San Miguel, all subject to pronounced tidal changes even though the surface water may taste fresh. Tidal ranges remain considerable as far as 70 odd nautical miles up Rio Tuira. Consequently, currents run fast and 3 knot velocities are common. Within the Gulf and rivers a multitude of sand and mud shoals may change seasonally so treat the guide's chartlets as rough aids only. A few stony banks and bars exist and if possible a navigator here should always proceed on a rising tide which will float the vessel promptly should she run aground. To explore the rivers along the north shore a yacht should start from the departure point of A at Lat. 08°22.0'N, Long. 078°20.3'W by GPS or about 1 nautical mile north of the east point of Isla Iguana.

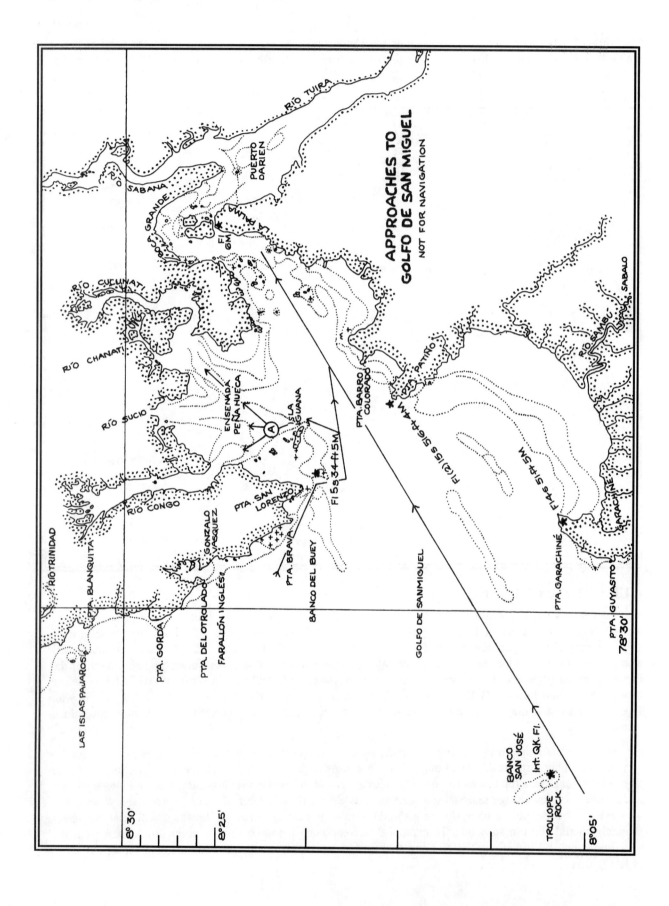

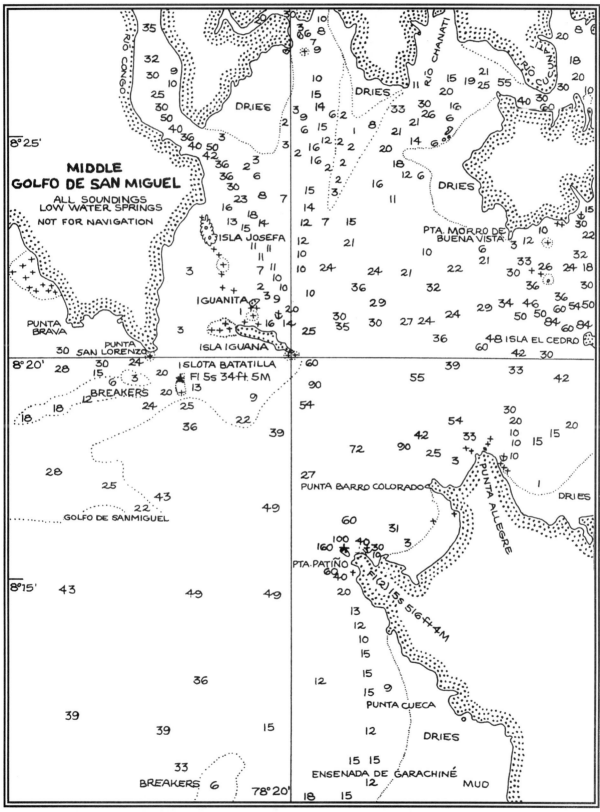

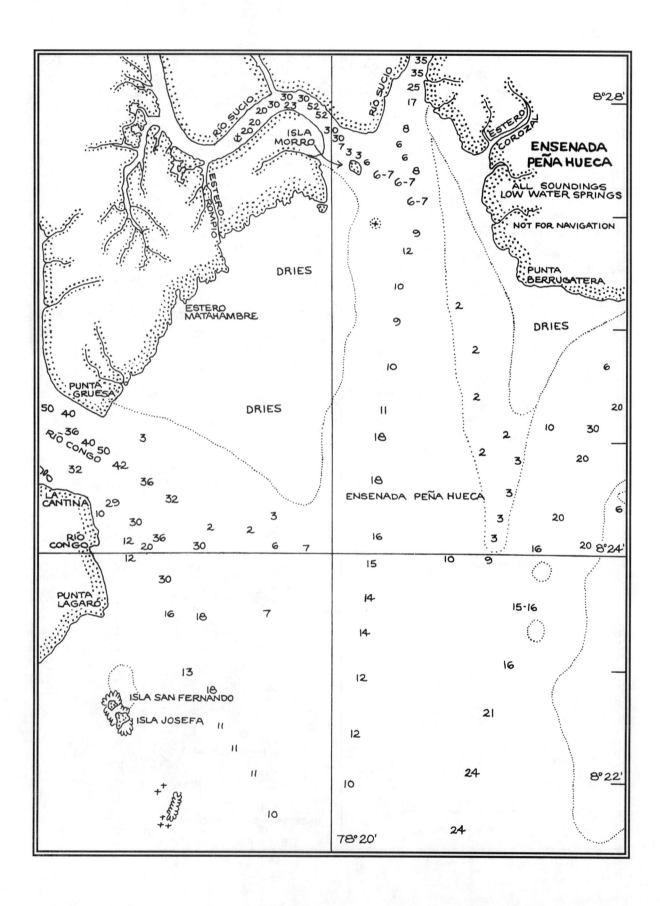

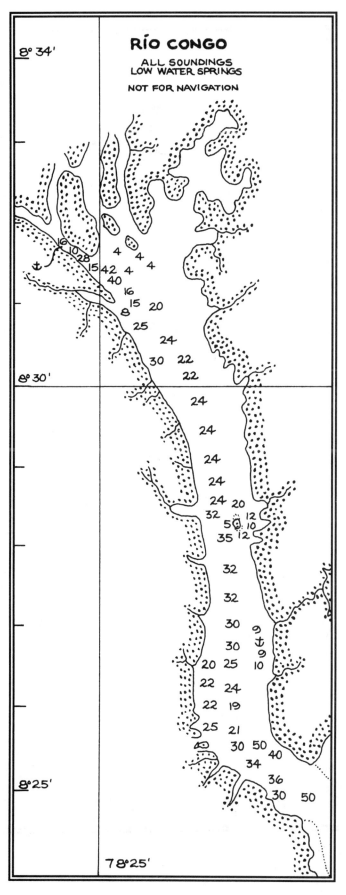

ISLA IGUANA

The 15 foot deep anchorage marked on the sketch chart and located at 08°20.8'N, 078°20.3'W by GPS has good holding in mud. Any closer and the muddy bottom begins to have large rocks embedded in it. At low water a dinghy can land on the south side of the easternmost point of Isla Iguanita and on Iguana on the sandy patch on the north side of the easternmost point.

RIO CONGO

From the departure point A off Isla Iguana a yacht can proceed straight to the mouth of Rio Congo, plainly visible to the NNW. Except at slack tides, it will be necessary to correct the heading to allow for tidal currents which may flow E or W across this course. Just before the river mouth a small village named Rio Congo (on some maps, La Paz) on the west bank has well water, gasoline and basic supplies. At times fresh shrimp, oysters and fish are available. When anchoring off the village do not come closer than about 12 feet LW as the bottom becomes very rocky. Because of the questionable holding off of the village we recommend anchoring inside Rio Congo for the night. The nearly mile wide Rio Congo is lined by tall mangrove trees backed by substantial hills on its seaward border and distant mountains to the north and east. Half way up the 7 mile long river off the east shore lies a small island facing the mouths of four creeks. An anchorage may be found here in 12 feet of water or further up at the head of Rio Congo. There, in a maze of islands and creeks one finds great bird watching and dinghy exploration possibilities. We did not see any people here although later we learned that Chitola, a village of indigenous Wounaan people, lies somewhere up the easternmost creek and not on the western bank of Rio Congo as some maps indicate. Congo is the word used for a type of catfish.

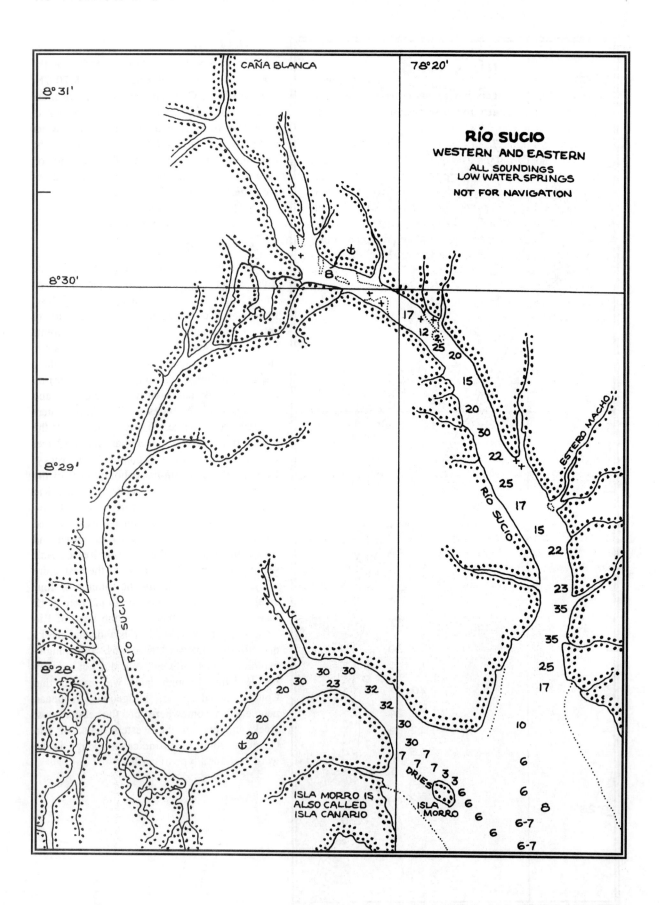

RIO SUCIO

To explore this river start again from point A and then steer slightly east of north for the mouth of Rio Sucio. Isla Morro (known as Isla Canario to the locals) should loom on the port bow. As you come closer to it, take great care to avoid a nasty rocky patch ½ n. mile SSE of Isla Morro - it disappears as the tide rises. Abeam of Isla Morro you will see the entrance to Rio Sucio West, a beautiful and deep river unfortunately plagued by mosquitoes which in the dry season are absent from the other rivers. Rio Sucio East deepens after the wide entrance and following the usual river tactics of keeping close to the outside of the river bends the boat will stay in deeper water until the river visibly narrows and several rocky bars run out far into mid-stream. They uncover only at spring tides and with our 5½ foot draft we could clear them at half tide. The sketch chart shows a good anchorage just before the river forks. Here, favor the south side of the river to avoid a drying sand bar that juts out of the opposite shore. It is also possible to anchor further up the left hand branch after negotiating more rocky bars. This left fork comes to three creeks and going in the dinghy up the one on the right you will come across a canoe landing. From the anchorage at the first fork in the river it takes 40 minutes to row there with a fair tide. The path from here leads a half mile to Caña Blanca, a Wounaan village. Women here, similar to other indigenous villages, weave the famous baskets bearing ancient designs whose meaning is now often forgotten. One of the most beautiful baskets we saw in Panama came from Caña Blanca. Water is available, seasonal fruits and vegetables also, but there are no dry goods. The people usually need sugar and coffee if you have any to spare.

RIO CUCUNATÍ

An easy entrance leads into this attractive river flanked by several densely wooded creeks and surrounding hills. The anchorage marked on the sketch chart and located at 08°27.8'N and 078°13.8'W by GPS will put a yacht close to two creeks which teem with water and land birds and are patrolled by a colony of howler monkeys whose ear shattering, awe inspiring roars always resound around Darién rivers. At low tide slinky gato solos may be seen lurking around the mangrove roots in the little creeks to the north. Further north, up Rio Cucunatí, you will see isolated family huts scattered along the eastern shore which eventually turns into a string of small islands and a wide shallow estuary. From this estuary a dinghy can take you to the large village of Cucunatí, a one hour ride in an inflatable powered by a 5 HP motor. At low tide you will have to leave the inflatable on a pebbly landing under low cliffs near the houses on the outskirts of Cucunatí. This pleasing village represents a cross section of Panamanians from all backgrounds and spreads over a large area. The road from here leads all the way to the Pan American Highway. Most of the traffic is by horseback and there are signs in front of gardens asking that horses be parked elsewhere. Several tiendas sell dry goods and cold soft drinks. Later, after leaving Rio Cucunatí, we learned that an indigenous village called Pijiba hides somewhere in the easternmost creeks of the estuary.

Low Tide in Rio Sucio, Golfo de San Miguel, Darién.

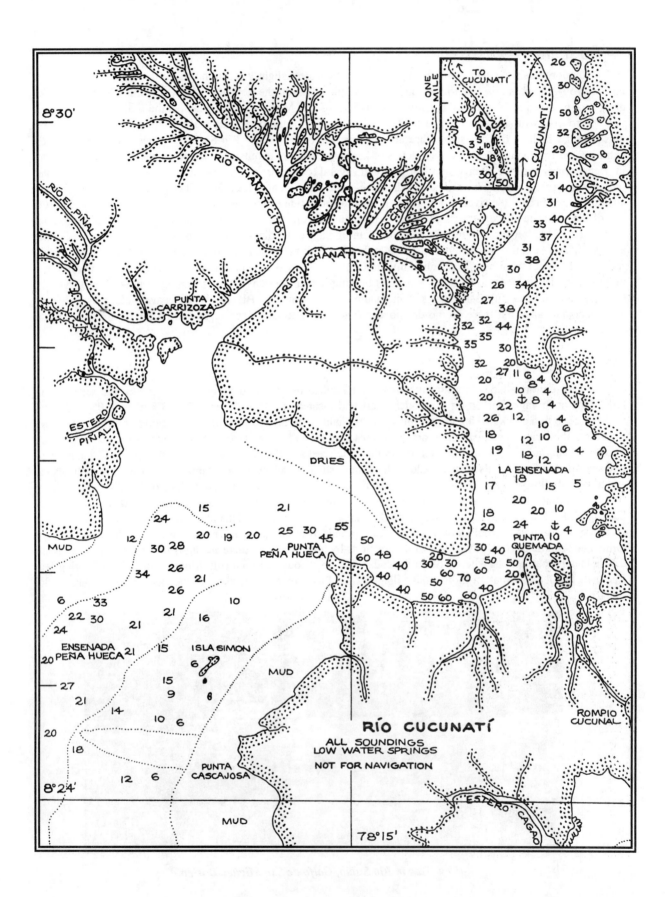

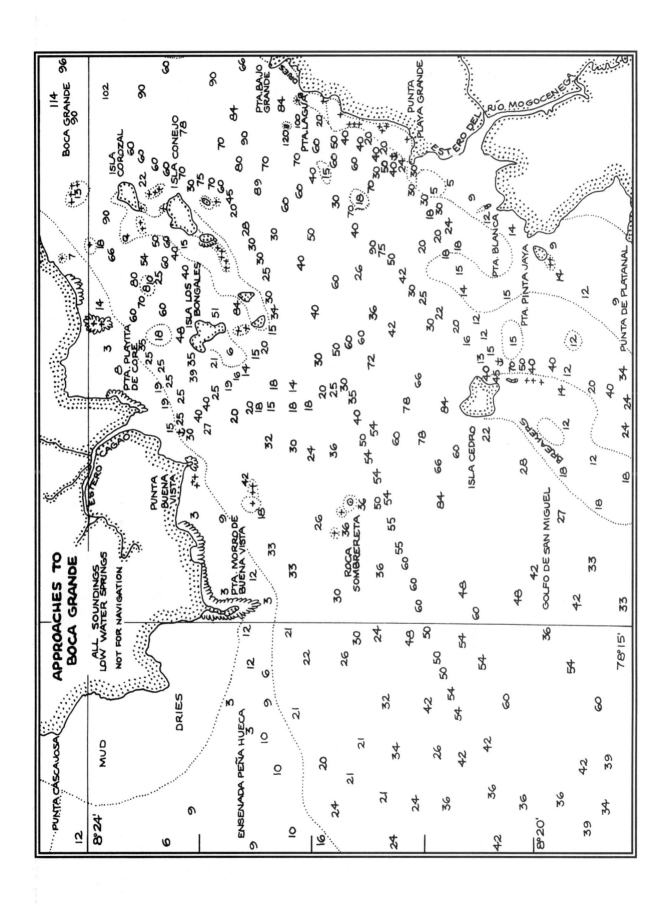

ISLA IGUANA TO BOCA GRANDE

A wide deep passage marked by the conspicuous Roca Sombrereta to the north and the bulky Isla Cedro to the south leads towards Boca Grande - the entrance to Rio Tuira. A few places suitable for anchoring line both shores. To the east of Punta Morro de Buena Vista, which appears as an island from afar, lies Punta Buena Vista and a group of islands: Los Bongales, Conejo, Corozal and others. The area inside this group suffers from strong eddying currents and very erratic soundings indicating a rocky bottom which rules it out as a possible anchorage. However, close to the mainland off Estero Cagao lies a quiet anchorage in mud with the estero, which means small river, offering interesting dinghy side trips.

ISLA CEDRO

Across the deep main channel to the south off the southeast coast of Isla Cedro there is a good anchorage in 15 feet. Very close to these islands on their eastern side the water deepens to 50 feet. A dinghy can land on the pebbly beaches on the eastern and southern sides of Isla Cedro. It is possible to climb a dry creek bed from the eastern beach and enter the dense vegetation to experience the eerie sounds of rich insect and bird life.

PUNTA PLAYA GRANDE

Further to the north another anchorage off Punta Playa Grande offers possible forays ashore. Anchor in 20 feet as shown on the sketch chart, or at 08°21.3'N and 078°10.7'W by GPS, and do not come closer inshore than 20 foot soundings. Many sharp rock outcroppings rise from the muddy bottom which shoals rapidly. A small bay close to the eastern end of Punta Playa Grande has a strip of sand which is a good low water dinghy landing. A walk over stones and rocks will bring you to the long beach overlooked by an abandoned hut. A good path behind it leads to a group of huts on the south side of Punta Playa Grande. However, if you stroll along the beach towards Punta Lagua you will pass a dirt road which ends at the beach and invites a detour into the interior. (This road joins the La Palma-Chepigana road.)

Mollymawk *anchored off Isla El Encanto in Boca Grande, Rio Tuira, Darién.*

BOCA GRANDE

Boca Grande, a very deep bend in the river, leads between high wooded hills. On the north shore a few huts on stilts dot the shores where subsistence farmers tend plots. A good anchorage out of the strong currents lies close to Rio Lagarto, north of Isla Lagarto. A tangle of mangrove trees along Rio Lagarto has several ribbons of dinghy creeks running through them. Although it is a very scenic sail through Boca Grande most vessels bound for Rio Tuira take Boca Chica, a shorter route through the narrow but deep channel between the uninhabited Isla El Encanto and the mainland. A small white lighthouse on the mainland side (eastern) marks the channel entrance. As you enter you may see high up on your left on Isla El Encanto the overgrown ruins of an old Spanish fort which used to guard Rio Tuira and the gold mines of the interior against raids by English buccaneers. A more modern ruin stands at the eastern end of the channel. Broken remains of a Gulf Oil pier and a defunct lumber mill wharf nestle against the tangled vegetation overlooked by an abandoned manager's house and company store which now provides shelter for a multitude of bats.

ISLA BOCA GRANDE

To the north from the east exit of Boca Chica, a group of picturesque uninhabited isles encircles a cozy anchorage close against the south shore of Isla Boca Grande. Enter from the south passing close to the islets on your port side and avoiding the tide rip area. Anchor as shown on the sketch chart in a soft mud bottom in 25 feet of water. If you decide to leave the anchorage by the channel between Isla Boca Grande and Isla El Encanto choose low tide to be able to see the rocky shoals which flank your course close to the east and west when you emerge into the main body of the river. The rocks disappear as the tide rises. The islets surrounding this Boca Grande anchorage abound in bird life, especially hundreds of grackles. Boca Grande, although uninhabited, is farmed making it possible to climb the hills for spectacular views of the river. The Boca Grande anchorage is one of the most beautiful on the river because of the proximity of the densely wooded hilly El Encanto and the view of the Sabana peninsula and the mountains to the east. Most historians agree that Balboa, the first European to see the Pacific Ocean, did so from the Sabana peninsula or nearby.

Not all ships make it up the River Tuira, Darién.

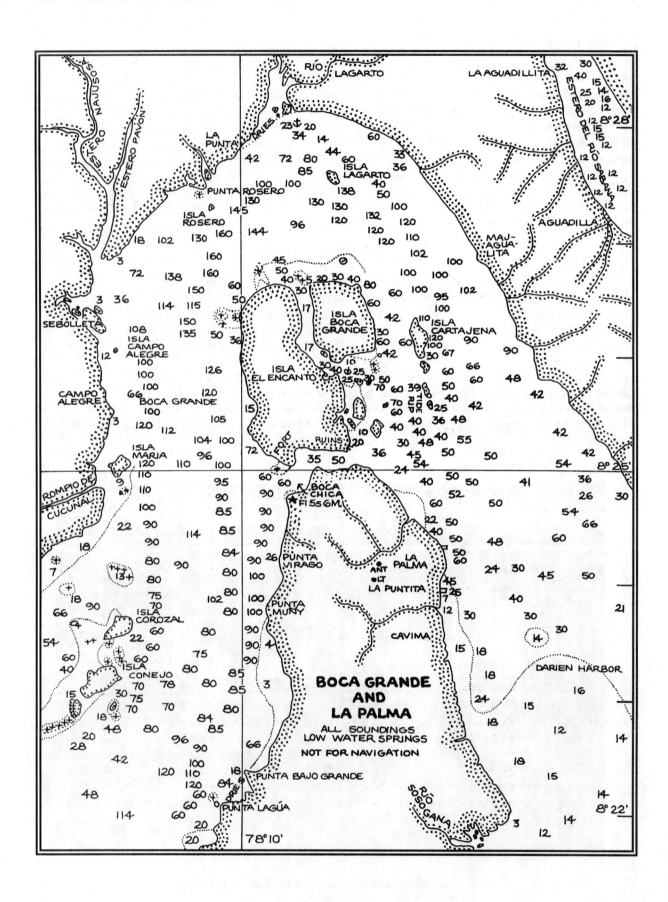

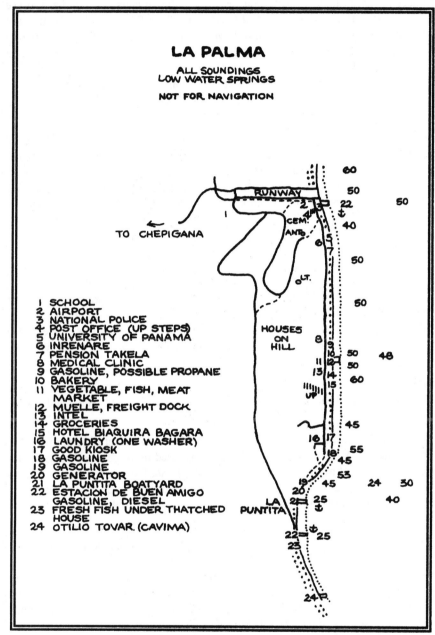

LA PALMA

South of Isla El Encanto channel you will see La Palma, the administrative center of the Province of Darién and its largest town with a population of around 4,600 people. Swift currents sweep past the town's water front and when the wind comes from the north the anchorage here gets choppy. It is better to sail past the town to La Puntita and anchor in about 20 feet in a bottom of mud with some shells between the short concrete pier jutting out from the shore at the foot of the La Palma power plant and a rickety wooden pier south of it. When you look ashore from your boat you might see a large yacht or another vessel under construction. Using Darién woods, the master shipwright, Rufino Gomez, started building a 90 foot plus ketch in 1994 for a New Yorker who in the past had a smaller yacht built by Rufino. You will find the best dinghy landing under the wooden pier at the Estacion Buen Amigo where they repair outboard motors, sell premixed or pure gasoline and diesel fuel. They also thresh local rice next door, you may want to sample this Darién product. The Estacion Buen Amigo sells homemade wooden saddles for $17.00. No drinking water is available at La Puntita. For this a yacht can go at high tide to the La Palma pier between small freighter visits and get good clean water from their hose. To do any shopping in La Palma you can walk there along the cliff path from La Puntita. If you decide to dinghy directly to town, do it close to high tide to avoid landing in soft mud and sharp pieces of garbage and other junk which abound when the water recedes. Several stores offer basic dry goods, hardware items and local produce. A diminutive open air market at the base of the town pier sells fresh meats, seafood and local produce. Ask at the market for ice, it comes from a private house. The market is open from 7:00-12:00AM and 2:00-4:00 or 5:00PM daily.

The INTEL office opens 8:00-12:00AM and 1:00-4:30PM Monday through Friday and has pay phones outside which, with luck, will connect you with the rest of Panama. For international calls you will have to use the operator inside the office. The post office is open 8:00-12:00AM and 2:00-5:00PM Monday through Saturday and is located close to the airport office at the north end of town. La Palma has daily flights to Panama City and is convenient for changing crew. Two simple hotels, Pension Takela, phone 299-6213, and Hotel Biaquira Bagara 299-6224, charge under US$20.00 for a double occupancy. Several small restaurants in town serve inexpensive meals. There are two banks in La Palma, the Banco Desarrollo Agropecuario and the Banco Nacional de Panama. An immigration office is next door to the town pier. La Palma has a busy medical clinic in the center of town.

South of La Puntita and visible from there on the west side of Rio Tuira sits a group of huts call Cavima. Otilio Tovar, a Wounaan originally from Rio Congo, lives in Cavima where he has created the little village which houses his extended family and where he welcomes visitors. He does not speak English but if you have any Spanish you will find Otilio a man with intimate knowledge of the area plants and their uses. He does not recommend anchoring close to Cavima because of the rocky and shallow bottom. However, it is only a short dinghy ride from La Puntita.

RIO SABANA

When you sail east from La Palma to Rio Sabana make sure to pass north of a dangerous rocky shoal 3/4 n. mile south of Punta Sabana. The shoal disappears with the rising tide. Along the east shore within the mouth of Rio Sabana several narrow deep creeks, Rio Iglesias, Estero Gregorio Diaz, and Estero Ñopo, penetrate far into the mangrove tree forests and lead inland. For solitude, these rivers are among the best. Only one of them, Rio Iglesias, has any signs of human activity, this in Puerto Quimba. Otherwise, all the creeks serve as havens for flocks of birds.

The west shore of Rio Sabana runs under a backbone of wooded hills, some 1,000 feet high, and as you move along only an occasional thatched hut pops into view - a fairy tale oasis under coconut palms and mango trees. The hills echo the roars of howler monkeys.

Rio Sabana was named by Europeans in the 16th century. Historians believe that at that time the area was cultivated and much more densely populated. Vasco Nuñez de Balboa encountered more people than you will. He sighted the Pacific from a ridge near the Gulf of San Miguel, probably the Punta Sabana peninsula. Balboa named the gulf and Punta San Lorenzo during the same period of time he claimed the Pacific Ocean for Spain. Now, the grasslands he viewed from that ridge are heavily wooded and the indigenous people greatly reduced in number.

The first three miles of Rio Sabana are relatively shallow at low water springs when deep draft vessels should use caution. After Aguadillita (a landing) the channel deepens and travels beside tall green hills to the west and distant mountains to the east. The river opens into a wide reach just before Islas Bellas (the Pretty Islands); an anchorage may be found southwest of the southernmost Bellas. Pass between Las Bellas as shown on the sketch chart to enter northern Rio Sabana. A deep channel runs along the eastern shore where it is wide enough for tacking. When the river begins curving follow the outside bends. Eventually, at the Wounaan village of about 30 huts called Boca de Lara, the river forks into two creeks, Rio Lara to the west and Quebrada Tumagantí to the east.

The tide arrives in Boca de Lara 1 hour and 45 minutes after the Balboa tabulated time and with less range so, at LW neaps the anchorage directly in front of the village will have about 6 feet. A deeper vessel will have to anchor in about 10 feet LW approximately ½ n. mile down stream from the village. Moor the boat bow and stern in the curve of the river along the deeper eastern shore to avoid swinging onto a pebbly bank that sticks out from the opposite side. Hang out an anchor light at night as a constant stream of fast taxi dugouts from La Palma passes day and night, most of them on the way to Santa Fé, a town further up Quebrada Tumagantí and close to the highway that eventually reaches Panama City.

Boca de Lara has a school, a clinic and three tiendas which sell cold drinks and basic goods. One tienda has gasoline. Women sell the famous baskets and men produce carvings of cocobolo wood and miniature animals sculpted out of tagua, or ivory nut, some absolutely exquisite. People here will barter their artifacts for T shirts, preferably with colorful imprints on both sides, cups, pots, towels and kerosene for their lamps as well as hooks and fishing line. Cash, of course, is most preferable.

On the return down river, anchor as indicated off Islas Bellas and take time to explore the creeks - at high tide, though, since almost all dry out at low tide.

In Rio Sabana, a tributary of Rio Tuira, Darién.

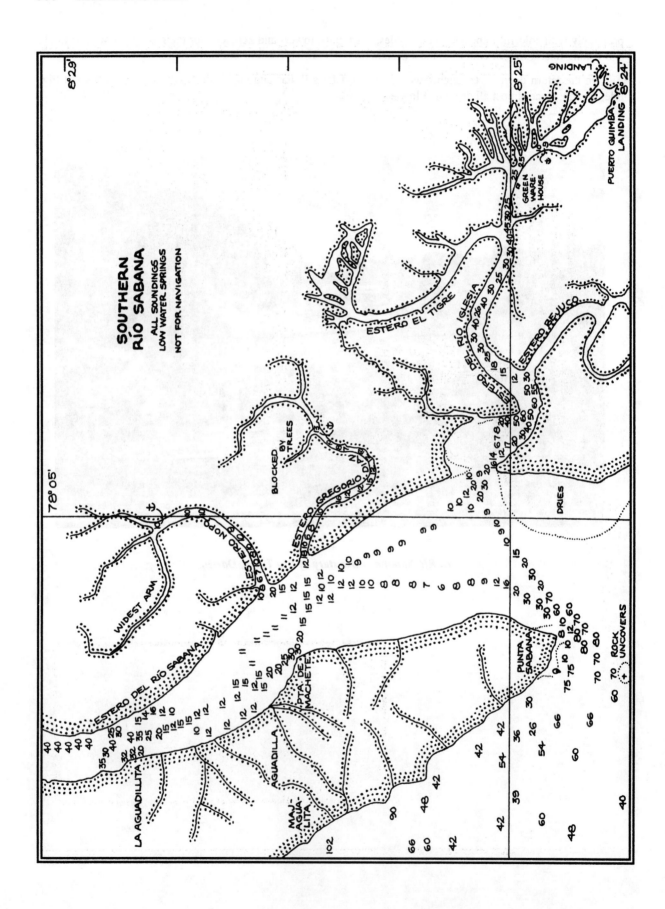

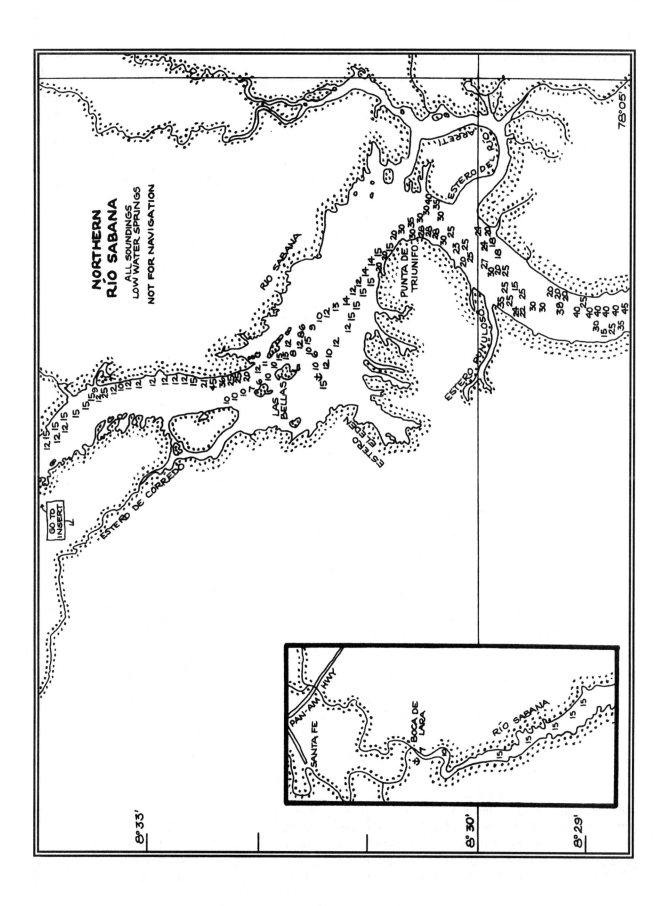

ESTERO ÑOPO

Keep to the north of middle when entering Estero Ñopo, then continue in mid-river. The current may be running fast in Sabana across the entrance to Ñopo so take care when entering the narrow mouth. An anchorage in mud may be found where the river breaks into three creeks. Ibis, great herons, little blue herons, whimbrels, willets, black mangrove hawks and screeching parrots constantly forage nearby. There are no human inhabitants on this river. We have seen land maps showing Puerto Quimba there and a road to Estero Ñopo, but these places are on Rio Iglesias.

ESTERO GREGORIO DIAZ

Keep to the north of middle when entering Estero Gregorio Diaz. To continue up river keep in the center of the narrow channel until the major curve. An anchorage may be found at the mouth of the first creek to the northwest. The holding is good in mud. We saw no one during the several days we spent here. Because the river is narrow the bird life is that much closer; black mangrove hawks were the most active.

RIO IGLESIAS

Keep to the south of the entrance to Rio Iglesias when crossing the bar and continue on favoring the south side of the channel. Anchoring is possible just within the mouth by edging carefully to the north. Low tide exposes a wide mud bank along the north shore extending to the east past the small creek to the northeast. To continue up river follow the outer curves of the river bends, pass the green warehouse on the southern shore and when the river begins to break up into numerous creeks choose a spot to anchor. The holding is good in mud. The river dries at low water around the islands. You may dinghy to the bald spot on the south shore behind the small islands and walk up to the newly paved road. The town of Rio Iglesias, also called Puerto Quimba, is a 30 minute walk to the left. Across the new road are Embera platform homes whose inhabitants will help with directions.

RIO TUIRA AND RIO BALSAS

The most direct way to sail up Rio Tuira from La Palma leads along the western shores. Steering roughly southeast from La Puntita your boat will have a minimum depth of 9 feet (at low water springs) all the way up to the conspicuous point on the west side of Tuira after which the river becomes considerably deeper.

CHEPIGANA

Chepigana, the next large settlement on Tuira, lies on the west bank of the river and you can anchor in 20 feet in a shallow bight off the pier. The pier dries completely at low tide. Chepigana, connected by road with La Palma (from where Chepigana's power comes) is a clean friendly town with a phone, post office and a clinic. Water and gasoline are available as well as some dry goods. The tienda has cold sodas and there is a bakery.

RIO TUIRA

South of Chepigana Rio Tuira takes a turn to the east and by heading that way you reach the town of Yaviza and the end of the Pan American Highway about 50 n. miles up the river. Navigating Rio Tuira requires playing the tides as many shoals pop up in unexpected places. Fortunately, all shoals on this river consist of soft mud and sand. By starting soon after low water the navigator will see most of the dangers as well as be assured of floating off any hidden shallow spots his boat hits. Follow the usual river tactics of keeping close to the outer curves. The sketch chart shows the recommended route until the island of Piriaque where the tide lags Balboa by 2½ hours. The deep channel follows the shore north of the island (you must go around Piriaque). Here the water turns fresh and the river narrows but remains fairly deep in the channel. Before deciding to anchor anywhere along the river make sure the place will have enough water to float your boat at low water. Fortunately, there are enough such deeper pools, which the locals call charcos - puddles in English, all the way to Yaviza. The main river ends at a fork where the shallow creek to the east leads to El Real. Take the left hand channel and you will enter Rio Chucunaque (on some maps called Rio Chico, although the locals call this Chucunaque and a river merging with it at Yaviza, Chico) where if you draw more than 3 feet you will need about half tide to get to Yaviza. High tide lags about 4 hours behind Balboa and rises only about half of the Balboa range. A water pipeline crosses over the river in the middle of Yaviza so anchor as soon as you reach a group of thatched huts and a building on your left. You will have the overhead pipeline in sight. We used a bow and two stern anchors to keep the boat from swinging into the center of the stream, only 120 feet wide here, and in the way of the occasional freight boats which call at Yaviza. One freighter makes it under the line and her mast is at least 15 feet high. Canoe traffic continues day and night so hang out a good anchor light.

A path from the dinghy landing on the north side of the river by the anchorage leads through the tuberculosis clinic grounds where patients sleep in thatched wall-less huts clustered around the medical building. A faucet of good water in front of the clinic is available to visitors. Yaviza, the largest town in the middle of Darién is a center of commerce, accessible by canoe to people living in the remote mountains. Here you meet mainland Kunas as well as Emberas and Wounaan who offer for sale their baskets and carvings. The Emberas and Wounaan are often referred to collectively as the Chocó, a term they do not use often. During the dry season trucks from Panama City come here to the end of the Pan-American Highway to collect agricultural products brought in by canoes up to 50 feet long which arrive loaded with roots and plantains until the gunwales are awash. These dugouts (hap in Wounaan and hampa in Embera) are measured not by feet but by the number of plantains they hold. A long dugout may hold 12,000 plantains. A good size police detachment tries to cope with drug traffic and illegal immigrants coming from Colombia via mountain trails. Instead of a regular phone connection, people in Yaviza patch their calls via radio from an office next door to the post office. Founded in 1638, Yaviza was equally busy in Spanish times and a small fort now in ruins, watched over the confluence of rivers to stop marauding pirates who crossed over from the Caribbean to attack Panama City or to plunder gold from the Cana and Tuquesa gold mines in the nearby mountains.

RIO BALSAS

Two channels, both requiring a rising tide to negotiate for all but shoal draft vessels, lead into Rio Balsas. The eastern entrance has only 4 to 5 feet depths near the mouth during low water springs before the channel deepens inside Rio Balsas proper, close to the northern bank. The western entrance by Isla Mangle, has a narrow channel 7 to 8 feet deep. However, if your boat strays a few yards the depth jumps to about 5 feet. This channel also gets deeper further inside and close to the southern river bank as the extensive shoals have taken over in the middle of the estuary. The channel which comes from south of Isla Mangle is of more interest to cruising people. The 10 foot anchorage at Isla Mangle is an excellent place to wait for a favorable tide for exploration into Rio Balsas.

When using the western entrance and the southern channel in Rio Balsas stick to the south side until the first large bend to the southeast, then gradually cross over to the north shore and follow the outside of the bend. The water will begin to shoal after rounding the curve and you must cross the river again. Continue in this fashion; favoring the outer curves then slowly crossing the river for the next outside curve. Past the small lumber mill on the starboard bank Rio Balsas becomes fresh, vegetation gets more varied and at the end of dry season flowers glow everywhere against the dark green foliage of the forest. The deep channel narrows progressively requiring even small boats to moor bow and stern to stay in the stream at low tide. Freight boats with 4½ foot draft go all the way to the settlement of Camogantí but they need at least 16 feet of tide and must moor there with cables to the shore. We suggest anchoring any time after passing the saw mill to enjoy a fresh water anchorage. From there many side creeks invite exploring in the dinghy.

ISLA MANGLE

The Isla Mangle anchorage off Rio Marea in 10 feet in mud allows dinghy exploration into that narrow river to watch a great variety of birds living in the dense tall woods on both sides. Look here for the bare throated tiger heron. Far in and accessible through a tunnel of branches interlocked overhead lies a small Embera community.

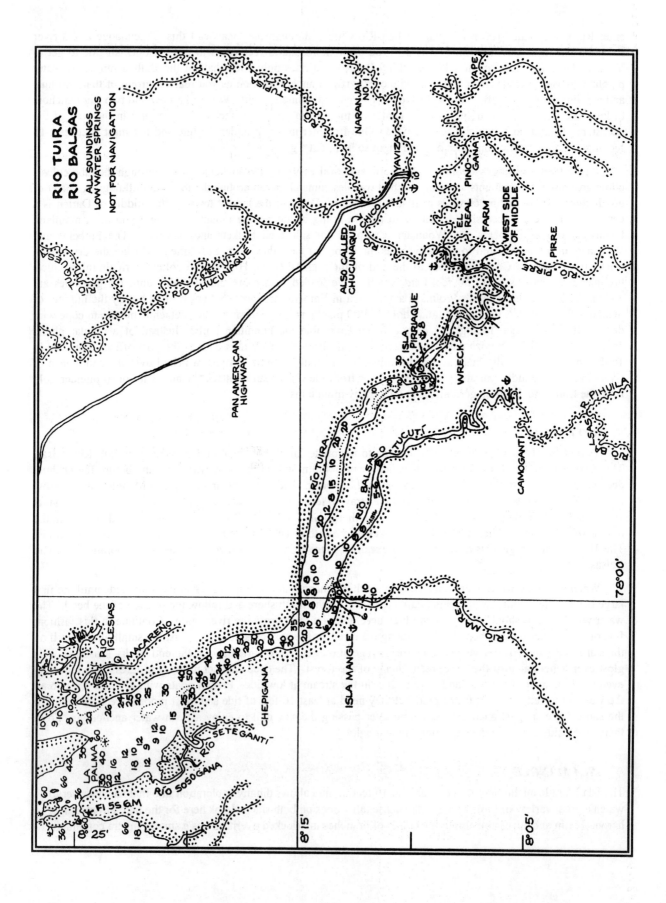

ANCHORAGES ON SOUTHERN SHORES OF THE GULF OF SAN MIGUEL

PUNTA ALLEGRE

After leaving Boca Grande a south bound yacht can anchor off Isla Cedro as mentioned earlier in this chapter and then move on to Punta Allegre off the fishing village of the same name. The anchorage shown on the sketch chart at the GPS position of 08°18'N and 078°14.8'W has 10 feet of water well clear of a multitude of rocks to the north and east of the point. In Punta Allegre one can hire a boat to go into Estero de Mogue to visit the indigenous village of Mogue where tourists are a familiar feature. Punta Allegre has water, gasoline and two tiendas with cold sodas and the usual dry goods. Ask for fresh seafood. The medical clinic is located near the school at the eastern end of town. When the phone works it will connect you with La Palma.

PUNTA PATIÑO

The 10 foot deep anchorage off Punta Patiño on the bearing of 264°T on the lighthouse has a very good holding ground and is free from the oceanic swell which sweeps into this part of Golfo de San Miguel from the Pacific. However, when the wind comes strong from the north as it frequently does between January and April, the anchorage gets uncomfortably choppy. In settled conditions one can dinghy ashore to visit the ANCON biological station in a conspicuous building on a hill near shore. ANCON, which stands for Association Nacional para Conservacion de la Naturaleza, works with the US Nature Conservancy to protect substantial parts of the forests as Darién National Park which has been declared a World Heritage Biosphere by UNESCO.

PUNTA GARACHINÉ

When navigating close to Punta Garachiné notice that the lighthouse stands on the tip of the point and not further southeast as charted on US DMA charts. The anchorage shown on the sketch chart and at 08°05.9'N and 078°24.4'W by GPS in 11 feet of water has excellent holding and a great shore background although it suffers from choppy waters when the wind comes whistling from the north during the dry months. Small cruise ships anchor off Garachiné and send their passengers in smaller boats into Rio Sambú to visit some of several indigenous hamlets along the river. All boats require high tide to go over the drying mud flats to get even close to the village of Garachiné, which is visible from the anchorage. Once past the flats Rio Sambú deepens giving access to the Embera villages of La Chunga, Puerto Indio, La Trampa and others.

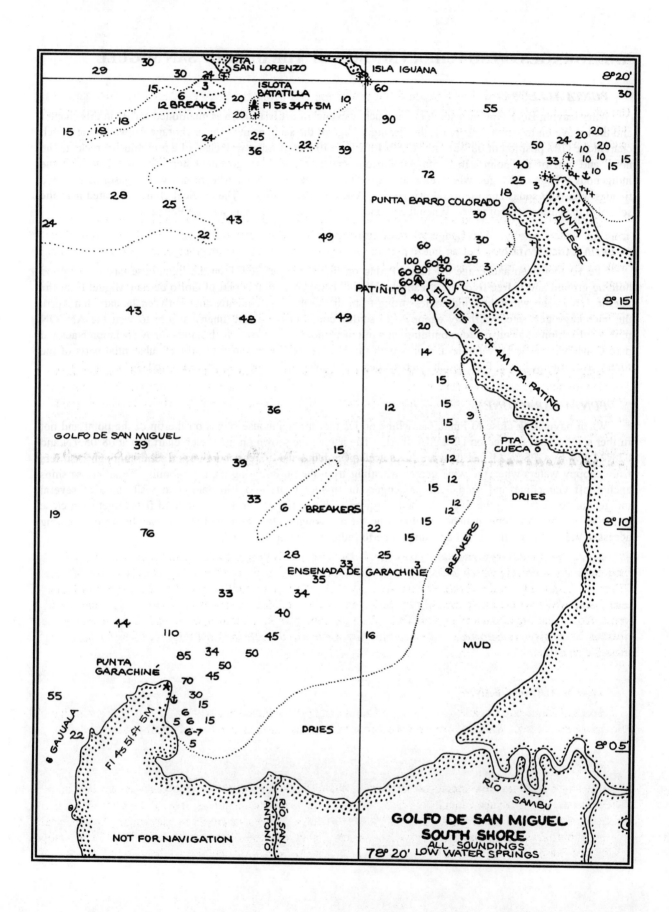

THE PACIFIC COAST TO THE BORDER WITH COLOMBIA

Sailing along this coast one looks at some of the world's few pieces of pure wilderness. Between Punta Garachiné and Bahía Piñas only isolated huts and a couple of villages stand at the edges of river mouths which tumble down through valley clefts in steep mountains. The beaches receive a full sweep of swells and it takes an exceptional day for a yacht dinghy to attempt a landing. However, the large Bahía Piñas offers perfect shelter in the northwest corner off the Tropic Star Lodge or if swell penetrates even there, in the northeast nook of the bay.

BAHÍA PIÑAS

Tropic Star Lodge caters to well-off sport fishing vacationers and well over 120 world fishing records come from the waters nearby. The Lodge tolerates cruising yachts, which can anchor just outside the moored club boats, in a friendly fashion but do not expect to use any facilities except in an emergency. However, you can walk on the beach in front of the Lodge and observe the black and yellow oronpendola birds whose long woven nests (we counted 108) hang like Christmas socks from a cluster of coconut palms. The Lodge also allows hiking on the Playa Blanca trail which leads uphill behind the club and ends on a pristine white beach after a walk through a chunk of exceptionally beautiful tropical forest. If you time your arrival at Playa Blanca at low tide you can continue over the rocks extending from the next point to the east and will suddenly find yourself at another larger beach at whose edge stand five huts on stilts - an indigenous community called Trinchera.

All the employees at the Lodge come from the villages of Bahía Piñas or Jaqué. To visit Bahía Piñas take your dinghy into the small river (the mouth dries at low water) at the western end of the long beach in front of the village as the breaking swells make landing on the beach itself risky most of the time. If you need fresh produce or fruit talk to the indigenous people who live on the outskirts of the village. They do most of the agricultural work here. Allow a day or so for them to harvest the produce and fetch it from their fincas. Their kids, who usually hang out around the Tropic Star end of the bay in small dugouts, will do the delivery duties and will take orders for produce. The small light dugout canoes seen around this area are raced around Christmas time. A substantial airstrip completed in 1994 allows regular air connections from Bahía Piñas to Panama City. Previously, all flights went to Jaqué, a large village at the mouth of the Rio Jaqué, 5 n. miles further south.

JAQUÉ

Ever present breakers mark the entrance to Rio Jacqué and only canoes and the shoal draft boats from Tropic Star enter this waterway which leads far inland to several indigenous villages. Trading vessels anchor offshore. Wounaan people live in the closest hamlet, Biroquira. A little further, Embera populate the villages of Mamey and Lucas, while Widocara, accessible only during high river conditions is inhabited by Wounaan. Almost every week Tropic Star organizes a trip up the river. You can join them for a reasonable fee and they will take you at least as far up river as Biroquira. One can also hire a motorized canoe in Bahía Piñas to go as far up river as possible on a tide.

FONDEADERO GRANDE

South of Jaqué one can anchor in 12 to 25 feet in Fondeadero Grande in a shallow bight on the north side of the first point of land. While it is rolly most of the time a dinghy can land on the beach close to a small stream.

GUAYABO

The shore becomes more rugged on the way further south, but Ensenada Guayabo has protected anchorages while the next bay, Guayabo Chiquita, gives the best sheltered anchorage in a little bight in the northwest corner, as shown on the sketch chart. Go in as far as your draft allows. Indigenous people live around the bays in small groups of huts drawing subsistence entirely from small plot agriculture, the sea and forest. The close proximity of the wild Darién mountains make this one of the most beautiful anchorages on the Pacific coast of Panama.

A WORD OF CAUTION

Small time bandits from Colombia have made robbing raids into these remote bays according to the people in Bahía Piñas. Apparently, the situation has improved after a strong reaction by the Panamanian police. The Embera in Guayabo Chiquita were very welcoming and assured us about the safety of staying there. Nevertheless, cruising in company and keeping an anchor watch at night might help avoid nasty surprises on this particular stretch of coast.

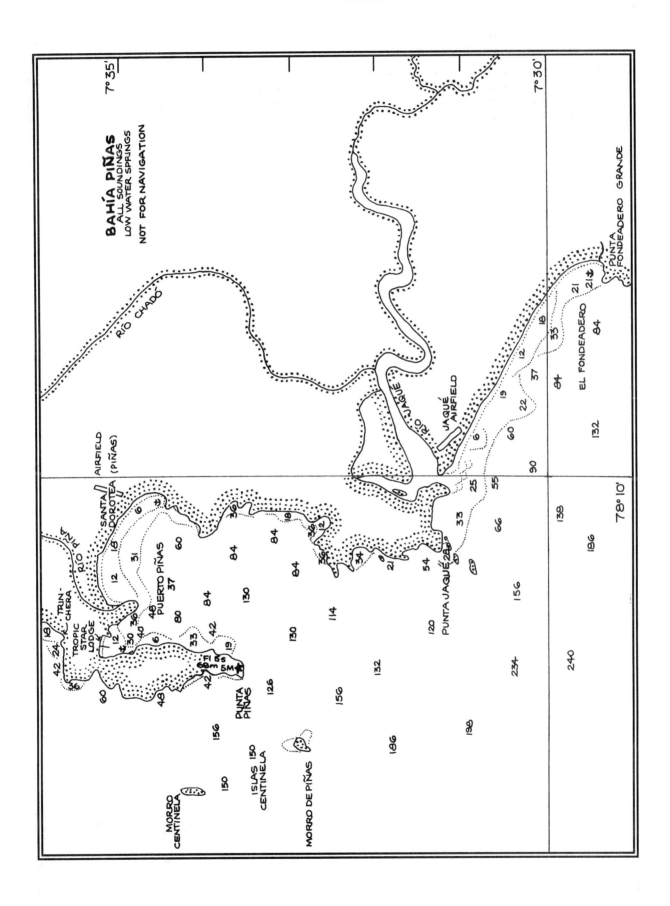

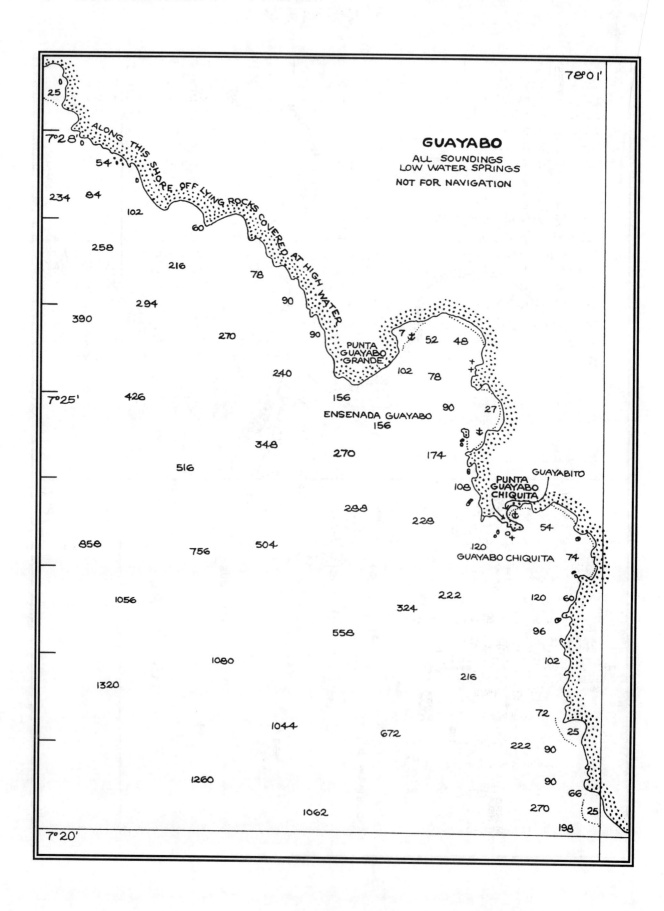

APPENDIX

FOOD!

Experimenting with strange, unknown foods brings another interesting and delicious dimension to a cruise. Shopping in a market filled with new fruits and vegetables changes a mundane chore into an exciting experience. In Panama, you will discover the most exotic foods when peering down into a dugout canoe that has come alongside. Many times the owner of the canoe has invited us home to show us how to prepare pifas and tamarind juice or hopped on board to cook corn cakes or coconut bread. An interest in food leads to all sorts of adventures! Here is a description and a few recipes for some of the most common exceptional Panamanian delicacies.

Pifa, Pijiba, Pejibaye, Piba, Pixbae

The names for this orange, yellow or green palm fruit which vary from location to location are worth learning. In pre-Columbian times this endemic starchy fruit played as an important a role in Central American diets as rice and wheat did elsewhere. Acknowledging this, the conquistadors destroyed many thousands of spiny pifa palms in an attempt to starve out the indigenous people. Today, pifa may be on the comeback, new groves are being planted with hopes of exporting the fruit.

Often sold on street corners from huge galvanized basins, pifas look like miniature coconuts and taste like a mixture of chestnuts and boiled peanuts. Because they need to be peeled (from the pointed end towards the stem) they make an excellent in-town snack. When buying fresh, uncooked fruit look for smooth skin without hairline cracks. Fresh and uncooked they will last about three days and around two if kept at room temperature after boiling them. Most vendors want to sell a whole grape-like cluster which generally leaves the yacht with too many. However, everyone loves pifas so they are excellent presents for the Balboa launch drivers, for night watchmen, kids, and people who stop by to visit.

Boiled Pifas

Place the fruit in boiling water to cover, return to boil, then simmer for 15 to 25 minutes. Store covered with water. Cooled, they make a great hors d'oeuvre. Skinned, seeded and ground they make a "flour" which mixed with a small amount of water may be formed into small cakes to be lightly sautéed. Use up to one cup of this "flour" in bread recipes. Add the "flour" to mashed potatoes. Skinned, seeded and sliced pifas make a great addition to salads, pizza toppings, stir fries or even spaghetti sauces. Cooked slices may be dried in the sun for longer term storage.

Pifa and Okra

1 large onion - halved and sliced thin

6 cloves garlic - sliced thin

1 large green pepper

2 cups sliced fresh okra

1 teaspoon dried basil

2 -3 large tomatoes, peeled, seeded and chopped

6 cooked pifas, peeled, seeded and quartered

½ teaspoon hot pepper flakes

Sauté the onion in a small amount of water until nearly transparent. Add the green pepper, cook 1 minute, add the okra, the tomatoes, the basil and the hot pepper flakes. Cook until the okra is tender. Add the pifas, cook until they are heated through. Throughout, add just enough water to keep the vegetables from sticking. Serve with rice, millet, kasha, pasta, potatoes or all by itself!

Pifa Dasheen Soup

1 large onion, chopped

½ head garlic, chopped

3 cups cooked, skinned and chopped pifas

3 cups diced dasheen

1 - 2 large bay leaves, crushed

1/8 teaspoon cayenne pepper

1 teaspoon salt

Optional: 2 tablespoons finely diced

dill pickles, or 1 diced plantain

diced otoe or ñampie

Sauté the onion in water to cover the bottom of the soup kettle until clear, add the diced dasheen (and any other vegetable to be added), bay leaves, cayenne and salt, bring to a boil, add chopped garlic and pifas. Cook 15 to 20 minutes or until the dasheen is done. This soup gains in flavor after letting it sit.

Roots

Working out recipes for cooking the great variety of available roots could make a lifelong project. The few described here appear under other names in many tropical countries.

Otoe - One of the smaller, thinner varieties, about the size of a sweet potato, otoe has encircling lines and is slightly hairy. A purple skin lies just under the brown outer skin and the meat will turn a light lavender like pig's feet when cooked. Mildly pork flavored and dry, otoe steams in 15 minutes but is better when added to soups or boiled.

Occasionally one finds delicious dark purple varieties of otoe.

Dasheen - A man in Bluefields (Chapter III) told us he once saw a dasheen that weighed 35 pounds. Most are about the size of a US football, heavy, have short roots all over and come with a lot of dirt on them. With the dirt left on and wrapped in newspaper, dasheen will last about a month. It also keeps well when a chunk has been cut off. A slightly sweet flavor makes this our favorite. It must be skinned and is delicious steamed, boiled and in root soups. Although dasheen is known on the Pacific side, it is most popular in the Bocas del Toro area.

Yuca - This brown root, as big around as a baking potato but up to two feet long with longitudinal lines, is often sold cut open for inspection. The meat should be white without long tough roots running the length of it. If the yuca has roots in the meat they should be cut out. Fresh yuca lasts only two or three days. Baking and steaming require nearly twice as long as boiling. Cooked, the waxy meat is sweet and when puréed with lentils, heavenly! Steamed yuca superbly complements hot garlicky black beans with a twist of lime. You can also slice the yuca very thinly and deep fry as chips.

Ñame - Small or large and brown, ñame has lateral lines in the skin and a few hairy, small rootlets. The skin has the texture of an Incan mummy, dry with small cracks, and when cut it is whiter than a mummy's bones. It turns slimy when cut open. Ñame can be as large as an American football or as small as a baking potato and they keep well. We had one from Isla Pedro Gonzalez (Chapter V) the shape and size an elephant's foot and when pieces were cut off the remainder kept very well. Steam ñames for 15 minutes, boil, mix in soups or bake sliced thin with onions and fresh fish. Serve steamed ñame with red beans and cumin.

Ñampi - Dusty brown ñampis are sold 4 to 12 inches long, sometimes longer. This root tends to grow in length rather than width. The slightly peeling dry skin shows faint lines running longitudinally. When it comes dirty, leave the soil on and keep it dry and it will last a couple of weeks. A purple to brownish skin becomes evident when peeling the vegetable and a slime appears over the cut white surface. Cooking will dissolve the slime. Steamed ñampi tastes as if mild sweet smoked ham was added to the pot. The texture is slightly waxy and mealy like a potato.

Corn

The favored variety of corn grown in Panama (for human consumption) dries well on and off the stalk. As Irene Castrellón from Isla Catalina in Rio Santa Lucia (Chapter IV) explained to me while she shaped a huge tortilla, "Everyone, rich or poor, eats something made of masa for breakfast."

Many northern urbanites may mistake the corn aisle in the big supermarkets in Panama City for the bird food section - there are so many varieties of dried corn. The availability of corn ground into several sizes and marketed by many companies attests to the importance of this food. The larger sizes, pelado and chichime should be presoaked. Chichime, normally used for a drink, makes a tasty breakfast when soaked overnight, drained, then cooked for 30 to 40 minutes in water twice the volume of the corn.

Irene Castrellón's Tortillas and Bollos

The evening before, cook the maiz pelado with a few grains of rice or a piece of yuca (to make the masa more elastic) until barely al dente. Cover with water and soak overnight. In the morning drain the water and grind the meal in a grain grinder. Make a dough (masa) by adding a small amount of water to produce a consistency similar to bread dough. A tortilla in Panama may be a small pancake size corn cake or a large 10 inches by 2 inches thick disk. Prepare a wet banana leaf by softening it over the stove burners. Form a thick tortilla the size of your frying pan, wrap it in the banana leaf as if wrapping a present, place in the pan and cook for one hour over a low flame. Turn after 30 minutes. Soften more wet leaf for "bollos". Shape the masa into double thick cigar shapes. Cut the leaf to cover each "bollo" twice, wrap them and tie the packages with string. Cook in rapidly boiling water for 10 to 15 minutes.

Kuna Cakes

The Kunas roast the corn before grinding it into a soft, floury meal. To two cups of roasted corn meal add barely a teaspoon of salt, mix in enough water to make a stiff dough. Form the dough into cakes similar to pancakes. These may be fried in hot oil as the Kunas do, or they are delicious steamed. (The more water you can work into the dough, the better because the corn needs to be rehydrated.) Hot pepper added to the dough makes them spicy. The Kuna words for roasted corn meal are ob tibialeubilet.

Coconut Bread

All over Central America people make coconut bread. For us the best comes from the province of Bocas del Toro. Specifically, from the tiny tienda at the end of a wooden dock in Cauchero and made by Lucrecia Chocón. If there isn't any ready she will make it to order. The two shops in Crawl Cay Channel also offer delicious coconut bread, ask for it everywhere in Laguna de Chiriquí and Bahía Almirante.

Lucrecia Chocón's Coconut Bread

1 mature coconut

1 tablespoon yeast

one palmful of salt

two palmfuls of sugar

10 cups of flour

Grate the coconut into a bowl, add the coconut water and a small amount of fresh water. Squeeze the coconut with your fingers in the water and drain through a colander. Repeat 3 times then strain through a strainer reserving the liquid.

Mix about 1 cup of water with the yeast, add 2 tablespoons of flour.

Add the salt to the flour on a large bread board and make a well in the center of the flour. Add the yeast mixture by pouring it into the well. Add the coconut milk a little at a time to make a rough, ragged mixture handful by handful. Push handfuls to the side and knead. Pull the dough apart and stretch open. Knead and pull apart again. Continue kneading until a soft pliable bread dough forms.

Shape the dough into a log and cut to make tennis ball size pieces. Roll and knead each ball until a finger can be punched into the dough and the hole remains. (When cut open there should be yeast holes in the dough.) Roll out each tennis ball with a glass to make hamburger size buns. Let the buns sit on the board. Cook in a 350° oven on a slightly oiled baking sheet until done, about 15 to 20 minutes.

A Few Fruits

Cacao - The seeds are dried, roasted and ground to make chocolate. Logs of unsweetened chocolate were available in most market places a few years ago but now are hard to find. A cacao disease spread though the Central American groves recently and many have been abandoned. Cacao trees require shade which is good for cool strolling. The fruit grows straight out of the tree trunks and may be cracked open and the white juicy membrane sucked off the seeds for a refreshing sweet-tart treat.

Cashews - Marañon - The poisonous (when raw) nuts hang off the bottom of the yellow and orange pear like fruits. Roasting these nuts requires extreme care as they splatter the poison dangerously and even the smoke can permanently affect the eyes. The juicy and edible fruit tastes slightly like the nut.

Mameys - Sapodillas - Two pale brown fruits with similar looking skin, sapodillas are the size of a tomato and taste like brown sugar. Mameys are 6 inches long or longer, have orange to red flesh which tastes rich and filling with a flavor all its own.

Guabas - Guabas are 10 to 20 inch long pods which when broken open reveal cotton candy covered inedible seeds. The cotton candy tastes better than the best at the fair.

Tamarinds - Tamarind trees proliferate along roadsides in hot climates. The dusty brown pods crack and crumble when the fruit is ripe. The dark brown sticky pulp has a sweet-sour flavor that will startle parched taste buds during a long hot walk.

Seagrapes - Seagrapes are a Caribbean beach treat. The lovely grape-like clusters are unmistakable and turn red or wine colored when ripe. A whole cluster will not ripen at once, each fruit has its own schedule. The salty sweet flavor (hot when the sun is high) comes surprisingly close to real grapes.

Genips - Sold on the street on small stems or in little bags, genips make the perfect on-watch snack. Each fruit is nearly all seed, the skin must be cracked open and the seed sucked for its juicy sweet-sour pulp.

BIBLIOGRAPHY

Erice, Jesus, *Diccionario de la Lengua Kuna*. Panama 1985.
Erice, Jesus, *Gramática Kuna*. Panama 1981.
Esquemeling, John, *The Buccaneers of America*. Dover Publications, New York 1967.
Forsyth, Adrian with Ken Miyata, *Tropical Nature*. Charles Scribner's Sons, New York 1984.
Hydrographic Office of the US Navy, *Central America and Mexico Pilot (East Coast)*. H.O. of US Navy 1927.
Iglesias, Marvel and Marjorie Vandervelde, *Beauty Is A Ring In My Nose?* Velde Press 1983.
Keller, Nancy J., *Central America On A Shoestring*. Lonely Planet Publications 1992.
Kelly, Joanne M., *Cuna*. South Brunswick, New York. A.S. Barnes, Thomas Yuschoff, London 1966.
Kricher, John C., *Neotropical Companion*. Princeton Univ. Press. 1989.
Labrut, Michéle, *Getting To Know Panama*. Focus Publications, Panama, 1993.
McCullough, David, *The Path Between The Seas, The Creation Of The Panama Canal Between 1870 - 1914*. Simon & Schuster, New York, 1977.
Morison, Samuel Eliot, with Mauricio Obregon, *The Caribbean As Columbus Saw It*. Chapter X, Panama and Colombia. 1964.
Nyrop, I and T.E. Weil, *Panama: A Country Study*. The American University, Washington, DC 1980.
Olaya, Clara Inéz, *Frutas De America*. Editorial Norma,S.A. Santa Fé de Bogota, Colombia 1992.
Parker, Ann and Neal, Avon, *Molas, Folk Art of the Cuna Indians*. Barre Publishing, Barre Massachusetts, 1977.
Prestán, Arnulfo, *Organizacion Social Y Politica de Kuna Yala*. In Hombre Y Cultura. Vol I No. 2, Univerity of Panama, 1991.
Ridgely, Robert and John A. Gwynne, *Birds Of Panama*. Princeton Univ. Press, 1989.
Sauer, Carl Ortiz, *The Early Spanish Main*. University of California, Cambridge University Press, 1966.
Steward, Julian H., *Handbook of South American Indians*. Volume 4, *The Circum-Caribbean Tribes*, Smithsonian Institution, Bureau of American Ethnology, Bulletin 143, United States Government Printing Office, Washington, 1948.
Tennin, J.V., *Roughing It In The San Blas Islands*. Panama, Panama-American Publ. Co. 1940.
Vandervelde, Marjorie and Marvel Iglesias, *Born Primitive*. Velde Press 1982.
Young, Philip D., *Ngöbe, Tradition and Change Among the Western Guaymi Of Panama*. University of Illinois, 1971.

INDEX

A

abbreviations, key to, 13
Abernathy, 38
Aboudi Tiwar, 119
Accuasir, Piedra 111-112
Accusichi, 109-111
Achutupu, 88, 104, 113-115, 117-118
Acla, 130
Acuacate Bay, 155
Acuadup, 76-77, 79
Acuakargana, 68, 70
Adentro, Isla de, 271
Admeasurer, 27, 41
Aduana, 6
advisors, 31, 41
Aeropuerto, Ensenada de, 282
Afuera, Isla, 231, 235, 237, 240, 271
Afuerita, Isla, 235
Agacatal, 270
Aglatomate, 126-128
Aguacate, 137-139
Aguadillita, 302, 304
Aguadulce, 11, 17, 212, 214
Aguja, Isla, 279
Aguja, Punta, 274-275
Ailigandi, 8-9, 112-113, 115-116
airplanes, 8, 64
Akuanusatupu, 99
Akwasuit Murru, 119-122
Allegre, Punta, 143, 145, 291, 309-310
Almacigos, 218, 220
Almirante, 12, 15, 172, 189-190
Almirante, Bahía, 3-4, 12, 135, 137, 144, 159, 174
Almongo, Diego de, 207
Amador, 36
Amarillos, Los, 229
Amateur radio license, 6
Ambrosio Bight, 189
ambulance numbers, 40
American Embassy, 24, 40
Amistad, La, 9
Ammen, Islas, 76, 79
Ampon, Isla, 267, 269, 272
Amponcito, Isla, 270
Anachucuna, 130-131, 133
ANCON, 9-10, 280, 309
Anderson, Sr., 140
Antón, Punta, 174, 176
Anton Viejo, Punta, 267
Apaitup, 106-107
Araus Museum, Reina Torres de, 10
Archibold, Guillermo, 10
Arenas, Bahía, 217
Argosy, 39

Aridup, 85, 104, 106, 109
Aritupu, 74-75
Armila, 133
Armuelles, Puerto, 260
Arnulfo, Hotel, 86
Associated Steamship Agency, 41
Astillero National Ltd., 41
Aston Cay, 186
Auree Cay, 184, 186
Azucar, Rio, 95, 97
Azuero Peninsula, 203-204, 213-214, 216-217

B

Bahía Almirante, 3-4, 12, 135, 137, 144, 155, 159, 174
Bahí Azul, 143, 145
Bahía Grande, 191, 193, 196
Bahía Honda (Bocas del Toro), 181, 183
Bahía Honda (Veraguas), 204, 231, 234, 237, 240
Bahía Hotel, 173-174
Bahía Las Minas, 44-45
Bahía Piñas, 11, 311-313
Baitel, Allan, 49
Bajo Boyarena, 264, 267-268
Bajo de Cartegena, 286
Bajo de Gumes, 286-287
Bajo de los Chepanos, 286
Bajo del Buey, 264, 272
Bajo Garcia, 171
Bajo San Pedrillo, 230
Balboa Yacht Club, 6-7, 11, 36-37, 40-41, 207
Balboa, 3-7, 9, 11-12, 23, 25, 27, 37-41, 203-205, 207-208, 223, 225, 263, 266, 288
Balboa, alternate anchorages, 37
Balboa, clearing in, 5, 38
Balboa, Vasco Nuñez de, 4, 130, 289, 299, 302
Ballena, Punta 233
Ballena, Rio 230, 233
Balsas, Rio, 308
Baltazar, Punta, 237-238
Bamboo Bight, 191, 193, 195
Banana Cut, 31-32
Banco de Las Matitas, 252, 255
Banco del Buey, 290
Banco del Medio, 264, 285
Banedup, 66-67, 69-70
Banerdup, 93, 96
Barren Rock, 143, 145
Barro Colorado, 3, 10, 31, 33
Barro Colorado, Punta (Darién), 310
Barro, Ensenada, 55
Bartolomé, Isla, 265
Bas Obispo Reach, 34
Bastimentos, 9, 144, 159, 174-175, 178, 182-188
Bastimentos, Isla, 144, 175, 178

Bastimentos, Punta, 175, 178
Batatilla, Isla, 289, 291, 310
batteries, 24, 39
Bayano Lake Dam, 288
Bayano, 4, 286-288
Bayoneta, Isla, 264, 269
Bejuco, 137, 139-140, 247-248, 250, 258
Bejuco, Ensenada de, 247, 258
Belén, 135, 137-139
Bellas, Islas, 302-303, 305
Benao, Ensenada, 213, 216
Benao, Punta, 213, 216
Bermudez Point Channel, 191, 197
Berraco, 254, 259
Biaquira Bagara, Hotel, 301-302
Bibliography, 319
Big Bight, 177, 182
Biroquira, 311
Black Christ, 9, 47
Blanditas, 224-225
Blauvelt, 143
Bluefield Rock, 143, 145
Bluefield, Laguna de, 142, 145
boatyard services, 10-11, 37
Boca Brava, 248-249, 251-253, 258
Boca Brava, Isla, 249-251, 258
Boca Chica (Chiriquí), 248, 252
Boca Chica (Gulf of San Miguel), 15, 299-300
Boca de la Trinidad, 224-225
Boca de Lara, 302-303, 305
Boca del Drago, 12, 135, 144, 174, 176
Boca del Toro Channel, 175
Boca del Toro, 12, 135, 144, 174-175, 178
Boca Grande (Darién), 290, 297, 300
Boca Grande, Isla (Darién), 300
Boca Torrito, Canal, 171, 201
Boca Torritos, 171, 193-194, 199-201
Bocas del Toro Province, 2
Bocas del Toro, 4-5, 8-9, 12, 15, 144, 151, 159
    172-174, 181-183, 186, 190-191, 196, 316-317
Bocatoreño bread, 155, 183-184
Bodega, Ensenada, 282
Bolaño, Isla, 264, 267
Bolaños, Isla, 249, 259
bollos, 253, 317
Bona, Isla, 210-211
Bongales, Los, 297-298
Bongo, Punta, 274, 279
Booby Cay, 140-141
Boquete, 9
Boqui Bajo, 244-245
Bordado Bohio, 32-33
Bordado Buena Vista, 33
Boyarena, 264, 267-268, 280
Brandon Point, 161, 186
Brava Point Channel, 111-112, 115
Brava, Playa, 271
Brava, Punta (Gulf of San Miguel), 289-291
Brava, Punta (San Blas), 58, 112, 115
Brava, Punta (Chiriquí), 251
Bridge of the Americas, 36

Brincanco, Isla, 240-241
Brisas, Hotel, 172-173
British Admiralty charts, ii
Brujas, Punta, 289
Bucaro, 214, 216
Bucaro, Ensenada, 216
Buen Nombres, Islotes, 267, 269
Buena Vista, Punta Morro de, 291, 297
Buenaventura, 45-46
Bueyes, Los, 50, 53
Bugori, 149
Burica, Punta 204, 302
Bus transportation, 8, 25, 38, 47, 49, 151, 223
business hours, 8
Buttonwood Cay, 171, 183-185

C

Caballitos, Los, 50
Cabeza Cays, 106, 109
Cabra, Isla, 48
Cabrito, Puerto, 249, 251
cacao, 155, 193, 318
Cacique, 46-47, 266, 277, 280
Cagao, Estero, 297
Caledonia, 123-124, 126, 130
Caleta Cayman, 218
Calovébora, 137, 139
Camacho Point, 191, 193, 196
Cambombia, Morro de, 275
Camera repair, 39
Camogantí, 307-308
Campamento, Punta del, 218, 221
Campana, Punta, 218-220
Caña Blanca, 295
Cana, 10, 307
Caña, Isla de, 272, 274-275
Caña, Rio, 153
Caña Cuenta, Punta, 269-270
Canal de Afuera, Isla, 231, 235, 237
Canal de Pinos, 119, 121-122
Canal de Tierra, xi, 231
Canal de Tigre, 143, 148
Canal Porter, 71-72
Canal Zone, 5
Canario, Isla, 294
Canglon, 8
Cangombia, 88-90, 92-93
Cangrejon, Bajo, 273
Cantina, La, 292
Caobos Cay, 69-70
Caobos Channel, 56, 82
Capurgana, 130-131
Caracoles, 272
Carate, Punta, 278, 281
Careening Island, 173, 175
Carenero, 173, 175
Carnaval, 8
Carreto, 129-131, 133
Carta Organica, 59

Cartagena, 57, 131
Cartagena, Isla, 300
Carter, Jimmy, 5
Cartí Grande, Rio, 78
Cartí Islands, 71-72, 78-80
Cartí Muladup, 79-80, 83
Cartí Sugdup, 71, 78
Cartí Tupile, 78-80
Casa Sola, Punta, 274
Casaya, 264, 267, 269-272
Casayeta, 264, 269-270
cashews, 318
Castillo de la Gloria, 46-47
Castillo San Jeronimo, 46
Castrellón, Irene, 317
Castrellón, Mario, 245
Catalina, Bahía, 259
Caté, Rio, 222, 229
Cativo, Punta, 230, 233
Cativon, Ensenada de, 233
Cauchero, v, 144, 154-155, 317
Cauro, Punta, 176
caution, Darién, 312
Cavada, Isla, 240, 246
Cavima, 300-302
Cayo Crawl, 183, 186
Cayo de Agua, 143-144, 146, 148
Cayo Guardo, 71
Cayos Gallego, 185, 188
Cayos Zapatillos, 9
Cébaco, 203-204, 218, 220-223
Cedro, Isla de, (Chiriguí), 250
Cedro, Isla, (Darién), 291, 297
Cedro, Mogotes de, 250, 252
Centinelas, Islas, 313
Central de Tuercas y Tornillos, 39
Centro Decorativo, 39
Centro Industrial, 39
Centro Marino, 38
Cerro Equi, 236
Cerro Punta, 9
chacaras, 151, 160
Chagres, Rio, 34, 134, 136-137
Chalapa, Punta, 251
Chama, Isla, 206
Chamé, Bahía, 205, 211
Chamé, Punta, 211
Chanati, Rio, 291
Changame, 40
Changuinola, 5, 8, 172, 174, 190
Chapera, Isla, 264, 267
Chapter I, 22-41
Chapter II, 42-133
Chapter III, 134-201
Chapter IV, 202-260
Chapter V, 261-314
Charco Azul, Bahía de, 204, 255, 260
charts, 25
Chepigana, 298, 306, 308
Chepillo, Isla, 286-287
Chepo, 4, 8, 287-288

Chepo, Rio, 287
Chibcha language, 58
chichime (the grain), 317
Chichime Cays, 57, 65-67
Chico, Rio, 308
Chimán, 289
Chiriquí Province, 2
Chiriquí, Golfo de, 204, 240
Chiriquí, Laguna de, 137, 144, 146-147, 149
Chiriquí, Rio, 137
Chiriquí Grande, 3, 5, 12, 141, 143-144, 151-152, 155, 159, 172, 190, 193
Chiriquí Marina, 253, 255
Chirre, Isla Punta, 234-235
Chitola, 293
Chitre, 5, 8, 264-265
Chiwadi, Rio, 75
Chocón, Lucrecia, v
Chocó, v, 3, 10, 307
Chocosana, 43
Chocoyos, 232
Chorro, Punta del, 284
Chu, Hotel, 207
Chucunaque, Rio, 308
Chunga, La, 309
Cimarrones, Islas, 233
clearing in and out, 5, 38, 61, 151, 172, 253, 256-257, 302
Cobler Rock, 187
Cocle Province, 2
Coco Alto, 96-98
Coco Bandero Cays, 96, 98
Coco Cay, 171, 191-193, 195-197, 199-200
Coco Solo, 7, 23, 29
Coco, Isla de, 272
coconut bread, 183, 315, 317
Cocos, Isletilla de Punta, 278, 281
Cocos, Punta de, 264, 272, 278, 281
Coetupu, 126-127
Coiba (San Blas), 78, 80
Coiba Explorer II, 236
Coiba National Park, 231, 236-237, 239
Coiba, 4, 9, 11, 78, 80, 204, 223, 231, 236-239
Coibita, 237-238
Colombia, 3-4, 9, 43, 57-58, 123, 131-133, 190, 262, 307, 312, 319
Colón, 2-3, 5, 7-10, 14, 24-25, 29-30, 45, 47, 49, 55, 57, 61, 108, 135, 137, 263
Colón, Isla, 144, 159, 173-174, 176-177, 182, 263
Columbus, 4, 45, 138, 177, 182, 319
Comarca de San Blas, 2, 4, 43, 58, 71
Commissioner's Rock, 208
communications, 79, 86, 123
Conch Point, 177, 182
Concholon, Punta del, 281
Conejo, Isla (Gulf of San Miguel) 297-298, 300
Conejo, Isla (Rio Santa Lucia) 243, 245
Congo dancing, 9
Congo, Rio, 290-293
congreso, 59-60, 80, 86, 95, 99, 104, 108, 114, 127, 130

Consular y Naves, 172
Contadora, 8, 264-266, 268, 280
Contadora, Resort Hotel, 266
Contractor's Hill, 31
Contreras, Las Islas de, 240-241
Corazon de Jesus, 70, 99, 101
Cordoba, Finca, 158-159
Corgidup (Lemon Cays), 65-66
Corgidup (Naguargandup Cays), 90-91
corn, 4, 113, 253, 315, 317
Coronado, Playa, 212
Corozal de Bayano, Punta, 286-287
Corozal, 16, 286-288, 298
Corral, Ensenada de, 210
Corriente, Punta 282
Costa Abajo, 8-9, 135
Costa Arriba, 8-9
Costa Rica, 3, 5, 9, 12, 190, 256-257
couriers, 3, 7, 151
Crawl Cay Channel, 160, 183-184, 186-187
Cricamola, Rio, 144, 150
Cristo, Punta, 238
Cristobal, 6-7, 11-12, 14, 23-24, 27, 29-31, 43, 45, 47, 50, 135
Cristóbal, Captain, v
Cristobal, Isla, 144, 171, 191-192, 195-197, 199-200
Cruce de Mono, 10
Cruz, Punta de, 282
Cuango, 8, 53, 55
Cuatro Calles, 251-252, 255
Cucaracha Reach, 35
Cucunatí, Rio, 290, 296
Cuili Cay, 50-51
Culebra Cut, 207
Culebra Island, 36
Culebra Reach, 35
Culebra Rock, 53, 104-105
Cupula, Punta, 77
Cusapin, 141-145

D

Damas, Bahía de Las, 237-238
Darién, v, 2-4, 7-10, 12, 262, 290, 295, 297, 300-301, 304, 307, 309, 311
Dark Land, 193, 198
dasheen, 151, 316
David, 3, 5, 7-9, 25, 151, 248-249, 253-254, 256, 319
Dávila, Pedrarias, 4, 130
de Lesseps, Ferdinand, 4
Deceano Bienjo, Punta, 153
Deer, Isla, 183, 186-187
Deliscanos, Ensenada, 144, 153
DHL, 7, 25, 151
Dia de la Raza, 9
Diablo Heights, 5, 35
Diaz Cay, 161, 186
Diaz, Ernest, 99
Diego Point, 175, 178

diesel, 24, 37, 51, 61, 141, 151, 174, 223, 226, 231, 253, 301
Dimar, S.A., 39
Direcion Consular y de Naves, 6, 172
Divorcio, 220
Do-it-yourself boat work, 10-11
Dolphin Island Resort, 114
Don Bernardo, 284-285
Don Jaime III, v
Donato, Punta, 176
Drake, Francis, 4, 45
Drake, Isla, 46
dry season, 3, 10, 43, 47, 49, 57, 70-71, 100, 131, 135, 203, 208, 280-281, 295, 307
drying out, 11, 280

E

Easter, 8
Eco Tours, 3, 130
Eden Channel, 65-66, 82
Egeo, 39
El Divorcio, 219
El Dorado, 7, 38-39
El Encanto, 299-300
El Jobo, 218, 221
El Real, 8, 10, 306, 308
El Rey, 23-24, 38
El Roble, 218
Electro Diesel, 39
Elefante, Bajo, 275
Elsie, Isla, 74
Embera, 10, 38, 262, 306-307, 309, 311-312
Empire Reach, 34
English language books, 38-39
English Rock, 222
Ensenada Indio, 50-51
Ensenada, Isla, 211
Ensenada, La, 272, 275, 279
Ensenada, Playa, 271
Entrada, Punta, 243
Esadi, Rio, 84-85
Escondido, Puerto, 195, 233
Escosés Channel, 56
Escosés, 4, 56-58, 127-130
Escribanos, 52-55
Escucha, Punta 45-46
Escudo de Veraguas, 14, 135, 137, 141, 144
Esmeralda, 272, 278-280
Esmetdup, 78
Esnatupile, 95, 98
Esperanza, Punta, 46-47
Espiritu Santo, 264, 272, 274, 279
Estacion Buen Amigo, 301
Estero Salado, 140
Estiva, Isla, 210-211
Euéro, Rio, 137-139

F

F anchorage, 23, 29
Farallon, Isla, 206
Farewell Islands, 101-102
Federal Express, 7, 25
Feria del Mar, 9
Ferro Cay, 160-161, 186
Festival de Bunde y el Bullerengue, 8
Festival la Cuadrilla, 9
Festival of Cristo Negro, 9
Fiesta of the Virgin Mercedes, 9
fishing, 4, 11, 38, 41, 55, 60, 67, 104, 137, 140, 182, 208, 214, 218, 223, 226, 245, 262, 281, 288, 303, 309, 311
Five Fathom Bank, 176
Flag Day, 9
Flamenco, 16, 36, 41
Flats, the, 23, 29
Fondeadero Grande, 311, 313
food shopping, 24, 61, 174
Food, 315
Fort Clayton, 35
Fort Kobbe, 36
Fort San Fernando, 46-47
Fort San Lorenzo, 135-136
Fort Sherman, 29
Fort St. Andrew, 127-130
Frailes, Norte and Sur, 216
Free Zone, 7, 23-25, 123
freighters, local, 7
French Canal, 23
Fresco Cay, 162, 171-172, 186
Fronteras, 256
fuel, 23-24, 37, 41, 61, 226, 253, 301

G

Gage, Thomas, 45
Gaigar, 80, 84-85
Gaillard Cut, 31, 34-35
Galera, Isla, 264
GALLEGA, 138
Gallego, Cayos, 171, 183, 185-186
Gallinazo, Punta, 191, 272
Gallo Cay, 65
Gambina, 221
Gamboa Reach, 31, 34
Gamdare International, 39
Gamez, Isla, 259
Gap, the, 181,183, 185
Garachiné, 8, 9, 15, 262, 290, 309-311
Garachiné, Punta, 290, 310
Garcia Cay, 190-191
Garote, 48-49
gasoline, 24, 37, 47, 49, 61, 86, 130, 140-141, 143, 148, 151, 155, 174, 183, 193-194, 214, 218, 223, 225-226, 231, 245, 248, 266, 288, 293, 301, 303, 306, 309

Gatun Lake, 26-27, 32-33, 135
Gatun Locks, 26, 29, 31, 41
Gauguin, Paul, 207
genips, 318
George, Isla, 74
Gerchow Cay, 189, 191
German Soldier Cay, 184, 186
Gertie, Isla, 74
Gibraleon, 264, 267, 269-270
Ginoves Point, 162, 171-172, 194
Gobernadora, Isla, 221-222
Golfo de Los Mosquitos, 135, 139
Golfo de San Miguel, 4, 290-291, 309-310
Gomez, Rufino, 301
Gorda, Punta, 275
Gorgas, Colonel William, 5
Gorua, Punta, 220
GPS, navigating with, 21, 43, 45
Gran Colombia, 4
Grande, Bahía, 191, 196
Grande, Isla, 48, 53, 196, 300
Granito de Oro, 236-238
Green Island, 93, 96-98
Gregorio Diaz, Estero, 304
Grey, Zane, 4
Ground Creek, 176, 182
Gruesa, Punta, 292
guabas, 318
Guacamayo, 142-143
Guanico, Punta, 216
Guarda, Canal de la, 265
Guarumo, Isla, 273
Guayabo Chiquita, 311-312, 314
Guayabo, 9, 311-312, 314
Guaymi, 3, 38, 140-141, 143, 148, 151, 159, 172, 183, 319
Guerro, Punta, 251
Guinea, Punta, 286
Gulf of Panama, 3, 12, 15, 203, 213, 262
Gulf of San Blas, 67, 71-73, 75
Gulf of San Miguel, 4, 290-291, 309-310
Gunboat Island, 85, 87

H

Hacha, 230, 234
ham radio, 47
Hannibal Bank, 4, 204
Haulover, 173
health matters, 9, 24, 40
Hermanas, Islas de las, 46
Hermosa, Ensenada, 238
Hermosa, Punta, 237-238
Herrera Province, 2
Hicaco, 222, 225-226, 229-230, 282-283
Hicaco, Isla de, 282
Hicaco, Punta, 229
Higueros, Isla, 255
Hijo Mocha, 256, 259
Hispanic Day, 9

History of Panama, 4-5
Holandes Cays, 68-70, 82
Holandes Channel, 56, 66, 82
holidays, 7-8, 10, 40, 331
Honda, Bahía (Bocas del Toro), 181, 185
Honda, Bahía (Veraguas), 234, 237, 240
Honda, Ensenada, 284
Horconcitos, 248
Hospital Bight, 175, 178-181, 183
Hospital Bight, Middle, 179
Hospital Bight, Short Cut, 180
Hospital Point, 14, 175, 178, 183
Hospital Reef, 178
Hospital San Fernando, 6
Hospital Santo Tomas, 6, 40
Hueca, Punta, 273

I

Iandu, 108, 110-111
Ibedi Tiwar, 123, 125
Icacos Island, 57, 66
Iglesias, Alcibiades, 9
Iglesias, Las, 250
Iglesias, Rio, 304, 308
Iguana Point, 191
Iguana, Isla (Gulf of Panama), 213-214
Iguana, Isla (Gulf of San Miguel), 289-291, 293, 298, 310
Iguana, Island (San Blas), 99, 102, 119, 121-122
Iguanita, Isla, 291, 293
Ikusa, Hotel, 113
Ilestu, 108, 110-112
immigration offices, 5, 61
immunizations, 9
Inapakiña, 8
Independence Day (from Colombia), 9
Independence Day (from Spain), 9
Indio, Puerto, 309
Indio, Rio, 50
Infierno, Punta, 286
Ingles Cays, 109, 111
INRENARE, 9, 182, 188, 207, 236
INTEL, 6, 23, 37
international couriers, 151
Intertrade, 7
Irish Bay, 150-151
Iskartupu, 107-108
Isla Colón, 9, 159, 174, 182
Isla de Pinos, 121-122, 124
Isla del Rey, 264, 271-281
Isla Grande, 8-9, 13, 48-49, 51-53, 57
Islamorada Int, S.A. 11, 25
Islandia, 113, 115-116
Isleta, La, 277
Islote Point, 108-109
ivory nut, 38, 262, 303

J

jagua, 38
Jaqué, 311, 313
Jaqué, Rio, 313
Jesus, Rio de, 224
Jetex, 7, 25, 151
Jicarita, 237
Jicaron, 204, 236-237
Jimenez, Max E., 39
John Crow Point, 191
Johnson Cay, 183, 186
José Pobre, 47
Juan Brown Point, 178
Juan Joaquin, Isla, 49
Juan, Punta, 191, 195
Juanita, Punta, 211
Jurel, Punta, 259

K

Kagandup, 65
Kaimou, 68-70
Kainora, 114-115, 117-118
Kalugirtupu, 69-70
Kanildup, 93, 96-98
Kanirdup, 127
Kapp, Kit, 127
Kaymatar, 104, 107
Knapp's Hole, 176, 182
Korbiski, 63-64
Kuadule, 99
Kuanidup, 82, 88
Kuba, 127
Kuna cakes, 317
Kuna Yala, 10, 43, 58-60, 64, 123, 130, 319
Kuna, v, xiv, 7-8, 10, 38, 43, 58-61, 64, 70-71, 75, 79-80, 88, 95, 99, 104, 108, 113-114, 119, 123, 130, 317, 319
Kwi Murru, 129, 133
Kwitupu, 119, 120

L

La Coquera Point, 104-105
La Guayra, 48-49
La Lavandera shoal, 48-49
La Muerta, Isla 249, 251-252
La Palma, 8, 298, 300-302, 306, 308-309
La Paz, 293
La Pelada Rock, 48-49
La Pluma, 225, 228
La Punta, 208, 221
Labor Day, 8
Lagarto, Isla, 300
Lagarto, Rio, 211
Lagua, Punta 298, 300
Laguna de Bluefield, 143, 145, 148

Laguna de Chiriquí, 12, 135, 141, 143-144, 151, 154-155, 159, 317
Lajas Reef, 135-136
Las Perlas, 3, 8, 203, 262-285, 298
laundry, 23, 37, 60, 95, 99, 114, 174
Laurel, Punta, 146-147, 156
Lemon Cays, Eastern, 66-67, 72, 82
Lemon Cays, Western, 65, 67, 72, 82
Lena, Isla, 74
Leones Arriba, 225, 228
Leones, Isla, 222, 228
Leve, Gerda, 283
Lighthouse Island, 93, 96-98
Lime Point, 174, 176
Limón, 14, 137-139
Limón, Punta, 138
Linarte, Isla, 250, 258
linehandlers, 27, 37
Linton, Isla, 48
List of lights, 13
locklines, 27-28
Log Rock, 171, 201
Logan Bight, 197
Loguovato, Isla, 250
Loma Partida, 144, 155
Lopez, Alvariño, 114
Los Grullos, 82, 88
Los Mogotes, 49
Los Octavios, Isla 230, 232
Los Santos, 2, 9
Lovaino, Rio, 239-240
Lucas, 311

M

Machete, Punta, 238, 304
Machorusio, Punta 259
Macolla, Punta, 52-53, 90-91
Madununudup, 93, 96
Mafafa, 280
Mafatita, Isletilla de, 277
Mafu Rocks, 48-49
Maiquipgandi, 70
Makemulu, 124, 126, 128, 130
Mala, Punta, 204, 213
Malaga, 269-270
Maldad, Punta La, 269
Mama Chi, 159
Mamartupu, 86
Mamey, 311
Mameys, 318
Mamimulu, 122-124
Mamitupu (eastern), 113-115, 117-118
Mamitupu (western), 63-64
Mandinga, Isla, 211
Mandinga, Rio, 72, 74-75
Mangle, Isla, 308
Mangles Channel, 82, 90, 96

Mangles Point, 90, 92
Mangrove Point, 173
Mann, John, 79-80
Mansukum, 119
Mantupkwa, 114, 117
Manx Cay, 183, 186
Manzanillo (Cébaco), 221
Manzanillo container terminal, 23
Manzanillo, Punta, 48, 50, 53
Map Link, 13
Maquina, 80
Marea, Rio, 308
Margarita, Bahía, 29
Margarita, Rio, 152
Mariana, Rio, 50
Marina Carenero, 174
Mariato, Punta 204, 214
Martin Cay, 162, 172, 186
Martin Perez, 272
Martin Pescador Rocks, 50-52
Martinez, Roy, 114
Martyr's Day, 8
Masargandi, Bahía de, 119-120
Matitas, Punta Las, 252, 255
Matupkwa, 114
Mauki, 70
Mayflower Channel, 82
McBride, Tina, 41
Medidor, Isla, 231, 234-235, 237
Medina, Punta, 271
Melones, Isla, 41, 205, 208
Membrillito, 267, 269
Membrillo, Isla, 267
Mercado Abasto, 38
methods of transiting, 28
Miel, Puerto La, 132-133
Miel, Punta de, 234-235, 237
Miguel de la Borda, 8, 135, 137
Milagir, 109, 111
Mina, Isla, 264, 269, 271
Minas, Bahía Las, 44
Ministerio de Hacienda y Tesoro, 5, 172
Minita, Isla de, 269
Miraflores Lake, 10, 27, 35, 37
Miraflores Locks, 26, 35
Miramar, 151, 153
Miria Murru, 120-121
Miria, 65
Miriadiadup, 68, 70
Mogo Mogo, 264, 267-268
Mogote de Adentro, 48
Mogote de Sepulcro, 256
Mogote, Isla, 46
Mogotes de Cedro, 250, 252
Mogotes de Manzanillo, Los, 50
Mogue, Estero de, 309
mola, 59-60, 86, 95
Molejones, Rio 151, 153
Mona, Isla (Chiriquí), 247, 250, 252
Mona, Isla (Veraguas), 242
Mona, Islote La (Bahía Honda), 231, 234

Monitas, Las, 247, 249, 258
Monkey Cay, 154-155
Mono Ajumado, 282-283
Mono, Culo de, Isla, 267, 269
Mono, Isla (Chiriquí), 250, 258
Mono, Isla (San Blas), 108, 110-113
Montijo, Bahía, 222, 224, 227-229
Montijo, Isla Leones, 228
Morales, Gaspar de, 280
Morgan, Henry, 4, 45
Mormaketupu, 80, 82, 84-85
Morodup, 68, 70
Moron Channel, 82
Moron Island, 82, 84-85, 87
Morro de Buena Vista, Punta, 291, 297-298
Morro de Puercos, 11, 17, 203
Morro de Taboga, 206-207
Morro, Isla, 292, 294
Morro, Punta del 210
Morti, Rio, v
Mosquito, Isla, 119-120
Mosquitos, Golfo de Los, 137, 139
Mosquitos, Punta, 120
Mother's Day, 9
Motor Sport Panama, 39
Mu Dummat, 58
Muelle Fiscal, 7
Muerta, Isla La, 229
Muerto, Ensenada, 242
Muerto, Isla de, 249, 251
Muertos, Bahía de, 251
Muertos, Punta, 240
Muladup, 78-80, 83
Mulatupu, v, 8, 122-125, 127, 130
Mulipe Murru, 129-130
Murrutuku, 114
Museum, Kuna, 79
museums, 10
Mutis, Puerto, 224

N

Nabsadi, Rio, 113, 116
Nabsadup, 95, 98
Naguargandup Cays, 82, 90-92
Naguargandup Cays, eastern, 88, 90, 92
Naguargandup Cays, western, 88, 90-91
Nalia, 63, 71
Nalunega, 62-64, 71
ñame, 316
ñampi, 317
Nancy Cay, 171, 175, 178-183, 185
Nancy Rock, 178
Nancy Shoal, 175, 178
Naos, 16, 36-37
Napakanti, 119, 121-122, 127-128
Naranjas, Punta, 214, 217
Naranjito, Punta, 221
Naranjo Grande, 79
Naranjo, Chico, 79

Naranjo, Ensenada (Azuero Peninsula), 214, 217
Naranjo, Ensenada del (Cébaco), 218
Naranjo, Islas (Abajo and Arriba), 44-45
Naranjo, Quebrada El (Cébaco), 218
Naraskandup, 84-85, 87-88
Narbagandup Dumat, 76, 79
Narbagandup Pipi, 76, 79
Nargana, 8, 70, 79, 88, 98-99, 101
Nargandi, Rio 77
Nasargandup, 66
National Day, 9
National Parks, 3, 9
navigation permit, 6
Negros, Ensenada Los, 256, 259
Nele Kantule, 9, 119
nele, 9, 59
Nellie, Isla, 74
Neloguichi, 71, 73
Nergala, Rio, 76
Ngöbe, 3, 38, 140-141, 143, 148, 151, 159, 172, 183, 319
Niadup, 102-103
Niagara, Roca, 284-285
Niakalubir, 68, 70
Niatupu, 65-66
NICOLA II, 254
Nicuesa, Rio, 72, 75
Nispero, Punta, 278
Nombre de Dios, 4, 45, 50-52
Nonomulu, 77, 79
Ñopo, Estero, 304
Noriega, Manuel, 5
Norte, Punta (Boca del Drago), 174, 176
Norte, Punta (Cayo de Agua), 146, 148
Norte, Punta, 146, 176
Ñotolente, 150-151
Novey Servi Center, 39
Nubadup, 124, 126-127
Nubasitupu, 85, 87
nuchus, 59
Nueva Granada, 4
Nugaruachirdup, 65
Nuinudup, 66-67
Nupnutupu, 74-75
Nurdupu, 82
Nusatupu, 84-86

O

Obaldia, Puerto, 131, 133
Octavios, Isla Los, 232
Oeste, Rio, 189
Ogoppiriadup, 69-70
Ogoppukib, 69-70
Ogopsibudup, 65, 93, 96-98
Ogumnaga 106-107
Old Bank Island, 178-180, 185, 187
Old Panama, 8
Old Point, 187
Ordup, 95, 98

Ordupbanedup, 95, 98
Orduptarboat, 95-96, 98
orenpendolas, 183
Orosdup, 74-75
Ortiz, Luis, 104
Oscuro, Punta, 275, 279
otoe, 316
Otoque, Isla, 205, 210-211

P

Pacheca, 15, 264-265, 268
Pacific Steamship Company, 207
Pacora, Isla, 234-235
Paitilla airport, 8
Pajaros, Isla, 121-122, 241
Palos Cut, Laguna, 199
Palos, Laguna, 197-199
Pan de Azucar, Cerro, 243-244
Pan de Azucar, Isla, 211
Panama Canal Comission, 10, 27
Panama Canal entrances, 18
Panama Canal system, 27
Panama Canal transit, 27-28, 31, 41
Panama Canal Yacht Club Annex, 48
Panama Canal Yacht Club, 6-7, 10, 23, 25, 29-30, 41, 48-49
Panama Canal, 3, 6-7, 10-12, 14, 16, 18, 23, 25-27, 29-31, 36, 38, 40-41, 47-49, 51, 57, 135, 172, 262, 319
Panama City, 3-5, 7-10, 12, 24-25, 38, 40-41, 47, 61, 64, 79, 99, 108, 127, 130-131, 207-208, 266, 288, 302, 307, 311, 317
Panama Outdoors, 39
Panama Province, 2
Panama Railroad, 4
Panama Yacht Services, 21
Panama, Bay of, 205
Panama, Gulf of, 15, 202-203, 261-262
Panamanian independence, 4
Pan-American Highway, 79, 223, 248, 252, 295, 302, 307
Papagayo, Isla, 227
Paraiso Reach, 35
Parida, Isla, 249, 259
Paridita, Isla, 259
Parita, Bahía, 204, 212, 214
Parque Nacional Interoceanico de Las Americas, 9
Parsamosukum, 71, 73
Pastores Pequeño, 190-191
Pastores, Isla, 190-191
Pata, Ensenada de, 210
Paterson, William, 127
Patiño, 290-291, 309-310
Patron Saint's Days, see holidays
Patronales of San Felipe, 8
Patronales of San Francisco, 8
Patronales of Virgen de la Carmen, 8
Patterson, Cayo, 144, 149
Paz y Salvo form, 5

Pedrarias, 4, 130
Pedregal, 11, 249, 252-256, 281
Pedro Gonzales, Isla, 264, 284-285
Pedro Miguel Boat Club, 6, 7, 10, 35
Pedro Miguel Locks, 10, 35
Pemasky National Park, 10
Peña Blanca Reach, 32
Peña El Mera, 224
Peña Hueca, Ensenada, 290, 292, 296-297
Peñas, Piedras Las, 210
Penitentiary colony, 236-238
Perdomo, Isla, 222, 224, 228
Perez Cay, 162, 186
Perez, Pablo Nuñez, 114
Perico Island, 36-37
Perlas, Las, 3, 8, 203, 262-285, 289
Perme, Puerto, 131, 133
Permiso de navegacion, 6, 38, 61, 151, 172, 253 256-257
permiso de salida, 5
Peru, 4, 25, 207
Pesqueros, 39
Pifa (pijiba, pijibaye, piba, pixbae), 315
Pifa and dasheen soup, 316
Pifa and okra, 315
Pifa, boiled, 315
Pigeon Creek, 171, 192-193
Pijiba, xiii, 295, 315
piloting by eye, 64, 71
Piña, Rio, 224, 313
Piñas, Bahía, 311, 313
Piñas, Punta, 313
Pinogana, 308
Pinos, Canal de, 56, 121-122
Pinos, Isla, 121-122, 124
Piriaque, 306, 308
Pitgandi Point, 111-112
Pixvae, Ensenada de, 242
Pizarro, Francisco, 207, 280
Plantain Cays (Big and Small), 141-142
Platanal, 218, 220
Platania, 270-272
Playa Blanca (Colón), 46-47
Playa Blanca (Darién), 311
Playa Brava (Las Perlas), 270-271
Playa Brava, Ensenada de, 240
Playa Cacique, 266
Playa Chiquita, 52-53, 55
Playa de Damas, 50-51
Playa de la Sueca, 266
Playa de San Juan, 280
Playa del Socorro, 256, 259
Playa Ejecutiva, 266
Playa Ensenada, 270
Playa Galeon, 266
Playa Grande, 259, 282-283, 297-298
Playa Grande, Ensenada, 282
Playa Grande, Punta (Gulf of San Miguel), 297-298
Playa Kobbe, 23, 40
Playa Raya, 145, 148
Playa, Punta, 83

Playita, Punta, 282
Playon Chico, 8, 104, 106-110
Playon Grande Channel, 105
Plaza, Isla, 258
police, 6, 99, 119, 123, 131, 135, 236, 288, 307
Pondsock, 15, 190-191
Ponedero, Punta, 221
Ponuga, Rio, 222, 224
Popa Numero Dos, Isla, 161, 186
Popa Numero Uno, Isla, 156, 158, 161
Popa, Ensenada, 161
Popa, Isla, 144, 146-147, 156-157, 161, 186-187
Porcada, Isla, 243-244
Porras, Laguna, 144, 171, 199-201
Porras, Puerto, 50
Port Geladi, 55
Porter Bight, 193, 195
Portobelo National Park, 9
Portobelo, 4, 8-9, 12, 45-47, 49, 51
Porvenir, 5, 8, 61-64, 71, 79, 82
postal services, 6
Pozo, Punta del, 259
Pretelt, Manuel, 24
propane, 24, 38, 49, 61, 174
Protecsa, 39
Providencia shoal, 53, 55
Providencia, 53, 57, 172, 190
Provinces, 2
Provision Island, 178-180, 182, 185
Puerco, Isla de, 275
Puerto Cabrito, 252
Puerto Escosés, 57, 128, 130
Puerto Indio, 309
Puerto Lindo, 48-49
Puerto Mutis, 223-225
Puerto Nuevo, (Rio Santa Lucia), 245
Puerto Obaldia, 7, 13, 61
Puerto Perme, 130-131, 133
Puerto Yate, 64
Pugadup, 99, 102
Punta Allegre, 143, 145, 291, 309-310
Punta Avispa, 143
Punta Brava (San Blas), 11, 58, 112-113, 115
Punta Brava (San Miguel), 289, 291
Punta Brujas, 288-289
Punta del Pozo, 254, 256
Punta Escosés, 4, 58, 127, 130
Punta Laurel Bay, 148
Punta Macolla, 52
Punta Norte, 148, 174, 288
Punta Playa, 52, 55, 80, 298
Punta San Blas, 11, 43, 55, 57, 63-64, 71
Puntita, La, 300-302
Purio, Puerto, 213
Putumayo, 126
Puyadas Channel, 99, 102

Q

Quarys Point, 189

Quebrada Paulino, 137
Quebrada Piedra, 245
Quemada, Punta, 296
Quimba, Puerto, 304
Quinquindup, 69
Quiros, 270
Quita Pampanillo, Punta, 228

R

Radicom Icom, 39
Radio Shack, 39
rainy season, 8, 43, 45, 47, 49, 57, 61, 131, 203, 230, 245, 254, 266
Ramirez Cay, 161, 186
Rancheria, 236-238
Rancho, Punta, 176
Ratones Cays, 104, 106, 109
Ratones Channel, 106
Redondo, Islote, 233
Redondo, Punta, 77
Remedios, 244-245
Repartideros, Los, 251-252
Republic of Panama, 3-7, 23, 37, 99, 131, 256
Restingue, Ensenada, 217
Revantazones Tigre, 143-145
Revantazones Valiente, 143, 145
Rey, Isla del, 264, 271-281
Ringrose, Basil, 245
Rio Azucar, 70, 93, 96-97
Rio Diablo, 98-99, 101
Rio Sidra, 71, 79, 84-86, 88
Robeson, George M., 71
Robeson, Islas, 74
Robinson, Charles, 8
Robinson, Sr. (Bluefields), 143
Robinson, Sr. (Holandes), 71
Roble, Punta, 220, 242
Roca Escosés, 58, 130
Roca Prosper, 237, 240-241
Roca Shag, 288-289
Rodelag, 39
Roldan Cay, 190-191
Roncador, Islote, 217
Roosevelt, Theodore, 4
Rosario, Ensenada de, 240, 242
Rosario, Playa, 238
Routes into the San Blas, 56
Rule of Twelves, 263

S

Sabana peninsula, 299, 302
Sabana, Punta, 302, 304
Sabana, Rio, 290, 304-305
Sabanilla, Punta, 46
Sabanitas, 47
Sabino, Punta, 255
Saboga, 264-265, 268

Sagariti, Rio, 289
sahila, 59-60, 104, 114, 119
Saigon, 173, 182
sail repair, 24
Sail Rock (Boca del Drago), 174, 176
Sail Rock (San Blas), 62, 64
Saino, Isla, 250, 258
Sajalices, Rio, 211
Salado, Estero, 137, 139
Salado, Rio El, 244
Salar, 88, 90-91
Salmedina Reef, 46-47
Salt Creek, 187-188
Sambú, 8, 309-310
Sambú, Rio, 310
San Andres, 172
San Blas, 56-133
San Blas, Canal de, 56, 65, 72, 82
San Blas, Cordillera, 58
San Blas, Golfo de, 72
San Blas, Punta, 63, 72
San Blas, routes into, 57
San Blas, shopping, 61
San Blas, the people, 58
San Cristobal, 50, 193
San Ignacio de Tupile, 109-111
San Jose, Banco, 290
San Jose, Isla (Chiriquí), 249, 258
San Jose, Isla de (Las Perlas), 264, 282
San Jose, south tip 282-283
San Juan, Morro de, 276
San Juan, Playa de, 276
San Juan, Rocas, 222
San Lorenzo, Bahía de, 247
San Lorenzo, Ensenada (Veraguas), 230, 232
San Lorenzo, Ensenada de (Chiriquí), 247-248
San Lorenzo, Punta (Gulf of San Miguel), 289-291
San Miguel, Gulf of, 289-291, 309-310
San Miguel, Isla del Rey, 264, 271-273
San Pablo Reach, 33
San Pablo, Isla, 274
San Pablo, Rio, 222, 227
San Pedro, Boca de, 249, 255
San Pedro, Isla, 274
San Pedro, Rio, 222, 224
San Telmo, 272, 276-278, 280
Sandfly Bay, 173, 175, 182
Sankanti Senik, 114, 117
Santa Catalina, 226, 230, 232, 259
Santa Catalina, Isla (Caribbean), 137
Santa Cruz, Ensenada de, 238, 259
Santa Lucia, Rio, 243-244
Santelmito Channel, 276, 280
Santelmito, Isla, 276
Santiago, 5, 8, 46, 223, 244-245
Santiago, Rio, 244
Sapé, Isla, 208, 211
Sapzurro, 131-132
Sarabeta, Punta, 176
Sasardi, v, 9, 122, 124-125
Sasogana, Rio, 308

Scottish settlement, 127
seagrapes, 318
Secas, Islas, 240, 246
Security warning, Coiba, 231
SEEPFERDEN, 283
Selfridge, Bajo, 76
Semana Santa, 8
Señora, Isla, 264, 284-285
Sepulcro, Mogote de, 256, 259
Servicio Maritimo Nacional, 278-279, 281
Seteganti, Rio, 308
Sevilla, Isla, 249, 251, 255
Shark Hole, 162, 172, 194, 201
Shelter Cove Marina & Lodge, 10, 25
Shepherd Bank, 173, 175
Shepherd, Ensenada, 190-191
Shepherd, Isla, 190-191
Shepherd, Samuel, Julian and Pedro, 190
Ship Identification Number, 27, 41
shopping, Panama City, 38
Short Cut, 180, 183
Sidra, Rio, 82, 84-86
Silico, Punta, 153-154
Silva de Afuera, Isla, 240
Silva de Tierra, Isla, 243, 245
Simondup, 93, 96-98
Simpson, Dave and Sharon, 254
Sindup, 104
Sister Cays, 191
Siufer, S.A., 39
Skynet courier, 7
Smithsonian, 3, 31, 39, 62-64, 319
Snug Harbor, 104, 106-108
Socorro, Playa del, 259
Solarte, 171, 175, 178-182, 185
Soledad Miria, 83, 85-86
Sombrereta, Roca, 297
Soná, 225
Soska palms, 119
Soskandup, 115
Soskantupu, 122, 124-127
Southwest Channel, 189-190
Split Hill, 144, 155-158
Spokeshave Reef, 58, 104-105
sportfishing, 3-4
SSB weather broadcasts, 19
Starbuck, Mike, 47
Stevens Circle, 38
Sucio West, Rio, 294-295
Sucio, Rio, 290, 292, 294
Sugandi Tiwar, 119
Sugar Island, 93, 96-98
Sugtupu, 78-80
Sukunya, 127-128, 130
Suledup, 108, 110-112
Suletupu, 126-128, 130
Sumwood Channel, 155-159
Super 99, 24, 38
surfing, 214, 230, 256, 288
Surrones, Punta 218
Swan Cay, 174, 176

T

Tabernilla Reach, 33
Taboga, 3, 7-8, 11, 41, 203, 205-208
Taboguilla, Isla, 206
Tabor, Isla, 211
Tadarguanet, 71-72, 74-75
Takela, Pension, 301-302
tamarinds, 318
Tambor, Isla, 48
Tannaquetupir, 108
Tapao, Ensenada, 144, 154
Tarpon Club, 137
Tasco, 24, 39
taxis, 23, 159, 174
Tembrillos, Isla, 264, 267
Terapa, Isla, 206
Terrain, Rio, 50
Themung, Punta, 156, 158
Three Brothers Bight, 146, 148
Tiadup, 67, 69-70, 95-96, 98
Tiburon, Bahía de, 63
Tiburon, Cape, 56
Ticantiqui, 70, 103-104
Tidal terms illustrated, 263
Tide tables, 263
Tides (Chapter V), 263
Tierra Oscura, 193, 198
Tigre, 8, 14, 70, 79, 102-104, 135
Tigre, Cayos, 143-146, 148
Tigre, Isla (Laguna de Chiriquí), 146, 148
Timon, Punta, 282
TIMONEER, 236
Tinta, Rio, 243
Tintorera, Isla, 259
Tiwar Bippi, 117
Tiwar Dumat, 114, 117
Tobobe, 135, 137, 141-144
Toe, King, 280
Tolé, 245
Tolomé, Canal, 265
Tommy Guardia, 12
Tonosí, Rio, 216
topographical maps, 12
Tori, Ensenada de, 150
Toro, Punta, 29
Torrijos, Omar, 5
Torrito, Boca, 199-201
Tortí, Rio, 74
tortillas, 317
Tovar, Otilio, 302
Toyopan Tesa, 39
Trampa, La, 309
Trans Express Worldwide, 7
Transcanal Yacht Services, 41
transiting, 27-28, 31, 41
Trapiche, Islote, 284-285
Tridente, Bajo, 74
Trinchera, 313
Trinidad, Rio, 224

Tropic Star Lodge, 4, 311, 313
Tuala, 95-96, 98
Tubasaniket, 84-85, 87
Tubo, Punta, 50
Tuborgana, 90, 92
Tubuala, 124, 126-127
Tucutí, Rio, 308
Tudor, Queen Mary, 270
Tuira, Rio, 289, 299, 306, 308
Tupbak, 121, 123-124
Tupile, San Ignacio de, 110
Tupisa, Rio, 308
Tupsuit Dumat, 71, 74-75
Tupsuit Pippi, 74-75
Tuquesa, 307-308
Tuwala, 9, 74-75

U

Uagitupu, 114
Uanokandi, 110-111
Uargandup, 96-97
Uarsadup, 83
Uastupu, 114-115, 117-118
Ubicantupu, 74-75
Ubigandup, 96-98
uchu, 59
Uchutupu Dumat, 64-67
Uchutupu Pippi, 64-66
Ukupseni, 104, 107, 109
Ukupsibu, 118-119
Ukupsui, 88, 90-91
Ukupsuit Tupu, 69-70
Ulartupu, 106, 109
ulus, 59, 71, 75, 80, 99, 114
Union de Chocó, v, 10
UPS, 7, 25
Urava, Isla, 206
Urgandi, 84-86
Urrutia, Florentino, v
Ursula, Punta, 237
Urusukun, 73
US DMA charts, 99, 263, 309
US Express Mail Service, 7
Ustupu, 8-9, 107-108, 118-120, 123
Uva, Isla, 237, 240-241
Uyama, Rio, 154

V

Vacamonte, 11, 16, 23, 40-41
Valdespino, Tilila, v
Valiente peninsula, 142
Valiente, Canal, 145
Valiente, Punta, 143, 145
Varedero, Ensenada del, 256, 259
Venaditos, Islas, 247
Venado, Isla (Bocas del Toro), 186
Venado, Isla (Chiriquí), 240, 247, 249

Ventana, Isla de, 248, 250, 258
Ventura Cruz, Canal, 271
Veraguas, 2, 14, 135, 137, 141, 144, 223, 234, 237, 240-242
Veraguas, Escudo de, 137, 141, 144
Verde, Isla (Las Perlas) 269
Verde, Isla (Montijo), 222, 224
Vernon, Admiral, 45
Viboras, Las, 50
Viejo, Port, 48
Viejo, Puerto, 221, 223
Virginia Rocks, 143, 145
visas, 5, 190, 256
Viscaino Cays, 162, 172, 186
Viudas, Islas, 258
Viveros, Isla, 264, 269, 271-272
Vivienda, La, 269-270
Volcan Baru National Park, 9

W

Wade, Phil, 236
Waisala Sukun, 120
Waisaladup, 65-66, 68, 70, 93, 96-98
Waisalamulhu, 78
Wakalatupu, 113, 115, 117-118
Wala Tiwar, 130
Warrie Point, 149
weather forecasts, 19
West Point, 140-141
Whaleback Rock, 222, 228

Wichubhuala, 62-64, 68
Widocara, 311
Wilson Cay, 161
World Courier, 7
Wounaan, 3, 262, 293, 295, 302, 307, 311
Wreck Rock, 174, 176

Y

Yabilikiña, 9
Yandup, 99
Yansaladup, 66-67
Yantupu, 78-80, 119
Yaviza, v, 7-8, 10, 306-308
Yebra, 138
Yellowtail Cay, 148-149
yuca, 316-317
Yurre, 243, 245

Z

Zancadillo, Punta, 284
Zapatilla Numero Dos, Cayo, 144, 187-188
Zapatilla Numero Uno, Cayo, 144, 187-188
Zapatilla, Cayos, 144, 182, 187-188
zarpe, 6, 151, 172, 212, 223
Zeisler, Dieter, 283
Zurron, Punta, 222

About The Authors

Nancy Schwalbe Zydler

The tidal creek twisting through a maze of marshland behind her home in Savannah, Georgia introduced Nancy to the enjoyment of exploring the currents and shifting sands in a coastal environment. The family's sloop and weekly Lightning and Penguin class sailing at the Savannah Yacht Club led to sailing adventures in inshore as well as offshore waters. Later, at the University of Georgia, she studied fine arts. Her paintings of tropical plant life have been exhibited at the Cheekwood Botanical Gardens and Art Museum in Tennessee, at the Hilton Head Museum of Art in South Carolina, and at galleries in South Carolina and South Florida.

In 1975, Nancy married and sailed away with Tom Zydler. Since that time, they have voyaged from the Great Lakes to Brazil, from Faeroe Islands to the Galapagos, and are still pursuing a life at sea. She has written articles about sailing for Cruising World, Sailing, Sail, Yachting Monthly, and Southern Boating. She holds a US Coast Guard 100 Ton Captains License.

Tom Zydler

Tom Zydler started racing dinghies at the age of 12 in his native Poland. He gradually moved up to ocean racing in the Baltic Sea, eventually becoming the youngest Polish holder of a yacht masters license for all oceans. He graduated from the Merchant Marine College and pursued a professional career at sea until receiving the first mate's position. Next, he moved ashore to study English Literature at the University of Lodz. After getting his M.A. with a thesis on Joseph Conrad, he stayed to teach English at the University while continuing to sail during the long vacations that academic life permitted. He led sailing expeditions as far as Iceland, Jan Mayen, and East Greenland. In 1972, he captained a 45 foot yawl from Poland to Cape Horn rounding it from the Atlantic to the Pacific. Next he served as a deck officer on German ships and in 1974, immigrated to the United States where he skippered large private and charter yachts after obtaining a US Coast Guard 500 Ton Masters License for all oceans.

Tom writes for yachting magazines and has been published in Cruising World, Yachting, Sailing, Sail, Southern Boating, Wooden Boat, and Professional Boatbuilder in the US, Classic Boat, Yachting World, and Yachting Monthly in the UK, and in Le Chasse Mareé in France. He markets his marine photography through Stock Newport in Portland, Maine.

Seaworthy Publications, Inc.

Financial Freedom aFloat
by
Charles Tuller
244 pages,
illustrations
bibliography
and index
ISBN 1-892399-06-7
$19.95 (US)

While there are many books that will tell you how to save money and cruise on a shoestring budget, *Financial Freedom aFloat* is the first book that tells you how to realistically pay for your cruising dreams without having to save for the rest of your life. The book is filled with ideas for using your existing talents to earn money while enjoying the cruising experience. The entire gamut of potential income opportunities available to cruisers, along with the advantages and disadvantages of each are examined in detail. *Financial Freedom aFloat* is designed for those who want to go cruising now, not ten or twenty years from now. It shows you how you can make your cruising dreams a reality. Even cruisers who view themselves as financially independent can benefit from this book by considering sections that discuss the realities of the cruising experience and making the time you spend cruising more rewarding and enjoyable.

Spanish for Cruisers Boat Repairs and Maintenance Phrase Book
by
Kathy Parsons
ISBN 0-9675905-0-7
$24.95 (US)

This easy-to-use phrase book provides all of the hard-to-find vocabulary you'll need to repair and maintain your boat, while you cruise the Spanish-speaking countries of the Americas and Caribbean.

You'll learn all the Spanish you need to:
√ Buy hardware and parts
√ Place orders, confirm prices, and schedule repairs
√ Find mechanics, repairmen, and canvas makers
√ Describe your problems, and the repairs you need
√ Haul, paint or store your boat
√ Call for help at sea, and get the assistance you need
√ Communicate with almost anyone

Race to Freedom
by
Vladislav Murnikov
321 pages
ISBN 0-9676657-0-1
$19.95 (US)

This inaugural book by Russian-born sailor and yacht designer Vladislav Murnikov chronicles the story of the first and only Soviet yacht (*Fazisi*) to ever compete in a Whitbread Round the World Race. *Race to Freedom* traces the original concept of Mr. Murnikov's dream through the trials and tribulations that eventually led to the successful campaign of the maxi-boat named *Fazisi*. She became the first private sports initiative in the slowly collapsing Soviet Union and truly a model of free enterprise at work that was inspirational for all involved.

The story has all the drama of an epic sailing adventure in the most treacherous waters on Earth, from the tragedy resulting from the loss of a co-skipper and a potentially mutinous crew, to the sheer elation of surfing down huge Southern Ocean waves in an 83-foot high-performance sailboat. Although built in the Soviet Union, *Fazisi* was equipped with Western sails, rigging and electronics. Being sponsored by Pepsi-Cola International and co-skippered by American Skip Novak, she was indeed an intriguing mix.

The Best Tips From Women Aboard
Edited by
Maria Russell
179 pages
illustrations
photographs
and index
ISBN 0-9663520-1-7
$14.95 (US)

Women Aboard is an organization dedicated to empowering women boaters

Here is just a sample of the useful tips inside
√ How to live in close quarters
√ Organization and dealing with clutter
√ How to welcome landlubbers aboard
√ Tips for boating with children
√ Problems with pets and how to solve them
√ Tips on having pets aboard
√ Making things stay put
√ Recommended galley supplies
√ Dealing with pests aboard
√ Multiple-use products
√ Tried and true products
√ Hints for holidays on board
√ What to take on extended trips
√ Plus loads of personal tips from **Women Aboard**

For further information, or to place an order please contact:

Seaworthy Publications, Inc.
215 S. Park St., Suite #1
Port Washington, WI 53074

Phone: (262) 268-9250, Fax: (262) 268-9208
e-mail: **publisher@seaworthy.com**
web site: **http://www.seaworthy.com**

Cruising Guides

The Abaco Guide
by
Stephen J. Pavlidis

The most comprehensive guide ever written covering the entire Abaco chain as well as the Grand Bahama region, and the Bight of Abaco. Its **66 detailed full-color charts** contain extremely accurate data which is based on independent surveys personally conducted by the author using a computer hydrographic system. Also included are GPS waypoints, piloting instructions, photos, approaches, services, routes, anchorages, dive sites, history, a chart index and more. **Features a new route into the Bight of Abaco from the north. Includes a special note on Hurricane Floyd and the Abacos.** Otabound (lay-flat binding), **173 pages.**
ISBN 1-892399-02-4, $29.95 (US)

The Turks and Caicos Guide
by
Stephen J. Pavlidis

The first-ever in-depth cruising guide providing coverage of the entire Turks and Caicos region, including parts of the northern coast of the Dominican Republic. The book contains full-color charts, piloting instructions, approaches, routes, anchorages, dive sites, and history. In addition, there is information on Puerto Plata and Luperón, in the Dominican Republic, with charts and photos. In this book, as in all other books by Pavlidis, the charts are extremely accurate and provide close-up views in much greater scale than standard navigation charts. The color scheme of the charts in this new book is designed to make navigation easier than black & white charts. Accurate charts of Luperón in the Dominican Republic reflect the latest changes as of 1998. Altogether, the book has **149 pages** with over **30 detaild full-color charts** of the region, Otabound (lay-flat binding).
ISBN 1-892399-01-6, $22.95 (US)

The Exuma Guide
by
Stephen J. Pavlidis

The most comprehensive and all-encompassing cruising guide ever written on the Exuma Cays. Much of what Steve has written in **The Exuma Guide** is not available from any other publication. Local knowledge is the key, and in **The Exuma Guide** you get information previously known only to those who live there. The guide contains lists of information on GPS waypoints, marine facilities, customs regulations, beacons and navigational aids, distances, ham and weather radio broadcasts and stations, anchoring tips, tides and currents, as well as phone numbers, reference reading, and even local recipes, holidays and customs. The books consists of **224 pages,** with **59 charts,** Otabound (lay-flat binding), chart index, aerial photographs, table of contents, and bibliography.
ISBN 0-9639566-7-1, $29.95 (US)

On and Off the Beaten Path
by
Stephen J. Pavlidis

The book has two sections. "On the Beaten Path" covers The Biminis, Andros, The Berry Islands, New Providence, Eleuthera, Little San Salvador, Cat Island, Long Island, Conception Island, Rum Cay, and San Salvador. "Off the Beaten Path" covers The Jumentos, The Crooked/Acklins District, Samana, The Plana Cays, Mayaguana, Inagua, and Hogsty Reef.
While a prudent skipper should still carry government charts for the region, This guide provides much local knowledge and greater detail on how to safely transit these waters. With this guide most cruisers can safely and confidently find their way into anchorages and through passes, that previously appeared somewhat daunting. Otabound (lay-flat binding) **320 pages, 32 charts,** chart index, photographs, and table of contents.
ISBN 0-9639566-9-8, $34.95 (US)

The Panama Guide Second Edition
by
Nancy Schwalbe Zydler &
Tom Zydler

The guide, as it is referred to in Panama includes specific piloting instructions covering all of coastal Panama, its major navigable rivers that reach the coast, as well as the San Blas Islands and Las Perlas.
The Panama Guide contains an 8-page color section featuring Tom Zydler's photography of Panama, also including GPS waypoints, instructions for transiting the Panama Canal, lists of navigational aids, local services, customs regulations, recommendations for on-shore activities, and a detailed index. The guide will make the waters surrounding Panama more accessible to yachtsmen by clearly showing routes for safe navigation, anchorage, rules and regulations, and suggestions for polite interaction with the Panamanian people. Otabound (lay-flat binding), **350 pages, 187 charts,** a full-color photo section, and index.
ISBN 1-892399-09-1, $44.95 (US)

Famous cruising couple Tom and Nancy Zydler's new book hits close to home. Nancy, a Georgia native, and Tom have taken two years to completely chart and describe the complex Georgia coast in this new book.
Filled with detailed information, charts, photos, and tables, their new book is the most comprehensive guide ever written about coastal Georgia. This book is for all types of boaters and fishermen, plus many other hobbyists from bird watchers to historians Nancy's clear, accurate charts and Tom's photography are coupled with their detailed text and information sections to create a guide that is as functional as it is informative.
The Zydlers have literally combed the entire coast of Georgia aboard their engineless yawl, *Mollymawk*, personally traveling up every channel and river in the region. The result is a work so comprehensive that it can only be described as monumental. All of the navigable rivers that reach the coast have been included with hundreds of charts and photos. 420 pages, color photo section, illustrations, charts, bibliography, index.
ISBN 1-892399-07-5, $39.95 (US)

Chartracker to the ICW Norfolk to Jacksonville
by
Katherine G. Redmond

√ The first true pilot guide to the ICW, containing both quick reference charts and piloting instructions in a side-by-side format

√ Quick references to services, mile markers, channel markers, local conditions, weather, and more

√ Simplified chart format, with bridge and lock restrictions noted on the charts, ICW distances in one-mile increments

√ Contains checkoff blocks for navigation aids/landmarks, plus county maps for NOAA weather tracking

√ Unique south to north orientation so the chart matches the channel ahead for southbound cruisers- especially helpful to the first-timer on the ICW

√ Includes complete charts and instructions for traveling the Great Dismal Swamp Route.

184 pages, with **132 full-color charts,** full-color uv coated cover, table of contents, text index, and bibliography,
ISBN 1-892399-00-8, $39.95 (US)

Hal Roth Recent Releases!

Two Against Cape Horn

Here's a tale of high adventure that's as fascinating as the voyages of Sir Francis Chichester or Joshua Slocum. Hal and Margaret Roth, veteran sailors, set out to take their famous 35-foot sloop, Whisper, through the little-known archipelago on the southwest coast of South America. As a finale, they planned to sail around Cape Horn, the greatest challenge of all. After a 7,600-mile voyage from California, they explored the vast archipelago in the wilds of southern Chile. They sailed in deep fjords between high mountains and glided past enormous, blue-fronted glaciers. Finally they arrived at the bottom of the world, ready to sail around Cape Horn.

One night Hal and Margaret anchored in a small bay in the uninhabited Wollaston islands. There, just twenty-four miles from Cape Horn, a violent storm slammed them ashore. They were wrecked in one of the most remote areas in the world. The Roths set up a camp ashore and survived for nine days until a Chilean warship saw their signals and took them off. Later, with help from the Chilean Navy, they re-vaged Whisper. After months of repairs, Hal and Margaret set out again. This time they successfully rounded Cape Horn, headed north in the Atlantic, and sailed back to the U.S. By the time they arrived in Maine, the Roths had logged 20,000 miles.

ISBN 1-892399-05-9, $22.95 (US)

We Followed Odysseus

This is the story of two legendary sailors–one from the distant past, the other from the very real present. Set against the backdrop of Homer's The Odyssey, and the fabled Greek isles of the Mediterranean Sea, Hal Roth tells the fascinating story of sailing a small boat in the wake of Odysseus. Crossing oceans and seas in pursuit of his cause, Roth, with help from his wife, Margaret, re-traces the voyages of Odysseus among the fabled Greek isles, the Italian and Sicilian coasts, Corsica, Malta, and an island off the coast of Tunisia. While writing the book, Roth talked to hundreds of people and discovered that while most have heard about Odysseus, they have never read The Iliad or The Odyssey. These are books they "are planning to read some day." Accordingly Roth summarizes very briefly and expertly each of the main chapters of The Odyssey. Maps, photos, 256 pages, hardcover.
ISBN 1-892399-03-2, $27.95 (US)

Whisper's Pacific Voyage

"Before we left we thought of lovely anchorages in turquoise lagoons, weeks of splendid sailing with the warm trade winds behind us, and getting to know such places as Samoa, Moorea, Rarotonga, and Kusaie. We looked forward to the fun of meeting Polynesians and Micronesians. I was anxious to hear Tahitian music first hand. Margaret was keen to see a coral atoll and to chop open a fresh coconut with her own hands.

"We hoped to visit a dozen harbors in far-off Japan. The Aleutian Islands, Alaska, and the islands off British Columbia in Canada where unknown mysteries. Like life itself we had a few storms, but we learned that the sun always comes out and the giant waves ease off.

"During nineteen months the two of us sailed 18,538 miles in a great circular route entirely around the Pacific. We stopped at seventy-five ports, met hundreds of people, and found nothing but friendship. We saw Tahitian dancing, listened to the singing of Samoan girls, and watched the tea ceremony in Japan. It  was our first great voyage and perhaps the most memorable because we were young, the yacht was simple, and we were unafraid."

ISBN 1-892399-04-0, $22.95 (US)

Hal Roth Classics!

Always a Distant Anchorage

The captivating story of Hal and Margaret Roth's 46-month, 30,000-mile east-west circumnavigation via the Panama and Suez canals. "A great adventure story...valuable, instructional..." - SAILING. "The Roth's showed guts, determination, and skill..." - Sail. Hal Roth excels...clear unencumbered writing...one who captures the sense and spirit of the adventure, and makes you 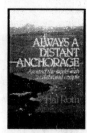 want to have one too. - New England Coastal News. Roth has an eye for detail and an enthusiasm for his tale that makes the reader feel that he is on the scene. Fun to read for sailors and non-sailors alike. - The Ellsworth American. Join Hal and Margaret on this truly incredible journey. Maps, photos, 348 pages, bibliography, index.
ISBN 0-9639566-5-5, $15.95 (US)

Two on a Big Ocean

Hal Roth and his wife, Margaret, won the CCA Blue Water Medal for 1971 for their 18,500-mile circumnavigation of the Pacific. "...Roth's books stand beside those written by Hiscock and others." - Sailor's Gazette. "...the author writes with grace, humor, and occasional poetic insight about the vastness and beauty of the ocean." - Library Journal "Roth is...a true explorer and adventurer..." - Yachting. "...a unique voyage through the islands of the Pacific." - Sail. "...polished and fast moving, telling an exciting story and teaching valuable lessons..." - SAILING. Maps, photos, 334 pages. ISBN 0-9639566-3-9, $15.95 (US)

Visit our web site at: www.seaworthy.com

Chasing the Long Rainbow
The Drama of a Singlehanded Sailing Race Around the World

This incredible account of Hal's first BOC Challenge race is a captivating, fast-paced, and highly personal story of the drama of his participation in the world's most demanding sailboat race. "... few have summed up the demands on singlehanders better than he does..." - Sail. "...dramatic account...from the perspective of the unsponsored sailor operating on a shoe-string budget. - Pacific Yachting. "Adventure lovers will find the book hard to put down." - Publisher's Weekly. "An extremely well-written book which will be enjoyed by both practical and armchair sailors." - Cruising World. Maps, photos, 334 pages.
ISBN 0-9639566-6-3, $15.95 (US)

A New Sailing Designs is Launched!
by Robert H. Perry

Next to a new boat there is probably nothing a sailboat lover will appreciate more than a new edition of Sailing Designs. Well, it's here—**Sailing Designs Volume—Five**, the most comprehensive, information-packed volume yet in the acclaimed series of design review books by **SAILING** Magazine technical editor Robert H. Perry. Featuring 228 reviews of sailboat designs introduced in the past five years, each presented on extra large 10 by 13 inch pages with detailed specifications and hull, accommodation and sail plans, the new **Sailing Designs** is a treasure of information and expert opinion. Perry, a respected yacht designer in his own right, pulls no punches in critiques that tell what's right and wrong about designs. A must-read for anyone who plans to buy a sailboat or simply appreciates intelligent writing about the art and science of sailboats. **Sailing Designs** is also vastly entertaining, perhaps the only nautical reference book that can be called a page turner.

Sailing Designs—Volume Five: 228 design reviews from 1995-1999, **240 pages**, index, 10"x13" tall. Robert H. Perry author, published September 1999, paperback. **ISBN 1-929006-04-7, $39.95 (US)**

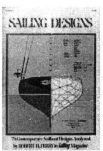

Sailing Designs—Volume One: 79 design reviews from 1974-1977, 5th printing, **96 pages**, index, 11"x15" tall. Robert H. Perry author, published 1977, paperback.
ISBN 1-929006-00-4
$14.95 (US)

Sailing Designs—Volume Two: 109 design reviews from 1977-1980, **120 pages**, index, 11"x15" tall. Robert H. Perry author, published 1980, paperback.
ISBN 1-929006-01-2
$18.95 (US)

Sailing Designs—Volume Four: 228 design reviews from 1987-1994, **240 pages**, index, 10"x13" tall. Robert H. Perry author, published 1994, paperback.
ISBN 1-929006-03-9
$29.95 (US)

Sailing Designs—Volume Three: 197 design reviews from 1981-1986, **208 pages**, index, 11"x15" tall. Robert H. Perry author, published 1986, paperback.
ISBN 1-929006-02-0
$24.95 (US)

Lightning and Boats
A Manual of Safety and Prevention
by Michael V. Huck

An insightful look at the phenomenon of lightning and provides the boater with a **three-tiered approach** to safety and strike prevention. The book describes low-cost equipment that any boater can employ to reduce the possibility of a strike occuring. Describes proper grounding and safety precautions to protect the crew and vessel, as well as the secondary effects of lightning and potential adverse effects on installed equipment caused by the electromagnetic pulse of near strikes. *"...does a good job of explaining to the layman the lightning phenomenon and how to protect boats from it."* - Practical Sailor. **80 pages**, illustrations, bibliography, glossary, **ISBN 0-9639566-0-4, $9.95 (US)**

The Meatless Galley Cookbook
by Anne Carlson

This is definately the cruisers cookbook. The book is designed for the boater who wants delicious, easy, healthful meals to prepare while on vacation, or enjoying the cruising lifestyle. With not only great recipes, the book provides advice and answers to boaters questions in many areas of meal preparation and related topics. There are sections on provisioning, menu plans, helpful hints, an introduction to offshore cooking, storage tips, and even spice substitutions. In addition, the book is beautifully illustrated throughout by nationally renowned marine artist, Bob Stewart. The books contains **180 pages** with 8 original sketches of boating scenes, full-color cover, table of contents, and text index.
ISBN 0-9639566-2-0, $16.95 (US)

For further information, or to place an order please contact:

Seaworthy Publications, Inc.
215 S. Park St., Suite #1
Port Washington, WI 53074

Phone: (262) 268-9250, Fax: (262) 268-9208
e-mail: **publisher@seaworthy.com**
web site: **http://www.seaworthy.com**

Seaworthy Publications, Inc.
Writer's Guidelines

Seaworthy Publications is a small press in southern Wisconsin dedicated to publishing books about sailing and boating. We actively solicit the unpublished works of authors interested in writing for us.

You can obtain a copy of our Writer's Guidelines by sending a self-addressed, stamped envelope to:

> Seaworthy Publications, Inc.
> 215 S. Park St., Suite #1
> Port Washington, WI 53074

You can also download a copy of our writer's guidelines from our web site at:

www.seaworthy.com